Praise for *Nurturing Children and Families*

"All the contributors are leaders in their particular discipline, and all express their debt to Brazelton's broad, inclusive vision of the mother-infant dyad."

CHOICE

"The book is an astounding collection of thirty-one chapters that reflect Brazelton's influence on many fields including child development, pediatrics, infant mental health, nursing, psychology, child psychiatry, social work, physical and occupational therapy, and policy. … I highly recommend this book to anyone – but especially to practitioners and teachers of infant mental health."

The Signal

"*Nurturing Children and Families* is a tribute to Brazelton's influence. It represents over half a century of work across disciplines, using the writing and teaching of this great man, and it presents key research and findings that reflect, tie to, or build upon his work."

Education, Practice, and Research

"In this marvelous collection of leading thinkers and practitioners, Lester and Sparrow have reflected the wisdom of T. Berry Brazelton in the words of the scholars he has inspired. *Nurturing Children and Families* is a timely volume which will undoubtedly enlighten both experts and students alike."

Matthew E. Melmed, Executive Director, Zero to Three

"This very impressive collection of papers by outstanding scholars is a fitting tribute to our nation's greatest living pediatrician. Like Brazelton himself has done, these papers move pediatrics from children's illnesses to their behavioral development with an emphasis on the all-important parent–child relationship."

Edward Zigler, Yale University

"This book is a treasure. Filled with the discoveries of brilliant scientists, it honors T. Berry Brazelton by mirroring his respectful approach to children and parents and his conviction that by really watching children we can find out what they need."

J. Ronald Lally, Co-Director, Center for Child & Family Studies, WestEd

"The distinguished contributors in this volume reflect the diversity of disciplines and perspectives that both mirror and honor the scientific, clinical, practice, and policy contributions of T. Berry Brazelton. Those who want to bask in and relive the exciting engagement with infants and families throughout the second half of the 20th century, can do so in these chapters. Those who want to engage in the transformations required in the 21st century, read, imagine, and take action, knowing that Brazelton's footsteps, though wide and encompassing, move quickly."

Hiram Fitzgerald, Michigan State University

This book is dedicated to Christina Brazelton

Nurturing Children and Families

Building on the Legacy of T. Berry Brazelton

Edited by Barry M. Lester
and Joshua D. Sparrow

A John Wiley & Sons, Ltd., Publication

This paperback edition first published 2013

Edition History: Blackwell Publishing Ltd (hardback, 2010)

Blackwell Publishing was acquired by John Wiley & Sons, in February 2007. Blackwell's publishing program has been merged with Wiley's global Scientific, Technical, and Medical business to form Wiley-Blackwell.

Registered Office
John Wiley & Sons, Ltd, The Atrium, Southern Gate, Chichester, West Sussex, PO19 8SQ, UK

Editorial Offices
350 Main Street, Malden, MA 02148-5020, USA
9600 Garsington Road, Oxford, OX4 2DQ, UK
The Atrium, Southern Gate, Chichester, West Sussex, PO19 8SQ, UK

For details of our global editorial offices, for customer services, and for information about how to apply for permission to reuse the copyright material in this book please see our website at www.wiley.com/wiley-blackwell.

Library of Congress Cataloging-in-Publication Data

Nurturing children and families : building on the legacy of T. Berry Brazelton / editors, Barry Lester and Joshua Sparrow.
p. cm.
Includes bibliographical references and index.
ISBN 978-1-4051-9600-0 (hbk.: alk. paper) ISBN 978-1-118-34465-1 (pbk.: alk. paper)
1. Child development. 2. Infants–Development. 3. Child psychology. 4. Infant psychology. 5. Parent and child. 6. Parent and infant. 7. Brazelton, T. Berry, 1918–
I. Lester, Barry M. II. Sparrow, Joshua D.
RJ131.N88 2010
618.92–dc22

2009053161

A catalogue record for this book is available from the British Library.

Cover image: Nicki Averill Design.
Cover design by Design Deluxe.

Set in 10.5/13pt Minion by SPi Publisher Services, Pondicherry, India

Printed in Malaysia by Ho Printing (M) Sdn Bhd

1 2013

Contents

Notes on Contributors

Heidelise Als, PhD is Associate Professor in Psychiatry, Harvard Medical School and Director of Neurobehavioral Infant and Child Studies at Children's Hospital Boston. Dr. Als has received numerous awards in recognition of her outstanding leadership in the developmental assessment and care of preterm and high-risk infants, and most recently was the recipient of the Stan and Mavis Graven Award for Leadership in Enhancing Physical and Developmental Environments for High-Risk Infants and their Families. She is the originator of the Newborn Individualized Developmental Care and Assessment Program (NIDCAP) approach for the care of preterm infants and their families, and the founder and President of the NIDCAP Federation International, a nonprofit organization which provides national and international training for advanced professionals in the field of NICU developmental care implementation.

Kathryn E. Barnard, RN, PhD is Professor Emeritus of Nursing and the founder and Director of the Center on Infant Mental Health and Development at the University of Washington. Her pioneering work to improve the physical and mental health outcomes of infants and young children has earned her numerous honors, including the Gustav O. Leinhard Award from the Institute of Medicine; the Lucille Petry Leone Award for Teaching; the M. Scott Award for Contributions to Nursing Science, Education and Service; the Martha May Eliot Award for Leadership in Maternal–Child Health; Nurse Scientist of the Year Award; and, from the American Academy of Nursing, both the Episteme Award, the highest honor in nursing, and the Living Legend Award.

Jessica Dym Bartlett, MA, MSW, LICSW is a psychotherapist who has worked with children and families, childcare programs, and school systems for over 15 years. She is an adjunct faculty member at the Boston University

School of Social Work where she teaches courses on resilience through the life span, human behavior in the social environment, and clinical practice with children and adolescents. Bartlett's research and publications focus on resilience, infant/early childhood mental health, and child maltreatment.

Rosemarie Bigsby, ScD, OTR/L, FAOTA is Clinical Associate Professor of Pediatrics and of Psychiatry and Human Behavior, and Coordinator of NICU Services at the Center for the Study of Children At Risk, Brown University, Alpert Medical School and Women & Infants' Hospital. Dr. Bigsby was named a Fellow of the American Occupational Therapy Association for her contributions to the practice of occupational therapy with infants and children. She is the author of a number of journal articles and book chapters, and is co-author of a textbook on NICU practice: *Developmental and Therapeutic Interventions in the NICU*, and a motor assessment tool: The Posture and Fine Motor Assessment of Infants (Psychological Corporation).

Kristie Brandt, CNM, MSN, DNP a board certified nurse-midwife, is the Director of the Parent–Infant & Child Institute in Napa, CA and co-developer and Director of the University of Massachusetts Boston Infant–Parent Mental Health Post-Graduate Certificate Program in Napa, CA, a 15-month training program for professionals. While Napa County's Chief Public Health Manager, she developed and researched the nation's first Touchpoints Perinatal Home Visiting Project, and she created and oversaw Napa's Therapeutic Child Care Center, serving high-risk children 0–5 in a full-day, full-year therapeutic program. Dr. Brandt is a visiting faculty member of the Brazelton Touchpoints Center at Children's Hospital Boston. She is author of the new book, *Facilitating the Reflective Process: An Introductory Workbook for the Infant–Family and Early Childhood Field* (2009).

Geoffrey Canada, MEd is the acclaimed author of *Fist Stick Knife Gun: A Personal History of Violence in America* and was the recipient of the first Heinz Award in 1994 for his work as President/CEO of Harlem Children's Zone in New York City. Since 1990, Mr. Canada has been the President and Chief Executive Officer for the Harlem Children's Zone. In a June 2004 cover story in the *New York Times Magazine*, the agency's Zone Project was called "one of the most ambitious social experiments of our time." The Project offers an interlocking network of social service, education and community-building programs to thousands of children and families in a 60-block area of Central Harlem.

Dante Cicchetti, PhD is McKnight Presidential Chair and Professor of Child Psychology and Psychiatry at the University of Minnesota. Dr. Cicchetti has received a number of awards, including the three highest honors of the Developmental Division of the American Psychological Association: the G. Stanley Hall Award for Distinguished Contribution to Developmental Psychology, the Urie Bronfenbrenner Award for Lifetime Contribution to Developmental Psychology in the Service of Science and Society, and the Mentor Award in Developmental Psychology. He has published over 400 articles, books, and journal Special Issues that have had far-reaching impact on developmental theory as well as science, policy, and practice related to child maltreatment, depression, mental retardation, and numerous other domains of development. Dr. Cicchetti is the founding and current editor of *Development and Psychopathology*.

M. Ann Easterbrooks, PhD is Professor in the Eliot-Pearson Department of Child Development at Tufts University. She is Co-Principal Investigator of the Massachusetts Healthy Families Evaluation, examining the efficacy of Healthy Families Massachusetts, a statewide child maltreatment prevention program. Dr. Easterbrooks's publications include chapters, research articles, and edited volumes on a range of topics, including: healthy social and emotional development in the context of psychosocial risk factors such as depression and trauma; father–child relationships in infancy and early childhood; the developmental course of parent–child attachment relationships; and promoting positive relationships in early education and care. She chairs the Publications Committee of the Society for Research in Child Development.

Tiffany Field, PhD is Director of the Touch Research Institutes at the University of Miami School of Medicine and Fielding Graduate University. She is recipient of the American Psychological Association Boyd McAndless Distinguished Young Scientist Award and has had a Research Scientist Award from the NIH for her research career. She is the author of *Infancy, The Amazing Infant, Touch, Advances in Touch, Touch Therapy, Massage Therapy Research,* and *Complementary and Alternative Therapies*, the editor of a series of volumes on *High-Risk Infants,* and on *Stress and Coping*, and the author of over 450 journal papers.

Myra D. Fox, BS is the former Director of Child Life Services at Children's Hospital Boston where she devoted her career to the special needs of hospitalized children and their families until her retirement in 2008. In later years her responsibilities included Director of Volunteer Services, with responsibilities for the Big Apple Clown Care Unit, music and art therapy. She also developed a comprehensive educational/tutoring program for hospitalized children that also included home teaching. Fox has been a consultant to pediatric hospitals and to children's television programs and has helped establish a child life program in Sao Paulo, Brazil.

Stanley I. Greenspan, MD was, until his death in April 2010, Clinical Professor of Psychiatry and Pediatrics at George Washington University Medical School, Chair of the Interdisciplinary Council on Developmental and Learning Disorders, and Chair of the Psychodynamic Diagnostic Manual Task Force, which represented many major psychoanalytic organizations. He was the founding President of Zero to Three: The National Center for Infants, Toddlers, and Families, and past Director of the NIMH Mental Health Study Center and the Clinical Infant Development Program. Dr. Greenspan was the recipient of many national and international awards, including the American Psychiatric Association's highest honor for child psychiatry research, author of over 100 scholarly articles and chapters and author or editor of over 40 books, translated into over a dozen languages, including *The Irreducible Needs of Children* co-authored with T. Berry Brazelton, MD.

William W. Harris, PhD is a senior fellow at the Jonathan M. Tisch College of Citizenship and Public Service at Tufts University. He founded KidsPac, a political action committee dedicated to sound public policies for poor children from birth to age six and their families. He has served on numerous advisory committees, including the American Psychiatric Association's Presidential Task Force on the Biopsychosocial Consequences of Childhood Violence. Harris has received several awards for his work on behalf of children, including the Advocacy Award, Division of Child, Youth and Family Services, from the American Psychological Association, the Dale Richmond Award from the American Academy of Pediatrics, the Leadership Award for Public Service from Zero to Three, and the Public Advocacy Award from the International Society for Traumatic Stress Studies.

Mikael Heimann, PhD is a Professor of Psychology at the Department of Behavioral Science, Linköping University, Sweden, Co-Director of the Swedish Institute for Disability Research, Linköping, and a senior researcher at the Norwegian Network for Infant Mental Health, Oslo, Norway. He worked clinically at the Clinic for Child and Adolescent Psychiatry, Gothenburg, Sweden, and was Professor and Head of a Centre of Child and

Adolescent Mental Health, University of Bergen, Norway. Dr. Heimann's research focuses on developmental processes (change processes and regression periods), infant cognition (imitation, memory, and attention), early social skills (neonatal imitation and mother–infant interaction), and early communicative development and developmental psychopathology (children with autism and sustained withdrawal in infancy). His interests also include intervention studies aimed at increasing social interaction skills as well as literacy (e.g., in children with autism and children with suspected dyslexia, "slow readers").

Myron Hofer, MD is Sackler Professor and Director of the Sackler Institute of Developmental Psychobiology in the Department of Psychiatry at Columbia University College of Physicians and Surgeons. Throughout his research career, Dr. Hofer has worked at the interface of biology and psychology, and helped to define the new field of Developmental Psychobiology as it emerged in the 1970s and 1980s. Through an experimental analysis of the psychobiological events that enmesh the infant rat and its mother, he discovered hidden regulatory processes that have become the basis for a new understanding of the early origins of attachment, the dynamics of the separation response, and the shaping of development by that first relationship. Dr. Hofer has served on the editorial boards of *Behavioral Neuroscience*, the *Journal of Psychosomatic Research, Developmental Psychobiology and Psychosomatic Medicine.* He is the author/co-author of five books – including *The Roots of Human Behavior* – as well as numerous journal articles, book chapters, monographs, and theoretical papers.

John Hornstein, EdD has worked in the field of early child development for over 30 years. His research focuses on the emotional development in young children with additional interest in cross-cultural issues, parenting, and creativity. He participated in the development of the AIMS Indicators of Emotional Health, and conducted research on its psychometric properties. Dr. Hornstein was on the faculty of the Department of Education at the University of New Hampshire for 13 years, teaching in early childhood education, special education, and undergraduate honors programs. As a research associate at Children's Hospital and Harvard Medical School in Boston, Dr. Hornstein serves as a faculty member of the Brazelton Touchpoints Center. Areas of focus at Touchpoints include work with Native American sites and the development of training in working with families of children with special needs.

Francine Jacobs, EdD is an Associate Professor in the Eliot-Pearson Department of Child Development and the Department of Urban and Environmental Policy and Planning at Tufts University. Her research focuses on programs and policies meant to improve the life circumstances for children and families, including those in early childhood education, child welfare and child protection, juvenile justice, and family support; she has evaluated a range of these interventions in the United States and elsewhere. She is the co-Principal Investigator of the Massachusetts Healthy Families Evaluation.

Jerome Kagan, PhD is Emeritus Professor of Psychology at Harvard University. His research has addressed infant cognitive development, morality, the role of culture, and the contribution of temperamental biases to personality development. Kagan is a fellow of the American Academy of Arts and Sciences, a member of the Institute of Medicine of the National Academy of Sciences, and recipient of distinguished scientist awards from the American Psychological Association and the Society for Research in Child Development. He is the author or co-author of several hundred articles and many books including: *Galen's Prophecy*; *The Nature of the Child*; *Three Seductive Ideas*; *The Long Shadow of Temperament*; *A Young Mind in a Growing Brain*; *The Three Cultures*; and a forthcoming book titled *The Temperamental Thread.*

Constance H. Keefer, MD is Assistant Professor of Pediatrics at Harvard Medical School and on the faculties of Newborn Medicine at Brigham and Women's Hospital and the Brazelton Institute and Brazelton Touchpoints Center at Children's Hospital. Dr. Keefer has done research on newborn behavior and child development, culture and parenting, and communication in healthcare. She focuses her teaching on development and behavior in pediatric primary care and application of the Touchpoints Approach. She co-authored *Understanding Newborn Behavior and Early Relationships: The Newborn Behavioral Observation (NBO) System Handbook*, and has contributed chapters on child development, newborn behavior, cultural perspective on behavior and development, the shy child, and nursery care of the newborn.

Sara Lawrence-Lightfoot, EdD, a MacArthur-prize-winning sociologist, is the Emily Hargroves Fisher Professor of Education at Harvard University. Educator, researcher, author and public intellectual, Lawrence-Lightfoot has written nine books including *The Good High School: Portraits of*

Character and Culture; *Balm in Gilead: Journey of a Healer*; *Respect: An Exploration*; *The Essential Conversation: What Parents and Teachers Can Learn From Each Other*; and her most recent, *The Third Chapter: Passion, Risk, and Adventure in the 25 Years After 50*. Her volume, *The Art and Science of Portraiture*, documents her pioneering approach to social science methodology which bridges the realms of aesthetics and empiricism. Lawrence-Lightfoot is the recipient of numerous honors including Harvard's George Ledlie Prize for research that "makes the most valuable contribution to science" and is for "the benefit of mankind." She is a Spencer Senior Scholar; and was named the Margaret Mead Fellow by the American Academy of Political and Social Sciences.

Barry M. Lester, PhD is Professor of Psychiatry and Human Behavior, Professor of Pediatrics and founding Director of the Center for the Study of Children at Risk, Brown University Alpert Medical School and Women and Infants Hospital. His research has addressed processes of development in children at risk due to biological and social factors. His research has been continuously funded by the NIH for over 25 years. Dr. Lester was a member of the Council at the NIH National Institute on Drug Abuse. He directs the Infant and Child Mental Health Post-Baccalaureate Certificate Program at Brown University and is past President of the International Association for Infant Mental Health. He is the author of several hundred peer-reviewed publications and 16 books, including *Why is My Baby Crying?*

Robert A. LeVine, PhD is Roy E. Larsen Professor of Education and Human Development, Emeritus, Harvard University. He worked with Dr. Brazelton in Kenya from 1974 to 1976; they are co-authors of *Child Care and Culture: Lessons from Africa* (1994). Dr. LeVine's most recent book is *Anthropology and Child Development: A Cross-Cultural Reader*, co-edited with Rebecca Staples (New Malden, MA: Blackwell Publishers).

Alicia F. Lieberman, PhD is Irving B. Harris Professor Endowed Chair, Professor and Vice Chair for Academic Affairs at the UCSF Department of Psychiatry and Director of the Child Trauma Research Program at San Francisco General Hospital. She is President of the board of directors of Zero to Three: The National Center for Infants, Toddlers and Families, and author of *The Emotional Life of the Toddler* and senior author of *Psychotherapy with Infants and Young Children: Repairing the Effects of Stress and Trauma on Early Attachment*; *Losing a Parent to Death in the Early Years: Treating Traumatic Bereavement in Infancy and Early Childhood*; and *Don't Hit my*

Mommy: A Manual for Child–Parent Psychotherapy with Young Witnesses of Family Violence; and of numerous articles and chapters.

J. Michael Murphy, EdD is a psychologist with the Child Psychiatry Service at the Massachusetts General Hospital where he has worked for more than 25 years, and Associate Professor of Psychology at the Harvard Medical School where he teaches research methodology to psychiatric residents. He has collaborated with the U.S. Government Department of Agriculture, Maternal and Child Health Bureau, the Center for Disease Control (CDC), and numerous states and cities and is currently working with the government of Chile to evaluate a large school-based mental health program there. He has published more than 50 papers in academic journals. For more than a decade Dr. Murphy has been a research consultant to Napa County Health and Human Services, helping to evaluate the implementation of the Touchpoints program there as well as the county's nurse home visiting programs and a therapeutic childcare center.

Julie C. Novak, DNSc, RN, CPNP, FAANP is Associate Dean for Practice, University of Texas Health Science Center San Antonio School of Nursing and Crow Endowed Professor. She continues to support special projects in the Center for Instructional Excellence at Purdue University where she served as School of Nursing Head and Director, DNP program and nurse-managed clinics and has grant support for two rural nurse-managed clinics. Her research addresses global child and family health promotion, public health safety and quality improvement, rural healthcare, and nursing education and practice. Dr. Novak is a Fellow of the American Academy of Nurse Practitioners and the National Association of Pediatric Nurse Practitioners. The recipient of numerous awards, Dr. Novak has authored or co-authored over 70 articles, book chapters, and a textbook.

J. Kevin Nugent, PhD is Founder and Director of the Brazelton Institute at the Division of Developmental Medicine, Children's Hospital Boston. He is Professor of Child and Family Studies at the University of Massachusetts at Amherst and a Lecturer in Psychology at Harvard Medical School. He is co-author with Dr. Brazelton of the *Neonatal Behavioral Assessment Scale (NBAS)*, 3rd edition. Recently, Dr. Nugent and his colleagues developed the *Newborn Behavioral Observations (NBO)* system, an adaptation of the *NBAS* as a clinical tool for clinicians in pediatric and intervention settings. Dr. Nugent is author or co-author of many articles and books including *The Newborn as Person: Enabling Healthy Infant Development Worldwide*;

Understanding Newborn Behavior and Early Relationships: The Handbook of the Newborn Behavioral Observations (NBO) System; *The Infant and Family in the 21st Century*; *The Cultural Context of Infancy*; *Using the NBAS with Infants and Families: Guidelines for Intervention*.

David L. Olds, PhD is Professor of Pediatrics, Psychiatry, Preventive Medicine, and Nursing at the University of Colorado, Denver, where he directs the Prevention Research Center for Family and Child Health. He has devoted his career to investigating methods of preventing health and developmental problems in children and parents from low-income families. The primary focus of his work has been on developing and testing in a series of randomized controlled trials a program of prenatal and infancy home visiting by nurses for socially disadvantaged mothers bearing first children, known today as the Nurse–Family Partnership. A member of the American Pediatrics Society, the Society for Prevention Research, and the Academy of Experimental Criminology, Professor Olds has received numerous awards for his work, including the Lela Rowland Prevention Award from the National Mental Health Association, a Senior Research Scientist Award from the National Institute of Mental Health, the Brooke Visiting Professorship in Epidemiology from the Royal Society of Medicine, and the Stockholm Prize in Criminology.

Howard J. Osofsky, MD, PhD is Kathleen and John Bricker Chair, Department of Psychiatry at Louisiana State University Health Sciences Center. He has served as Co-Director of the Louisiana Rural Trauma Services Center, part of the National Child Traumatic Stress Network. In the aftermath of Hurricane Katrina, he was asked to be Clinical Director for Louisiana Spirit. Dr. Osofsky received the award as "Best Department Chair" from the American Academy of Child and Adolescent Psychiatry in recognition of his efforts for children and adolescents. He has received the Sarah Haley Award for Clinical Excellence from the International Society for Traumatic Stress Studies, the Public Citizen of the Year Award by the Louisiana Chapter of the National Association of Social Workers and the Department of Psychiatry, and the Distinguished Partners in Education Award by the Board of Elementary and Secondary Education of the State Department of Education for their work in schools following Hurricane Katrina.

Joy D. Osofsky, PhD is a psychologist and psychoanalyst and Professor of Pediatrics and Psychiatry at Louisiana State University Health Sciences Center (LSUHSC) in New Orleans. She is Head of the Division of Pediatric

Mental Health. Dr. Osofsky is Co-Director of the Louisiana Rural Trauma Services Center, a center in the National Child Traumatic Stress Network and Director of the Harris Center for Infant Mental Health at LSUHSC. She is editor of *Children in a Violent Society* and *Young Children and Trauma: Intervention and Treatment*. Dr. Osofsky is past President of Zero to Three: National Center for Infants, Toddlers, and Families and past President of the World Association for Infant Mental Health. She has received the Sarah Haley Award for Clinical Excellence for work with trauma from the International Society for Traumatic Stress Studies. The LSUHSC team from the Department of Psychiatry was awarded the Distinguished Partners in Education Award by the Board of Elementary and Secondary Education of the State Department of Education for their work in schools following Hurricane Katrina.

Daniel Pedersen, MA is founding President of the Buffett Early Childhood Fund, which invests in education where America is most underinvested: the first five years of life. Under Pedersen's leadership, the foundation also is helping to build a coast-to-coast network of independently evaluated, highly effective Educare schools. Each school serves nearly 200 infants, toddlers and preschoolers in families facing the most difficult odds. Each school also functions as a catalyst for broader policy change within its community and state. In addition, Pedersen chairs the Birth to Five Policy Alliance and the executive policy council of the First Five Years Fund. The Alliance galvanizes state-based advocacy groups and more than a dozen national organizations committed to improving state early childhood policies. The First Five Years Fund forges change in federal policy making and national communications about early childhood. Pedersen was instrumental in creating the Educare network and both policy entities. Today, all three enterprises are backed by several nationally significant charitable foundations which are intent on finding new ways to work together on behalf of children at risk of school failure.

Frans X. Plooij, PhD is Director of the International Research-Institute on Infant Studies. He studied animal psychology with Adriaan Kortlandt, University of Amsterdam, the Netherlands, and biology of behavior with Gerard Baerends, University of Groningen, the Netherlands. He worked with Jane Goodall in the Gombe National Park on infant development in free-living chimpanzees; with Robert Hinde in the MRC-unit on the Development and Integration of Behaviour, University Sub-Department of Animal Behaviour in Madingley, Cambridge, England; at the department of Developmental Psychology, University of Nijmegen, the Netherlands, where he studied and filmed babies in the home environment. He has served as Vice-President for Information of the International Society for Human Ethology, Vice-President of the Institut Européen pour le Développement des Potentialités de tous les Enfants (IEDPE), and on the editorial board of the international journal *Ethology and Sociobiology*, and he is a member of the panel of assessors of the *Journal of Clinical Child Psychology and Psychiatry*.

Amy L. Salisbury, PhD, APRN, BC trained as a clinical nurse specialist in child and family psychiatry and holds a PhD in developmental psychobiology. Her research examines prenatal and postnatal neurobehavioral development within a larger biopsychosocial framework. Dr. Salisbury heads the Fetal Behavior Studies Program at the Center for the Study of Children At Risk, Brown University, Alpert Medical School and Women and Infants' Hospital examining fetal and infant neurobehavioral development. Dr. Salisbury and her colleagues have developed an organized a method of assessing fetal neurobehavior, called the Fetal Neurobehavior Coding System (FENS), which is currently being used to study the effects of fetal exposure to maternal depression, anxiety, antidepressant medications, opiates, and maternal smoking.

Allan N. Schore, PhD is on the clinical faculty of the UCLA David Geffen School of Medicine. He is author of three seminal volumes, *Affect Regulation and the Origin of the Self*, *Affect Dysregulation and Disorders of the Self*, and *Affect Regulation and the Repair of the Self*, as well as numerous articles and chapters. He is editor of the acclaimed Norton Series on Interpersonal Neurobiology, and a reviewer on the editorial staff of 35 journals across a number of scientific and clinical disciplines. He is a member of the Society of Neuroscience, and of the American Psychological Association Divisions of Neuropsychology and of Psychoanalysis, from which he received its Scientific Award.

Jack P. Shonkoff, MD is the Julius B. Richmond FAMRI Professor of Child Health and Development at the Harvard School of Public Health and the Harvard Graduate School of Education; Professor of Pediatrics at Harvard Medical School and Children's Hospital Boston; and Director of the university-wide Center on the Developing Child at Harvard University. He also chairs the National Scientific Council on the Developing Child, a multi-university collaboration comprising leading scholars in neuroscience, psychology, pediatrics, and economics, whose mission is to bring credible science to bear on policy affecting young children. Under the auspices of the National Academy of Sciences, Dr. Shonkoff chaired a blue-ribbon committee that produced a landmark report entitled, *From Neurons to Neighborhoods: The Science of Early Childhood Development*. He has received multiple honors, including elected membership to the Institute of Medicine of the National Academy of Sciences, designated National Associate of the National Academies, the C. Anderson Aldrich Award in Child Development from the American Academy of Pediatrics, and the Award for Distinguished Contributions to Public Policy for Children from the Society for Research in Child Development. He has authored more than 150 publications.

Jayne Singer, PhD, a clinical psychologist, is Clinical Director of the Child and Parent Program in the Developmental Medicine Center at Children's Hospital Boston. She is an Assistant Professor of Pediatrics and Psychiatry at the Harvard Medical School, and serves as President of the Massachusetts Association for Infant Mental Health. Dr. Singer serves as a faculty member of the Brazelton Touchpoints Center where she provides leadership for the Early Care and Education (ECE) Initiative and is the primary contributor to the ECE Training Materials.

Joshua D. Sparrow, MD is Director of Special Initiatives at the Brazelton Touchpoints Center, Children's Hospital, Boston, and Assistant Professor in Psychiatry at the Harvard Medical School. He has co-authored eight books with Dr. T. Berry Brazelton, and revised with him the second edition of *Touchpoints Birth to Three: Your Child's Emotional and Behavioral Development*. His work focuses on the social determinants of development and health, and culturally informed adaptations of interventions that catalyze community healing and self-strengthening processes.

Ann C. Stadtler, MSN, CPNP, one of the original faculty members and curriculum developers at the Brazelton Touchpoints Center (BTC), Children's Hospital Boston, is Director of Site Development and Training. She has received numerous awards including the Touchpoints Distinguished Leader Award. She co-designed "Toilet School," a group treatment approach to failure to toilet train. Stadtler's work at the Brazelton Touchpoints Center includes the integration of parent voices into a systems theory-based approach for infants and families.

Daniel N. Stern, MD is Professeur Honoraire in the Faculté de Psychologie, University of Geneva, Switzerland, Adjunct Professor in the Department of Psychiatry, Cornell University Medical School, and New York Hospital

Lecturer at the Columbia University Center for Psychoanalysis. Professor Stern is the author of several hundred journal articles and chapters, as well as six books, including *The First Relationship: Infant and Mother* – his first book – and *The Motherhood Constellation: A Unifying View of Parent–Infant Psychotherapies*. Professor Stern has been awarded an Honorary Doctorate at the University of Copenhagen, Denmark, the University of Mons Hinault, Belgium, and the University of Palermo, Italy.

Mallary I. Swartz, PhD is Director of Research and Evaluation at Connected Beginnings Training Institute in Boston, Massachusetts. Dr. Swartz has worked on multiple research and evaluation studies related to early care and education at Frank Porter Graham Child Development Center at the University of North Carolina at Chapel Hill, at the University of Pittsburgh, at the Children's Museum of Pittsburgh, and at Tufts University, where she worked as a research analyst on the Evaluation of the Touchpoints Early Care and Education Initiative. Dr. Swartz also worked with organizations in New Orleans to rebuild and enhance the quality of childcare and to develop a family childcare curriculum for the state of Louisiana.

Sheree L. Toth is an Associate Professor of Clinical and Social Psychology at the University of Rochester and the Director of Mt. Hope Family Center. She has published in the areas of the developmental consequences of child maltreatment and the impact that Major Depressive Disorders exert on offspring and has completed a randomized clinical trial of Interpersonal Psychotherapy with low-income depressed mothers. Dr. Toth is an Associate Editor for the journal *Development and Psychopathology* and a past Associate Editor of *The Journal of Child and Family Studies*. She has contributed chapters to numerous books, including *The Handbook of Child Psychology and Developmental Psychopathology*, and she has co-edited *The Rochester Symposium on Developmental Psychopathology*. She received the 2006 award from the American Professional Society on the Abuse of Children for the publication of an outstanding research article in the area of child maltreatment.

Ed Tronick, PhD is a University Distinguished Professor of Psychology at the University of Massachusetts, Boston, Director of the Child Development Unit at Children's Hospital, a Lecturer in Pediatrics, Harvard Medical School and an Associate Professor at both the Graduate School of Education and the School of Public Health at Harvard. He is a faculty member at the Fielding Graduate Institute and a member of the Boston Psychoanalytic

Society and Institute. With Dr. Kristie Brandt, he is Co-Director of the Napa Parent–Infant Mental Health Fellowship Program and he is a faculty member of the Brazelton Touchpoints Center. He has published more than 200 scientific articles and four books. His research has been funded by the National Institute on Drug Abuse, the National Institute of Child Health and Development, the National Institute of Mental Health (NIMH), the National Science Foundation, and the McArthur Foundation. He has also served as permanent member of an NIMH review panel, and reviews for the National Science Foundations of Canada, the USA and Switzerland.

Charles H. Zeanah, MD is the Mary K. Sellars-Polchow Chair in Psychiatry, Professor of Clinical Pediatrics, and Vice Chair for Child and Adolescent Psychiatry in the Department of Psychiatry and Neurology at Tulane University School of Medicine in New Orleans. He is also Executive Director of the Institute for Infant and Early Childhood Mental Health at Tulane. He is the recipient of the Rieger Award for Service Excellence and the Irving Phillips Award for Prevention from the American Academy of Child and Adolescent Psychiatry (AACAP), the Presidential Citation for Distinguished Research and Leadership in Infant Mental Health from the American Orthopsychiatric Association, the Sarah Haley Memorial Award for Clinical Excellence from the International Society for Traumatic Stress Studies, and the Blanche F. Ittelson Award for Research in Child Psychiatry from the American Psychiatric Association. Dr. Zeanah is a Fellow of AACAP, a Distinguished Fellow of the American Psychiatric Association, and a Board Member of Zero to Three. He is the editor of the *Handbook of Infant Mental Health*.

Paula Doyle Zeanah, PhD, MSN, RN is Professor of Clinical Psychiatry and Pediatrics at the Tulane University School of Medicine, and adjunct faculty, School of Public Health and Tropical Medicine at Tulane. Dr. Zeanah serves as Chief of the Psychology Division in the Department of Psychiatry at Tulane, and Co-Director of the Pediatric Psychiatry Consultation-Liaison service at Tulane Hospital. She has served for more than a decade as a mental health consultant for the Louisiana Office of Public Health, Maternal Child Health section, and has conducted numerous large-scale research projects.

Libby Zimmerman, PhD, LICSW was, until her death in August 2009, founding Executive Director of Connected Beginnings Training Institute in Boston, Massachusetts. She held a PhD from the Heller School for Social

New ideas may also emerge and take hold at fertile places, in times when a host of conditions are ripe for their gestation. As the many contributors to this volume demonstrate, and the many more equally meritorious ones that could not be included within these several hundred pages, a generation that labors together under related conditions, facing related challenges, struggling with related dilemmas, can participate in a process of cross-pollination that leads to the most transformational ideas of all. In some instances, great observers and thinkers come together, as in the Center for Cognitive Studies at Harvard in the 1960s and 1970s to stimulate each other's insights. Brazelton's understanding of the fundamentally relational nature of human development runs parallel to his analogous position on the social origins of scientific thought and learning. Throughout his career he sought to create opportunities for the intercourse of exciting minds: for example, at the National Center for Clinical Infant Programs (NCCIP), which he helped to found, which later became Zero to Three and where the infant mental health field was born; in the fellowship he created at Children's Hospital, Boston and Harvard Medical School that helped give birth to the subspecialty of Behavioral and Developmental Pediatrics and was a precursor of behavioral and developmental pediatric fellowship training programs; through the work of the Brazelton Institute and its international network of Neonatal Behavioral Assessment Scale (NBAS) trainers which continually revises, updates, and adapts that scale; or yet again through the national site network of the Brazelton Touchpoints Center which seeks to bring together clinicians from all of the fields dedicated to children and their families as a learning community to catalyze innovative new approaches to practice and service delivery. Brazelton was far in advance of his time in breaking down barriers between disciplinary silos, stimulating interdisciplinary collaborations, and paving the way for what is now called translational "bench to bedside to practice" science.

Brazelton's creativity and openness to new possibilities and ways of understanding allowed him to see connections among new ideas emerging around him and his observations. But the potency and influence of ideas also depend on their articulation. Brazelton's unusual talent for communication positioned him to bring together these ideas, make them comprehensible, and express their power. As the most eloquent and effective spokesperson of his generation for new understandings of infants, children, families, and their development, he must also be credited with both stirring up the choir in his midst to sing more loudly, and with readying the broadest audience ever for its message.

As a result of this confluence of talents, Brazelton was able to take his scientific findings and those of his colleagues and help parlay them into dramatic, nationwide changes in practice, service delivery, and policy. Research on the effects of anesthesia during labor on newborns contributed to the resurgence of natural childbirth. Findings on the effects of overstimulation on infants born preterm led to the reduction of detrimental sensory exposures in neonatal intensive care units. Observations of the effects of separation from parents on hospitalized children as they recovered from illness or surgery led to family-friendly pediatric hospitals and rooming in. Hospitals continue their quest for family-centered care opportunities: new neonatal intensive care, units are being built with individual rooms where parents can stay with their babies, participate in their care, and provide the kind of individualized stimulation appropriate for their babies' level of development. Elucidation of the effects of environmental toxins on newborn and infant behavior contributed to the removal of lead from gasoline in the USA. Studies of the astonishing advances in the parent–child relationship in the first three months of life helped make the case for the Family Leave Act, guaranteeing all mothers three months of (unpaid) maternity leave. Hypotheses about the remarkable plasticity of infant brains before radiation-free brain imaging techniques became available to prove them fueled legislation to mandate early intervention for children under age three with special needs. It is also the purpose of this book to demonstrate the critical link between observation and communication, between science and advocacy, and how fortunate infants, children, parents, and professionals who serve them are that such gifts need not be mutually exclusive and indeed may reside, however rarely, within a single individual.

Given the breadth of Brazelton's influence, and to guide readers to those chapters most relevant to their interests, this book's thirty-one chapters are grouped into twelve sections and presented in three parts – proceeding from research to practice to considerations of dissemination and scaling: (I) A Scientific Revolution in Behavioral and Developmental Research; (II) From Theory to Practice: Innovations in Clinical Intervention; and (III) Translational Science: Implications for Professional Development, Systems of Care, and Policy. It is hoped that the organization of this book and its inclusion of experts from such a wide range of disciplines and sectors will point to some of the exciting and fruitful new connections that emerge when traditional divisions among disciplines and fields are overcome. The reader is likely to find, as well, that there is a set of overarching principles that emerges to order and organize these new connections in new ways.

The first section, Changing Paradigms, sets the stage by outlining the fundamental transformations in approaches to newborns, development, relationships, and health/development-promoting human systems, as well as to research design and methodology, brought about by Brazelton's research. The following five sections, Advances in Understanding Fetal and Newborn Behavior, Self-Regulatory and Relational Processes, Regression and Reorganization in Relational Models of Development, Relational and Contextual Developmental Models, and Neuroscience Perspectives on Relational and Developmental Models, highlight exciting research that builds on Brazelton's pioneering contributions to the basic sciences of human development and relationships. The next three sections – Preventive Interventions: Home Visitation, Early Interventions: The Care of Infants Born Preterm, and Infant Mental Health and the Treatment of Early Trauma – focus on promising and proven applications of the principles that have emerged from the research to current clinical challenges. Implications of practice change – for example, relationship-based and family-centered care – for professional development, systems of care, and policy are taken up in the sections on Changing Practice and Improving Care through Professional Development and Innovating Change in Service Delivery, Systems of Care, and Policy. The book closes with a section entitled Changing Ways of Being which distills the ways of being that underlie and sustain Brazelton's transformative impact on research, practice, systems of care, and social policies that deploy scientific innovation to nurture infants, children, and families.

Beyond documenting Brazelton's pathbreaking contributions, and the new knowledge and ways of knowing that have emerged from his singular yet expansive vision, this book also intends to set forth some of the as yet uncharted territories for the biological and social sciences of human development that remain to be mapped upon the Brazelton legacy. Brazelton's ideas are not only transformative, but highly generative ones – and there remains much more to be done with them. Brazelton has mentored several generations of the most innovative and influential researchers, clinicians, and policy makers in the fields he has impacted, of whom only a regrettably small fraction could be included within the confines of this book. It is hoped that future generations of researchers and clinicians will find inspiration in this book for their continued exploration of the power of these ideas to nurture infants, children, and their families.

Joshua D. Sparrow
Barry M. Lester

Acknowledgments

A book about the work of one individual who has touched so many understandably could not have been written without the work of many. The editors wish to express their gratitude to Lee Breault, at the Center for the Study of Children at Risk, Brown University Alpert Medical School, to Kim Alleyne, Cathy Ayoub, Lisa Desrochers, Barbara Dorant, Terry Ann Lunt, Suzanne Otcasek, Holly Scott, and Alisa Serraton-Cazeau at the Brazelton Touchpoints Center, Children's Hospital, Boston, for the myriad ways in which they helped to cajole and nurture this uniquely personal and professional project, and to Chris Cardone and Constance Adler at Wiley-Blackwell for their clarity and guidance along the way.

As befits a book about the wide reach of T. Berry Brazelton's lifetime accomplishments into many fields beyond his own and well into the future, this book has been written by highly influential innovators in these fields who span several generations. The caliber of their contributions has been matched by their enthusiasm and generosity in participating in this project, no doubt a mark of the joy experienced in celebrating a central inspiration for their own life's work. To the contributors to this book, and to Brazelton's other students, teachers, mentors, colleagues in research, practice, politics, and philanthropy around the world, who for more than half a century have labored with him to generate not only new knowledge and practice but whole new fields in which to apply it, we offer our gratitude.

The revolution in our understanding of human behavior and development described in this book would not have been possible without all of the infants, children, and families across the globe who shared their intrinsic truths with Brazelton and the generations of colleagues whom he helped to inspire. To them, too, we give thanks. All of us who have benefited from Brazelton's contributions are also deeply grateful to his wife, Chrissie, and his children, Kitty, Polly, Stina, and Tom, who have been his most stalwart supporters all along.

Like the Brazelton scale, the face-to-face/still face paradigm has also been used in other cultures. Again, there are important cultural differences. In Kenya, for example, the Gusii show some of the same patterns of reciprocal interactions as U.S. mothers (Brazelton, Dixon, Keefer, & Tronick, 1981), suggesting the universality of these early patterns of social interaction.

Models of Development

Brazelton always had a questioning attitude toward science. His unwillingness to equate the scientific models of the day with eternal truths has led to revolutionary changes in our models of development, especially in terms of our understanding of the meaning of variability and change in behavior. Brazelton challenged prevailing views that significant amounts of variability in infant behavior, for example, on the Brazelton scale, were problematic. He argued, on the contrary, that for babies to stay the same on the scale would be problematic and potentially clinically worrisome. What others called error or "noise," he viewed as a critical part of the "signal." He urged the scientific community not to throw out the baby with the bathwater (Brazelton, 1990). Behavioral instability is part, in fact a critical part, of normal processes of developmental change. Infancy is a period of rapid development and while a "moving target" may be more difficult to study, the study of change is key to our understanding of development. Saving the bathwater has had a major impact on our models of child development because it meant rejecting simplistic "nature–nurture" models of development that were linear or additive. The idea that one could take different genotypes, add in the environment and sum up the child's development was replaced by models that incorporated change. From a psychometric or measurement point of view, this was nightmarish because it meant that traditional ways of partitioning the variance to estimate what was "error" and what was not were no longer viable. As a result there have been substantial advances in statistical models that include change such as nonlinear, growth, trajectory, and systems models.

Developmental models were constructed that were complex, multifaceted, and took a broad systems approach extending from factors proximal to the infant, such as the parent–infant interaction, to the far reaches of factors more distal to the infant such as community organizations, cultural values and the greater social fabric of society (Bronfenbrenner, 1979). Arguably the transactional model (Sameroff, 1982) became the most influential of these and had at its core Brazelton's idea that development is the product of reciprocal interactions (transactions) in which infant behavior modifies parent behavior which in turn modifies infant behavior and that this is an ongoing dynamic process. Brazelton's work changed our fundamental understanding about how development unfolds and the very processes of development. *Touchpoints* (Brazelton, 1992) was a further advance. One of the remarkable features of *Touchpoints* is that it is both a book for parents on child rearing and a major theoretical advance in our understanding of child development. *Touchpoints* is based on the model that development is nonlinear and uneven. Psychological growth takes place in many directions at once. There are spurts in development but there are also regressions. Regressions are seen as not only normal, but necessary for normal development. There is order in the system. These spurts and regressions are predictable and *Touchpoints* is a blueprint that provides the schematic for these processes.

The Conduct of Research

It is, of course, tautological to say that a productive scientist influences research in his field but it is nonetheless interesting to see some of the ways in which Brazelton's work has changed the way we go about the business of research. The dynamics of newborn behavior, the infant's contribution to his or her own development, and processes of reciprocity in the infant–parent relationship have become major areas of research of their own. Even in studies not focusing on these areas, these issues still need to be accounted for or addressed in their research design. For example, studies of parenting need to include measurement of the mother–child interaction. Similarly, the bathwater of change including the normative nature of regression is both studied and serves as a platform to frame other research agendas and establish new areas of programmatic research.

Methodologically, the Brazelton scale and the face-to-face/still face paradigm have become industry standard tools in the field. These measures are based on direct observation and measurement of behavior in contrast to parent report. Using parents' reports of their infants' behavior to measure, for example, temperament or mother–infant interaction introduces bias and may not be as objective as measuring these behaviors directly. The advent of these tools contributed to methodological advances in measurement of infant behavior through direct observation.

The Brazelton scale, in addition to being a research instrument, is also used as an intervention to help parents get to know their babies (Kusaka, Ohgi, Gima, & Fujimoto, 2007). The scale has also been used with chimps in studies of cross-species comparisons of newborn behavior (Bard, Platzman, & Lester, 1992) and to study the molecular genetics of newborn behavior in chimps (Champoux et al., 2002). There have also been adaptations of the Brazelton Scale designed for special purposes such as the Assessment of Preterm Infant Behavior (Als, Lester, Tronick, & Brazelton, 1982), the NICU Network Neurobehavioral Scale (Lester, Tronick, & Brazelton, 2004) and a fetal neurobehavioral scale, the Fetal Neurobehavioral Assessment System (Salisbury, Fallone, & Lester, 2005). The NNNS was designed to expand the scope of behavior in the Brazelton scale for applicability to high-risk infants including substance exposed and preterm infants. The NNNS groups infants into discrete neurobehavioral profiles that reflect patterns of individual differences. In addition, the profiles have been shown to identify infants with medical problems, including brain damage, and infants that will go on to have cognitive and behavioral problems, including problems with school readiness (Liu et al., 2009). This could lead to the Brazelton scale goal of early identification and the development of interventions to prevent future deficits in children.

As mentioned earlier in this chapter, the cognitive revolution gave us the mind but not the brain. The Brazelton revolution gave us the baby and, once we knew what the baby could do, it only made sense to try and figure out how. Where do these individual differences come from? Why does one baby have one set of behaviors and another baby have a different set of behaviors – at birth? How does the baby know what behaviors to use to change the caregiving environment? Brazelton always argued that these behaviors and behavioral systems are not random and simply reinforced by the environment. They have a purpose. They have adaptive value. How does this work?

The answer may lie in modern neuroscience. These are exciting times as we have probably learned more about the brain in the past 20 years than in all of recorded history, including fetal programming. Fetal programming is based on developmental plasticity, which enables the organism to change (i.e. reprogram) structure and function in response to environmental cues. These are evolved mechanisms that monitor the environment to adjust set points of brain circuits. The adaptive significance is that plasticity enables a range of phenotypes to develop from a single genotype depending on environmental influences. Developmental plasticity sets the template or "programs" the fetus

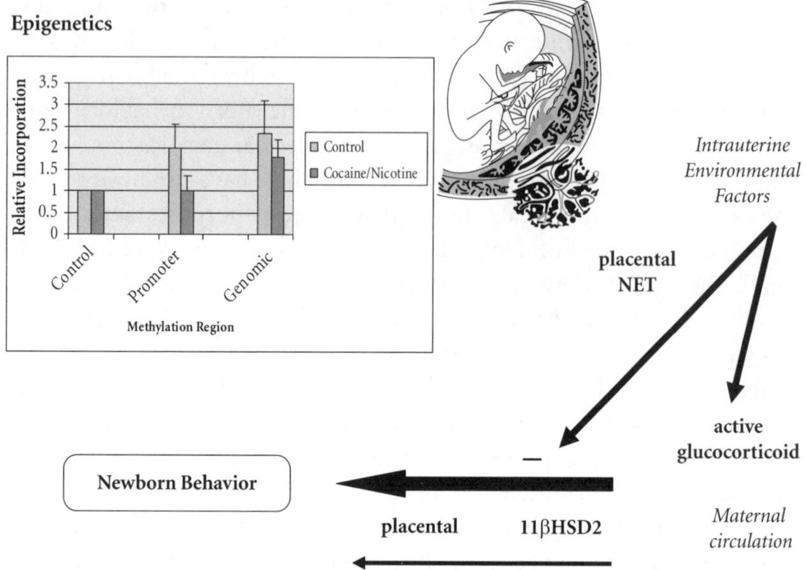

Figure 1.1 Factors in the intrauterine environment can affect genes in the placenta that determine fetal exposure to the stress hormone cortisol which, in turn, affects the behavior of the newborn
Source: Adapted from Lester & Padbury (2009).

for postnatal adaptation to the environment. The fetus "reads" characteristics of its environment and prepares to adapt to the external environment. Most of the work on fetal programming has been directed toward studying adult chronic disease. Observations that low birthweight was related to the later development of cardiovascular disease and metabolic disorders (Barker & Fall, 1993) led to the concept of the "fetal origins" of adult disease. The idea is that fetal metabolic pathways are reprogrammed in response to undernutrition but, in a postnatal environment with adequate nutrition, this becomes maladaptive and leads to the adult development of chronic disease.

The fetal origins of adult disease invite speculation about the possibility of the fetal origins of behavioral outcomes. It is understood that undernutrition is but a proxy for specific processes that may involve, for example, the neuroendocrine system. Figure 1.1, adapted from Lester and Padbury, shows a model in which factors in the intrauterine environment can affect genes in the placenta that determine fetal exposure to the stress hormone cortisol which, in turn, affects the behavior of the newborn (Lester &

Collaborative consultation anticipates that there will be differences in perspectives, beliefs, values, practices, and goals, and that deliberate strategies can be used to heighten understanding of these differences, to arrive at an overarching sense of common purpose. The force driving this process is not the motivation of one group to impose on, extract from, or dominate another, but a focus on the natural tendency of humans to engage in relationships with each other, and to rally together to nurture and protect their young. The relational basis of collaborative consultation can be a way of grappling with the self–other duality that arises across cultures and other differences, and with the alienation that 'otherness' can confer (Scheper-Hughes, 1992).

Carefully adapted strategies are needed to engender the engaging and sustaining qualities of the relationship – equal, respectful, mutually supportive, present, authentic, connected. Borrowing from Brazelton's procedure for observing infants, collaborative consultation may begin with an initial period of quiet, observing presence. Finding out where the "other" appears to be begins the process of "joining," of overcoming "otherness." This may remain unattainable, yet the expression of this intent and these aspired-to ideals through a shared, experiential process is powerful. The experience of trust, intimacy, shared understandings and purposes brings into clearer focus similarities across cultures. In practice, this also requires times for being physically present with each other, in each other's worlds.

The process of quiet observation, shared discovery, and meaning making used to communicate about newborn behavior can be readily applied to the process of collaborative consultation. Purely objective descriptions of observable behaviors are not the goal, but careful monitoring for the leap from observations to inferences and judgments can be one way in which collaborators discover their differences, their similarities, their shared understandings, and where they have more to learn about each other to more fully understand each other. Attention to these leaps can also help restore and keep on track the moments of authentic presence with each other that constitute for all partners the lived experience of coming together, of connection.

Collaborative consultation is about the potential of relationships across perceived differences to bring about growth in all parties. Brazelton carefully attends to examiners' impact on newborn behavior, and holds them responsible for eliciting the newborn's "best performance." Examiners will be changed in the process and will understand themselves and the baby better if they reflect on the baby's effects on them. The same baby may leave one examiner exhausted, another elated; one examiner may feel ready to adopt one baby, and indifferent about another. Analogously, collaborative consultation encourages all partners as equals to carefully consider their effects on each other.

Collaborative consultation is not intended to increase one group's success in foisting its views and practices on another. The interaction of peoples across perceived differences has often caused more harm than good, particularly in the context of power imbalances, and this must be vigilantly guarded against. When a new technology is offered to a people of a different culture, it may be rejected or ineffective. It may cause blatant damage, or more subtle harm, for example in the form of undermining and supplanting the local culture's time-tested and carefully adapted ways and wisdom. One instance of this is the "science" of childrearing's unintended effect of undermining parents' sense of competence and of connection to their cultural identity which guides their parenting. On the other hand, of course, just because a practice is deemed "cultural" does not necessarily mean that it promotes children's health, wellbeing, and development (Scheper-Hughes, 1992).

The coming together of two or more groups must be desired by both, with full foreknowledge of these risks. These may be avoided, for example, when partners can serve as catalysts for each other's discovery of their own strengths and potential, when they can arrive at common ground to overcome an impasse, when their mutual positive regard, support and respect helps them experience an alternative to the isolation and disempowerment of historical trauma and current oppression, and to listen with more hope to their own voices (Yellow Horse Brave Heart & Debruyn, 1998). Re-equilibration of power imbalances is also both a part of the process of collaborative consultation and one of its goals.

Applying Brazelton's model of developmental change to the process of transformation that occurs within these deepening relationships, one might expect periods of disorganization within each partner or within their relationship to each other. As assumptions are questioned and biases revealed, disorganization may take the form of confusion, doubt, conflict, or withdrawal. Such disorganization might also be expected to precede subsequent phases of greater trust, constructive risk-taking, and intimacy. For higher level reorganization to follow periods of developmental disorganization, specific supports are needed, just as they are for all humans undergoing developmental processes – parents, adult caregivers, and, of course, children. These supports include ongoing relational connections and a belief in one's capacity to positively influence one's self and environment, one's present and future. Hope holds out the template for future configurations of development, whether for the child, the parent, the practitioner, or the community. Along with hope, the affirmation of strengths and of the need for self-determination help keep the parallel developmental crises of children, parents, professionals, institutions, and collaborative consultations in touch with their potential for better adapted reorganizations.

Future Challenges

Developmental disorganization and reorganization in children, families, professionals, institutions, communities and collaborations; the relational, contextual, and systemic bases of development in all of these areas; the importance of and challenges to social connectedness, empowerment, and self-determination in collaborative efforts and community building: none of these meet the current fragmentary demand for a single silver bullet, for fast and cheap results. "Parachute" programs, e.g., distributing soap bars to communities where there is insufficient water to use them, or book bags to children who go to school hungry, or condoms to sex workers whose clients violently forbid them to use them, are misguided responses to this demand. Although their shortcomings are predictable and well documented, they continue to attract support. They are based on simple concepts, simple enough to be conveyed in a sound bite or elevator pitch. But because they are inherently singly focused, non-relational and unilateral, they cannot bring about changes that go deep enough to sustain themselves (Mitchell, 2009).

Like most calls for substantive change, applications of Brazelton's ideas to collaborative community building raise resistance. "Relational" sounds touchy-feely, like unnecessary fluff, and stirs up primitive fears of boundary loss and fusion. Strategies for empowerment and self-determination represent another kind of threat. Yet these transformative ideas are a direct response to the limits of where past theory and practice can take us, and suggest a promising path to the future. Perhaps the processes by which they will be disseminated, understood, adapted, and applied will also be guided by these ideas themselves.

The importance of collaborations respectful of the imperative of self-determination is now understood by many nongovernmental and community-based organizations. Brazelton has perhaps wisely but not entirely avoided the thorny dilemma of cultural relativism and a universal ethics raised by self-determination and globalization that many others (Farmer, 2005; Scheper-Hughes, 1992; United Nations General Assembly, 1989) have attempted to tackle. Globalization is perhaps the largest scale for connectedness, yet in its current form, change is certainly not transacted through the equipotent ripples of mutually adapting circles described here. To some extent, collaborative consultation might be used to try to protect against the domination of one culture by another in this increasingly interconnected world. It might help guard against the shortcomings and unintended harm to all of us that can accompany attempted redistribution from one culture to another of knowledge, services, or resources, including those that may be considered universal rights – food, clean water, shelter, access to healthcare and education, among others. But collaborative consultation will not suffice if there *are* indeed some universal rights, unless this process itself is ultimately guided by them.

Here, too, Brazelton's transformative ideas may help. His approach has been to mobilize the political will and the resources for protection, nurturance, and the fostering of health, growth and wellbeing of infants and children. Yet he has been clear that this is not a matter of simply rallying around the "best interests" of the child. The infant, as Winnicott, one of Brazelton's heroes, has said, does not exist without the mother (Winnicott, 1964/1987). So might we add to the rights and best interests of the child a more comprehensive stance to protect, nurture, and support the health, growth, and wellbeing of the child's caregiving environment – defined widely to also include the child's local community, physical environment, and as affected by global forces (Sparrow, in press)? As overly simple as it may sound, is there not some merit to using this idea that springs from Brazelton's transformative ones, as a fundamental criterion against which to consider the compromises that collaborating cultures propose?

References and further reading

Brazelton, T. B. (1973). *Neonatal behavior assessment scale.* Philadelphia: Lippincott.

Brazelton, T. B. (1992). *Touchpoints – The essential reference: Your child's emotional and behavioral development.* Cambridge, MA: Perseus Books.

Brazelton, T. B., & Nugent, K. (1995). *Neonatal behavioral assessment scale* (3rd ed.). London: Mac Keith Press.

Brazelton T. B., & Sparrow J. D. (2006). *Touchpoints 0–3: Your child's emotional and behavioral development* (2nd ed.). Cambridge, MA: Da Capo Press.

Bronfenbrenner, U. (1979). *The ecology of human development: Experiments by nature and design.* Cambridge, MA: Harvard University Press.

Farmer, P. (2005). *Pathologies of power: Health, human rights, and the new war on the poor.* Berkeley: University of California Press.

Fogel A., King B. J., & Shanker S. G. (Eds.) (2008). *Human development in the twenty-first century: Visionary ideas from systems scientists.* Cambridge: Cambridge University Press.

Heimann, M. (Ed.) (2003). *Regression periods in human infancy.* Mahwah, NJ: Erlbaum.

Mitchell, S. (2009) *Unsimple truths: Science, complexity, and policy.* Chicago: University of Chicago Press.

Murray, L., Cooper, P., & Hipwell, A. (2003). Mental health of parents caring for infants. *Archives of Women's Mental Health, 6*, 71–77.

Sameroff, A. J. (1975). Transactional models in early social relations. *Human Development. 18*(1–2), 65–79.

Scheper-Hughes, N. (1992). *Death without weeping: The violence of everyday life in Brazil.* Berkeley: University of California Press.

Sparrow, J. D. (in press). Child justice, caregiver empowerment and community self-determination. In B. S. Fennimore & A. L. Goodwin (Eds.), *Promoting social justice for young children.* New York: Springer.

United Nations General Assembly, Convention on the Rights of the Child (1989), United Nations, accessed June, 2009, from: http://www.ohchr.org/english/law/crc.htm

van de Rijt-Plooij, H. H. C., & Plooij, F. X. (1992). Infantile regressions: Disorganization and the onset of transition periods. *Journal of Reproductive and Infant Psychology, 10*, 129–149.

Winnicott, D. W. (1964/1987). *The child, the family, and the outside world.* Reading, MA: Addison Wesley.

Yellow Horse Brave Heart, M., & Debruyn, L. M. (1998). The American Indian holocaust: Healing historical unresolved grief. *American Indian & Alaska Native Mental Health Research, 8*(2), 60–82.

Section II

Advances in Understanding Fetal and Newborn Behavior

3

Before Infant Assessment
Fetal Neurobehavior

Amy L. Salisbury

Historical Influences of Fetal Neurobehavioral Assessment

The early work of T. Berry Brazelton was instrumental in demonstrating the power of direct observation of infant behavior in a social context. He contributed to our understanding of the infant's behavioral repertoire as spontaneous as well as elicited by physical or social stimuli (Brazelton, 1973; Brazelton & Robey, 1965). His work demonstrated that infants are born with awareness, responsiveness, and social competence and that these attributes showed profound individual differences that helped the infant interact with the environment and caregivers in an adaptive manner. These observations became the basis for teaching parents about their newborns' capacities and an opportunity for infants and caregivers to learn about each other (Brazelton, Tronick, Adamson, Als, & Wise, 1975; Brazelton & Young, 1964).

Prior to direct observations of infants in isolation and with caretakers, understanding infants' biological, behavioral, and social capacities from the earliest hours of life was not fully realized. Infants were viewed as reflexive organisms with little ability to interact with the world around them (Irwin & Weiss, 1930). Contemporary theories of human development not only accept that the infant is an active participant from birth, but celebrate the notion that young infants often initiate as well as respond to their environment and the people in it, playing at least some role in shaping their relationships with caretakers. For example, developmental systems theory, derived from general systems theory, is based on the premise that biological, behavioral, and environmental systems dynamically influence each other over time. In this model, the infant is part of a developmental system and is as much a driver in the system as the surrounding environment. Infant development is dependent upon genetic encoding of proteins, but also upon mutual experience with the environment (Denenberg, 1980). This results in an evolving course of development over time. Epigenetic and organismic models of developmental theory suggest that we will only truly understand a developing system if we study its organization of form and structure as it moves toward a teleological state (Bertalanffy, 1968; Gottleib, 1991). Developmental study is often just a snapshot of this evolving system and would be incomplete without consideration of the shared influences involved.

Early observations of infant behavior provided a wealth of information about behavior patterns and response to stimuli in the earliest days of postnatal life (Brazelton, 1961; Cobb, Grimm, & Dawson, 1967; Gilmer, 1933; Korner, 1969; McGraw, 1939; Pratt, 1935; Wolff, 1959). The seminal work of Brazelton and others, in both human and non-human research, exemplified how systematic assessment of infant development as a part of its larger system brought us greater understanding of the infant's capacities (Brazelton, 1961; Cobb et al., 1967; Gilmer, 1933; Korner, 1969; McGraw, 1939; Pratt, 1935; Thoman, Turner, Leiderman, & Barnett, 1970; Wolff, 1959), and how even seemingly small influences can have profound effects on development (Denenberg, DeSantis, Waite, & Thoman, 1977; Denenberg & Whimbey, 1963; DeSantis, Waite, Thoman, & Denenberg, 1977).

The current work in the study of infant development remains heavily focused on the infant from the time of birth. However, if the infant truly possesses the ability to interact socially and react selectively to various stimuli from the moment of birth, it is a logical extension that these capacities exist prior to the event of birth.

Fetal Neurobehavioral Assessment

Neurobehavior is a construct originally introduced into the field of infant development over 30 years ago (Brazelton, 1961) as a means of determining neurological integrity by looking at various behaviors of the infant. In the newborn, examining reflexes, motor activity and tone, responsivity, attention, and habituation in the context of behavioral state operationally define neurobehavior. Brazelton developed the Neonatal Behavioral Assessment Scale (NBAS) to systematically observe and measure infant neurobehavioral domains in the first months of life (Brazelton, 1978). Based on the NBAS, Lester and Tronick developed the NICU Network Neurobehavioral Scale (NNNS) to measure processes of biobehavioral organization in infants at risk due to multiple factors in premature and as well as term newborn infants (Lester & Tronick, 2004). Because the NNNS was designed to accommodate the unique needs of the premature infant, it was a natural extension to use these principles to assess the infant before birth.

Fetal neurobehavior is an extension of the original construct in that similar behaviors can be assessed to determine neurologic integrity of the fetus (DiPietro, 2001). Operationally, fetal neurobehavioral development is accomplished by the measurement of four domains: fetal heart rate, motor activity, behavioral state, and responsiveness to external or extrauterine stimuli (DiPietro, Hodgson, Costigan, Hilton, & Johnson, 1996b). The use of ultrasound technology enables visualization of the fetus to observe specific fetal action patterns, motor activity, quality and amplitude of movements, and eye movements. Additional monitoring equipment, such as the fetal cardiograph, provides the measurement of fetal heart rate. There is currently not enough data about the full repertoire of human fetal behavior or normative development over gestation to accept a standardized "scale" to describe fetal neurobehavior. However, with the collective work of the researchers studying fetal development, the time for such an assessment may not be far away.

Several methods of fetal behavioral assessment have been developed over the years to examine different aspects of fetal neurobehavior. Fetal behavior patterns were observed by ultrasound observations at weekly intervals throughout gestation (de Vries, Visser, & Prechtl, 1982). The authors were able to describe a broad range of behaviors that are also observed in the newborn infant. Morokuma et al. (2007) proposed a standardized assessment of fetal behaviors using ultrasound observation of key behaviors they found to be related to compromised neurological outcome. Others in the field examined fetal heart rate responsiveness to stimuli, including the voice of the mother versus a stranger (Kisilevsky & Muir, 1991) and reactivity to a vibroacoustic stimulus (Kisilevsky, 1995). DiPietro and her co-authors examined the fetal–maternal system by utilizing fetal actocardiograms in conjunction with maternal physiology measures (DiPietro, Hodgson, Costigan, Hilton, & Johnson, 1996a; DiPietro, Irizarry, Costigan, & Gurewitsch, 2004). Kisilevsky and DiPietro investigated fetal neurobehavior in the context of the social or physical environment of the fetus. Their work has expanded the field of fetal assessment to include important aspects of the fetal developmental system. They have shown the fetus to be selectively responsive to the mothers voice (Kisilevsky et al., 2009) as well as maternal physiology (DiPietro, Costigan, Nelson, Gurewitsch, & Laudenslager, 2008; DiPietro et al., 2004).

Using the NNNS, systems theory, and the collective history provided by prior infant and fetal research as a basis, we have been developing and testing a method for a comprehensive neurobehavioral assessment of the fetus, including fetal behavior patterns, fetal heart rate, activity, and reactivity to stimuli, called the Fetal Neurobehavioral Assessment System (FENS) (Salisbury, Fallone, & Lester, 2005). The FENS is a standardized method of monitoring, observing, and scoring fetal neurobehavior. It is not a measurement scale, but it is hoped that we will be able to have some standard, normative data of fetal neurobehavior in the near future.

Methods

The FENS includes direct observation and measurement of fetal behaviors, heart rate, activity, and reactivity to stimuli. The FENS uses the observation of these parameters to assess fetal central nervous system maturation. The system includes a behavioral coding scheme that was adapted from the work of others in the field (de Vries et al., 1982; de Vries, Visser, & Prechtl, 1985; Nijhuis, Prechtl, Martin, & Bots, 1982; Pillai & James, 1991) and is based on our own experiences observing fetal and infant behavior in a wide variety of contexts (Salisbury et al., 2007; Salisbury, Minard, Hunsley, & Thoman, 2001; Stroud et al., 2009). Assessment of fetal neurobehavior is limited to visual observation and physiological measures, but includes behaviors that enable reliable measurement within the core domains of neurobehavioral assessment.

Real-time ultrasound (Toshiba diagnostic ultrasound machine model SSA-340A with a 3.75 MHz transducer) is currently used to examine fetal behaviors in conjunction with a fetal actocardiograph (Toitu MT325) to monitor fetal heart rate (FHR) and activity (DiPietro, Costigan, & Pressman, 1999). While the pregnant woman reclines in a semi-recumbent position, the fetus is monitored for a baseline period of time (40–60 minutes), followed by a single, 3-second Vibroacoustic Stimulus (VAS) applied to the maternal abdomen and an additional 10–30 minutes of post-VAS observation. Alternative stimuli may be used in the FENS, such as light, voice, and airborne sounds (Kisilevsky et al., 2009; Kisilevsky, Pang, & Hains, 2000). The

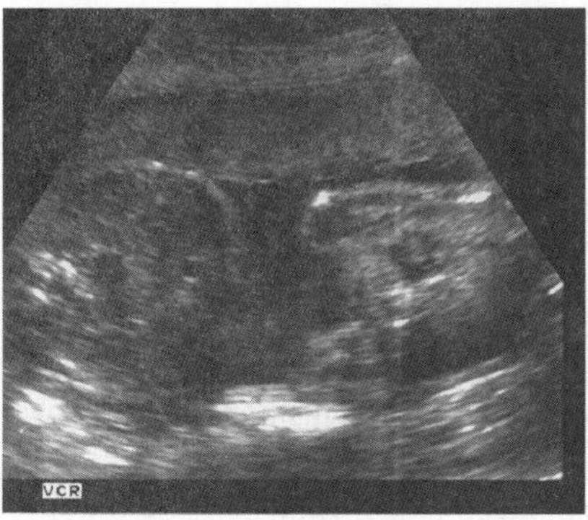

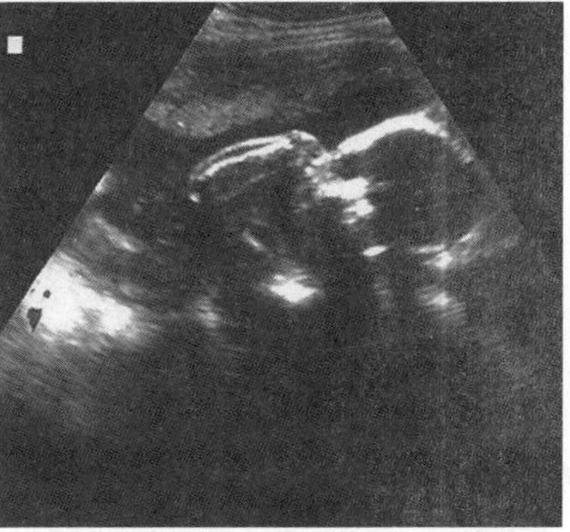

Figure 3.1 Fetal ultrasound images representing the view obtained for coding behaviors. The fetal head is to the right in both images, with at least one limb, a portion of the chest, and the fetal face visible

Source: From van de Rijt-Plooij, H. H. C., & Plooij, F. X. (1992). Infantile regressions: Disorganization and the onset of transition periods. *Journal of Reproductive and Infant Psychology*, 10, 129–149. Reproduced by permission of Taylor & Francis Ltd.: www.informaworld.com

maximum observation time is limited to 60 minutes of intermittent ultrasound scanning. Fetal behavior is observed using a single ultrasound transducer focused on a longitudinal view of the fetal face, trunk, and upper limbs (see Figure 3.1). An actocardiograph machine (Toitu m325; H&A Medical) is used to collect simultaneous fetal heart rate (FHR), fetal heart patterns, and fetal movement (amplitude, duration, frequency) (DiPietro et al., 1999; Maeda, Tatsumura, & Nakajima, 1991; Maeda et al., 1988). The data from the ultrasound video recordings and the actocardiogram are synchronized for scoring of fetal behaviors, fetal heart rate, activity, and fetal behavioral state.

The ultrasound observation is recorded on to a digital mpg video file for coding of specific fetal behaviors at a later time. A video coding software program (Mangold-International, Atlanta, GA) is used to view the video in 10-second epochs and score each epoch for the presence or absence of each of the behaviors listed in Table 3.1. Based on the observations and data from the NNNS, we are coding behaviors that represent the typical behavioral repertoire of the fetus at varying gestational ages, including those behaviors that may be more frequently observed in infants who are in distress (e.g., the drug-exposed neonate), such as tremors, backarching, and startles. Further testing will determine if fetuses in distress exhibit certain different behavior patterns than those that are not stressed. Inter-rater reliability has been demonstrated for video coding, with Percent Agreement scores of 81–100% and Intraclass correlations of 0.84–1.0.

Table 3.1 Fetal behaviors coded in the FENS ultrasound coding scheme

Summary Variable	*Variable*	*Description*
Fetal Eye Movement	Present	Clear movement of the pupil or eyelid
	Absent	A clear view of the eye is obtained and there is no movement
Fetal Breathing Movements	Regular	Displacement of the diaphragm with movement of the abdomen, may be rhythmic or non-rhythmic
	Vigorous	FBMs that are large enough to move the entire fetus's body
	Hiccup	Consists of a jerky, repetitive contraction of the diaphragm
General Body Movements	Smooth	Pattern of movement involving smooth, simultaneous movement of a limb, trunk and head that results in a change of position
	Jerky	GBM that involves jerky movements of limbs or entire body
	Incomplete	GBM that is not fluid or coordinated and does not result in change in position
	Flexion	Flexion of the trunk
Patterned Body Movements	Stretch	A single event including a back extension or upward movement of the shoulder with retroflexion of the head; typically includes a pause at the peak of the movement with subsequent relaxation
	Backarch	Extension of the trunk and maintenance in this position for greater than 1 second
	Startle	A quick, generalized movement, involving abduction or extension of the limbs with or without movement of the trunk and head, followed by a return to a resting position
	Fidget	Nearly continuous limb movements that are not part of a GBM or other patterned movement
Head Movements	Rotation	Movement of the head in the lateral plane for at least a 30-degree angle from starting position

Table 3.1 (*Cont'd*)

Summary Variable	*Variable*	*Description*
	Extension	A small movement of the head that extends upward in the vertical plane
	General	Small movement of the head that is not an extension or rotation
Mouthing Movements	Rhythmic	Rhythmical bursts of jaw opening and closing at least 4 times in 10 seconds (sucking)
	NonRhythmic	Mouth opening and closing that is isolated or limited to less than 4 at one time, often with tongue protrusion or lapping (drinking)
	Yawning	The timing of a yawn is similar to a stretch that includes prolonged wide opening of the jaws followed by relaxation; often accompanied by a stretch or a subsequent GBM
Limb Movements	Smooth	Movement of an extremity that is generally fluid
	Jerky	Movement of an extremity that is generally forceful and/or abrupt in nature
	Indeterminate	Upper limb movement is evident but quality cannot be determined
	Lower Limb	Lower limb is moving but quality of movement cannot be determined
	Multiple	Repetitive limb movement in the same plane in a single epoch.
	Hand to Face	The hand slowly touches the face or mouth
	Tremor	Small rhythmic, jerky movement of an extremity

Source: Adapted from Salisbury et al. (2009)

Research Applications

Normative development

The FENS can be used to assess normative fetal development as well as to assess at-risk fetuses.

In several pilot studies, we demonstrated consistent developmental changes over gestational age (Salisbury, Yanni, Lagasse, & Lester, 2004) as well as significant correlations between FENS and NNNS measures (Salisbury et al., 2005). In agreement with others, we found that large fetal movements decrease over gestational age, with increases in fetal breathing movements and more coordinated rest–activity cycles (Salisbury et al., 2004). Fetal jerky movements typically decrease with advancing gestational age, with an increase in smooth movements, and are most likely dependent upon the behavioral state of the fetus. We found that quality of movement at 25 weeks gestational age, determined by the ratio of smooth to jerky movements, was positively related to the NNNS measure of infant self-regulation, and negatively related to infant excitability on the NNNS at 2 days post delivery (Salisbury et al., 2005).

Clinical Research

The FENS is being used to examine fetal responses to maternal mood, anxiety, and substance use in clinical research samples. In pilot studies, fetal heart rate reactivity to a vibroacoustic stimulus was shown to be heightened in fetuses whose mothers reported higher amounts of depressive symptoms compared to fetuses whose mothers had lower depression scores (Allister, Lester, Carr, & Liu, 2001). In another pilot study, we replicated this finding and demonstrated that fetuses of women with depressed mood also have a concomitant heightened behavioral reactivity to a VAS (Salisbury et al., 2004).

We have preliminary evidence that fetuses exposed to SRI medications in utero may have poorer quality of movement at 36 weeks gestational age (GA) compared to nonexposed fetuses as well as lower amounts of fetal breathing movements at 36 weeks GA (Salisbury, Ponder, Padbury, & Lester, 2009).

The FENS methods are also currently being used to examine fetal neurobehavioral development in fetuses exposed to maternal smoking, opiates, and psychotropic medications. In addition, the FENS is being used to assess fetuses that have an older sibling with an autism spectrum disorder to determine if there are markers of autism prior to birth.

Clinical Applications

As discussed previously, the maternal–fetal system is a system rather than merely fetal reflexes and reactivity. The idea that fetal behaviors and physiology can influence maternal physiology and behaviors has been accepted and studied for the last few decades and is summarized in Lecanuet, Fifer, Krasenegor, and Smotherman, 1995. A clinical application of these ideas is the use of ultrasound images as an intervention with at-risk populations of pregnant women, including women with depression (Boukydis et al., 2006) and smoking during pregnancy (Stotts et al., 2009). The intervention is based on the idea that visualizing the fetus and seeing behavioral patterns in utero will increase a woman's sense of attachment to the fetus and in turn increase her motivation for self-care and avoidance of risky behaviors such as smoking or drinking alcohol during the pregnancy. There are limited studies in this area and consideration needs to be given to the possibility that the intervention could cause excessive anxiety in some women that would not be beneficial.

In our work, we do not use the FENS as an intervention per se. Due to the author's training in child psychiatry and on the clinical use of the NNNS assessment, it became a natural extension to use the same process of involving the caretakers in learning about the behavioral and social strengths of their unborn child. The FENS procedures begin with a general assessment of fetal position in the uterus. We use the time to share our observations with the mother and other caretakers if present. They are able to focus on the behavior, rather than anatomical structures as is the case in a diagnostic ultrasound, of their unborn child for the first time. Although not yet studied systematically, we have observed that even women who present with profound anhedonia and very low energy display an increase in bright affect and vocalization during the assessment. This is in agreement with the recent study by Boukydis et al. (2006) showing a similar effect during routine diagnostic ultrasound assessments. Given the vast range of intensity of human reaction to a pregnancy itself, it should not be surprising that an infant, before birth, could have such an influence on maternal mood, thoughts, and behaviors.

Conclusions

The FENS is a method of observing and measuring fetal behaviors in utero during the second half of pregnancy that assesses fetal central nervous system (CNS) maturation, including neurological development and behavioral reactivity, in typically developing and at-risk fetuses. The FENS is based on the idea that direct observation of behavior patterns in social and physical environmental contexts are ideal for understanding human development and, perhaps, for shaping more optimal relationships and stronger foundations for the infant system to grow.

References and further reading

Allister, L., Lester, B. M., Carr, S., & Liu, J. (2001). The effects of maternal depression on fetal heart rate response to vibroacoustic stimulation. *Developmental Neuropsychology, 20*(3), 639–651.

Bertalanffy, L. V. (1968). *General systems theory*. New York: Brazilier.

Boukydis, C. F., Treadwell, M. C., Delaney-Black, V., Boyes, K., King, M., Robinson, T., & Sokol, R. (2006). Women's responses to ultrasound examinations during routine screens in an obstetric clinic. *Journal of Ultrasound in Medicine, 25*(6), 721–728.

Brazelton, T. B. (1961). Psychophysiologic reactions in the neonate. I. The value of observations of the neonate. *Journal of Pediatrics, 58*, 508–512.

Brazelton, T. B. (1973). Assessment of the infant at risk. *Clinical Obstetrics & Gynecology, 16*(1), 361–375.

Brazelton, T. B. (1978). The Brazelton Neonatal Behavior Assessment Scale: Introduction. *Monographs of the Society for Research in Child Development, 43*(5–6), 1–13.

Brazelton, T. B., & Robey, J. S. (1965). Observations of neonatal behavior: The effect of perinatal variables, in particular that of maternal medication. *Journal of the American Academy of Child Psychiatry, 4*(4), 613–637.

Brazelton, T. B., Tronick, E., Adamson, L., Als, H., & Wise, S. (1975). Early mother–infant reciprocity. *Ciba Foundation Symposium* (33), 137–154.

Brazelton, T. B., & Young, G. C. (1964). An example of imitative behavior in a nine-week-old infant. *Journal of the American Academy of Child Psychiatry, 19*, 53–67.

Cobb, K., Grimm, E. R., & Dawson, B. (1967). Reliability of global observations of newborn infants. *Journal of Genetic Psychology, 110*, 253–267.

de Vries, J. I., Visser, G. H., & Prechtl, H. F. (1982). The emergence of fetal behaviour. I. Qualitative aspects. *Early Human Development, 7*(4), 301–322.

de Vries, J. I. Visser, G. H. & Prechtl, H. F. (1985). The emergence of fetal behaviour. II. *Quantitative Aspects. 12*, 99–120.

Denenberg, V. H. (1980). General systems theory, brain organization, and early experiences. *American Journal of Physiology, 7*, R3–13.

Denenberg, V. H., DeSantis, D., Waite, S., & Thoman, E. B. (1977). The effects of handling in infancy on behavioral states in the rabbit. *Physiology & Behavior, 18*(4), 553–557.

Denenberg, V. H., & Whimbey, A. E. (1963). Behavior of adult rats is modified by the experiences their mothers had as infants. *Science, 142*, 1192–1193.

DeSantis, D., Waite, S., Thoman, E. B., & Denenberg, V. H. (1977). Effects of isolation rearing upon behavioral state organization and growth in the rabbit. *Behavioral Biology, 21*(2), 273–285.

DiPietro, J. A. (2001). Fetal neurobehavioral assessment. In P. S. Zeskind & J. E. Singer (Eds.), *Biobehavioral assessment* (pp. 43–80). New York: Elsevier.

DiPietro, J. A., Costigan, K. A., Nelson, P., Gurewitsch, E. D., & Laudenslager, M. L. (2008). Fetal responses to induced maternal relaxation during pregnancy. *Biological Psychology, 77*(1), 11–19.

DiPietro, J. A., Costigan, K. A., & Pressman, E. K. (1999). Fetal movement detection: comparison of the Toitu actograph with ultrasound from 20 weeks gestation. *Journal of Maternal–Fetal Medicine, 8*(6), 237–242.

DiPietro, J. A., Hodgson, D. M., Costigan, K. A., Hilton, S. C., & Johnson, T. R. (1996a). Development of fetal movement–fetal heart rate coupling from 20 weeks through term. *Early Human Development, 44*(2), 139–151.

DiPietro, J. A., Hodgson, D. M., Costigan, K. A., Hilton, S. C., & Johnson, T. R. (1996b). Fetal neurobehavioral development. *Child Development, 67*(5), 2553–2567.

DiPietro, J. A., Irizarry, R. A., Costigan, K. A., & Gurewitsch, E. D. (2004). The psychophysiology of the maternal–fetal relationship. *Psychophysiology, 41*(4), 510–520.

Gilmer, B. V. H. (1933). An analysis of the spontaneous responses of the newborn infant. *Journal of Genetic Psychology, 42*, 392–405.

Gottleib, G. (1991). Experiential canalization of behavioral development: Results. *Developmental Psychobiology, 27*, 35–39.

Irwin, O. C., & Weiss, A. P. (1930). A note on mass activity in newborn infants. *Journal of Genetic Psychology, 38*, 20–30.

Kisilevsky, B. S. (1995). The influence of stimulus and subject variables on human fetal responses to sound and vibration. In J. P. Lecanuet, W. P. Fifer, N. A. Krasnegor & W. P. Smotherman (Eds.), *Fetal development: A psychobiological perspective* (pp. 263–278). Hillsdale, NJ: Lawrence Erlbaum.

Kisilevsky, B. S., Hains, S. M., Brown, C. A., Lee, C. T., Cowperthwaite, B., Stutzman, S. S., … Wang, Z. (2009). Fetal sensitivity to properties of maternal speech and language. *Infant Behavior & Development, 32*(1), 59–71.

Kisilevsky, B. S., & Muir, D. W. (1991). Human fetal and subsequent newborn responses to sound and vibration. *Infant Behavior & Development, 14*, 1–26.

Kisilevsky, B. S., Pang, L., & Hains, S. M. (2000). Maturation of human fetal responses to airborne sound in low- and high-risk fetuses. *Early Human Development, 58*(3), 179–195.

Korner, A. F. (1969). Neonatal startles, smiles, erections, and reflex sucks as related to state, sex, and individuality. *Child Development, 40*(4), 1039–1053.

Lecanuet, J. P., Fifer, W., Krasenegor, N. A., & Smotherman, W. P. (Eds.). (1995). *Fetal development: A psychobiological perspective.* Hillsdale, NJ: Lawrence Erlbaum.

Lester, B. M., & Tronick, E. Z. (2004). History and description of the Neonatal Intensive Care Unit Network Neurobehavioral Scale. *Pediatrics, 113*(3 Pt. 2), 634–640.

Maeda, K., Tatsumura, M., & Nakajima, K. (1991). Objective and quantitative evaluation of fetal movement with ultrasonic Doppler actocardiogram. *Biology of the Neonate, 60* (Suppl. 1), 41–51.

Maeda, K., Tatsumura, M., Nakajima, K., Ida, T., Nagata, N., & Minagawa, Y. (1988). The ultrasonic Doppler fetal actocardiogram and its computer processing. *Journal of Perinatal Medicine, 16*(4), 327–331.

McGraw, M. B. (1939). Swimming behavior of the human infant. *Journal of Pediatrics, 15*, 485–490.

Morokuma, S., Fukushima, K., Yumoto, Y., Uchimura, M., Fujiwara, A., Matsumoto, M., ... Nakano, H. (2007). Simplified ultrasound screening for fetal brain function based on behavioral pattern. *Early Human Development, 83*(3), 177–181.

Nijhuis, J. G., Prechtl, H. F. R., Martin, C. B., Jr., & Bots, R. S. G. M. (1982). Are there behavioural states in the human fetus? *Early Human Development, 6*, 177–195.

Pillai, M., & James, D. (1991). Human fetal mouthing movements: A potential biophysical variable for distinguishing state 1F from abnormal fetal behavior; report of 4 cases. *European Journal of Obstetrics & Gynecology and Reproductive Biology, 38*(2), 151–156.

Pratt, K. C. (1935). The organization of behavior in the newborn infant. *Psychological Bulletin, 32*, 692–693.

Salisbury, A. L., Fallone, M. D., & Lester, B. (2005). Neurobehavioral assessment from fetus to infant: The NICU network neurobehavioral scale and the fetal neurobehavior coding scale. *Mental Retardation & Developmental Disabilities Research Reviews, 11*(1), 14–20.

Salisbury, A. L., Lester, B. M., Seifer, R., Lagasse, L., Bauer, C. R., Shankaran, S., et al. (2007). Prenatal cocaine use and maternal depression: Effects on infant neurobehavior. *Neurotoxicology and Teratology, 29*(3), 331–340.

Salisbury, A. L., Minard, K., Hunsley, M., & Thoman, E. (2001). Audio recording of infant crying: Comparison with maternal crylogs. *International Journal of Behavioral Development, 25*(5), 458–465.

Salisbury, A. L., Ponder, K. L., Padbury, J. F., & Lester, B. M. (2009). Fetal effects of psychoactive drugs. *Clinics in Perinatology, 36*(3), 595–619.

Salisbury, A. L., Yanni, P., Lagasse, L. L., & Lester, B. (Eds.). (2004). *Maternal–fetal psychobiology: A very early look at emotional development*. Oxford, UK: Oxford University Press.

Stotts, A. L., Groff, J. Y., Velasquez, M. M., Benjamin-Garner, R., Green, C., Carbonari, J. P., & DiClemente, C. C. (2009). Ultrasound feedback and motivational interviewing targeting smoking cessation in the second and third trimesters of pregnancy. *Nicotine & Tobacco Research, 11*(8), 961–968.

Stroud, L. R., Paster, R. L., Papandonatos, G. D., Niaura, R., Salisbury, A. L., Battle, C., et al. (2009). Maternal smoking during pregnancy and newborn neurobehavior: Effects at 10 to 27 days. *Journal of Pediatrics, 154*(1), 10–16.

Thoman, E. B., Turner, A. M., Leiderman, P. H., & Barnett, C. R. (1970). Neonate–mother interaction: Effects of parity on feeding behavior. *Child Dev, 41*(4), 1103–1111.

Wolff, P. H. (1959). Observations on newborn infants. *Psychosomatic Medicine, 21*, 110–118.

4

The Development of the NBAS
A Turning Point in Understanding the Newborn

J. Kevin Nugent

Background and History

To better appreciate the contribution of the Neonatal Behavioral Assessment Scale to our understanding of the human newborn, a retrospective review of the field of infant assessment and development is apposite. After all, for the first part of the twentieth century it was still assumed that the newborn infant was a "blank slate," a reflex organism, operating at a brain-stem level. The dominant view – even in the fields of psychology and medicine – was that infants were generally passive recipients of sensory stimulation, who could neither see nor hear and only responded to environmental input with innate programmed reflexes. Newborn assessment scales reflected these assumptions.

The earlier neonatal scales had focused on the assessment of the so-called "primitive reflexes" and "postural reactions" (e.g., Andre-Thomas and Dargassies, 1960; Peiper, 1963; Prechtl & Beintema, 1968). These scales were designed specifically to assess brain functioning by examining newborn reflexes. In clinical settings, the assessment of neonates was confined to Apgar scores and pediatric examinations of physical competence.

Until the 1960s and early 1970s, it was still generally believed that newborns could see only shadows at birth and that their capacities for learning were extremely limited, even nonexistent. But just then, Robert Fantz, using an innovative novelty preference research paradigm, demonstrated that newborns could not only see but they had clearcut visual preferences (Fantz, 1961). In terms of their auditory capacities, the prevailing assumption among both researchers and clinicians was that newborns' fluid-filled ears impaired their hearing for the first few days. However, Murphy and Smyth (1962) demonstrated that infants respond to auditory stimuli even before birth. These findings gave research on infant learning and development a new thrust. But, because they were not based on any particular model of development, these studies contributed little to an understanding of newborn and infant development.

A New Model of Newborn and Infant Development

In the late 1950s, a number of advances, especially in the fields of psychology and psychiatry, were contributing to a dramatic shift in thinking about infants and their development. Three "grand systems" for understanding child development held sway – Piaget's cognitive developmentalism, psychoanalysis, and learning theory. All three systems set the stage for the development of a new paradigm that would reframe thinking on infant development and early parent–infant relations. Brazelton first began to examine individual differences in infant crying patterns (Brazelton, 1962a, 1962b). Then at the Center for Cognitive Studies at Harvard, he worked with Jerome Bruner, Tom Bower, Martin Richards, Colwyn Trevarthen and Edward Tronick on new microanalytic observational techniques in an effort to develop a more detailed and complex understanding of individual differences in infant behavior and early infant–parent transactions. This body of research confirmed Brazelton's hypothesis that newborns were equipped with powerful innate reciprocal communicative abilities. He could also see that they were also capable of the kind of "organized" behavioral responses Peter Wolff had demonstrated earlier in his seminal work on "newborn behavioral states" (Wolff, 1959). This provided a conceptual foundation for the development of the Neonatal Behavioral Assessment Scale.

The First Iteration of the Neonatal Behavioral Assessment Scale (NBAS)

The Graham Scale (Graham, Matarazzo, & Caldwell, 1956) and the Graham–Rosenblith Scale (Rosenblith, 1961) were the first scales to attempt to outline behavioral differences among neonates. Shortly thereafter, the first iteration of the NBAS appeared – The Cambridge Neonatal Scales – developed by Brazelton and Daniel Freedman (Brazelton and Freedman, 1971). Using this scale, Freedman and his colleague were able to identify behavioral differences between Caucasian and Chinese neonates

(Freedman & Freedman, 1969). Intrigued by these findings, Brazelton and John Robey then went to southern Mexico to study the Zinacanteco Indians in the highlands of Chiapas (Brazelton, Robey, & Collier, 1969). Here, their ideas on neonatal differences were confirmed. They discovered that, compared to their Caucasian counterparts, these infants, even after delivery, "lay quietly on the blanket looking around the room with alert faces for an entire hour" (Brazelton et al., 1969, p. 279).

Confident that the scale could capture individual differences in newborn behavior, the next challenge was to develop a system that could describe, identify, and ultimately code these differences with a high degree of inter-rater reliability (Brazelton, 1973, 2009). With the help of Daniel Freedman, Frances Degan Horowitz, Barbara Koslowski, Henry Riciutti, John Robey, Arnold Sameroff and Edward Tronick, Brazelton developed a new scoring system, which was incorporated into the first edition of the NBAS (Brazelton, 1973). Because it yielded a comprehensive description of newborn competencies, on the one hand, and was able to identify individual differences in newborn behavior, on the other, the NBAS can be said to have begun where other scales left off.

The NBAS – Contents and Scoring

The NBAS assesses the newborn's behavioral repertoire with 28 behavioral items, each scored on a 9-point scale. It also includes an assessment of the infant's neurological status on 20 items, each scored on a 4-point scale. The reflex items are used to identify gross neurological abnormalities through deviant scores or patterns of scores, but they are not designed to provide a neurological diagnosis. The NBAS items cover the following domains of neonatal functioning:

Autonomic/physiological regulation: the infant's homeostatic adjustments of the central nervous system as reflected in color change, tremors and startles

Motor organization: the quality of movement and tone, activity level and the level of integrated motor movements

State organization and regulation: infant arousal and state lability, and the infant's ability to regulate his/her state in the face of increasing levels of stimulation

Attention/social interaction: the ability to attend to visual and auditory stimuli and the quality of overall alertness

In the two most recent editions of the NBAS (Brazelton, 1984; Brazelton and Nugent, 1995), a set of supplementary items was added in an attempt to better capture the range and quality of the behavior of fragile high-risk infants. The usefulness of these items has been supported by studies of high-risk infants (e.g., Dreher, Nugent, & Hudgins, 1994; Eyler, Behnke, Conlon, Woods, & Wobie, 1997; Sagiv, Nugent, Brazelton, Choi, & Korrick, 2007).

Unlike other psychological and neurological scales, the NBAS is unique in that it was never conceptualized as a series of discrete stimulus-response presentations. It is best described as an interactive assessment, since the examiner plays a major role in facilitating the performance and organizational skills of the infant. Because the reliability and validity of research data were predicated on the maintenance of the highest standards in eliciting the infant's "best performance," all NBAS examiners were required to be trained to a 90 percent inter-rater reliability level.

Since the NBAS contains 28 behavioral items and 20 reflex items, the search for the most effective data reduction and data analysis procedures challenged researchers from the beginning. Item-by-item comparisons across the individual NBAS items gave way to approaches based on factor analysis (e.g., Azuma, Malee, Kavanagh, & Deddish, 1991; Jacobson et al., 1986; Lester et al., 1976; Sostek, 1985), but it was Lester's seven-cluster system that became the most widely used system among researchers (Lester, 1984; Mayes, Granger, Frank, Schottenfeld, & Bornstein, 1993; Sagiv et al., 2007).

Research Uses

Since the time it was first published, the NBAS has been used in hundreds of studies to examine the effects of a wide range of pre- and perinatal variables on newborn behavior (see Brazelton & Nugent, 1995 for a review of these studies). Because it is sensitive to even subtle environmental effects, the NBAS has demonstrated that newborn behavior and development can be affected by many variables including intrauterine growth restriction, low birth weight, and prematurity (e.g., Costas, Botet, & Ortolà, 1989; Eyler et al., 1997); environmental polychlorinated biphenyls (PCBs) (e.g., Lonky, Reihman, Darvill, Mather, & Daly, 1996; Sagiv et al., 2007); different modes of delivery and obstetric medication (e.g., Lester, Als, & Brazelton 1982; Sepkoski et al., 1992); gestational and pregestational diabetes (e.g., Botet et al., 1996); infant massage (e.g., Field, 2009); neonatal hyperbilirubinemia (e.g., deCaceres et al., 1991) and maternal ingestion of cocaine, tobacco, alcohol, and caffeine (e.g., Mayes et al., 1993).

The model of development on which the NBAS is based assumes that developmental outcome is a function of the interaction of organismic and environmental factors, so that most researchers who have used the NBAS to examine the relationship between newborn behavior and later outcome have combined the NBAS scores with measures of the infant's environment (e.g., Linn & Horowitz, 1984; Nugent, 1991; Ohgi, Takahashi, Nugent, Arisawa, & Akiyama, 2003; Stjernqvist & Svenningsen, 1995; Van den Boom, 1991).

Uses of the NBAS in Different Cultural Settings

From the time it was first published, the NBAS has been used to examine neonatal differences and their natural variations in different cultural settings. These studies have been reviewed by Lester and Brazelton (1982) and Super and Harkness (1982), while Nugent, Lester, and Brazelton (1989, 1991) later presented a series of NBAS studies from 24 different cultures in Europe, Asia, North and South America, and Africa.

While this body of cross-cultural research constitutes a fraction of the canon of cultural and cross-cultural studies, the NBAS studies have made a unique contribution to the field by showing that, while the basic organizational processes in infancy may be universal, the range and form of these adaptations are shaped by the demands of each individual culture. Moreover, these studies expand our understanding of the range of variability in newborn behavioral patterns and the diversity of child-rearing practices and belief systems.

Clinical Uses of the NBAS

Since the NBAS was first published, it has been used as a way of sensitizing parents to their infants and thus promoting a positive relationship between parent and child (e.g., Nugent, 1985; Nugent and Brazelton, 1989, 2000). A number of follow-up studies have consistently reported positive effects of exposure to the NBAS on variables such as maternal confidence and self-esteem, parent–infant interaction, and developmental outcome (e.g., Achenbach, Howell, Aoki, & Rauh, 1993; Beeghly et al., 1995; Gomes-Pedro et al., 1995; Kaaresen et al., 2006; Myers, 1982; Parker, Zahr, Cole, & Braced, 1992; Rauh et al., 1988).

Although many of these intervention studies are characterized by small sample sizes, the evidence for short-term positive effects of NBAS-based interventions is consistent for both high-risk and low-risk samples. A meta-analysis of 13 parenting intervention studies based on the NBAS by Das Eiden and Reifman (1996) concluded that the NBAS interventions had beneficial effects on the quality of later parenting. But, although the longitudinal data show positive effects, the results are not used to argue for *direct* long-term effects as an exclusive function of NBAS-based interventions. In the case of Rauh et al.'s (1988) Vermont follow-up study and the Kaaresen et al. (2006) longitudinal study in Norway, the initial NBAS-based intervention was complemented by other interventions at later points. We can therefore conclude that, although there may not be persistent *direct* effects as a result of NBAS-based interventions, long-term effects may derive from *indirect* transactional effects.

Scales Inspired by the NBAS

The NBAS also stimulated the development of a number of assessment scales for use with different populations and in different settings – a testament to its theoretical richness and generativity. The NBAS-K (Kansas version) was developed by Horowitz and colleagues "to identify individual 'outlier' infants whose behavioral organization can be said to be very different from normal" (Horowitz & Linn, 1984, p. 97). The Assessment of Premature Infant Behavior (APIB) was derived from the NBAS and has become the most widely used instrument to assess preterm infant behavior (Als et al., 1982). The Neonatal Intensive Care Unit Network Neurobehavioral Assessment Scale (NNNS) (Lester & Tronick, 2005) was designed for the neurobehavioral assessment of drug-exposed and other high-risk infants, including preterm infants. A number of clinical approaches, based on the NBAS, were also developed as a form of parent support or intervention. The Mother's Assessment of the Behavior of the Infant (MABI), (Widmayer & Field, 1980) and the Family Administered Neonatal Activities (FANA) (Cardone and Gilkerson (1990) were adapted from the NBAS, while Keefer (1995) based the PEBE (the combined physical and behavioral neonatal examination) on the NBAS. The recently developed Newborn Behavioral Observations (NBO) system (Nugent, Keefer, Minear, Johnson and Blanchard, 2007) was also inspired by the clinical uses of the NBAS. The NBO is a flexible interactive relationship-building instrument and is used extensively in clinical settings as a means of sensitizing parents to the capacities and individuality of the newborn infant and fostering the relationship between parent and child and between clinician and parent.

Conclusion – Looking Toward the Future

The NBAS has now established itself as an invaluable neurobehavioral assessment tool in research and clinical settings across the world (Nugent, Petrauskas and Brazelton, 2009). With the growing interest in viewing development through the lens of developmental psychobiology, the history of the NBAS suggests that it can play a key role in the emerging field of cognitive neuroscience. Combining NBAS observations with emerging neuroimaging techniques, such as ERPs and fMRIs, should make possible a more comprehensive exploration of newborn behavioral functioning and a greater understanding of the neural underpinnings of newborn behavioral patterns (Nelson, Thomas, & de Haan, 2006; Stern and Bruschweiler-Stern, 2009). Finally, because the model on which the NBAS is based is by nature both flexible and adaptable, it can be predicted that the NBAS will continue to enrich the lives of researchers, clinicians and parents in years to come and make a unique contribution to the field.

References and further reading

Achenbach, T. M., Howell, C. T., Aoki, M. F., & Rauh, V. A. (1993). Nine-year outcome of the Vermont intervention program for low birth-weight infants. *Pediatrics, 91*, 45–55.

Als, H., Lester, B. M., Tronick, E., and Brazelton, T. B. (1982). Manual for the Assessment of Preterm Infants' Behavior (APIB). In H. E. Fitzgerald, B. M. Lester, & M. Yogman (Eds.), *Theory and research in behavioral pediatrics* (Vol. 1, pp. 65–132), New York: Plenum.

Andre-Thomas, C. I., & Dargassies, S. S. (1960). *The neurological examination of the infant.* London: The Spastic Society Medical Education and Information Unit.

Azuma, S. D., Malee, K. M., Kavanagh, J. A., & Deddish, R. B. (1991). Confirmatory factor analysis with preterm NBAS data: A comparison of four data reduction models. *Infant Behavior and Development, 14*, 209–225.

Beeghly, M., Brazelton, T. B., Flannery, K., Nugent, J. K., Barrett, D., & Tronick, E. Z. (1995). Specificity of preventative pediatric intervention effects in early infancy. *Journal of Developmental and Behavioral Pediatrics, 16*(3), 158–166.

Botet, F., de Cáceres, M. L., Rosales, S., & Costas, C. (1996). Behavioral assessment of newborns of diabetic mothers. *Behavioural Neurology, 9*, 1–4.

Brazelton, T. B. (1962a). Observations of the neonate. *Journal of the American Academy of Child Psychiatry, 1*, 38–58.

Brazelton, T. B. (1962b). Crying in infancy. *Pediatrics, 29*, 579–588.

Brazelton, T. B. (1973). *Neonatal Behavioral Assessment Scale.* Clinics in Developmental Medicine, No. 50. London: Heinemann Medical.

Brazelton, T. B. (1984). *Neonatal Behavioral Assessment Scale* (2nd ed.). Clinics in Developmental Medicine, No. 88. London: Spastics International.

Brazelton, T. B. (2009). The role of the Neonatal Behavioral Assessment Scale: personal reflections. In J. K. Nugent, B. Petrauskas and T. B. Brazelton (Eds.), *The newborn as a person: enabling healthy infant development worldwide.* Hoboken, NJ: John Wiley and Sons.

Brazelton, T. B., & Freedman, D. G. (1971). The Cambridge Neonatal Scales. In G. B. A. Stodinga & J. J. van der Werften Bosch (Eds.), *Normal and abnormal development of brain and behavior* (pp. 104–32). Leiden: Leiden University Press.

Brazelton, T. B., and Nugent, J. K. (1995). *The Neonatal Behavioral Assessment Scale.* London: Mac Keith Press.

Brazelton, T. B., Robey, J. S., & Collier, G. A. (1969). Infant behavior in the Zinancanteco Indians in southern Mexico. *Pediatrics, 44*, 274–281.

Cardone, I. A., & Gilkerson, L. (1990). Family administered neonatal activities: A first step in the integration of parental perceptions and newborn behavior, *Infant Mental Health Journal, 11*, 127–131.

Costas, C., Botet, F., & Ortolà, M. E. (1989). Behavior of the small-for-date newborn, according to the Brazelton Scale. *Anales Españoles de Pediatría, 1*, 37–40.

Das Eiden, R., & Reifman, A. (1996). Effects of Brazelton demonstrations on later parenting. *Journal of Pediatric Psychology, 21*(6), 857–868.

deCáceres, M. L., Costas, C., Botet, F., & Rosales, S. (1991). Assessment of newborn behavior and serum bilirubin levels. *Anales Españoles de Pediatría, 37*, 466–468.

Dreher, M., Nugent, J. K., & Hudgins, R. (1994). Prenatal marijuana exposure and neonatal outcomes in Jamaica: An ethnographic study. *Pediatrics, 93*, 254–260.

Eyler, F. D., Behnke, M., Conlon, M., Woods, N. S., & Wobie, K. (1997). Birth outcome from a prospective, matched study of prenatal crack/cocaine use: II. Interactive and dose effects on neurobehavioral assessment. *Pediatrics, 101*, 237–241.

Fantz, R. L. (1961). The origin of form perception. *Scientific American, 204*, 66–72.

Field, T. (2009). The effects of newborn massage. In J. K. Nugent, B. Petruaskas, & T. B. Brazelton (Eds.), *The newborn as person: Enabling healthy infant development worldwide.* Hoboken, NJ: Wiley.

Freedman, D. G., & Freedman, N. C. (1969). Behavioural differences between Chinese-American and European-American newborns. *Nature, 24*, 1227.

Gomes-Pedro, J., Patricio, M., Carvalho, A., Goldschmidt, T., Torgal-Garcia, F., & Monteiro, M. B. (1995). Early intervention with Portuguese mothers: A two-year follow-up. *Developmental and Behavioral Pediatrics, 16*, 21–28.

Graham, F. K., Matarazzo, R. G., & Caldwell, B. M. (1956). Behavioral differences between normal and traumatized newborns. 1. The test procedures. *Psycho. Monogr., 70*(20), 1–16.

Horowitz, F. D., & Linn, P. L. (1984). Use of the NBAS in research. In T. B. Brazelton (Ed.), *Neonatal behavioral assessment scale* (2nd ed., pp. 97–104). Philadelphia: J. B. Lippincott.

Jacobson, J. J., Fein, G. G., Jacobson, S. W., & Schwartz, P. M. (1984). Factors and clusters for the Brazelton Scale: An investigation of the dimensions of neonatal behavior. *Developmental Psychology, 20*, 339–353.

Kaaresen, P. I., Rønning, J. A., Ulvund, S. E., & Dahl, L. B. (2006). A randomized, controlled trial of the effectiveness of an early-intervention program in reducing parenting stress after preterm birth. *Pediatrics, 118*(1), 9–19.

Keefer, C. H. (1995). The combined physical and behavioral neonatal examination: A parent-centered approach to pediatric care. In T. B. Brazelton & J. K. Nugent (Eds.), *The Neonatal Behavioral Assessment Scale.* Mac Keith Press: London.

Lester, B. M. (1984). Data analysis and prediction. In T. B. Brazelton, *Neonatal Behavioral Assessment Scale* (2nd ed.). London: Mac Keith Press.

Lester, B. M., & Brazelton, T. B. (1982). Cross-cultural assessment of newborn behavior. In D. Wagner & H. Stevenson (Eds.), *Cultural perspectives on child development* (pp. 20–53). San Francisco: W. H. Freeman.

Lester, B. M., Als, H., & Brazelton, T. B. (1982). Regional obstetric anesthesia and newborn behavior: A reanalysis toward synergistic effects. *Child Development 53*(3), 687–692.

Lester, B. M., Emory, E. K., Hoffman, S. L., & Eitzman, D. V. (1976). A multivariate study of the effects of high risk factors on performance on the Brazelton Neonatal Assessment Scale. *Child Development, 47*, 515–517.

Lester, B. M., & Tronick, E. Z. (2005). *NICU network neurobehavioral scale (NNNS) manual.* Baltimore: Paul H. Brookes.

Linn, P. L., & Horowitz, F. D. (1984). The relationship between infant individual differences and mother–infant interaction in the neonatal period. *Infant Behavior and Development, 6*, 415–427.

Lonky, E., Reihman, J., Darvill, T., Mather, J., & Daly, H. (1996). Neonatal Behavioral Assessment Scale performance in humans influenced by maternal consumption of environmentally contaminated Lake Ontario fish. *Journal of Great Lakes Research, 22*(2), 198–212.

Mayes, L., Granger, R. H., Frank, M., Schottenfeld, R., & Bornstein, M. (1993). Neurobehavioral profiles of neonates exposed to cocaine prenatally. *Pediatrics, 91*(4), 778–783.

Murphy, K., & Smyth, C. (1962). Response of fetus to auditory stimulation. *Lancet, 1*, 972–973.

Myers, B. J. (1982). Early intervention using Brazelton training with middle class mothers and fathers of newborns. *Child Development, 53,* 462–471.

Nelson, C.A., Thomas, K. M., & de Haan, M. (2006). Neural bases of cognitive development. In W. Damon and R. M. Lerner (Eds.), *Handbook of child psychology* (6th ed.). Hoboken, NJ: John Wiley.

Nugent, J. K. (1985). *Using the NBAS with infants and their families: Guidelines for intervention.* White Plains, NY: March of Dimes Birth Defects Foundation.

Nugent, J. K. (1991). Cultural and psychological influences on the father's role in infant development. *Journal of Marriage and the Family, 53*(2), 475–485.

Nugent, J. K., & Brazelton, T. B. (1989). Preventive intervention with infants and families: The NBAS model. *Infant Mental Health Journal, 10,* 84–99.

Nugent, J. K., & Brazelton, T. B. (2000). Preventive infant mental health: Uses of the Brazelton Scale. In J. Osofsky & H. E. Fitzgerald (Eds.), *WAIMH handbook of infant mental health* (Vol. II, pp. 159–202). New York: John Wiley.

Nugent, J. K., Keefer, C. H., Minear, S., Johnson, L., & Blanchard, Y. (2007). *Understanding newborn behavior and early relationships: The newborn behavioral observations (NBO) system.* Baltimore: Paul H. Brookes.

Nugent, J. K., Lester, B. M., & Brazelton, T. B. (Eds.) (1989). *The cultural context of infancy* (Vol. 1). *Biology, culture and infant development.* Norwood, NJ: Ablex.

Nugent, J. K., Lester, B. M., & Brazelton, T. B. (Eds.) (1991). *The cultural context of infancy.* (Vol. 2). *Multicultural and interdisciplinary approaches to parent–infant relations.* Norwood, NJ: Ablex.

Nugent, J. K., Petrauskas, B., & Brazelton, T. B. (Eds.) (2009). *The newborn as person: Enabling healthy infant development worldwide.* Hoboken, NJ: John Wiley.

Ohgi, S., Takahashi, T., Nugent, J. K., Arisawa, K., & Akiyama, T. (2003). Neonatal behavioral characteristics and later behavioral problems. *Clinical Pediatrics, 42,* 679–686.

Parker, S., Zahr, L. K., Cole, J. C. D., & Braced, M. L. (1992). Outcomes after developmental intervention in the neonatal intensive care unit for mothers of preterm infants with low socioeconomic status. *Journal of Pediatrics, 120,* 780–785.

Peiper, A. (1963). *Cerebral function in infancy and childhood* (3rd ed.). New York: Consultants Bureau.

Prechtl, H. F. R., & Beintema, D. (1968). The neurological examination of the full-term infant. *Clinics in Developmental Medicine, 28.* London: Heinemann Medical.

Rauh, V., Achenbach, T., Nurcombe, B., Howell, C., & Teti, D. (1988). Minimizing adverse effects of low birthweight: Four-year results of an early intervention program. *Child Development, 59,* 544–553.

Rosenblith, J. F. (1961). The modified Graham Behavior Test for neonates: test-retest reliability, normative data, and hypotheses for future work. *Biologica Neonatorum, 3,* 174–193.

Sagiv, S., Nugent, J. K., Brazelton, T. B., Choi, E., & Korrick, S. (2007). Prenatal organochlorine exposure and measures of behavior in infancy. *Environmental Health Perspectives, 116*(5), 666–673.

Sepkoski, C. M., Lester, B. M., Ostheimer, G. W., & Brazelton, T. B. (1992). The effects of maternal epidural anesthesia on neonatal behavior during the first month. *Developmental Medicine and Child Neurology, 34*, 1072–1080.

Sostek, A. M. (1985). On the use of a priori cluster scales for the Brazelton Neonatal Behavioral Assessment Scale: A response to Maier et al. (1983). *Infant Behavior and Development, 8*, 245–246.

Stern, D. N., & Bruschweiler-Stern, N. (2009). Future dialogue between the neurosciences and the behavioral observation of infants. In J. K. Nugent, B. Petruaskas, & T. B. Brazelton (Eds.), *The newborn as person: Enabling healthy infant development worldwide.* Hoboken, NJ: Wiley.

Stjernqvist, K., & Svenningsen, N. W. (1995). Extremely low-birth-weight infants (less than 901g): Development and behaviour after 4 years of life. *Acta Paediatrica, 84*: 500–506.

Super, C., & Harkness, S. (1982). The infant's niche in rural Kenya and metropolitan America. In L. Adler (Ed.), *Cross-cultural research at issue.* New York: Academic Press.

Van den Boom, D. (1991). The influence of infant irritability on the development of the mother–infant relationship in the first 6 months of life. In J. K. Nugent, B. M. Lester, & T. B. Brazelton (Eds.), *The cultural context of infancy* (Vol. 2). Norwood, NJ: Ablex.

Widmayer, S., & Field, T. (1980). Effects of Brazelton demonstrations on early interaction of preterm infants and their teenage mothers. *Infant Behavior and Development, 3*, 79–89.

Wolff, P. (1959). Observations on human infants. *Psychosomatic Medicine, 221*, 110–118.

5

Keys to Developing Early Parent–Child Relationships

Kathryn E. Barnard

In the early 1970s at the University of Washington we were designing a study entitled the Nursing Child Assessment Project (Barnard, 1979; Barnard & Eyres, 1979), a product of the Johnson's Administration Great Society efforts contracted by the United States Public Health Service, Division of Nursing to identify risk factors for later child development. T. B. Brazelton came to consult, bringing a vibrant sense of enthusiasm for our work. His perspective on newborn behavior as evidence for how much the infant's brain was processing and responding to the environment changed our whole paradigm of infants and caregivers. We included the Brazelton Neonatal Behavioral Assessment Scale (BNBAS) (Brazelton, 1973/1984) as a primary measure in our study to evaluate how the infant's beginning capacity for sensing and reacting to her caregivers might influence later developmental outcomes.

From that time until this writing, over four decades later, Dr. Brazelton and the author have both been involved in influencing our respective professions of nursing and pediatrics to focus on early development, advancing the agenda of infant mental health in our respective fields by the research and training programs we created. These training programs, the Nursing Child Assessment Satellite Training (NCAST) and the Brazelton Touchpoints Center (BTC), have continued beyond our leadership to provide scores of professionals in all disciplines with knowledge of infant behavior and development, parenting, parent–child relationships and strategies for improving healthcare for young children and their families.

This chapter describes both the concepts Brazelton advanced about infant behavior and parent–infant interactions that were incorporated into a version of NCAST developed for health professions and parents called *Keys to Caregiving* (Sumner, 1995), as well as the author's work in infant state, state modulation and parent–child interaction.

The Knowledge Base for Infant Caregiving

The infant as the informant

When their infant is born, parents have no manual to deal with the novelty and individuality of her nonverbal communication, the cycles of sleep–wakefulness–fussiness. Hopefully, they will have supportive family and friends. Hopefully, they will have received information from books, the internet, healthcare professionals, and friends to help them through the early days, when both they and the infant are learning to be together in this world, brand new for the infant. Gone are the warmth, fluidity, sounds, activity cycles that structured fetal life. What might make it easier for parents and infant to develop their relationship? What knowledge would be useful? Can professionals help parents develop confidence in their parenting? These are some of the questions we considered in developing our program to support early parenting. When the first year gets off to a good enough start, the child's and family's futures will be on track to develop their full potential.

Who has the responsibility to support parenting in the first year of life? Families have played an important role in the past but, as we become a global and traveling world with less frequent physical contact, the geographical closeness that makes family support work for new parents becomes less available. Healthcare professionals involved in pregnancy, labor and delivery, post-partum, and well childcare visits have filled in some of the information and supportive roles. Models from other countries illustrate how programs such as birth doulas and special care during the first month can create an environment that will support the development of parent–child, parent–parent, and family relationships. The development of a sense of security and trust is important for both parents and children – increasingly important in the stressful world we live in.

What knowledge do parents of new babies need and how can this information and support be provided? We have integrated Brazelton's discoveries about infant behavior (Brazelton, 1973/1984) into training materials for professionals and parents. *Keys to Caregiving* was developed in the 1990s to teach professionals about infant state, infant behavior, modulation of infant state, and parent–child interaction (Sumner, 1995). This training series has been disseminated widely to hospitals, nursing education programs, and public health agencies. Each parent has the right to information that will enhance their early caregiving. It is the author's ambition to make this information available to every parent and caregiver.

Infant states

There are two sleep states, one transitional state, and three awake states. State is important since infants behave differently depending on what state they are in. For instance in quiet sleep (Non-REM), infants do not feed well. They feed better in Active (REM) sleep or when awake. The greatest difference between states of consciousness is the infant's degree of responsiveness, manifest in observable behaviors. In quiet sleep, there are few body or arm/leg movements and respiration is even. In active sleep, there are small, jerky body and eye movements and respiration is irregular. In the drowsy/transitional state, there is a mixture of movements with eyes opening and closing. Awake states are recognizable by eyes being open. Quiet alert is characterized by open eyes and limited body movement. Quiet alert is the best state for learning. Active alert involves open eyes and frequent body movements. Crying is a state that most people recognize, a distress signal telling caregivers that something is wrong.

States of consciousness are organized into a pattern of sleep and waking. During sleep, the infant alternates between active and quiet sleep. This sleep cycle lasts about 60 minutes, after which the infant will either transition to an awake state or shift into sleep again. As the infant matures the periods of both sleep and wakefulness become longer. By the end of the first month, the infant sleeps 13–14 hours a day. By three months, the infant is able to combine several 60-minute sleep cycles and have a good nap. Understanding their infant's sleep and wakefulness pattern and learning to predict it builds parents' confidence (Barnard, 1999).

State modulation

Infants born prior to 32 weeks of gestation lack the brain maturation needed to maintain the same type of sleep or to modulate state control as seen in the term baby. The author's dissertation study (Barnard, 1973; Barnard & Bee, 1983) investigated the use of mild repetitive stimuli – a maternal heart beat and a gentle rocking motion – to assist the preterm baby in maintaining the quiet sleep state. The finding that these stimuli did increase quiet sleep prompted an interest in the modulation of state by altering environmental stimuli: repetition to calm or soothe and variety to arouse or awaken. Soothing stimuli include comforting actions such as rocking, stroking or talking in a soft and rhythmical way. The slow, rhythmical and unchanging pacing promotes negative learning, i.e., learning to shut out (or "habituate," as Brazelton terms this phenomenon) stimuli by shifting to a state of lower arousal. To wake the baby, the opposite strategy is used: a variety of new and changing stimuli are presented in a nonintrusive way: undressing, repositioning, talking to, and touching are good examples. Before feeding, a variety of stimuli can be presented to bring the baby to greater arousal. In an awake state, the infant will have more control over breathing, sucking and swallowing, so that feeding will be easier. The infant will then have a chance to alert during the feeding and engage the parent in eye-to-eye interaction. This information about how to manage the baby's state can be very helpful to parents, especially when their infant finds it hard to transition from sleep to awake or vice versa.

Infant Behaviors

Guide for Parents and Caregivers

We developed a format to describe infant behaviors based on Brazelton's infant assessment clinical and research tools (Brazelton, 1973/1984). The behaviors we chose were ones that we felt were meaningful to parents and caregivers: alertness, visual and auditory responsiveness, habituation, consolability, self-consoling, consoling by caregiver, cuddliness, smiling, motor behavior, irritability, and readability.

Table 5.1, a framework for healthcare providers to use as they orient parents to their newborn, lists seven infant behaviors, characteristics, state usually present in, and recommendations for caregiving. While we have not entitled it the "Brazelton Parent Scale", that is the purpose: a map for parents to explore their newborn's capacities for learning and responding that creates a basis for interaction. This interaction creates a feedback loop for parent and infant through which each learns about and becomes responsive to the other. Table 5.1 outlines the behaviors of interest to caregivers and the context and meaning of infant behavior (Blackburn, 1978, 1994).

Take, for example, alertness. Table 5.1 offers suggestions on how to encourage alert behavior by providing stimulation: unwrapping the infant, placing her in an upright position, talking to her, showing one's face to her, and by eliciting reflexes such as rooting or grasping. Quiet alertness is a state in which the infant can take in information and is a useful one to attain for feedings. Parents are also encouraged to promote babies' visual and auditory responses. The experience of talking to a baby

Barnard, Hammond, Booth, Bee, Mitchell, & Spieker, 1989) and family stress (HOLMES stress scale) (Holmes & Rahe, 1967). All four categories – baby's behavior, environment, parent–child interaction, and family stress levels – had separate correlations with developmental outcomes, including cognitive and language measures (Barnard & Eyres, 1979). However, the best predictors were the environment and parent–child interaction (Bee et al., 1982).

The parent–child interaction scales, developed by the study team and several consultants, including T. B. Brazelton, Leon Yarrow and Evelyn Thoman, are known as the NCAST Parent–Child Interaction (PCI) Scales (Barnard & Kelly, 1989; Barnard et al., 1989). The theoretical construct for the scale items specifies parent/caregiver characteristics (sensitivity to cues, response to distress, social-emotional growth fostering and cognitive growth fostering) and child characteristics (responsiveness to the caregiver and clarity of cues). There are two PCI versions, one for observation during feeding and one during parent–infant teaching. Feeding was selected as a typical non-stressful time, compared to teaching interactions, when parent and child are mildly stressed as the parent teaches the child a new behavior. To date, the best predictor of later child development is the parent's score on the PCI. The parent's score is positively related to parent educational level.

For the teaching scale, we evaluated ethnic differences in the Early Longitudinal Childhood Study (ELCS-B) sample in the first year of life. The five ethnic populations sampled in a representative manner to reflect the population makeup of the United States included European American, African American, Hispanic American, Asian American, and Native American. At nine to eleven months, there were no ethnic differences for children's scores and few for mothers (Conrad, 2007).

There is a well-designed training program for the PCI Scales, the most widely used scales for measuring parent–child interaction today in both clinical practice and research throughout the United States and in at least 14 communities internationally. They are a reliable and valid means of observing and rating caregiver–child interaction for the purpose of assessing a dyad's strengths and areas needing improvement. They are used as pre- and posttest measures and contain a well-developed set of observable behaviors that describe the caregiver–child communication and interaction during either a feeding situation, birth to twelve months, or a teaching situation, birth to thirty-six months.

In summary, newborns are special human beings. Their capacity to communicate, at first, is mainly receptive. They sense differences in their environment and changes in their wellbeing. They have the capacity to respond to their internal and external environments by state changes and motor activity. This capacity for responsiveness is but one piece of evidence for previously unrecognized neonatal neurological functioning brought to light by Brazelton's documentation of newborn behavior. Parents and other caregivers can learn to understand infant behavior as nonverbal communication, to interpret the infant's special communication, and to develop cycles of responsiveness that build the foundation of parent–infant attachment. Learning the Brazelton Scale and the NCAST are a first step toward understanding the emergence of the parent–child relationship in the context of ongoing communication within the dyad.

References and further reading

Barnard, K. E. (1973). The effects of stimulation on the sleep behavior of the premature infant. *Communicating Nursing Research, 6*. Boulder, CO: WICHE.

Barnard, K. E. (1979). Instrumentation and findings: Infant characteristics. *Child health assessment part 2: The first year of life*. DHEW Pub. No. (HRA) 79-25, Stock No. 017-041-00131-9. Washington, DC: U.S. Government Printing Office.

Barnard, K. E. (1999). *Beginning rhythms: The emerging process of sleep wake behavior and self-regulation*. Seattle: NCAST Publications, University of Washington.

Barnard, K. E., & Bee, H. L. (1983). The impact of temporally patterned stimulation on the development of preterm infants. *Child Development, 54*, 1156–1167.

Barnard, K. E., & Eyres, S. J. (Eds.) (1979). *Child health assessment part 2: The first year of life*. DHEW Pub. No. (HRA) 79-25, Stock No. 017-041-00131-9. Washington, DC: U.S. Government Printing Office.

Barnard, K. E., & Kelly, J. F. (1989). Assessment of parent–child interaction. In S. J. Meisels & J. P. Shonkoff (Eds.), *Handbook of early childhood intervention*. New York: Cambridge University Press.

Barnard, K. E., Hammond, M. A., Booth, C. L., Bee, H. L., Mitchell, S. K., & Spieker, S. J. (1989). Measurement and meaning of parent–child interaction. In F. J. Morrison, C. E. Lord, & D. P. Keating (Eds.), *Applied developmental psychology* (Vol. III). New York: Academic Press.

Bee, H. L., Barnard, K. E., Eyres, S. J., Gray, C. A., Hammond, M. A., Spietz, A. L., Snyder, C., & Clark, B. (1982). Prediction of IQ and language skill from perinatal status, child performance, family characteristics, and mother–infant interaction. *Child Development, 53*, 1134–1156.

Blackburn, S. (1978, original). State-related behaviors and individual differences. In M. L. Duxbury (Ed.), *Early parent–infant relationships. Module 3*. New York: The National Foundation March of Dimes.

Blackburn, S. (1994, adapted). Infant-related behavior chart. In G. Sumner (Ed.), *Keys to caregiving: Self-instructional video series.* Seattle: NCAST Publications, University of Washington.

Bradley, R., & Caldwell, B. (1988). Using the HOME inventory to assess the family environment. *Pediatric Nursing, 14,* 97–102.

Brazelton, T. B. (1973/1984). *Neonatal behavioral assessment scale.* Philadelphia: J. B. Lippincott.

Conrad, L. (2007). *Ethnicity: A secondary analysis of national data with the NCAST teaching scale: Data.* (Dissertation, University of Washington).

Holmes, T., & Rahe, R. (1967). Holmes–Rahe life events rating scale. *Journal of Psychosomatic Research, 11,* 213–219.

Kilbride, H. W., Johnson, D. L., & Streissguth, A. P. (1977). Social class, birth order and newborn experience. *Child Development, 48,* 1686–1688.

Sumner, G. (1995). Keys to caregiving: A new NCAST program for healthcare providers and parents of newborns. *Zero to Three* (August/September), 33–35.

6

Prenatal Depression Effects on Neurobehavioral Dysregulation

Tiffany Field

T. Berry Brazelton has made countless contributions to the fields of child development and pediatrics, among them the development of the Brazelton Neonatal Behavior Assessment Scale (Brazelton, 1984). The scale has been used with many different samples of newborns to identify infants born at risk. Among those are the infants of prenatally depressed mothers. This chapter reviews data on prenatal depression effects on newborns and pregnancy massage to reduce those negative effects.

Birth Complications

Depression is prevalent in pregnant women, affecting 10–25% of women (Stowe, Hostetter, & Newport, 2005). Depressed women are more likely to deliver prematurely (Moncuso, Schetter, Rini, Roesch, & Hobel, 2004). Neonates of depressed mothers are also at greater risk for being born low birth weight (<2500 g) and small for gestational age (<10th percentile), with low birth weight being one of the leading causes of fetal morbidity and mortality (National Center for Health Statistics, 2004).

Behaviorally, biochemically, and physiologically fetuses and neonates of depressed mothers also differ. Fetuses of depressed women show elevated heart rates (Allister, Lester, Carr, & Liu, 2001), greater activity levels (Dieter et al., 2001), and greater physiological reactivity (Monk et al., 2004). As described below, newborns of depressed mothers perform less optimally on the Brazelton Neonatal Behavior Assessment Scale, and they show less positive affect on that scale (Abrams, Field, Scafidi, & Prodromidis, 1995; Field et al., 2004a; Lundy, Field, & Pickens, 1997; Lundy et al., 1999).

During behavior observations, the high cortisol group infants showed more crying, fussing and negative facial expressions.

Comorbid Effects of Other Moods

These prenatal depression data are confounded by moods that are comorbid with depression. Other prenatal moods or emotions have been noted to differentially affect fetal and infant development including anxiety and anger. Because these are comorbid with prenatal depression, the depression effects would appear to be confounded. Anxiety during midpregnancy has predicted lower mental and motor development scores at 8 months (Buitelaar, Huizink, Mulder, de Medina, & Visser, 2003).

In a prenatal anxiety study by our group, 166 women were classified as experiencing high or low anxiety during the second trimester of pregnancy (Field et al., 2003). The high-anxiety women also had high scores on depression and anger scales. The high-anxiety mothers' low dopamine levels were followed by their neonates having low dopamine levels (dopamine, being an activating neurotransmitter, may be contributing to the depressed affect in these newborns). The high-anxiety mothers' newborns also had greater relative right frontal EEG (electroencephalographic) activation (which usually is accompanied by withdrawn behavior) and lower vagal tone (which has been associated with withdrawn, depressive behavior). Finally, the newborns of high-anxiety mothers spent more time in deep sleep and less time in quiet and active alert states and showed more state changes and less optimal performance on the Brazelton Neonatal Behavior Assessment Scale (motor maturity, autonomic stability, and withdrawal).

In a data analysis on the same sample, the 166 women were classified as experiencing high or low anger during the second trimester of pregnancy (Field et al., 2002). The high-anger women also had high scores on depression and anxiety scales. The high-anger mothers' high prenatal cortisol and low dopamine levels were mimicked by their neonates' high cortisol and low dopamine levels. The high-anger mothers and infants were also similar on their greater relative right frontal EEG activation and their lower vagal tone. The newborns of high-anger mothers also had disorganized sleep patterns (greater indeterminate sleep and more state changes) and less optimal performance on the Brazelton assessment (orientation, motor maturity, and depression scales).

Therapies for Reducing Prenatal Depression and Neonatal Problems

Interventions are, of course, needed to help depressed mothers reduce their depression, anxiety, and anger and to provide medical, economic, and social support. Psychotropic medications have been tried with mixed results. A very large literature has debated the efficacy of psychotropic medications for prenatal depression. Although some have concluded no efficacy (Gentile, 2005; Misri et al., 2004), others have reported negative effects on the neonates including lower Apgar scores and lower Bayley developmental scores (Casper et al., 2003).

Stress reduction therapies for depressed pregnant women have led to lower depression scores, less negative affect and lower cortisol levels (Urizar et al., 2004). Other therapies that have been effective include massage therapy (Field, Diego, Hernandez-Reif, Schanberg, & Kuhn 2004) and acupuncture (Manber, Schnyer, Allen, Rush, & Blassey, 2004). Following massage therapy provided by the pregnant woman's significant other, the women had lower levels of anxiety and depressed mood and less leg and back pain (Field, Diego, Hernandez-Reif, et al., 2004b). In addition, by the end of the study, they had higher dopamine and serotonin levels and lower cortisol and norepinephrine levels. These changes may have contributed to the reduced fetal activity and the better neonatal outcome for the massage group. Fewer infants were born prematurely (0% in the massage group versus 17% in the control group), fewer were born low birth weight, and the massage group newborns had better performance on the Brazelton habituation, range of state, autonomic stability, and withdrawal scales.

In another study using partners as therapists, pregnant women diagnosed with major depression were provided with 12 weeks of twice per week massage therapy by their significant other or received standard treatment as a control group (Field et al. 2008). The therapy group women versus the control group women had reduced depression during the postpartum period. Their newborns were also less likely to be born prematurely and low birth weight, and they had lower cortisol levels and performed better on the Brazelton Neonatal Behavior Assessment habituation, orientation, motor and depression scales (see Table 6.1).

Newborns whose mothers received moderate pressure massage versus those who received light pressure massage therapy during pregnancy (month 5 through month 8) were also compared on their behaviors

Table 6.1 Means for Brazelton Neonatal Behavior Assessment Scale scores (standard deviations in parentheses)

Groups				
Variables	*Control*	*Massage*	*F*	*p*
Brazelton Scales				
Habituation	4.6 (2.3)	5.7 (1.4)	5.12	.03
Orientation	5.0 (1.5)	5.6 (1.2)	4.61	.05
Motor	4.6 (1.2)	5.3 (0.6)	12.17	.001
State Organization	3.7 (1.1)	3.8 (0.8)		NS
State Regulation	5.9 (2.8)	5.4 (1.2)		NS
Autonomic Stability	5.5 (1.4)	6.0 (1.2)		NS
Reflexes	3.2 (3.3)	2.3 (2.0)		NS
Depression	2.8 (2.0)	2.1 (1.4)	4.13	.05

during 15-minute sleep–wake behavior observations and on their performance on the Brazelton Neonatal Behavior Assessment Scale (Field, Hernandez-Reif, & Diego, 2005). The group of neonates whose mothers received moderate pressure massage spent a greater percent of the observation time smiling and vocalizing, and they received better scores on the orientation, motor, excitability, and depression clusters on the Brazelton Scale.

Conclusion

Newborns of prenatally depressed mothers have shown inferior performance on the Brazelton Neonatal Behavior Assessment Scale which together with their less positive affect and their physiological and biochemical profile (elevated cortisol, low dopamine, right frontal EEG activation and low vagal tone) suggest neurobehavioral dysregulation. Thus, this scale can be effectively used with these infants for identifying newborns who may be at risk for nonoptimal development. In addition, the scale has differentiated newborns whose mothers received pregnancy massage, suggesting that pregnancy massage can impact neurodevelopment of the newborn. Without scales of this kind and scholars like T. Berry Brazelton, these high-risk mothers and their newborns may have gone unnoticed and untreated.

References and further reading

Abrams, M., Field, T., Scafidi, E., & Prodromidis, M. (1995). Newborns of depressed mothers. *Infant Mental Health Journal, 16,* 233–239.

Allister, L., Lester, B. M., Carr, S., & Liu, J. (2001). The effects of maternal depression on fetal heart rate response to vibroacoustic stimulation. *Developmental Neuropsychology, 20,* 639–651.

Brazelton, T. B. (1984). *Neonatal Behavior Assessment Scale.* Philadelphia: Lippincott.

Buitelaar, J. K., Huizink, A. C., Mulder, E. J., de Medina, R G., & Visser, G. H. (2003). Prenatal stress and cognitive development and temperament in infants. *Neurobiology Aging, 24,* 53–60.

Casper, R. C., Fleishen B. E., Lee-Ancajas, J. C., Gilles, A., Gaylord, E., DeBattista, A., & Noyme, H. E. (2003). Follow-up of children of depressed mothers exposed or not exposed to antidepressant drugs during pregnancy. *Journal of Pediatrics, 142,* 402–408.

de Weerth, C., Zijl, R. H., & Buitelaar, J. K. (2003). Development of cortisol circadian rhythm in infancy. *Early Human Development, 73,* 39–52.

Diego, M. A., Field, T., Cullen, C., Hernandez-Reif, M., Schanberg, S., & Kuhn, C. (2004). Prepartum, postpartum and chronic depression effects on infants. *Infant Behavior & Development, 28,* 155–164.

Dieter, J. N. I., Field, T., Hernandez-Reif, M., Jones, N. A., LeCanuet. J. P., Salman, E. A., & Redzepi, M. (2001). Maternal depression and increased fetal activity. *Journal of Obstetrics and Gynaecology, 21,* 468–473.

Field, T., Diego, M., Dieter, J., Hernandez-Ralf, M., Schanberg, S., Kuhn, C., … Bendell, D.(2004). Prenatal depression effects on the fetus and the newborn. *Infant Behavior and Development, 27,* 216–229.

Field, T., Diego, M., Hernandez-Reif, M., Salman, F., Schanberg, S., & Kuhn, C. (2002). Prenatal anger effects on the fetus and neonate. *Journal of Obstetrics and Gynecology, 22,* 260–266.

Field, T., Diego, M., Hernandez-Reif, M., Schanberg, S., Kuhn, C., Yando, R., & Bendell, D. (2003). Pregnancy anxiety and comorbid depression and anger effects on the fetus and neonate. *Depression and Anxiety, 17,* 140–151.

Field, T., Diego, M. A., Hernandez-Reif, M., Schanberg, S., & Kuhn, C. (2004). Massage therapy effects on depressed pregnant women. *Journal of Psychosomatic Obstetrics & Gynaecology, 25*(2), 115–122.

Field, T., Fox, N., Pickens, L., & Nawrocki, T. (1995). Relative right frontal EEG activation in 3- to 6-month-old infants of "depressed" mothers. *Developmental Psychology, 31,* 358–363.

Field, T., Hernandez-Reif, M., & Diego, M. (2005). Newborns of depressed mothers who received moderate versus light pressure massage during pregnancy. *Infant Behavior and Development, 29,* 54–58.

Field, T., Hernandez-Reif, M., Diego, M., Figueiredo, B., Schanberg, S., & Kuhn, C. (2006). Prenatal cortisol, prematurity and low birthweight. *Infant Behavior and Development, 29,* 268–275.

Field, T., Figueiredo, B., Hernandez-Reif, M., Diego, M., Deeds, O. & Ascencio, A. (2008). Massage therapy reduces pain in pregnant women, alleviates prenatal depression in both parents and improves their relationships. *Journal of Bodywork and Movement Therapies.*

Field, T., Pickens, J., Fox, N., Nawrocki, T., & Gonzalez, J. (1995). Vagal tone in infants of depressed mothers. *Development and Psychopathology, 7,* 227–231.

Gentile, S. (2005). The safety of newer antidepressants in pregnancy and breast feeding. *Drug Safety, 28,* 137–152.

Jones, N. A., Field, T., Fox, N. A., Davalos, M., Lundy, B., & Hart, S. (1998). Newborns of mothers with depressive symptoms are physiologically less developed. *Infant Behavior and Development, 21,* 537–541.

Lundy, B., Field, T., & Pickens, J. (1997). Newborns of mothers with depressive symptoms are less expressive. *Infant Behavior and Development, 19,* 419–424.

Lundy, B. L., Jones, N. A., Field, T., Nearing, G., Davalos, M., Pietro, P., ... Kuhn, C. (1999). Prepartum depression effects on neonates. *Infant Behavior and Development, 22,* 121–137.

Manber, R., Schnyer, R. N., Allen, J. J., Rush, A. J., & Blassey, C. M. (2004). Acupuncture: A promising treatment for depression during pregnancy. *Journal of Affect Disorder, 83,* 89–95.

Misri, S., Oberlander, T. F., Fairbrother, N., Carter, D., Ryan, D., Kuan, A. J., & Reebye, P. (2004). Relation between prenatal maternal mood and anxiety and neonatal health. *Canadian Journal of Psychiatry, 49*(10), 684–689.

Moncuso, R. A., Schetter, C. D., Rini, C. M., Roesch, S. C., & Hobel, C. J. (2004). Maternal prenatal anxiety and corticotrophin-realising hormone associated with timing and delivery. *Psychosomatic Medicine, 66*(5), 762–769.

Monk, C., Sloan, R. P., Myers, M. M., Ellman, L.,Werner, E., Jeon, J., ... Fifer, W. P. (2004). Fetal heart rate reactivity differs by women's psychiatric status: An early marker for developmental risk? *Journal of the American Academy of Child and Adolescent Psychiatry, 43,* 283–290.

National Center for Health Statistics (2004). Health, United States, with chartbook on trends in the health of Americans. Hyattsville, MD.

Stowe, Z. N., Hostetter, A. L., & Newport, D. J. (2005). The onset of postpartum depression: Implications for clinical screening in obstetrical and primary care. *American Journal of Obstetric Gynecology, 192,* 522–526.

Urizar, G. G. Jr., Milazzo, M., Le, H. N., Delucchi, K., Sotelo, R., & Munoz, R. F. (2004). Impact of stress reduction instructions on stress and cortisol levels during pregnancy. *Biology Psychology, 67,* 275–282.

Neonatal Behavioral Assessment Scale (NBAS). Attention to preterm infant arousal has led to widespread rethinking of neonatal intensive care environments and practices.

Brazelton's NBAS is designed to evaluate newborns' individual capabilities, as well as their ability and style of regulating arousal levels in various stimulation contexts: visual, auditory, tactile (Brazelton, 1973, 1995). Responses to each stimulus, including state changes, are quantified, as is the baby's capacity to habituate to repeated stimuli. All of the baby's "answers" consist of his movements. The dynamic quality of the movements further specifies the "answers."

The NBAS is also used as a prevention–intervention tool (Bruschweiler-Stern, 2000, 2003). When performed in parents' presence as a focus to discuss relational problems, it has special clinical value. Again, the dynamic aspects of the baby's behavior are key.

After two to three months, infants become remarkably social, with smiles, vocalizations, and the play of visual regard. Face-to-face play becomes a major interactional activity. The secret of this activity is to negotiate and balance the strength of stimulation from the parents with the level of tolerable and pleasurable arousal of the infant. Parents use their facial expressions, vocalizations, gestures, and movements to adjust the strength of their stimulation from moment to moment while playing. They are like a "sound-light show" for the infant. The infant expresses in his behavior his level of pleasurable arousal, and where his state is tending (Stern, 1971, 1977, 1985). The wide range of parents' stimuli repertoire, and the spectrum of nuanced behaviors infants use to adjust their arousal level, has been well studied (Beebe, Jaffe, Feldstein, Mays, & Alson, 1985; Brazelton, Koslowski & Main, 1974; Fogel, 1982; Jaffe, Beebe, Feldstein, Crown, & Jasnow, 2001; Stern, 1971, 1977, 1985; Trevarthen, 1977, 1985, 2008; Trevarthen & Hubley, 1978; Tronick, 1989; Tronick, Als & Adamson, 1979; and others).

Neuroscientific thinking and behavioral observation accord with the idea that the earliest laid down structures, such as the brain-stem, progressively become integrated into the more complex organization of later emerging higher centers. The temporal development of the brain is an ascending process both in evolution and ontogeny (Jackson, 1931; Luria, 1966; Luu & Tucker, 1996; Schore, 2003). This view implies that the arousal systems can function largely unregulated by frontal cortical areas, at least for a stretch of early postnatal life.

At birth, only the amygdala (involved with emotional regulation) is on line to regulate brain-stem arousal systems (Chugani, 1996). It matures rapidly over the first two months after birth. The cerebral cortex does not start to mature rapidly until the eighth week post-partum when a general psychobiological developmental leap occurs (Emde, Gaensbauer, & Harmon, 1976; Yamada et al., 2000) and then goes through a critical period of growth from roughly 10 to 18 months (Schore, 2003).

These data, mostly from postnatal development observations, support the ideas and findings already described of an early relative independence of arousal systems from regulation by higher centers and the remarkable potential specificity of the arousal systems. The primacy of movement and its dynamic features is the developmental infrastructure for what will follow.

The large role the arousal systems play in creating dynamic forms suggests that in earliest life the infant is predominantly sensitive to dynamic information. Movement, the most primary and salient event, does not come alone. Movement takes time to unfurl, necessarily tracing a temporal profile. Once the infant has experienced intentional action and effort, even in a primitive form, motion will be imbued with force. The elements for generating gestalts of dynamic forms are present, of which, "forms of vitality" are one type (Stern, 2010).

Along with this, the infant's early experience is multisensory because the qualitative aspects of the modalities are not yet fully discriminated. But if the dynamic forms are, stimulation from any sensory modality would first be experienced as a dynamic flow of movement, contoured in time, imbued with force and an intentional direction: dynamic forms of experience predominate.

Dynamic forms could thus exist for the very young but with multimodal content. This notion takes up again concepts such as the "sensori-tonic field" (Werner, 1940; Werner & Wapner, 1949).

One could ask, do fetuses and young infants have or need modality-specific sensory information in the womb or right after birth? Such information could be acquired after birth with appropriate experience. This idea is compatible with new findings on multisensory neurons in many "specialized" parts of the brain and on interconnectivity.

Stimuli can be divided into mainly static and dynamic stimuli. We would expect the ability to discriminate dynamic stimuli to be in place first, developmentally, and to discriminate static stimuli later. This is often but not universally true. Responses to some static stimuli are slower to develop: only at about 2 months of age can infants discriminate color, when brightness is controlled (Bornstein, 1981). Small changes in musical amplitude (of ten decibels) cannot be discriminated until five to eight months (Olsho,

Schoon, Sakai, Turpin, & Sperduto, 1982). On the other hand, different smells, like that of a mother's milk, are discriminated days after birth (MacFarlane, 1975), but not before infants have had several exposures to their mother's smell. Sweetness can be discriminated at birth from other basic tastes; however, young infants appear not to discriminate between salt, bitter, and sour. Infants only one month old can discriminate the syllables /ba/ and /pa/. These appear to be categorical differences but at a closer look they are microdynamic, having to do with the rise time of sound in "plosives" (the "p" and "b") (Eimas, Siqueland, Jusczyk, & Vigorito, 1978). Different modalities may have different timetables for discrimination among static stimuli because of anatomic, physiological, evolutionary factors, as well as how they are "psychologically" packaged. Still, the possibility exists that for many modalities the dynamic features may be registered psychologically very early and, most importantly, before the static features.

Along the same lines, the right side of the neonatal brain is dominant (Chivron Jambaque, Nabbout, Lounes, Syrota, & Dulac, 1997) and is better for holistic, synthetic and multisensory tasks such as grasping the dynamic. This suggests that early nonverbal representations are built around a central core of dynamic forms.

To capture this in clinical-human terms, why is it such a pleasure to watch a greatly gifted clinician like Berry Brazelton work with a baby? He seems to enter into and swim with the dynamic flows. It is as if he had an intuitive familiarity with this world of dynamics, hidden in full sight but acting all around. When one watches him, one becomes inspired to be able to do what he can with a baby. Only partially connected to knowledge, this is far more about how to be with a baby.

One of the aims of this chapter has been to sensitize clinicians and researchers to the world of dynamic experience in the hope that it leads them further as researchers and clinicians.

References and further reading

Als, H. (1984). *A manual for the naturalistic observation of the newborn (preterm and fullterm)* (rev.). Boston, MA: Dept of Psychiatry, Harvard Medical School.

Als, H., Lawhon, G., Duffy, F., McAnulty, G., Gibes-Grossman, R., & Blickman, J. (1994). Individualized developmental care for the very low-birth-weight preterm infant, medical and neurofunctional effects. *Journal of the American Medical Association, 272*(11), 853–858.

Anders, T., & Keener, M. (1985). Developmental course of nighttime sleep wake patterns in full-term and pre-term infants during the first year of life. I. *Sleep, 8,* 173–192.

Beebe, B., Jaffe, J., Feldstein, S., Mays, K., & Alson, D. (1985). Interpersonal timing. In F. M. Field & N. Fox (Eds.), *Social perception in infants* (pp. 217–247). Norwood, NJ: Ablex.

Bornstein, M. H. (1981). "Human infant color and color perception" reviewed and reassessed: A critique of Werner and Wooten (1979). *Infant Behavior and Development, 4*(5), 119–150.

Brazelton, T. B. (1973). Neonatal behavioral assessment scale. *Clinics in Developmental Medicine No. 50.* Philadelphia: J. B. Lippincott.

Brazelton, T. B. (1995). *Neonatal behavioral assessment scale* (3rd ed.). London: Mac Keith Press.

Brazelton, T. B., Koslowski, B., & Main, M. (1974). The origins of reciprocity: The early mother–infant interaction. In M. Lewis and L. A. Rosenblum (Eds.), *The effects of the infant on its caregiver.* New York: Wiley.

Bruschweiler-Stern, N. (2000). Modèle d'intervention préventive au cours de la période néonatale. *Prisme, 33,* 126–139.

Bruschweiler-Stern, N. (2003). Neonatal interventions for relationship problems. In A. J. Sameroff, S. C. McDonough, and K. L. Rosenblum (Eds.), *Treating parent–infant relationship problems: Strategies for intervention* (pp. 188–212). New York, NY: Guilford Press.

Chivron Jambaque, I., Nabbout, R., Lounes, R., Syrota, A., & Dulac, O. (1997). The right brain hemisphere is dominant in human infants. *Brain, 120,* 1057–1065.

Chugani, H. T. (1996). Neuroimaging of developmental nonlinearity and developmental pathologies. In R. W. Thatcher, G. R. Lyon, J. Rumsey, & N. Krasnegor (Eds.), *Developmental neuroimaging: Mapping the development of brain and behavior* (pp. 187–195). San Diego: Academic Press.

DeCasper, A. J., & Fifer, W. P. (1980). Of human bonding: Newborns prefer their mothers' voices. *Science, 208,* 1174–1176.

Eimas, P. D., Siqueland, E. R., Jusczyk, P., & Vigorito, J. (1978). Speech perception in infants. In L. Bloom (Ed.), *Readings in language development.* New York, NY: Wiley.

Emde, R. N., Gaensbauer, T., & Harmon, R. (1976). Emotional expression in infancy: A biobehavioral study. *Psychological Issues Monograph Series, 10*(1), 37.

Field, F. M., & Fox, N. (Eds.) (1985). *Social perception in infants.* Norwood, NJ: Ablex.

Fogel, A. (1982). Affect dynamics in early infancy: Affective tolerance. In T. Field & A. Fogel (Eds.), *Emotion and early interaction.* Hillsdale, NJ: Erlbaum.

Gallese, V., & Lakoff, G. (2005). The brain's concepts: The role of the sensory-motor system in conceptual knowledge. *Cognitive Neuropsychology, 21*(3–4), 1–25.

Hebb, D. O. (1949). *The organization of behavior: A neuropsychological theory.* New York: John Wiley.

Jackson, J. H. (1931). *Selected writings of J. H. Jackson* (Vol. 1). London: Hodder and Stoughton.

Jaffe, J., Beebe, B. Feldstein, S. Crown, S. & Jasnow, M. (2001). Rhythms of dialogue in yearly infancy. *Monographs of the society for research in child development, 66*(2), 264.

Lakoff, G., & Johnson, M. (1980). *Metaphors we live by*. Chicago: University of Chicago Press.

Luria, A. R. (1966). *Higher cortical functions in man*. New York: Basic Books.

Luu, P., & Tucker, D. M. (1996). Self-regulation and cortical development: Implications for functional studies of the brain. In R. W. Thatcher, G. R. Lyon, J. Rumsey, & N. Krasnegor (Eds.), *Developmental neuroimaging: Mapping the development of brain and behavior* (pp. 297–305). San Diego: Academic Press.

MacFarlane, A. (1975). Olfaction in the development of social preferences in the human neonate: Parent–infant interaction. *Proceedings of the CIBA Foundation Symposium 33, ASP*. Amsterdam.

Olsho, L. W., Schoon, C., Sakai, R., Turpin, R., & Sperduto, V. (1982). Preliminary data on frequency discrimination in infancy. *Journal of the Acoustical Society of America, 71*, 509–511.

Panksepp, J. (1998). *Affective neuroscience: The foundations of human and animal emotions*. New York: Oxford University Press.

Parmelee, A. H., & Stern, E. (1972). Development of states in infants. In C. D. Clemente, D. P. Purpura & F. R. Meyer (Eds.), *Sleep and the maturing nervous system* (pp. 85–98). New York: Academic Press.

Pfaff, D. W. (2006). *Brain arousal and information theory: Neural and genetic mechanisms*. New York: Basic Books.

Pfaff, D. W., & Kieffer, B. L. (Eds.). (2008). Molecular and biophysical mechanisms of arousal, alertness and attention. *Annals of the New York Academy of Science, 1129*.

Piontelli, A. (2001). Startles: Activators during early prenatal life. In C. Einspieler, P. Wollf, & H. F. R. Prechtl (Eds.), *Acts of the international symposium on time and timing in developmental neurology* (pp. 11–12). Graz, Austria: University of Graz.

Piontelli, A. (2007). On the onset of fetal behavior. In M. Mancia (Ed.), *Psychoanalysis and neuroscience* (pp. 391–418). Amsterdam: Springer Verlag.

Prechtl, H. F. R. (1984). Continuity and change in early neural development. In H. F. R. Prechtl (Ed.), *Continuity of neural functions from prenatal to postnatal life* (pp. 1–15). London: Mac Keith Press.

Robbins, T. W., & Everitt, B. J. (1987). Psychopharmacological studies of arousal and attention. In S. M. Stahl, E. C. Goodman, & S. D. Iversen (Eds.), *Cognitive neurochemistry* (pp. 21–56).Oxford: Oxford University Press.

Schore, A. N. (2003). *Affect regulation and the repair of the self*. New York, NY: W. W. Norton.

Sheets-Johnstone, M. (1999). *The primacy of movement.* Amsterdam/Philadelphia: John Benjamins.

Stern, D. N. (1971). A micro-analysis of mother interaction: Behaviors regulating social contact between a mother and her three and a half month-old twins. *Journal of the American Academy of Child Psychiatry 10*, 501–517.

Stern, D. N. (1977). *The first relationship: Infant and mother.* Cambridge, MA: Harvard University Press.

Stern, D. N. (1985). *The interpersonal world of the infant.* New York, NY: Basic Books.

Stern, D. N. (2004). *The present moment: In psychotherapy and everyday life.* New York, NY: W. W. Norton.

Stern, D. N. (2010). *Forms of vitality: Dynamic experience in psychology, neuroscience and the arts.* New York: Oxford University Press.

Trevarthen, C. (1977). Descriptive analysis of infant communication behavior. In H. R. Schaffer (Ed.), *Studies in mother–infant interaction: The Loch Lomond Symposium* (pp. 227–270). London: Academic Press.

Trevarthen, C. (1985). Facial expressions of emotions in mother–infant interactions. *Human Neurobiology*, *4*, 21–32.

Trevarthen, C. (2008). The musical art of infant conversation: Narrating in the time of sympathetic experience, without rational interpretation, before words. In M. Imberty & M. Gratier (Eds.), *Musicae Scientiae*, Special Issue: Narrative in Music and Interaction, 15–46.

Trevarthen, C., & Hubley, P. (1978). Secondary intersubjectivity: Confidence, confiding and acts of meaning in the first year. In A. Lock (Ed.), *Action, gesture and symbol: The emergence of language.* London: Academic Press.

Tronick, E. Z. (1989). Emotions and emotional communication in infants. *American Psychologist, 44*(2) 112–119.

Tronick, E. Z., Als, H., & Adamson, L. (1979). Structure of early face-to-face communicative interactions. In M. Bullowa (Ed.), *Before speech: The beginning of interpersonal communication* (pp. 349–370). New York: Cambridge University Press.

Werner, H. (1940). *Comparative psychology of mental development.* New York: Harper.

Werner, H., & Wapner, S. (1949). Sensory-tonic field theory of perception. *Journal of Personality, 18*, 88–107.

Yamada, H., Sadato, N., Konishi, Y., Kimura, K., Tanaka, M., Yonekura, Y., Ishii, Y., & Itoh, H. (2000). A milestone for normal development of the infantile brain detected by functional MRI. *Neurology*, *55*, 218–223.

8

Infants and Mothers
Self- and Mutual Regulation and Meaning Making

Ed Tronick

Introduction

The focus of this chapter is on the nature of how people live in the world and how they change both themselves and their relation to the world over time. Why are some infants, children, and adults happy and robust and others sad and withered? What are the developing infant's capacities for neurobehavioral self-organization? How are early infant–adult interactions organized? What is the relation between therapeutic interactions and infant–adult interactions? Is there a process that can explain normal as well as abnormal development? Is the process of "meaning making," in which humans make sense of their self in relation to the world, only in their heads, or is it in their bodies as well?

Brazelton (Brazelton, 1973, 1974; Brazelton, Koslowski, & Main, 1974) saw infants as trying to communicate with those around them; their behavior was a language. Bruner (1990) argued that humans are *makers of meaning* about their relation to the world. The Mutual Regulation Model (MRM) weds these views of meaning with open systems theory. It sees humans as complex open psychobiological systems that constantly work to garner energy and meaningful information to gain a sense of their relation to the world. This sense-of-oneself in the world equals the totality of meanings, purposes, intentions, and biological goals operating in every moment on every component and process in the human system. This totality of meanings is a *psychobiological state of consciousness.* In the Brazelton examination (Brazelton, 1973), one can see behavioral organization of the infant when looking at a person or looking at an object to see this totality: one is a state of communicating with people, the other a state of acting on objects. Yet another state is contemplative, a quite calm self-focused attentiveness. Thus even infants without awareness, self-reflection, and explicit forms of meaning have states of consciousness that organize their being in the world.

Expanding States of Consciousness

The successful growth of states of consciousness is governed by principles from dynamic systems theory that require all living systems to garner energy and information from the world in order to maintain and increase the complexity and coherence of the organization and structure of their states of consciousness. The three ways of expanding complexity and coherence are: (1) interacting and communicating with people; (2) acting on things; and (3) as Modell (1993) would argue, engaging our private selves. When humans are successful in appropriating meaning into themselves, their biopsychological state moves away from entropy and the edge of chaos, and new properties (meanings) emerge. When humans are unsuccessful in appropriating meaning, the biopsychological state dissipates, loses complexity, and properties of the system are lost or become fixed.

A particularly effective way of growing and expanding complexity occurs when two or more individuals convey and apprehend meanings from each other to create a dyadic state of consciousness. Brazelton (Brazelton, Koslowski & Main, 1974) pointed toward this in his pioneering study of reciprocity in mother–infant interactions. This dyadic state contains more information than either individual's state and individuals can appropriate meanings from it into their own states of consciousness and increase its complexity. This is the Dyadic Expansion of States of Consciousness Model.

The Mutual Regulation Model (MRM)

Infant self-organizing neurobehavioral capacities

The MRM is related to meaning making, the Dyadic Expansion of States of Consciousness Model, and the complexity and coherence of individuals' ways of being in the world (Beeghly & Tronick, 1994; Tronick, 1989). The MRM views infant and caretaker as components of a larger *dyadic* regulatory system. The MRM postulates that infants have self-organizing neurobehavioral capacities that organize behavioral states (from sleep to alertness) and biopsychological processes that they use for making sense of themselves and their place in the world. Early work on neurobehavioral capacities was carried out with Brazelton using the Neonatal Behavioral Assessment Scale (NBAS) (Brazelton, 1973; Tronick, 1987). When Brazelton first created the scale the infant was viewed as undifferentiated and disorganized, reflexive with only all-or-none states of distress or sleep. Brazelton's (Brazelton, 1994; Brazelton & Cramer, 1990) work made it clear that this was incorrect.

Later research utilized more sophisticated techniques to investigate infant neurobehavior including kinematic analysis of movement and brain imaging techniques to explore how brain lesions might compromise infant self-organization (Fetters, Chen, Jonsdottir, & Tronick, 2004). We found that infants with almost identical lesions would have radically different outcomes (e.g., cerebral palsy versus normal motor organization), suggesting that self-organization and unknown features of experience (perhaps, caretaker carrying patterns) play key roles in determining the quality of movement. We also developed a new neurobehavioral scale, the NICU Network Neurobehavioral Scale (NNNS) (Lester & Tronick, 2004), that provides a detailed assessment of the interplay between stressors and infant self-regulatory abilities. Using the NNNS, we developed standardized data on newborn neurobehavioral organization (e.g., percentiles for different neurobehavioral performances on the items) (Tronick et al., 2004). In longitudinal studies we saw the relations of different NNNS profiles to medical and behavioral outcomes through 4 years of age (Liu et al., in press) and in current work to behavioral problems at 7–8 years of age. These data will aid clinicians' evaluation of newborn neurobehavior and suggest forms of clinical interventions.

Mutual regulation

Despite infants' impressive self-organizing capacities, they clearly have limits. An infant can utilize a number of mechanisms (e.g., crying, moving, and "fetaling up") to self-regulate body temperature but eventually these resources will be exhausted and the effort will fail. However, an infant is a self-contained system within a larger dyadic regulatory system. The other subsystem is the caregiver who functions to scaffold an infant's limited regulatory capacities. How is this regulation guided and directed? Following Brazelton (1992, 1994; Brazelton & Greenspan, 2000), it seemed that regulation was accomplished by the operation of a communication system in which the infant communicated its regulatory status to the caregiver, who responded to the *meaning* of the communication. An infant cry might mean "I am in trouble," and a bright alert look might mean "I am fine." A parent does not see a baby's clenched hand as a fist, but without awareness intuitively knows the baby is stressed.

"Messy" interactions, intersubjectivity, and reparation

Work on regulation and communication led to studies of the organization of infant–adult (mothers and fathers and strangers) face-to-face interaction (Tronick, 2007). We devised a technique using videotape recorders and slow motion to micro-analytically code the communicative expressions of infants and adults and their interactions. We discovered the temporal organization of the dyadic communication system, contingencies of signaling (of meaning), synchrony and attunements (Cohn & Tronick, 1988; Tronick & Cohn, 1989; Tronick, 1989). Considering the mutuality of infant–adult interaction led to the inclusion of Habermas's concept of intersubjectivity (Trevarthen & Hubley, 1978). In the infant–adult interaction, there is a mutual apprehension in which each understands what the other *intends*. Intersubjectivity is a precognition to meaning making, states of consciousness, and their dyadic expansion.

Initially, the organization of the infant–mother interaction seemed bidirectional, synchronous, and coordinated. But findings emerged showing that much of the time there was lack of coordination between infant and adult. There was a "messiness" to the interaction – a mismatch of affective states and relational intentions that occurred when infant and adult were conveying nonmatching meanings: Infant: "I want you to look at me." Adult: "I want to look away." Re-achieving a matching state from a mismatching state was a mutually regulated process of reparation.

The Still-Face perturbation

The Face-to-Face/Still-Face (FFSF) paradigm developed to evaluate a simple deduction from the MRM: If infants are regulating the interaction and themselves by responding to adult regulatory input, meanings, and intentions, then if the adult's communications are perturbed, the infant should detect this disruption, attempt to correct it, and react to it in meaningful ways. We instructed the adult to hold a still face and not move or talk after a period of normal interaction with the infant. Infants attempted to solicit mother's attention and when their efforts failed they looked away, withdrew, and expressed sad and angry affect. The implication from the SF was that in normal exchanges when things are hard to see infants also apprehend and respond to the adult's meanings expressed in their affective and other displays.

We then began the first observational studies of face-to-face interactions of depressed mothers and infants. These studies opened up a field of developmental observations of infants with parents with a variety of behavioral disorders (Apter-Danon, Devouche, Valente, & Le Nestour, 2004), the effects of interventions (Downing, 2003), and some of the first microanalytic studies of infants' or parents' blindness or deafness, infant facial anomalies, and medical status (e.g., drug exposure, prematurity). All of these disturbances of the communicative regulatory system had effects – but not always ill effects – as dyads, such as how a sighted mother and a blind infant found ways to mutually regulate their interaction with each other and to communicate.

Culture and other perturbations

This work was expanded to include naturally occurring perturbations, such as the relation of culturated forms of regulation, and showed that Western models of child rearing and development are severely limited and narrow. The study of Quechua child-rearing practices in Peru demonstrated a form of "normal" caretaking that Western theorists would consider to be stimulus deprivation leading to pathological development (Tronick, Thomas, & Daltabuit, 1994) but did not. The multiple caretaking system of Efe foragers living in the Ituri forest did not conform to universalist or evolutionary hypotheses or attachment theory, with its concept of monotropy in human evolution (Tronick, Winn, & Morelli, 1985). Yet the system was "normal," and Efe infants became acculturated adults who "naturally" made sense of the world in an Efe way.

In Kenya, Gusii mothers do not often engage in the face-to-face play thought to be required for normal development (Brazelton, 1974; LeVine, 1973). When *asked* to engage in face-to-face play, Gusii mothers turned away from their infants just as the infants were most focused on them. This behavior would be labeled as pathological in the West, but functions to shape normal Gusii infants' state of consciousness of the world as a Gusii. Thus, not only do these different culturated individuals-in-groups have different experiences, but the very processes that generate their states of consciousness are culturated (Tronick & Morelli, 1991).

Meaning Making

The human communication system is not about *how much* information is being conveyed but what the information is *about*. Process terms can make vastly different phenomena equivalent. For example, privileging the qualities of the process of dancing (synchrony, complexity) masks differences in the dance being done (tango, hip hop). Such process terms are not uninteresting, but they ignore the kind of dance the dancers are doing. People need some level of mutual regulation when they are doing something together, but they cannot be in synchrony without actually doing something together and interactions that are sensitive have to be sensitive about the something being done.

Likewise, the communication system is not always coordinated and smooth but must be filled with something, and the "somethings" are meaning, intentions, purposes, and the like. These meanings can be conveyed with different communication qualities (smoothly, disjointedly) and via different channels (language, facial expressions, moods, gestures), but some*thing* must be communicated: the individual's state of consciousness, experiential state, intentions to act in the world, cultural and somatic meanings, and relational intentions to be with and to create new meanings with others.

Using the Theory to Think about Practice

Therapy, like infant–adult interactions, is a messy process of match–mismatch and reparation, with two active meaning-making individuals in the room. Reparation of messiness is a key change-inducing process in therapy and development. In development, reparation has the effect of the infant and adult coming to experience and implicitly know that the negative experience of a mismatch can be transformed into a positive affective match, the partner can be trusted, and one can be effective in acting on the world. Also, in repairing interactive messiness new implicit ways of being together for the infant and adult are co-created and come to be known.

In the Boston Process of Change Group, we saw therapy as a sloppy process with change occurring during moments of meeting when the sloppiness was repaired (Tronick, 1998). Thus, in the reparation of mismatches in therapy the patient who may be stuck in negative affect experiences its transformation into positive affect. Further, by working on the messiness of the therapeutic relationship, patient (and therapist) come to know new ways of being with the therapist and, in turn, with others. The reparation model and its findings imply that relationships are dyadically regulated and that infant and patient are active, intentional, and capable of making reparations in the relationship. But, unlike the Boston Process of Change Group's findings, the implicit knowing that comes with being together is not sufficient to produce change. Something else is needed: a change in meaning, made by the infant or the patient, about their place in the world.

Successful creation of a dyadic state of consciousness, and selective appropriation of meaning by the individuals creating it, expands the complexity of their individual states of consciousness and fulfills the principle of dynamic systems (i.e., to continually maintain and increase complexity and live, or to fail and perish). But how is this systems theory experience-near and clinically relevant? The Dyadic Expansion of States of Consciousness Model is experience-near because there are experiential consequences to the success or failure of the process of expanding the complexity and coherence of states of consciousness. When new information is incorporated, the individual experiences a sense of expansion, joy, and movement into the world: a willingness to take a risk for something new. A successful increase in complexity leads to a sense of connection to the other person in the dyadic state, and a relationship emerges. Importantly, a sense of connection to one's self develops, accompanied by a feeling of solidity, stability, and continuity of self.

When meaning is not incorporated, or incorporated unsuccessfully, the complexity of the state dissipates. The individual experiences a sense of shrinkage, sadness and/or anger, withdrawal and disconnection from the world, from others, and from him- or herself. The feeling of continuity in time is compromised. Thus, a variety of powerful experiential consequences travel with the success or failure of expansion, not the least of which is that successful meaning making is the constitutive process of relationship formation. Furthermore, according to dynamic systems theory, letting go of old meanings requires giving up organization and certitude, and threatens the unpredictable but implicitly hoped for outcome of expansion. Change for a patient means risking dissipation and experiencing fear or even the terror of annihilation and the dissolution of the self. But change also means hope.

Because meanings come from multiple levels in the individual, some meanings may only be available to the therapist and/or patient in certain states of receptivity, just as the infant can only do certain things in certain states. Alert interpretative states may detect meaning in cognitions and language and produce insight, but reverie states (Ogden, 1997) may be needed to apprehend meanings from preconscious or unconscious levels. And because we have not identified all the ways that a therapist or patient comes to reach certain levels of meaning, there will be meanings that may be available to one or the other that are not apprehended and cannot be formulated yet produce change. Change may emerge from what can never be formulated.

There also is the somewhat vicious clinical implication of complexity-governed selection. The selective force of complexity operates moment-to-moment to maximize coherence and complexity of the individual's state of consciousness and, like natural selection, it is blind to the state of the system it is moving toward. The principle is something like "maximize complexity and coherence" now in the moment, in the short run. As a consequence, complexity is not necessarily adaptive in either the short or long run because increasing complexity hardly equals successful adaptation. For example, an individual may stay in a destructive relationship or have a self-debilitating sense of place in the world because these may be the only ways in which to maintain or perhaps increase complexity in the moment. These are solutions in the moment, but in the long run they may preclude engagement with the social world or other ways of being in the world that could be expansive. In these patients, dissipation and terror are a constant threat and the need for therapist and patient to co-create mutual strategies to modulate these affective states, the meaning of these affective states, is essential.

Conclusion

This theoretical perspective can be used to address other questions: What are the different types of meaning-making processes? Is meaning and its making and the remembrance of the past actually a multileveled, biopsychological process or is meaning only in the mind? What induces change? What is the nature of psychological change and what principles govern it? What is the relation between meaning making and mutual regulation? Why and how are relationships so important to human development? What makes relationships unique, and is there such a thing as a prototypical (attachment) relationship? What makes us stay in a painful relationship? What principles govern our moment-to-moment actions versus our developmental pathway over a lifespan (Tronick, 2007)?

Certainly, these MRM and the dyadic states of consciousness models, reparation, and complexity-governed selection will not answer all of these questions, but they may provide purchase on many of them. Importantly, rather than being purely descriptive in nature, the biopsychological instantiation of these ideas in dynamic systems theory will allow us to make deductions about how people experience and live in the world and how they change both themselves and their relation to the world.

References and further reading

Apter-Danon, G. G. R., Devouche, E., Valente, M., & Le Nestour, A. (2004). *Role of maternal mood and personality disorder in mother–infant interactive and regulatory capacities: Implications for interventions.* Symposium. Paper presented at the International Conference of Infant Studies, Chicago.

Ball, W., & Tronick, E. Z. (1971). Infant responses to impending collision: Optical and real. *Science, 171*, 818–920.

Beeghly, M., & Tronick, E. Z. (1994). Effects of prenatal exposure to cocaine in early infancy: Toxic effects on the process of mutual regulation. *Infant Mental Health Journal, 15*(2), 158–175.

Bollas, C. (1987). *The shadow of the object: Psychoanalysis of the unthought known.* New York: Columbia University Press.

Boston Change Process Study Group (Harrison, A. M., Lyons-Ruth, K., Morgan A. C., Bruschweiler-Stern, N., Nahum, J. P., Stern, D. N., Sander, L. W., & Tronick, E. Z.) (2002). Explicating the implicit: The local level of microprocess of change in the analytic situation. *International Journal of Psychoanalysis, 83*, 105–162.

Brazelton, T. B. (1973). *Neonatal behavioral assessment scale.* London: Spastic International Medical Publications.

Brazelton, T. B. (1974). Does the neonate shape his environment? In *The infant at risk: Birth defects.* Original Articles Series, *The National Foundation, 10*(32), 131–140.

Brazelton, T. B. (1992). *Touchpoints: Your child's emotional and behavioral development.* Reading, MA: Addison-Wesley.

Brazelton, T. B. (1994). Touchpoints: Opportunities for preventing problems in the parent–child relationship. *Acta Paediatrica, Supplement, 394*, 35–39.

Brazelton, T. B., & Cramer, B. G. (1990). *The earliest relationship: Parents, infants, and the drama of early attachment.* Reading, MA: Addison-Wesley.

Brazelton, T. B., & Greenspan, S. (2000). *The irreducible needs of children.* New York: Perseus.

Brazelton, T. B., Koslowski, B., & Main, M. (1974). The origins of reciprocity: The early mother–infant interaction. In M. Lewis, & L. A. Rosenblum (Eds.), *The effect of the infant on its caregiver* (pp. 49–76). New York: John Wiley Interscience.

Brazelton, T. B., & Yogman, W. M. (1986). Introduction: Reciprocity, attachment, and effectance: Analage in early infancy. In T. B. Brazelton, & M. W. Yogman (Eds.), *Affective development in infancy* (pp. 1–10). Norwood, NJ: Ablex.

Bruner, J. (1990). *Acts of meaning*. Cambridge, MA: Harvard University Press.

Cohn, J. F., & Tronick, E. (1988). Mother–infant face-to-face interaction: Influence is bidirectional and unrelated to periodic cycles in either partner's behavior. *Development Psychology, 24*, 386–392.

Downing, G. (2003). Video Microanalyse Therapie: Einige Grundlagen und Prinzipien. In H. Scheuerer-English, G. J. Suess, & W. Pfeifer (Eds.), *Wege zur Sicherheit: Bindungswissen in Diagnostik und Intervention* (pp. 51–68.). Göttingen: Giessen: Psychosozial Verlag.

Fetters, L., Chen, Y. P., Jonsdottir, J., & Tronick, E. Z. (2004). Kicking coordination captures differences between full term and premature infants with white matter disorder. *Human Movement Science, 22*, 729–248.

Freeman, W. J. (2000). *How brains make up their mind*. New York: Columbia University Press.

Gottman, J. M., & Levenson, R. (1988). The social psychophysiology of marriage. In P. Noller, & M. A. Fitzpatrick (Eds.), *Perspectives on marital interaction* (pp. 182–200). San Diego, CA: College-Hill.

Harrison, A. M. (2003). Change in psychoanalysis: Getting from A to B. *Journal of the American Psychoanalytic Association, 51*, 221–257.

Lester, B. M., & Tronick, E. Z. (2004). The Neonatal Intensive Care Unit Network Neurobehavioral Scale (NNNS). *Pediatrics, 113*(3), 631–699.

LeVine, R. (1973). *Culture, behavior and personality*. Chicago: Aldine.

Liu, J., Bann, C., Lester, B., Tronick, E., Das, A., LaGasse, L. et al. (in press). Neonatal neurobehavior predicts medical and behavioral outcome. *Pediatrics*.

Modell, A. (1993). *The private self*. Cambridge, MA: Harvard University Press.

Ogden, T. (1997). *Reverie and interpretation: Sensing something human*. Lanham: Rowland & Littlefield.

Trevarthen, C., & Hubley, P. (1978). Secondary intersubjectivity: Confidence, confiding and acts of meaning in the first year. In A. Lock (Ed.), *Action, gesture and symbol: The emergence of language* (pp. 183–229). New York: Academic Press.

Tronick, E. (1987). The Neonatal Behavioral Assessment Scale as a biomarker of the effects of environmental agents on the newborn. *Environmental Health Perspectives, 74*, 185–189.

Tronick, E. (1989). Emotions and emotional communication in infants. *American Psychologist, 44*(2), 112–119.

Tronick, E. (1998). Interactions that effect change in psychotherapy: A model based on infant research. *Infant Menalt Health Journal, 19*, 1–290.

Tronick, E. (2007). *The neurobehavioral and social emotional development of infants and children*. New York: Norton Press.

Tronick, E., & Cohn, J. (1989). Infant–mother face-to-face interaction: Age and gender differences in coordination and the occurrence of miscoordination. *Child Development, 60*, 85–92.

Tronick, E., & Morelli, G. (1991). Foreword: The role of culture in brain organization, child development, and parenting. In J. K. Nugent, B. M. Lester, & T. B. Brazelton (Eds.), *The cultural context of infancy: Multicultural and interdisciplinary approaches to parent–infant relations* (2nd ed., pp. ix–xiii). Norwood, NJ: Ablex Publishing.

Tronick, E., Olson, K., Rosenberg, R., Bohne, L., Lu, J., & Lester, B. M. (2004). Normative neurobehavioral performance of healthy infants. *Pediatrics, 112*(3), (part 2 of 2), 676–679.

Tronick, E., Thomas, R., & Daltabuit, M. (1994). The Quechua manta pouch: A caretaking practice for buffering the Peruvian infant against the multiple stressors of high altitude. *Child Development, 65*, 1005–1013.

Tronick, E., & Weinberg, M. K. (1997). Depressed mothers and infants: Failure to form dyadic states of consciousness. In L. Murray, & P. J. Cooper (Eds.), *Postpartum depression and child development* (pp. 54–81). New York: Guilford Press.

Tronick, E., Winn, S., & Morelli, G. (1985). Multiple caretaking in the context of human evolution: Why don't the Efe' Know the Western prescription for child care? In M. Reite, & T. Field (Eds.), *The psychobiology of attachment and separation* (pp. 293–322). Denver, CO and Miami, FA: Harcourt Brace Jovanovich.

Tronick, E., Wise, S., Als, H., Adamson, L., Scanlon, J., & Brazelton, T. B. (1977). Regional obstetric anesthesia and newborn behavior: Effect over the first ten days of life. *Pediatrics, 58*, 94–100.

Winnicott, D. W. (1964). *The child, the family, and the outside world.* Baltimore: Penguin Books.

1976; Elman et al., 1996; Fischer & Rose, 1994; Kozulin, 1990; van de Rijt-Plooij & Plooij, 1992; Smith & Breazeal, 2007; Trevarthen, 1982; Trevarthen & Aitken, 2003; Munakata & McClelland, 2003). As one example, van Geert (1991) proposed a dynamic systems model of competitive growth in which regression is found in the intermediary stage whereas Plooij (1990, 2003) has promoted the idea that the perceptual control theory developed by Powers (1973) better explain regressions within early infancy. According to this theory, infants are born with few and limited levels of control, but with age develop a hierarchy of perceptual control. Each change in perception is the result of important changes within the nervous system and each change also signals the development of a new skill or strategy, and causes regression. These changes momentarily destabilize the infant's inner world and thus affect the mother–infant relationship. The reaction of the infant changes and the mother (parent) has to understand those new responses and renegotiate the relationship. The underlying brain changes also mean that, at the end of a period, the infant's understanding of the world will have changed to some degree.

The remaining part of this chapter summarizes the results from a European project that, during the 1990s, brought together research groups from Spain, Sweden, and Great Britain to test if indicators of regression could be found at the ages proposed in the original studies (Plooij & van de Rijt-Plooij, 1989; van de Rijt-Plooij & Plooij, 1992).

Observations from Spain

Sadurni and Rostan (2002, 2003) studied regression periods among eighteen Catalan children in Spain. The children were between three weeks and 14 months and each child was followed longitudinally for about five months within one of four cohorts. Data were collected through questionnaires, semi-structured interviews and direct observations; the protocol followed van de Rijt-Plooij and Plooij's (1992) original suggestions. A regression period was coded if three behavioral indices were co-occurring: (1) an increase in bodily contact, (2) an increase in crying/irritability, and (3) one of several possible distortions; e.g., a shift in the child's sleep–wake cycle, a change in the child's activity level or drowsiness. The agreement between coders for specifying a regression period was around 80 percent.

The findings from the Spanish study show a close fit with the regression periods proposed by van de Rijt-Plooij and Ploij (1992) (see Figure 9.1).

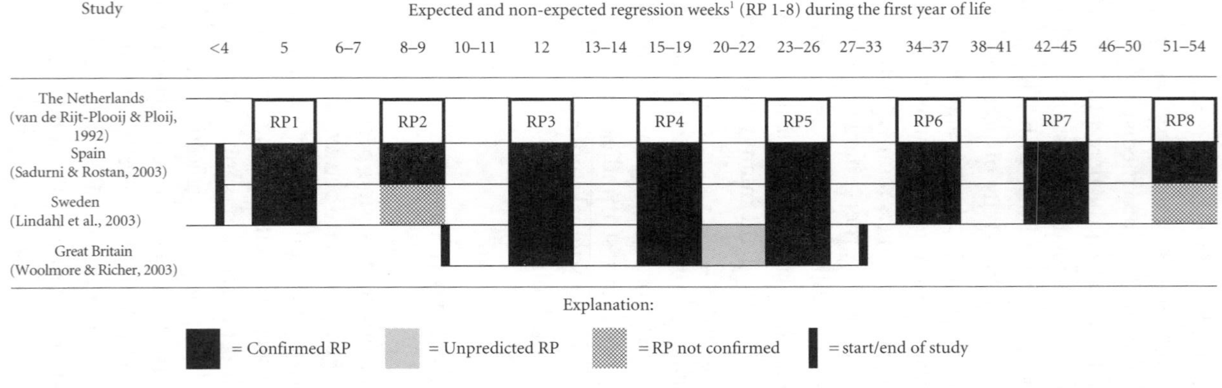

[1]Each regressive week has been estimated based on data presented by van de Rijt-Plooij and Ploij (1992) using 50+ as criterion. Thus, over 50% of the children participating in a study must be judged as regressive for a regressive week to be declared. Exceptions: (1) In RP1 in Lindah1 et al.'s study, the number of regressive children is exactly 50%. (2) Woolmore and Richer used a different statistical procedure when identifying regression (z test of proportions).

Figure 9.1 Regressive periods (RP) replicated in Spain, Sweden and Great Britain using findings from the Netherlands as gold standard. For each study a hit is counted if one or more regressive weeks is overlapping completely or in part with the Dutch report. A miss is counted if a RP lies completely outside expected periods (thus, a hit would be noted for RP 4 if a study identifies regression for weeks 14–17). An unconfirmed RP indicates that less than 50% of the children in a study are judged as regressive

Source: Figure from H. H. C. van de Rijt-Plooij, & F. X. Plooij (1987), Growing independence, conflict, and learning in mother–infant relations in free-ranging chimpanzees, *Behaviour*, 101, 1–86. Reproduced by permission of Koninklijke Brill NV

Sadurni and Rostan report peaks at 5, 8, 12–13, 18, 26–27, 35, 43 and 52 weeks, observations that matched almost perfectly the expected weeks.

The original Dutch study never reported fewer than 80 percent of the children as regressive within any RP while the level of reported regression in the Spanish study varied from 42 to 100 percent. The highest percentages were observed for RP 2 (100%), RP 5 (85%) and RP 1 (80%) while lowest figure was noted for RP 3 (42%). For the other four RPs, the reported percentages varied from 50 to 62 percent.

Each regression period lasted on average for two weeks with a range from one to four weeks. It was obvious that some children had quite concentrated RPs while for others the regression periods were prolonged over several weeks. Possible reasons for this variability can, according to Sadurni and Rostan, be attributed to either individual (e.g., temperamental differences between children) or relational factors influencing both members of the dyad.

Observations from Great Britain

Based on weekly phone interviews with thirty mothers from 10 to 26 weeks postpartum, a study from Great Britain found clear support for three regression periods (Woolmore & Richer, 2003). Beside the obvious aim to replicate the Dutch findings, Woolmore and Richer also made a point of developing a rigorous protocol for detecting regression periods. A computerized algorithm was used for deciding if any specific week should be categorized as regressive or not. They underscore that it is difficult to decide if a regression period exists or not due to the high level of "noise" in the system under observation (= the mother–infant dyad). The information indicating regression is seen as a "weak signal" in a noisy environment.

The computer algorithm developed by Woolmore and Richer (see Figure 9.2) analyzed the information and classified any particular week as either a regression week or a nonregression week. To be classified as a regression week, the score had to be one or two in category A (Fractious or changeable mood) and B (Attachment-related behavior) and two or more in category C (Additional regression items). The categorizations made with the computer program were checked for reliability by having an independent rater evaluate twelve infants who were selected randomly. The achieved reliability was excellent (Kappa = .82).

The final analysis revealed a pattern that fit well with the expected weeks (see Figure 9.1); clear support was found for the three expected peaks,

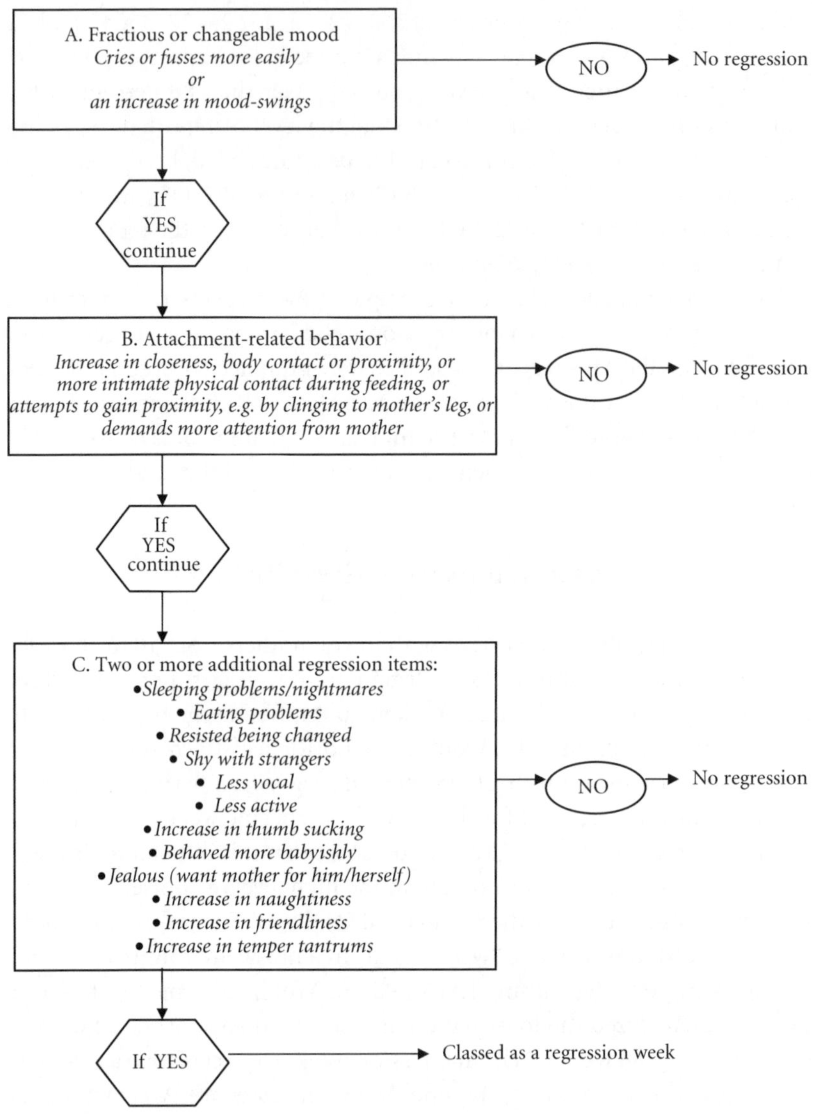

Figure 9.2 The Plooij algorithm for determining regression weeks
Source: Adapted from Woolmore and Richer (2003, p. 25)

at 12, 17 and 24 weeks ($p < .01$; z test of proportions). In addition two additional peaks were initially found around week 14 and 20. Of these two, the peak around 14 weeks disappeared when a correction for age was instigated so that a deviance of +/– one week was accepted. The regression peak at week 20 did however not disappear and represents a regression week not previously reported by van de Rijt-Plooij and Plooij (1992). This week has previously been linked to an increase in conflicts within the mother–infant dyad by van de Rijt-Plooij and Plooij (1993) and Woolmore and Richer suggest that this regressive peak signifies something else than a pure regression period. In addition, they claim that this peak disappears for dyads in which the mother is depressed (Plooij & van de Rijt-Plooij, 2003).

In sum, the British study highlights the importance of adopting a rigorous methodology when studying regression during the infancy period. This is important in order to reduce the possibility of reporting chance findings. It is, however, as important to be aware of the opposite risk, to not see regression when it is actually there.

Observations from Sweden

As for the studies carried out in Spain and Great Britain, the main goal of the Swedish project (Lindahl, 1998; Lindahl, Heimann, & Ullstadius, 2003) was to replicate van de Rijt-Plooij and Plooij's (1992) findings. A definition of regression that closely matched the one used in the original studies was chosen, a definition that emphasizes regression as an interpersonal phenomenon: "The regressive phenomenon we are dealing with . . . belongs to the emotional domain. It consists mainly of the temporary decrease/disappearance of the growing independence of the baby as measured through mother–infant body contact, combined with an increase in crying" (van de Rijt-Plooij & Plooij, 1992, p. 131).

Seventeen infants (9 girls) and their mothers were followed from birth to 15 months and data on regression was collected through both questionnaires and observations. A significant correlation was observed between the numbers of observed and expected regression weeks ($r = .90$), which suggests a connection stronger than could be expected by chance. Overall a cyclical pattern matching the original findings was found, although these periods did not always coincide perfectly with the expected RPs (about 70% of the observed regressive weeks matched the expected weeks). The percentage of infants judged as regressive during the expected weeks revealed support for six of the hypothesized periods (see Figure 9.1): Fifty percent or more of the children were identified as regressive during RP 1 (54%), RP 3 (50%), RP 4 (70+), RP 5 (53%), RP 6 (80+), and RP 7 (80+) weeks. In contrast, no or weak support was found for RP 2 (29%), RP 8 (44%), and RP 9 (36%).

The lack of support for RP 2 in the Swedish study is somewhat surprising since this period around two months of age is one of the more accepted periods of change or transition in the literature (e.g., Fischer, 1987; Trevarthen & Aitken, 2003). Moreover, both the original study by van de Rijt-Plooij and Plooij (1992) and the Spanish replication study (this chapter) found clear indications of regression during this period. A re-analysis of the Swedish data did not resolve the issue but did hint at a possible explanation: Five additional infants had been judged as "close-to-be-regressive" by their mothers but not strong enough to indicate a RP. A similar pattern of "borderline regression" was not found for any of the other expected regression periods and, if these five infants had been included together with the four previously identified infants, support for RP 2 would have been evident (69% displayed regression or borderline regression). Moreover, the low number of regressive infants for RP 9 might have been masked by illness since four children (= 29%) were reported ill and not regressive during this regression period.

The role of the primary caregiver changed when the infants were between 8 and 12 months old and might explain why no support for RP 8 was found. For about half the sample, the mother went back to work and the father stepped in as caregiver, a change that might have had an impact on the parental–infant relationship and also on how behavioral changes were reported back to the research team.

Conclusions

The combined findings from Spain, Sweden, and Great Britain are in concert with the overall picture presented by van de Rijt-Plooij and Plooij (1992, 1993); the phenomenon of regression periods in early infancy seems to be real and warrants the attention of both clinicians and researchers. It is notable that the regression periods investigated in the research presented in this chapter to a large degree overlap with the "touchpoints" in development as suggested from clinical experience by Brazelton (Brazelton & Sparrow, 2006).

Campos et al. (2008) recently suggested that regressive phenomena have been neglected in contemporary research. Much of current research has, for good reasons, focused on finding links between early and late versions of early competencies resulting in a better understanding of the capacities the infant has and of early starting points for important social and cognitive skills. However, the overwhelming support for early competencies might also overshadow the fact that similar or identical behaviors might be governed by different neural structures. Thus, there is a risk that we over-interpret early competencies and early changes in the development.

This means that for understanding the regression phenomena described here we need to focus on the detailed behavioral and neurological development of the infant. Social and cognitive functions emerge as the result of interactions between different brain regions as well as of interactions between the brain and the psychosocial environment (Johnson et al., 2009). Moreover, Johnson et al. also argue that "the same behavior could be supported by different neural substrates at different ages during development" (p. 152) which might affect how we understand the changes taking place at each regression period. Plooij (2003) presents a list of possible perceptual changes underlying each regression period. Understanding of events is, for instance, highlighted at RP 4, relationships at RP 5, and categories at RP 6. These are possible links that need to be coupled with direct behavioral evidence. It is however also possible, if we follow the line of argument put forward by Johnson et al., that each RP does *not* represent a completely new competence but instead a further development of skills already to some degree within the child's repertoire.

Finally, it must be stressed that more research is needed. We lack knowledge of how individual differences might influence how regressive behaviors are expressed and interpreted; we lack a deeper understanding on how culture exerts its influence; and we lack knowledge of possible consequences on the development of attachment by how the parent–infant dyad handles the stress induced by regression. We do, however, have good grounds to suspect that how parents react to or understand their infant will impact development. Thus, a parent with less knowledge, with less social support or with mental health problems (e.g., depression) increases the risk of a nonoptimal outcome of recurrent stressful conflicts between the parent and the infant induced by repeated regressions. The one-time smooth interaction might instead become characterized by an increase in crying, fewer moments of positive interactions and maybe even sustained withdrawal on the infant's part (Guedeney, 2007).

Acknowledgment

Writing this chapter has in part been made possible by a grant from the Swedish Council for Working Life and Social Research (grant # 2006–1040).

References and further reading

Bates, E. (1976). *Language and context: Studies in the acquisition of pragmatics.* New York: Academic Press.

Bever, T. G. (1982). Introduction. In T. G. Bever (Ed.), *Regression in mental development: Basic phenomena and theories* (pp. 1–4). Hillsdale, NJ: Erlbaum.

Brazelton, T. B., & Sparrow, J. D. (2006). *Birth to three: Your child's emotional and behavioural development.* Cambridge, MA: Da Capo Press.

Campos, J. J., Witherington, D., Anderson, D. I., Frankel, C. I., Uchiyama, I., & Barby-Roth, M. (2008). Rediscovering development in infancy. *Child Development, 79,* 1625–1632.

Elman, J. L., Bates, E. A., Johnson, M. H., Karmiloff-Smith, A., Parisi, D., & Plunkett, K. (1996). *Rethinking innateness: A connectionist perspective on development.* Cambridge, MA: MIT Press.

Fischer, K. W. (1987). Relation between brain and cognitive development. *Child Development, 58,* 623–632.

Fischer, K. W., & Rose, S. P. (1994). Dynamic development of coordination of components in brain and behavior: A framework for theory and research. In G. Dawson, & K. W. Fischer (Eds.), *Human behavior and the developing brain* (pp. 3–66). New York: The Guilford Press.

Guedeney, A. (2007). Withdrawal behavior and depression in infancy. *Infant Mental Health Journal, 28,* 393–408.

Hall, W. G., & Oppenheim, R. W. (1987). Developmental psychobiology, Prenatal, perinatal and early postnatal aspects of behavioural development. *Annual Review of Psychology, 38,* 91–128.

Heimann, M. (1991). Neonatal imitation: A social and biological phenomenon. In T. Archer, & S. Hansen (Eds.), *Behavioral biology: The neuroendocrine axis* (pp. 173–186). Hillsdale, NJ.: Erlbaum.

Johnson, M. H. (2005). The ontogeny of the social brain: A tribute to Michael Posner. In U. Mayr, E. Awh, & S. W. Keele (Eds.), *Developing individuality in the human brain* (pp. 125–140). Washington, DC: American Psychological Association.

Johnson, M. H., Grossman, T., & Cohen Kadosh, K. (2009). Mapping functional brain development: Building a social brain through interactive specialization. *Developmental Psychology, 45*(1), 151–159.

Kagan, J. (2008). In defense of qualitative changes in development. *Child Development, 79,* 1606–1624.

Kozulin, A. (1990). The concept of regression and Vygotskian developmental theory. *Developmental Review, 10,* 218–238.

Lindahl, L. B. (1998). *Gender and age related developmental processes during infancy.* Doctoral dissertation, Göteborg University, Sweden.

Lindahl, L. B., Heimann, M., & Ullstadius, E. (2003). Occurrence of regression periods in the normal development of Swedish infants. In M. Heimann (Ed.), *Regression periods in human infancy* (pp. 41–55). Mahwah, NJ: Erlbaum.

Munakata, Y., & McClelland, J. L. (2003). Connectionist models of development. *Developmental Science, 6*, 413–429.

Plooij, F. X. (1990). Developmental psychology: Developmental stages as successive reorganizations of the hierarchy. In R. J. Robertson, & W. T. Powers (Eds.), *The control theory view – Introduction to modern psychology* (pp. 123–133). Gravel Switch, KY: The Control Systems Group.

Plooij, F. X. (2003). The trilogy of mind. In M. Heimann (Ed.), *Regression periods in human infancy* (pp. 185–203). Mahwah, NJ: Erlbaum.

Plooij, F. X., & van de Rijt-Plooij, H. H. C. (1989). Vulnerable periods during infancy: Hierarchically reorganized systems control, stress and disease. *Ethology and Sociobiology, 10,* 279–296.

Plooij, F. X., & van de Rijt-Plooij, H. H. C. (2003). The effects of sources of "noise" on direct observation measures of regression periods: Case studies of four infants' adaptations to special parental conditions. In M. Heimann (Ed.), *Regression periods in human infancy* (pp. 57–80). Mahwah, NJ: Erlbaum.

Powers, W. T. (1973). *Behavior: The control of perception*. Chicago: Aldine.

Sadurni, M., & Rostan, R. (2002). Regression periods in infancy: A case study from Catalonia. *The Spanish Journal of Psychology, 1*, 36–43.

Sadurni, M., & Rostan, C. (2003). Reflections on regression periods in the development of Catalan infants. In M. Heimann (Ed.), *Regression periods in human infancy* (pp. 7–22). Mahwah, NJ: Erlbaum.

Smith, L. B., & Breazeal, C. (2007). The dynamic lift of developmental process. *Developmental Science, 10*, 61–68.

Trevarthen, C. (1982). Basic patterns of psychogenetic change in infancy. In T. G. Bever (Ed.), *Regressions in mental development: Basic phenomena and theories* (pp. 7–46). Hillsdale, NJ: Erlbaum.

Trevarthen, C., & Aitken, K. (2003). Regulation of brain development and age-related changes in infants' motives: The developmental function of regressive periods. In M. Heimann (Ed.), *Regression periods in human infancy* (pp. 107–184). Mahwah, NJ: Erlbaum.

Tronick, E. (2006). The inherent stress of normal daily life and social interaction leads to the development of coping and resilience, and variation in resilience in infants and young children. *Annals of the New York Academy of Science, 1094*, 83–104.

van de Rijt-Plooij, H. H. C., & Plooij, F. X. (1987). Growing independence, conflict and learning in mother–infant relations in free-ranging chimpanzees, *Behaviour, 101*, 1–86.

van de Rijt-Plooij, H. H. C., & Plooij, F. X. (1992). Infantile regressions: Disorganization and the onset of transition periods. *Journal of Reproductive and Infant Psychology, 10*, 129–149.

van de Rijt-Plooij, H. H. C., & Plooij, F. X. (1993). Distinct periods of mother–infant conflict in normal development: Sources of progress and germs of pathology. *Journal of Child Psychology and Psychiatry, 34*, 229–245.

van Geert, P. (1991). A dynamic systems model of cognitive and language growth. *Psychological Review, 98*, 3–53.

Woolmore, A., & Richer, J. (2003). Detecting infant regression periods: Weak signals in a noisy environment. In M. Heimann (Ed.), *Regression periods in human infancy* (pp. 23–39). Mahwah, NJ: Erlbaum.

Zeanah, C. H., Neil, W. B., & Larrieu, J. A. (1997). Infant development and developmental risk: A review of the past 10 years. *Journal of American Academy of Child & Adolescent Psychiatry, 36*, 165–177.

10

The Four Whys of Age-Linked Regression Periods in Infancy

Frans X. Plooij

Introduction

Niko Tinbergen's "four why" questions (Tinbergen, 1963) concerning the evolution, development, causation, and function of behavior provide a fertile approach to the study of behavior. This chapter applies this approach to "regression," which refers here to an infant's temporary reversion to the higher proportions of time spent seeking maternal contact characteristic of earlier periods of development, and corresponds to the 'disorganization' within Brazelton's touchpoints of development.

Evolution of Regression Periods

Evolutionarily speaking, the regression phenomenon is old, and has been observed in humans, primates, and nonprimate mammals. One author reported peaks in nipple contact in 12 monkey species and two nonprimate mammals (Horwich, 1974) that occur at similar times in development, if corrections are made for each species' rate of development. The peaks are thought to emerge during emotional states of insecurity.

In the Gombe National Park, we studied the behavioral development and growing independence of free-living chimpanzee infants (Plooij, 1984; van de Rijt-Plooij & Plooij, 1987), and expanded Horwich's findings (Figure 10.1). Growing independence appeared not to be a gradual process, but to occur in leaps and bounds.

The top row of Figure 10.1 delineates six categories of infant–mother distance: "ventral," "not ventral," "in contact, but not supported by mother's body," "off mother within arm's reach," "out of arm's reach within 5 meters," "beyond 5 meters within 15 meters." The left column presents the age in

distance categories / month	ventral	not – ventral	in contact	within arm's reach	between 1.5–5m	between 5–15m	
1	1						
2	1						
3	1		2				
4	1	3	2				
5	1	4	3	2	5		
6	1	4	2	3	4		
7	1		2	2	4		
							A
8	2	4	1	3	4		
9	3		1	2	4		
10	1	5	3	2	4		
11	2	4	1	3	5		
							1
12	3	5	2	1	3	6	
13	2	5	3	1	3	6	
14	3	5	2	1	4		
15	2	5	4	1	3		
16	4	6	2	1	3	5	
17	1	5	4	2	3	6	
18	3	5	4	1	1	6	
							2
19	4	5	5	2	1	2	
20	4	5	3	2	1	6	

A = drop in ventro – ventral contact
1 = first drop in contact
2 = second drop in contact

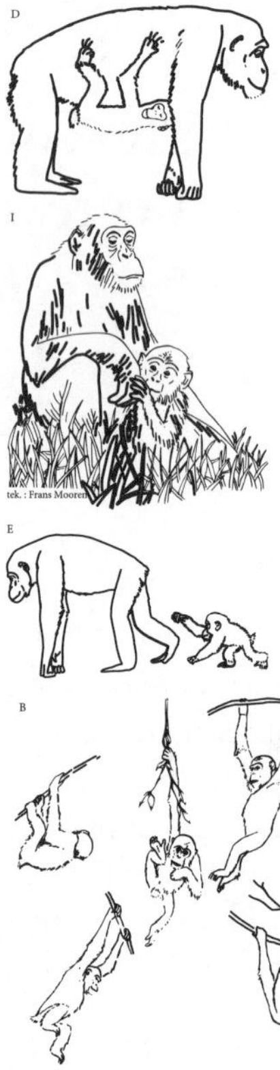

Figure 10.1 Rank order of the amount of time spent in each of six distance-categories for the mother–infant dyad FF and FD

Source: Figure from H. H. C. van de Rijt-Plooij, & F. X. Plooij (1987) Growing independence, conflict, and learning in mother–infant relations in free-ranging chimpanzees, *Behaviour*, 101, 1–86. Reproduced by permission of Koninklijke Brill NV. Line drawings by Dr. David Bygott, from F. Plooij (1984) The behavioral development of free-living chimpanzee babies and infants. In L. P. Lipsitt (Ed.), *Monographs on infancy* (Vol. 3). Norwood, NJ: Ablex. Copyright (©) 1984 by Ablex Publishing Corporation. Reproduced by permission of ABC-CLIO, LLC

months. In the other columns, numbers 1–6 refer to the rank order of that particular distance category as an observed percentage of time spent in any distance category. The top rank orders number 1 are connected by a solid line, indicating the change over time in the distance category the infant spent most time in. From top to bottom, the first dotted line (A) marks a leap from staying mainly in ventro-ventral contact with the mother to staying mainly off the body of the mother, but still in contact. The second

Figure 10.2a Mother Passion is trying to get her son Prof off her nipple and belly. She is pulling, pushing and bite-gnawing, trying to loosen his hands, feet, and mouth holding tight to her hair and nipple

Source: From H. H. C. van de Rijt-Plooij & F. X. Plooij (1987) Growing independence, conflict and learning in mother–infant relations in free-ranging chimpanzees, *Behaviour, 101*, 1–86. Reproduced by permission of Koninklijke Brill NV

dotted line (1) marks the leap from mainly staying in contact to mainly staying out of contact, within arm's reach. And the third dotted line (2) marks the leap from mainly staying within arm's reach to mainly staying out of arm's reach, within 5 meters. These top distance categories are illustrated in the right margin. Before each 'leap' in independence, a regression period occurred. Regression was expressed, first, in a temporary shift back to mainly staying closer to mother and, second, in a temporary increase in the amount of ventro-ventral contact.

The regression period was followed by a period of mother–infant conflict over body contact (van de Rijt-Plooij & Plooij, 1988). Mother Passion, for example, is shown (Figure 10.2a), trying to get her son Prof off her nipple and belly. She is pulling, pushing and bite-gnawing, trying to loosen his hands, feet, and mouth holding tight to her hair and nipple. This time Passion failed and travels on with Prof still ventral and sucking

Figure 10.2b This time Passion failed and travels on with Prof still ventral and sucking
Source: From H. H. C. van de Rijt-Plooij & F. X. Plooij (1987) Growing independence, conflict and learning in mother–infant relations in free-ranging chimpanzees, *Behaviour, 101*, 1–86. Reproduced by permission of Koninklijke Brill NV

(Figure 10.2b). The conflict is about the privilege of being ventral and sucking, and is not directed at the infant. Mother Fifi (Figure 10.2c), by contrast, succeeds in scooping her baby Freud from the ventral to the dorsal position. Mother–infant conflict was followed by a leap to greater independence.

Regression Period Development

After studying chimpanzee mothers and infants, we examined regression periods in human infants with direct observation of mother–infant interaction in the unrestricted home environment, weekly questionnaires, and indepth interviews of the mother (van de Rijt-Plooij & Plooij, 1992).

The main results are shown in Figure 10.3. The lower part B of this figure is another way of representing data presented in the upper half A. Part B presents the percentage of mothers reporting regressive infant behaviors over age and shows that these are age-linked.

Figure 10.2c Mother Fifi, by contrast, succeeds in scooping her baby Freud from the ventral to the dorsal position

Part A (Figure 10.3) shows how the lower part of this figure was generated. Each row stands for one infant. In each row two horizontal black bars are shown repeatedly. The top black bar stands for the weeks in which the mother confirmed the question "Was your baby more difficult than usual this week?" in the weekly questionnaire. Together, these horizontal black bars show a vertical striping, indicating that the difficult weeks are age-linked.

The bottom black bar in each horizontal row stands for actual infant behaviors (the three Cs: Crying, Clinging, Cranky) observed each week by the mother that are typical for regression periods. The babies seek proximity to their mothers. Any behavior that helps reach that goal is used. Sometimes mothers report such behaviors while not experiencing their baby as more difficult than usual. In these cases, a bottom black bar is shown where the top black bar is missing. Altogether, the bottom black bars give an even more complete picture and confirm the overall results based on the experiences of the mothers.

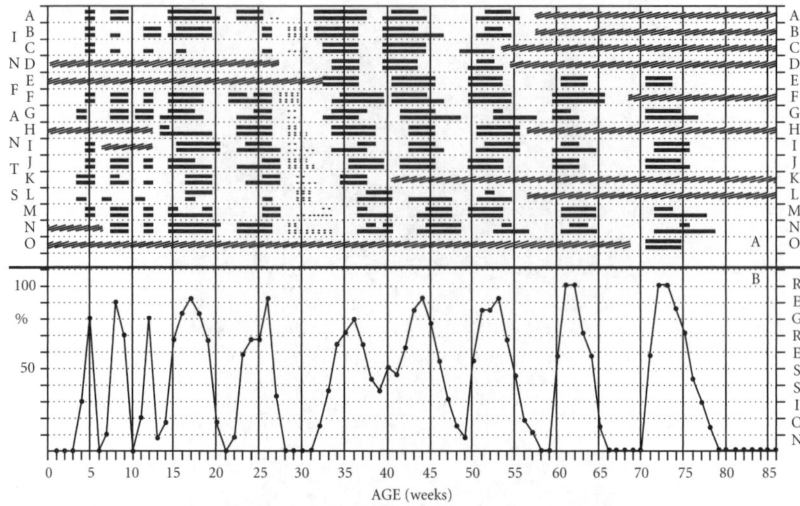

Figure 10.3 Age-linked regression periods
Source: From H. H. C. van de Rijt-Plooij & F. X. Plooij (1992) Infantile regressions: Disorganization and the onset of transition periods. *Journal of Reproductive and Infant Psychology, 10*, 129–149. Reproduced by permission of Taylor & Francis Ltd.: www.informaworld.com

The thick horizontal bars refer to weeks when no data were available. The dotted horizontal bars refer to the "checking back pattern" reported by Mahler and coworkers (Mahler, Pine, & Bergman, 1975). This behavior is new and not regressive.

As in the chimps, there was mother–infant conflict in humans (van de Rijt-Plooij & Plooij, 1993). These data are based on weekly questionnaires combined with indepth interviews. The mother–infant conflict was divided into three categories (see Figure 10.4).

First, annoyance: typical with younger babies. Initially, mothers worried that something was wrong with their babies during a regression period and might even visit the pediatrician,[1] only to learn that nothing was wrong. Then worry would change into annoyance. In the first few months, mothers would not act on their annoyance.

At later ages, especially the second half of the first year, they would. This was called "promoting progress," because the mothers sensed that their babies were able to do more, so would demand more of them. At this age they used mild strategies, diverting the attention of their babies, who would acquiesce.

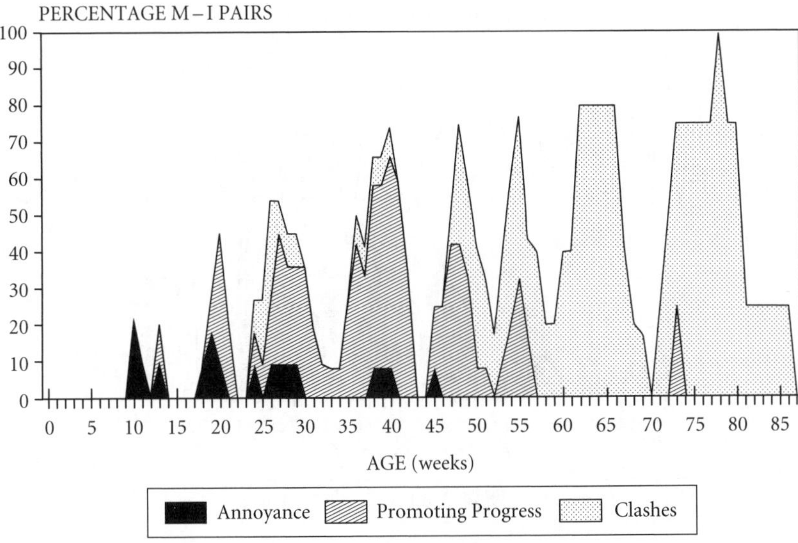

Figure 10.4 Conflict periods

Source: From H. H. C. van de Rijt-Plooij & F. X. Plooij (1993), Distinct periods of mother–infant conflict in normal development: Sources of progress and germs of pathology. *Journal of Child Psychology and Psychiatry, 34*, 229–245. Reproduced by permission of Blackwell Publishing, Oxford, England.

Soon, though, especially during the second year of life, the babies would no longer accept diversion, and straightforward "clashes" would result. At around 18 months, all mothers reported clashes.

As in the chimps, conflict periods followed regression periods. At the top of Figure 10.5, the regression periods are depicted upside down with peaks pointing downwards. Regression peaks precede conflict peaks. This was verified through separate statistical analysis of individual infant data. Onset of regression periods preceded onset of conflict periods more frequently than expected by chance, using the sign test (Siegel, 1956).

Our original findings having been replicated by independent research groups in Sweden, Spain, and England (Lindahl, Heimann, & Ullstadius, 2003; Sadurni & Rostan, 2003; Woolmore & Richer, 2003) and validated by direct observation (Plooij & van de Rijt-Plooij, 2003). We then sought completely different evidence. The line of argument was as follows: relationships between regression (or disorganization) and progression (or reorganization) have been proposed for almost a century by scientists from various backgrounds. Disorganization throws the whole organism off

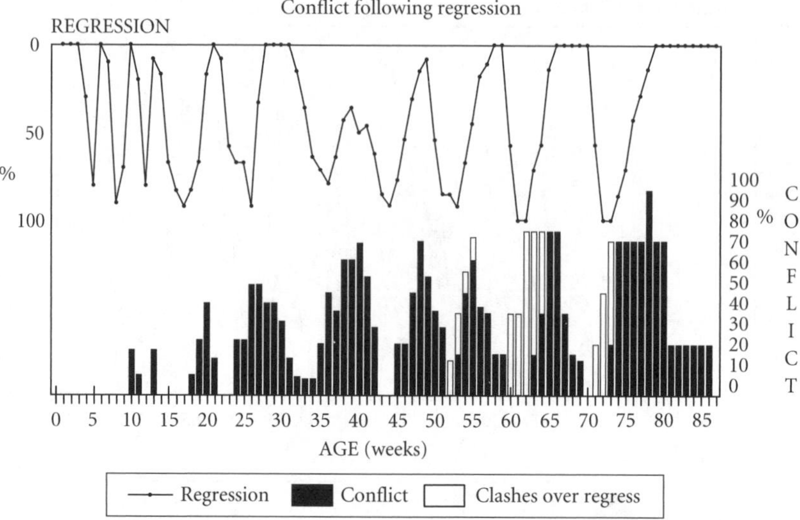

Figure 10.5 Conflict following regression
Source: From H. H. C. van de Rijt-Plooij & F. X. Plooij (1993) Distinct periods of mother–infant conflict in normal development: Sources of progress and germs of pathology. *Journal of Child Psychology and Psychiatry, 34,* 229–245. Reproduced by permission of Blackwell Publishing, Oxford, England

balance, so it should appear not only in behavior associated with regression periods, but also in other domains. Progress in psychoneuroimmunology during recent decades has revealed complex interactions between behavior and the central nervous, endocrine, and immune systems (Ader, Felten, & Cohen, 2001). When the organism is disorganized, the immune system and health of the organism might also be expected to be disorganized. As long ago as 1935, Walter Cannon suggested that normal experiences of life – such as the onset of puberty, fatigue, and everyday worry – all make a physical impression on the body: "the whole gamut of human diseases might be studied from this point of view" (Cannon, 1935). This notion implies that age-linked disorganization might be manifest in domains beyond behavior.

We studied illness distribution over the course of infancy, predicting peaks in a nonlinear, multimodal distribution at ages corresponding to regression periods during the first 20 months of life. Superposed on an inverted U-shaped curve we found small but statistically significant peaks in illness following the regression periods (Plooij, van de Rijt-Plooij, van der Stelt, van Es, & Helmers, 2003). The inverted U-shaped curve can be explained from the literature on the development of the immune system, but the superposed illness peaks had never been reported.

We then studied Sudden Infant Death Syndrome (SIDS) distribution over infancy using the same statistical techniques and found similar, small peaks of SIDS superposed onto the well-known inverted U-shaped curve (Plooij, van de Rijt-Plooij, & Helmers, 2003). The ages at which these small peaks are found overlap with the regression period ages.

Regression Period Causation

The suggestion that sudden brain changes might underlie regression periods and peaks in illnesses and SIDS brings us to the third of the "four whys": causation.

Trevarthen and Aitken's extensive literature review on prenatal brain development cites evidence for a predictable, gene-regulated, developmental neuroanatomical history of the adaptive motive systems of the mind. They proposed that "the core regulatory systems of interneurons in the brain stem, which in the adult regulate attentional orientations, coordinate purposeful movements of the body and its parts, and mediate the equilibria between autonomic and exploratory or executive states, first emerge in the embryo brain as regulators of morphogenesis in emerging cognitive systems." Such development does not stop at birth. The same or similar intrinsic regulations of brain development may underlie the emergence of motives in the growing human brain to perceive and learn in new ways. Age-linked brain developments occur from infancy to senescence. Trevarthen & Aitken (2003) report sudden postnatal brain changes co-occurring with 7 out of the 10 regression periods in the first 20 months.

Regression Period Function

Regressive behavior and difficult periods do have a function. Marten de Vries studied survival rates of Masai children with and without difficult temperaments in times of famine. Better able to trigger caring behavior of their mothers, difficult children had higher survival rates (de Vries, 1984).

Using three temperamentally different subgroups from a large birth cohort, Maziade and coworkers undertook a longitudinal study of the association between temperament measured in children at 4 and 8 months and

IQ assessed at 4.7 years. The data suggested a strong effect of extreme temperament traits on IQ development in middle and upper socioeconomic classes and in families with superior functioning in terms of communication. The temperamentally difficult group unexpectedly displayed higher IQs, and the well-replicated effect of socioeconomic status on IQ development was observed mainly in this group. These data support the hypothesis that difficult infants activate special family resources, stimulating intellectual development (Maziade, Côté, Boutin, Bernier, & Thivierge, 1987).

We developed a parental support and education program called "Leaping Hurdles" (LH) for a group of single mothers at risk of abusing their infants (van de Rijt-Plooij, van der Stelt, & Plooij, 1996). We made parents aware of regression periods and that their babies could not help being difficult, and how they could comfort their babies in these difficult periods and facilitate consequent learning. In an evaluation study with a quasi-experimental, nonequivalent control group design, we compared an experimental group receiving LH with a control group. After establishing that the two groups did not show statistically significant differences on 30 covariables, we found the following statistically significant differences in the dependent variables. LH parents' views on their babies' temperament became more informed by their babies' behavior than by their rules, and by their babies' mental rather than motor development. Parents' internal locus of control increased. The LH infants scored higher on Bayley Scale cognitive subsets, with females, typically testing below males in the general population, achieving similar results in this context. Infants were less fearful and more open to strangers. Attachment types were similar across groups. Health outcomes improved, especially for girls.

Regression periods have the function of activating family resources to promote intellectual and social development as well as physical health.

Epilogue

Niko Tinbergen's classic "four whys" have triggered a wide variety of research on regression periods. These studies provide additional lines of evidence supporting nonlinear, discontinuous models of development such as Brazelton's touchpoints and ours, and lead to the emergence of the following picture.

At gene-regulated ages, brain changes generate a new motive, directing babies' attention to a new type of perception, disrupting behavioral organization. Infants withdraw from the world and seek greater parent contact.

A more intensive caretaking period follows, culminating in parent–infant conflict. In the process, parents become acquainted with their infants' new motive and perceptual abilities. Babies explore the new perceptual world, resulting in a new type of learning and a progression toward a greater independence. Infants work out a set of new skills, behaviors, and task performances typical for that perceptual world. Each baby 'selects' a preferred set of skills. Rates of skill acquisition depend on babies' personal preferences and prevailing conditions in the physical and social environment. With each new motive, babies enter the next perceptual world, one level higher in the representational hierarchy. Then the whole process starts all over again.

Acknowledgment

In September 2003 my late wife, pal, colleague, and co-author, Hetty van de Rijt-Plooij, died far too young. Based on our lifelong joint venture, this chapter is dedicated to her. She deserves as much, if not more, credit.

Note

1 It is here that Berry Brazelton's parenting book, *Touchpoints* (1992), is linked to our Dutch parenting book, *Oei, ik groei!* (van de Rijt & Plooij, 1992), that was later translated into American English as *The Wonder Weeks* (van de Rijt & Plooij, 2010). While we collected our data underlying *Oei, ik groei!* in the home environment, Brazelton collected his data underlying *Touchpoints* in his clinical practice. Independently we discovered the same phenomenon in two different environments.

References and further reading

Ader, R., Felten, D. L., & Cohen, N. (Eds.) (2001). *Psychoneuroimmunology* (3rd ed., Vol. 2). New York: Academic Press.

Brazelton, T. B. (1992). *Touchpoints.* Reading, MA: Addison-Wesley.

Cannon, W. (1935). Stresses and strains of homeostasis. *The American Journal of the Medical Sciences, 189*(1), 13–14.

de Vries, M. W. (1984). Temperament and infant mortality among Masai of East Africa. *American Journal of Psychiatry, 141*, 1189–1194.

Horwich, R. H. (1974). Regressive periods in primate behavioral development with reference to other mammals. *Primates, 15*, 141–149.

Lindahl, L., Heimann, M., & Ullstadius, E. (2003). Occurrence of regressive periods in the normal development of Swedish infants. In M. Heimann (Ed.), *Regression periods in human infancy* (pp. 41–55). Mahwah, NJ: Erlbaum.

Mahler, S., Pine, F., & Bergman, A. (1975). *The psychological birth of the human infant: Symbiosis and individuation*. New York: Basic Books.

Maziade, M., Côté, R., Boutin, P., Bernier, H., & Thivierge, J. (1987). Temperament and intellectual development: A longitudinal study from infancy to four years. *American Journal of Psychiatry, 144*(2), 144–150.

Plooij, F. X. (1984). The behavioral development of free-living chimpanzee babies and infants. In L. P. Lipsitt (Ed.), *Monographs on infancy* (Vol. 3). Norwood, NJ: Ablex.

Plooij, F. X. (2003). The trilogy of mind. In M. Heimann (Ed.), *Regression periods in human infancy* (pp. 185–205). Mahwah, NJ: Erlbaum.

Plooij, F. X., & van de Rijt-Plooij, H. H. C. (2003). The effects of sources of "noise" on direct observation measures of regression periods: Case studies of four infants' adaptations to special parental conditions. In M. Heimann (Ed.), *Regression periods in human infancy* (pp. 57–80). Mahwah, NJ: Erlbaum.

Plooij, F. X., van de Rijt-Plooij, H. H. C., & Helmers, R. (2003). Multimodal distribution of SIDS and regression periods. In M. Heimann (Ed.), *Regression periods in human infancy* (pp. 97–106). Mahwah, NJ: Erlbaum.

Plooij, F. X., van de Rijt-Plooij, H. H. C., van der Stelt, J. M., van Es, B., & Helmers, R. (2003). Illness-peaks during infancy and regression periods. In M. Heimann (Ed.), *Regression periods in human infancy* (pp. 81–95). Mahwah, NJ: Erlbaum.

Sadurni, M., & Rostan, C. (2003). Reflections on regression periods in the development of Catalan infants. In M. Heimann (Ed.), *Regression periods in human infancy* (pp. 7–22). Mahwah, NJ: Erlbaum.

Siegel, S. (1956). *Nonparametric statistics for the behavioral sciences*. Tokyo: McGraw-Hill Kogakusha.

Tinbergen, N. (1963). On aims and methods of ethology. *Z Tierpsychol, 20*, 410–433.

Trevarthen, C. (1977). Descriptive analyses of infant communicative behavior. In H. R. Schaffer (Ed.), *Studies in mother–infant interaction* (pp. 227–270). London: Academic Press.

Trevarthen, C., & Aitken, K. (2003). Regulation of brain development and age-related changes in infants' motives: The developmental function of regressive periods. In M. Heimann (Ed.), *Regression periods in human infancy* (pp. 107–184). Mahwah, NJ: Erlbaum.

van de Rijt, H. H. C., & Plooij, F. X. (1992). *Oei, ik groei!* Ede/Antwerpen: Zomer & Keuning.

van de Rijt, H. H. C., & Plooij, F. X. (2010). *The Wonder Weeks: How to stimulate your baby's mental development and help him turn his 10 predictable, great, fussy phases into magical leaps forward.* Arnhem, The Netherlands: Kiddy World Promotions B. V.

van de Rijt-Plooij, H. H. C., & Plooij, F. X. (1987). Growing independence, conflict and learning in mother–infant relations in free-ranging chimpanzees, *Behaviour, 101*, 1–86.

van de Rijt-Plooij, H. H. C., & Plooij, F. X. (1988). Mother–infant relations, conflict, stress and illness among free-ranging chimpanzees. *Developmental Medicine and Child Neurology, 30*, 306–315.

van de Rijt-Plooij, H. H. C., & Plooij, F. X. (1992a). Infantile regressions: Disorganization and the onset of transition periods. *Journal of Reproductive and Infant Psychology, 10*, 129–149.

van de Rijt-Plooij, H., & Plooij, F. (1993). Distinct periods of mother–infant conflict in normal development: Sources of progress and germs of pathology. *Journal of Child Psychology and Psychiatry, 34*, 229–245.

van de Rijt-Plooij, H. H. C., van der Stelt, J., & Plooij, F. X. (1996). *Hordenlopen: Een preventieve oudercursus voor de eerste anderhalf jaar*. Lisse: Swets & Zeitlinger.

Woolmore, A., & Richer, J. (2003). Detecting infant regression periods: Weak signals in a noisy environment. In M. Heimann (Ed.), *Regression periods in human infancy* (pp. 23–39). Mahwah, NJ: Erlbaum.

Section V

Relational and Contextual Developmental Models

11

An Ethical Framework for Educating Children with Special Needs and All Children

Stanley I. Greenspan

Educators feel pressured to focus on "academics," yet academics build on a series of stages of emotional and social learning. Berry Brazelton's pioneering work inspires the ethical approach to educating children, especially those with special needs, presented here. This approach conceptualizes emotional, social, and academic learning as inseparable.

The cornerstone of academics is the ability to think. A child unable to relate to other children, or with limited language, might be able to say, "Open door" but can't answer "Why do you want it open?" This child can engage in certain kinds of thinking but not causal thinking. Without this ability – for example, to answer when he is asked why he wants to go outside, "Because I want to play, Mommy" – reading comprehension will be difficult. Even if he can decode "Johnny had a big smile on his face when he got a new bicycle," he will not be to answer "How did Johnny feel when he got his new bicycle?" He can sound out words but can't comprehend. Nor will he fully understand 2 + 3 = 5, that two apples plus three apples equals five apples, that he can give five apples to his friends, if he has only memorized the addition equation. For this kind of understanding, various brain structures must work in coordination (Greenspan & Shanker, 2004).

This chapter describes an educational approach for all children, especially for children with special needs, and explains why, as Brazelton was among the first to urge, "affect" is at the core. The stages that infants, toddlers, and young children progress through build on one another to promote healthy social and emotional development, and set the stage for academics (Greenspan & Lewis, 1999).

Stage 1

Regulation and Interest in the World

Within the first months of life, babies learn to transfer emotions arising from inner sensations (e.g., a gas bubble in the tummy) to perceptions of the outer world: parents' faces, voices, smells, and touch. To perceive the outer world, they must *want* to look or listen. Although born with a tendency to perceive some basic patterns, they are enticed by the emotional rhythm of voices, smiles, and gleaming eyes – interesting sounds and sights. Rhythmic patterns between parents' and infants' movements or vocalizations enable infants to begin relating to the outside world.

As Brazelton observed, infants are born with individual differences in their processing of sensory perceptions. They organize perceptions in accordance with affective experience, for example, pleasure in turning to Mommy's voice and smiling face. Pleasurable affect mobilizes and coordinates various brain functions. Interest in the outside world, academics' first step, begins with affect.

Stage 2

Engaging and Relating

In the second stage (two to five months), interactions engage babies' emotional interest in their world and help form first relationships. With warm nurturing, they become progressively more invested in certain people. No longer will just any face or smell do. It must be Mommy's or Daddy's. From birth, they begin distinguishing primary caregivers from others; now this ability reaches a crescendo through joyful smiles, coos, and a deep sense of pleasurable intimacy.

Higher levels of learning depend on sustained relationships that build trust and intimacy rather than simply fulfilling concrete needs.

The concrete person who just wants "things" never becomes a fully reflective thinker. If people are viewed as "things," their thoughts and feelings cannot be understood. Understanding and empathy for others comes from investing other human beings with one's own feelings, beginning with first relationships in which nurturing care creates a sense of intimacy.

As infants become invested in their main caregivers, they begin to perceive patterns in them. They can perceive more than just the mouth and eye, but more of the face as a whole. Pattern recognition is another step in academic work. For example, reading depends on recognizing patterns of sounds that form words. Pattern recognition emerges from early emotional interactions – academic life's second step.

Stage 3

Intentionality

Beyond intimacy and engagement, emotions are now transformed into signals for communication as caregivers read and respond to babies' signals and challenge them to read and respond to theirs. Infants begin to engage in back-and-forth emotional signaling, opening and closing circles of communication. Six-month-olds smile eagerly at their mothers, receive a smile back, then smile again, closing a circle of communication. Different gestures, facial expressions, and vocalizations become part of this signaling. By eight months, these exchanges usually occur in sequence and help infants to begin separating perceptions from actions.

Intelligence reaches an important new level as babies purposefully smile to get a smile back, vocalize happiness to get a happy sound back, and reach for father's nose to get a funny "toot-toot" sound back. These new lessons on causality are gradually applied to the spatial world and to planning actions (motor planning). When the rattle falls to the ground, babies follow it with their eyes as though looking for it. They look at and touch their father's hand because it just hid the rattle. The beginning sense of causality marks a beginning sense of "reality," based on understanding the actions of others as purposeful rather than random. Language development begins before ideas or words with the discovery that the world is a logical place where babies can predictably make things happen.

Stage 4
Problem Solving, Mood Regulation, and a Sense of Self

Explosive development takes place between nine and eighteen months. Infants learn to engage in a continuous flow of emotional signaling and use this ability to solve problems. They may take mother by the hand, gesture with eyes and hands so that she'll open the door to the backyard, and then point to the swing. True social problem solving emerges as caregivers read and respond to toddlers' emotional signals and engage with them in long chains of communication. Toddlers learn to regulate moods and behavior, to perceive and organize patterns to form a more complete sense of self.

Through a wide range of emotional interactions that are part of daily life, children learn to predict patterns of adult behavior and act accordingly. They learn that when their father comes home and looks grumpy, it's best to stay out of his way; that before their mother has had her morning coffee, they'd better walk and talk softly. These savvy adaptations are based on, and facilitate, an ability to recognize patterns. Pattern recognition, ideally learned first through social interactions, can be applied to solve problems in the physical world.

Children who take a parent by the hand to search for a toy, for example, are coming to understand the elements of a pattern. These include their emotional needs (what they want), the action patterns involved in finding a toy, the visual-spatial patterns involved in going from ground level to upper-shelf level where the toy resides, the vocal pattern involved in attracting their father's attention (whimpers at not having what they want, then gleeful exclamations of triumph), and the social patterns involved in working together with parents toward a common goal. Pattern recognition allows children to fit pieces of behavior together meaningfully, propelling them beyond piecemeal behavior. Elaborate negotiations or play with others bring experiences of the world in larger integrated patterns.

Toddlers now engage in scientific thinking, realizing that patterns have several steps. Pattern recognition enables a continuous flow of back and forth interactions using gestures and a few words. Patterns of increasing complexity emerge. Foundations for understanding quantity are laid down. Toddlers know the difference between a little and a lot before they can say these words. They are learning that saying two words together, like "Mommy hug" will get them a hug; that ideas and words can be sequenced to generate and express more complex meanings. Language depends on affect's mediation of meaning.

Children who memorize a book or a few words without comprehending are not learning to think. The ability to decode is based on a back and forth exchange of sounds and vocal gestures. Basic reading will depend on distinguishing different sounds and sound sequences and matching them to different visual experiences, experiences occurring first during this period.

Emotional signaling proceeds from the catastrophic, all-or-nothing reactions of the early first year to a separation between sensory perceptions and perception in action – the beginning of freestanding symbols or images. Once infants generate freestanding mental images – the image of Mommy or Daddy or the apple – interactions with those images stimulate emotional experiences, and symbol formation begins. Further experiences with parents and siblings add deeper meaning to symbols.

Symbol formation is essential to reading, writing, and math. This critical part of academics begins before children learn to use ideas, visual ideas, and language.

Stage 5

Creating Symbols, Using Words and Ideas

The emergence of formal symbols, words, and ideas involves a momentous transformation. Given many early opportunities for emotional exchanges, children can now more easily separate action from perception, hold onto freestanding images, and invest them with emotions. If they have had many emotionally relevant experiences, they can create a broad range of meaningful symbols. If not, a child may be able to label objects and perform rote memory tasks, but won't be able to say "Mommy, play with me!" or "I don't like that." Later on, she might learn to decode and repeat what she reads but won't have meaningful language or reading comprehension.

Images acquire meaning through emotional interactions, as when children learn what an apple is, what love is. They can use words ("Love you") or pictures to convey the feeling of giving mom a big hug. They can symbolize hitting and screaming by saying, "Me mad!" and use pretend play to symbolize real or imagined events, such as tea parties or monster attacks. Children can now also use symbols to manipulate ideas in their minds without having to carry out actions. This allows tremendous flexibility in reasoning because they can now solve problems in their minds.

New words acquired become meaningful to the degree that they refer to lived emotional experiences. The twelve or eighteen months of exchanges children have already experienced with caregivers provide a foundation for the emergence of meaningful language. Continuous interaction with others and the world maintains this progress throughout life.

This stage of developing ideas and language (between eighteen and thirty months and continuing thereafter) also moves through several levels based on the complexity of the ideas used and how the ideas are used to express wishes or actions or feelings:

- Ideas, words, actions used together (ideas are acted out, but words are also used to signify the action). Ideas or words not yet used instead of actions.
- Action words used instead of actions and convey intent ("Hit you!").
- Feelings conveyed through ideas, but treated as real rather than as signals ("I'm mad," "I'm hungry," "I need a hug," as compared with "I feel mad" or "I feel hungry" or "I feel I need a hug").
- Words used to convey bodily feeling states ("My muscles are exploding," "My head is aching").
- Words convey feelings, but mostly global feeling states ("I feel awful," "I feel okay"). The feeling states are generally polarized (all good or all bad). Polarized uses of ideas may characterize the next stage, when logical bridges are created to link ideas together.
- Words begin to convey more differentiated feelings ("I feel sad" or "I feel angry") and are beginning to more fully represent specific feelings not tied to action. This more differentiated use of ideas characterizes the relative mastery of this stage.

Intelligence, ordinarily thought to begin with symbol formation, starts developing far earlier. Despite the emphasis on verbal symbol acquisition, a cornerstone of many intellectual endeavors, symbol formation occurs in many domains and gives rise to higher levels of intelligence in all of them, e.g., visual-spatial symbols (preschoolers can build a house and elaborate on each part of it) as well as planned actions which serve symbolic goals (taking the toy bus from the house to the school to pick up some children).

As children use ideas through pretend play and imagination, they are learning creativity, important to thinking, reading and elaborating on it, and understanding mathematical principles. Writing an essay requires taking in information and saying something fresh and exciting about it, a kind of pretend play. Pretend play mobilizes creative thinking. Einstein talked about the importance of pretend outer space travel in his preschool years for his concept of the time/space continuum, formalized later into mathematical principles.

Stage 6

Emotional Thinking, Logic, and a Sense of "Reality"

In addition to constructing new meanings, children have already begun to infuse formal symbols with previously established meanings. Now, from approximately thirty to forty months, children learn to connect symbols together logically. When a child is asked "Why do you want to go out and play?" the child answers, "Because it's fun" or "Because I want to go down that slide." Now the child can combine symbols to think causally about her behavior. "Why are you so mad?" "Because Sally took my toy!"

Children learn to connect symbols in a variety of contexts, understanding one event's link to another ("The wind blew and knocked over my card house"), how ideas operate across time ("If I'm good now, I'll get a reward later"), and space ("Mom is not here, but she is close by"). Ideas help explain emotions – "I got a toy so I'm happy"– and organize knowledge of the world.

Connecting ideas logically is the basis for reality testing because children now connect internal experiences with external ones and categorize them accordingly (fantasy versus reality). Ongoing emotional interactions with someone who is "not me" provide constant contact with an external reality. Emotional investment in relationships enables children to recognize the difference between their fantasies and the actual behavior of others. While "reality testing" might appear to be a purely cognitive capacity, it requires an ability to organize an emotional sense of self that is distinct from one's sense of others. Such "reality testing" is a critical foundation for logical thinking. Without it, facts are often used to support irrational beliefs.

Logical thinking enables new skills to flow, including those involved in reading, math, writing, debating, scientific reasoning, and the like. Children can now create new inventions of their own, such as a new "game," and play games with rules.

General "reasoning" emerges from understanding emotional interactions and is applied to the more impersonal world. Cause-and-effect thinking with symbols comes from dealing logically with someone else's intentions or feelings: "When I'm mean, my mom gets annoyed with me." Once a sense of causality has been established at the symbolic level, children can understand how the light from the sun causes "day time."

The ability to build bridges between ideas leads to a new level of intelligence. Children can apply their new reasoning ability not only to arguing about "why I should watch more TV" (because it's fun) but also to why certain letters make up a word (reading) or why adding numbers together can help them figure out how many apples there are.

Mathematical and scientific understanding, reading comprehension, connecting letter shapes with words are all based on the mastery of logic. Some children do this strictly from memory, but that is not the same as mastering the thinking-based ideas that support the meanings.

Stage 7
Multiple-Cause and Triangular Thinking

From simple causal thinking, children progress to recognizing multiple causes, often experiencing a rapid growth in this capacity between four and seven years of age. If someone won't play with them, instead of concluding, "She hates me," children can say, "Maybe she has someone else she wants to play with today." They can set up multiple hypotheses. Or, "Maybe she doesn't want to play with me because I always play house. Maybe if we play something else she'll want to come over." Children are becoming multiple-cause thinkers in many contexts.

They can compare friends – "I like Sally better than Stephanie because she has fun toys." Multiple-cause thinking makes "triangular" thinking possible. If mother is annoyed, children can try to make mother jealous by going to father and being coy with him. They can become friends with Sally so as to get to know Sally's friend Judy.

Children become more flexible thinkers as a result of multicausal thinking. It may seem to be purely social, without academic relevance, but this ability helps children understand, for example, that there are many reasons for why the Civil War happened or many reasons for a certain scientific fact, such as why it takes so long to get to Mars, i.e., "Because it's far away, because we don't have fast rocket ships." This kind of thinking helps children comprehend why book characters' actions have many causes. Eventually they come to understand more intricate literary plots, multiple causes for historical events, and physical phenomena requiring scientific explanation. Multiple-cause thinking constitutes a higher level of reflective thinking in all spheres.

Stage 8
Comparative, Gray-Area Thinking

Once children are able to give many reasons for something, they move to the stage of comparative and gray-area thinking. At this stage, they can compare two things, two friends for example, and say why they like Johnny better than Harold, "Because Johnny likes to play the same kinds of games that I do."

Understanding quantity requires comparative thinking, in terms of gradations – gray-area thinking: "These are a lot of cookies, but not as much as I want." Children might use a 10-point scale to describe how much they like cookies. Understanding how degrees of quantity affect one another is the basis for multiplication, division and higher level mathematics.

The ability to engage in gray-area or emotionally differentiated thinking enables children to understand the different degrees, or "relative" influence of, different feelings, events, and phenomena. In school, they not only look at multiple reasons for events but can weigh the degree of their influence as well. "I think opinions about slavery were a lot more important than where people lived (the North versus the South) in causing the Civil War." With peers they can compare feelings in a graduated way: "I like Sally a lot more than Stephanie because she is much nicer to me when I'm upset."

Gray-area thinking enables children to comprehend their role in a group and deal with increasingly complex social systems ("I'm third best at spelling and fifth best at telling stories"). All future complex thinking requires mastery of this stage, whether it involves looking at the relative influence of variables in science and math or understanding one's social group and society. Children's ability to engage in gray-area, comparative thinking includes a new appreciation of both the world and themselves, essential to higher level thinking in science, math and language.

Stage 9
Reflective Thinking – A Growing Sense of Self and an Internal Standard

Between the ages of nine and ten years children arrive at the stage of reflective thinking (continuing throughout life), where they can evaluate their own thoughts and feelings. They can take a step away and say, "I'm angrier today than I usually am. I wonder why?" They can ask, "I wonder why I like Mark Twain better than Tolstoy?" and then write an essay on their reflections, i.e., "Maybe Twain's background was more similar to mine than Tolstoy's."

As early as 10 or 12 years, these more complex emotional interactions and thinking establish an internal standard based on a growing internal sense of self that, in turn, constitutes an inner standard by which to judge experience. For the first time they can say, "I shouldn't be so angry because the insult wasn't that great." They can consider peers' behavior and conclude, "I shouldn't do that because it isn't the right thing for me to do. It may be okay for them." A child this age can feel inadequate at the playground and still feel like a good person. In contrast, an eight year old might feel like a bad person instead of being able to apply her inner standard. Using that internal standard, children can now look at history and say, "I agree with the North (or South) for the following reasons."

Children become able to make inferences, i.e., thinking in more than one frame of reference at the same time or creating a new idea from existing ones. One of the two frames of reference compared must be based on an organized sense of self that is the product of meaningful experience. Sophisticated rather than naive inferences involve all developmental levels as well as emotionally meaningful experience in the sphere of knowledge where the inference is being made.

The highest levels of thinking require combined emotional and cognitive development because they involve comparing frames of reference, necessarily based both on ongoing emotional experiences and a complex internal sense of self. The new ability to think in two perspectives – objective reality and personal opinion – opens the door to higher levels of intelligence and reflection characteristic of adolescent and adult thinking.

These nine stages constitute basic functional emotional development and create the very "structure of thinking." From childhood on, these skills are applied to an ever broadening range of experiences.

Future Challenges

Individual Differences and Education

For the complex world of the future, all children will need to become complex learners who have benefited from the kinds of early experiences described here. The key will be to help parents, educators, and pediatricians, as Brazelton has been doing for many years, to understand the inseparability of social, emotional, and cognitive development, and to respond to children in accordance with their individual differences.

The cornerstone of the approach to development presented in this chapter is Brazelton's discovery of individual differences in newborns. His Neonatal Behavioral Assessment Scale (Brazelton & Nugent, 1995) is used worldwide to systematically assess the unique features of each newborn's nervous system, for example, sensory thresholds and responses, and state regulation. Many of these characteristics persist throughout life and shape each child's individual negotiation of the nine stages described here. Educational environments should be adapted to these unique aspects of each child's development.

Rather than separating children into groups based on their limitations, each child should be allowed to learn at his own pace and determine his own potential. They should be provided with learning relationships with adults trained to understand individual differences and the developmental steps of learning. Individual differences should guide strategies to help children develop their capacity for self-regulation. Schools organized according to these principles can help children become better learners and overcome difficulties with behavior, attention, focus, etc., so that they can successfully climb the developmental "ladder" of stages necessary for academic success. This is essential to a bioethical approach to educating children, rather than one that just "works."

References and further reading

Brazelton, T. B., & Nugent, J. K. (1995). *Neonatal behavioral assessment scale (NBAS)* (3rd ed.). London: Mac Keith Press.

Greenspan, S. I., & Lewis, N. B. (1999). *Building healthy minds: The six experiences that create intelligence and emotional growth in babies and young children*. Cambridge, MA: Perseus.

Greenspan, S. I., & Shanker, S. G. (2004). *The first idea: How symbols, language and intelligence evolved in early primates and humans*. Reading, MA: Perseus.

12

Protective Environments in Africa and Elsewhere

Robert A. LeVine

In the late 1960s, Berry Brazelton collaborated with the author on a joint project in sub-Saharan Africa. The idea behind the project was that African mothers, operating on their own without pediatric or institutional support, must have time-tested ways of nurturing infants at risk that deserved to be understood in detail. Earlier work on child rearing in Kenya and Nigeria had lacked the knowledge and attention to early infancy that Brazelton could bring to our understanding. Our collaboration on the Gusii Infant Study began in 1974, after Brazelton and Tronick had already shown the impressive performance of urban Zambian mothers with their small neonates within the first two weeks after birth. What particularly impressed Brazelton was the confidence of the Zambian mothers that they knew how to deal with a small and dehydrated newborn, a confidence confirmed by the observations of the Brazelton and Tronick study. By the time we actually began working together on the Gusii Infant Study in 1974, Brazelton, with Barbara Koslowski and Ed Tronick, had carried out a study showing the impressive performance of urban Zambian mothers with their small neonates within the first two weeks after birth (Brazelton, Koslowski, & Tronick, 1976).

The Gusii as studied by the author from 1955 to 1957 were an agricultural and pastoral people who inhabited a fertile highland region located between the "White" Highlands of the Rift Valley on the east and Lake Victoria on the west. They were known in Kenya as hard-working farmers isolated from major political and social changes taking place in Nairobi and other places in the country. By the time of the infant study in 1974, much had changed: After Kenya became an independent country in December 1963, there had been major improvements in road networks, education, and employment opportunities, and a new consciousness among the Gusii that they were Kenyan citizens. Not all the changes were beneficial, however, and the rise in population numbers and density on a fixed land base was especially ominous.

Based on colonial census figures, the author had estimated the Gusii population in the mid-1950s as 300,000, but the current (2006) population is 1.6 million – a more than fivefold increase in 50 years. By 1974, 17 years after the author's earlier study, the consequences of this growth in its early phases were becoming evident in periodic food shortages when the rains were delayed, conflict among neighbors over land ownership, and a high rate of labor migration (i.e., men working outside the district, with their wives and children increasingly dependent on remittances and less on agriculture and animal husbandry). The impact of population growth on infants is described below.

Although we are inclined, with good reason, to view the effects of Gusii population growth in apocalyptic terms, it is equally important to understand that it represents a reproductive success story – these are people who knew how to bear and raise large numbers of children despite the substantial risks to health and survival that existed before the recent onslaught of HIV/AIDS and drug-resistant malaria. Thus Gusiiland (Kisii District) was an appropriate place to seek an answer to Brazelton's question: How do African mothers facilitate growth and development in the face of risk and with minimal medical support?

Before examining the findings, we must acknowledge some qualifications: Up to the 1980s there was little malaria, indeed few mosquitoes, in the higher areas that form the largest part of Kisii, so the mothers in our study did not have to deal with this greatest threat to infant survival in Africa. Furthermore, although mothers in the area did not generally give birth in hospitals or use modern healthcare as much as their counterparts in developed countries, they had already (by the 1970s) been the beneficiaries of infant immunization efforts, preventive measures like the use of wells instead of rivers for water (preventing the typhoid epidemics of the 1950s), and other preventive and emergency medicine that resulted in substantial declines in infant and child mortality between 1950 and 1974. Thus the Gusii infant study was conducted in an environment that had some natural advantages for child survival not present everywhere in tropical Africa (lack of malaria) and some public health advantages (immunization, clean water, emergency services) not available to previous generations of Gusii mothers. Yet these advantages by themselves could not account for the declining mortality/high fertility pattern without a strong maternal commitment to child survival and an organized strategy to fulfill reproductive goals.

That Gusii mothers and families had an extraordinary commitment to the survival of their children can be illustrated by the nurturing of disabled individuals. A striking example from fieldwork in the 1950s is a man with arms and legs shrunken to stumps (possibly from polio, which was rampant at that time) who moved along the ground lying face-forward on a wheeled board (like a widened skateboard). The researchers were amazed to discover that he suffered no stigma in the community but was a respected elder with four wives and many children and grandchildren. Like other polygynous elders, he exercised influence in dispute settlement negotiations and other community events. Twenty years later his descendants spoke of him with reverence without mentioning his disability. During that same period a young woman in one of the families included in the study had a hydrocephalic baby, and the author recorded her devotion to the child during the last months of this project. Returning for a brief visit seven years later in 1964, the author was told the child had died only a few months before, meaning that for six or more years this mother and her family had not given up on this child. In the 1970s, Suzanne Dixon recorded a similar case of an infant born with a metabolic deficiency who was never able to lift his head or walk, in the same Gusii neighborhood. At that time, the parents sought medical help in Nairobi, but once again were remarkable in their dedication to this child. And during the Gusii infant study, Sarah LeVine, Constance Keefer and Suzanne Dixon found well-functioning blind and deaf women who had been nurtured into adulthood by caring parents and families. In contrast to peoples practicing infanticide or the neglect of disabled children, the Gusii startled us with their level of commitment to nurturing a child regardless of disability – and regardless of the fact that the average married woman in the 1970s had about ten children.

In the Gusii infant study we were able to discover the strategies Gusii women used to ensure the survival, health, and growth of their infants. Their goal was to bear as many children between marriage and menopause as they could reasonably expect to reach maturity. This meant in effect attempting to bear a child about every two years. A birth interval as short as 18 months would arouse the criticism of neighbors; one as long as 30 months would arouse the mother's anxiety about her continued ability to reproduce. In our sample, we found an average birth interval of 21 months. This was associated with 17 months of breastfeeding (reduced by two months from the 19-month mean of the 1950s) and sleeping at the mother's breast at night. Maintaining the period of lactation was regarded as necessary *protection* for the infant before the mother became pregnant again. In the first six months the 28 mothers we observed took care of their babies without help from others; we called this the period of "post-partum incubation." After that, older sisters helped their mother with daytime care and, by 17 months, the toddler was regarded as ready to join, and be socialized by, the group of her older siblings. With mothers bearing an average of ten children, most did have older sibs and were socialized by them. (Oldest children often joined a group of older children at nearby, closely related, households.)

Mothers made little effort to engage their babies in mutual gaze or verbal interaction, on the grounds that that was the job of the other children in the sibling group and would happen soon enough. The mother's job was protection, and that included monitoring the child for growth, motor development and signs of illness, seeking medical help if needed (interrupting whatever other tasks she had been performing and taking as much time as necessary), and directing older sibs to carry the baby on their backs long after the infants were able to walk (at nine to ten months of age).

These practices, along with responsive breastfeeding, co-sleeping, and supplementary feeding, constituted the envelope of protective maternal care designed to reduce risk and nurture health and growth during the birth interval. The emphasis on protection, physical nurturance, and soothing (with much less crying than American children) can be interpreted as a strategy for infant survival that produces a healthy, compliant toddler ready to become a respectful and obedient member of the domestic work team while gaining other social skills through interaction with older siblings.

Setting aside the question of whether this strategy puts too much emphasis on protection and too little on stimulation and communicative interaction during the first year of life, let us explore the question of whether it adequately protected Gusii children. These mothers had neither the economic resources nor the access to medical care to protect their infants from disease risks as well as mothers in many Western, industrialized societies. Given their situation, their practices may well have minimized risks as much as possible, but only if one assumes it necessary for women to bear an average of ten children. During the period we observed them, there was a crop failure that made numerous children malnourished – an outcome clearly exacerbated by the number of mouths there were to feed. As we evaluated this situation in our book (LeVine et al., 1994), we had to include the high fertility of Gusii mothers as a factor *increasing* the risks to children, not only at the time we studied them but to an even greater extent in the foreseeable future. Thus the protective practices of care for the individual child may be vitiated by the sheer number of children born.

Why did the Gusii mothers we studied continue to bear so many children in a situation of increasing scarcity? Among the Gusii, as among many of the other agricultural peoples of Africa, fertility has long been not only highly valued but also the primary measure by which each woman and her community judge her worth. A woman who leaves many children is celebrated at her funeral; barren women are reviled and feared. Gusii women use their continued fertility during adulthood as an indicator of their physical and spiritual health: A woman who does not become pregnant again when she expects to tends to believe that something is wrong with her that requires healing, and her husband will be called upon to consult diviners and perform sacrifices (LeVine, 1980). Furthermore, if her husband is a polygynist whose other wives are continuing to bear children, she will suspect witchcraft or sorcery, and her suspicions will generate tensions and require other remedies. Finally, women who have only had daughters will anxiously go on bearing children until they have a son to help take care of them in their old age.

There is nothing in Gusii thought that calls high fertility into question. This made economic sense in earlier times, when land was so abundant that the more wives and children a man had, the more land they could bring under cultivation and pasturage – thus the greater product in grain and cattle which could be exchanged as well as used for subsistence. In those days the fertility of women was an essential part of the pathway toward wealth. But this abundance came to an end by the 1940s, when the land was filled in and Gusii began to defend their property claims in court. In the next two decades the high fertility pattern continued to be supported by the high mortality of children due to infectious diseases. An elderly woman told us in the 1950s that she had borne 16 children, only eight of whom lived to adulthood. In the 1970s infant and child mortality rates were drastically reduced (due to public health measures, primary health care services, and rising incomes), yet fertility goals and attitudes remained unchanged. Family planning programs in the area were not seriously undertaken until it was too late: In the 1977 Kenya National Fertility Survey, only 1 percent of Gusii women said they were using contraception.

A Gusii man we knew in the 1970s exemplifies the problem as it affected families. He had inherited twenty fertile acres from his father decades earlier, and he married four wives with whom he had many children and grandchildren. In 1976, there were 58 persons living on that parcel of land, with other members of the family (who could claim to inherit a part of it) living in Nairobi and other towns outside the district. No one could inherit more than a fraction of the land, which no longer produced enough to support its many residents. Indeed, the owner himself was a small businessman who supported himself and his fourth wife through trade, and most of the sons had become educated and were employed outside the district. Thus in one generation this man's land was transformed from a subsistence farm to a residential homestead dependent on cash income from outside sources. This pattern was repeated many times throughout Kisii District. The land of the Gusii people, once so abundant in relation to its population, could no longer support it.

By the turn of the century, Kisii District achieved the dubious honor of having the highest population density in Kenya – a remarkable accomplishment, given the long-term overcrowding in the areas of the Abaluyia to the north and the Kikuyu to the east. This demographic distinction brought with it a variety of unprecedented consequences. Those with sufficient education, other marketable skills, or wealth had left the district to take jobs in towns throughout Kenya, farm in the Rift Valley, or migrate to the United States, settling in cities along the east coast as well as in Minnesota and Texas. Those they left behind were relatively poor and old, creating socioeconomic strata among the Gusii. Like other migrants, those of the Gusii diaspora sent remittances on which the people at home became increasingly dependent. Improvident parents, often those addicted to alcohol, sold all their land and some became so desperate that they lived off wages received for the childcare services of their immature children to prosperous families.

The new trends were not all negative: there were more schools, mobile phones, and urban-style services in Kisii District; Gusii were less likely than before to suffer the disadvantages of isolation within Kenya. But poverty and unemployment, resulting from population growth and Kenya's economic misfortunes of the late twentieth century, bred crime on a scale that overwhelmed law enforcement agencies. Furthermore, Kenya's post-election disorders of 2008 brought Gusii residents in the Rift Valley back to Kisii District seeking safety after having been violently driven from their homes of many years. As the district gained from its greater involvement in the national society, so it lost its buffer against Kenya's political and economic problems.

One distressing symptom of the malaise fueled partly by population growth has been the eruption of "witch-killings" among the Gusii in the late twentieth century. These began in 1992 but have continued to the present day. In the early 1990s, persons (usually older women) accused of witchcraft resulting in the deaths of their neighbors were burnt to death in their houses by mobs consisting of their kin and neighbors as well as gangs of young men. As many as 100 of these killings occurred in 1992, and in some cases men were involved in the mobs that killed their own mothers – something unimaginable to Gusii in the past (Ogembo, 2001). An instance in 2009 was brought forcibly to our attention and later to the attention of all who watch the BBC World Service; it consists of a video of five Gusii elders, at least one man among the women, looking frail and bewildered after being doused with kerosene, being burnt alive in a ditch as young men stoke the fire and occasionally beat them with sticks. The cameraman, who works for a local TV station, said he feared that had he interfered the perpetrators would turn on him. The police, upstaged by the distribution of this horrific video, arrested and charged twenty people with crimes; the Kenya National Human Rights Commission has publicly deplored the incident.

This is not the place to attempt an explanation of this social pathology that now haunts Gusiiland. Increased social density in the face of limited resources has long been thought to result in violence, though the particular forms that violence will take depend on the local symbolism of a community. What this points to is the tragedy of a people whose practices were organized to provide protection for the lives and development of their children and who are now facing the insecurity of violence within their own community. The Gusii as we observed them were adept at providing conditions in which a maximum number of infants could thrive but they failed to foresee the consequences of successful childbearing for future generations. The Gusii of the early twentieth century were, like Americans, a "people of plenty" whose ideals and habits were predicated on an endless abundance the environment could not endlessly supply. Their tragedy, so different in many ways, and condensed into only half a century, may yet become ours.

One final word: The pediatric clinic that Berry Brazelton, Herb Leiderman, and Connie Keefer established in 1975 at Keumbu, and which was kept going into 1976 by Suzanne Dixon and David Feigal, was later sustained by Gusii people themselves as an outpatient clinic and then became a government hospital in time for the epidemics of HIV/AIDS and drug-resistant malaria. We thank the agencies that funded our research (the National Science Foundation; the National Institute of Mental Health; Children's Hospital Medical Center, Boston; Stanford University Medical Center) for enabling us to give something to the Gusii whose children we studied and whom the author had known for many years.

References and further reading

Brazelton, T. B., Koslowski, B, Tronick, E. Z. (1976). Neonatal behavior among urban Zambians and Americans. *Annual Progress in Child Psychiatry. 15*, 97–107.

LeVine, R. A. (1980). Adulthood among the Gusii of Kenya. In N. Smelser, & E. Erikson (Eds.), *Love and work in adulthood.* Cambridge, MA: Harvard University Press.

LeVine, R. A., Dixon S., LeVine S., Richman A., Keefer C., Leiderman P. H., & Brazelton T. B. (1994). *Child care and culture: Lessons from Africa.* New York: Cambridge University Press.

Ogembo, J. M. (2001). Cultural narratives, violence and mother–son loyalty: An exploration into Gusii personification of evil. *Ethos, 29*, 3–29.

Section VI

Neuroscience Perspectives on Relational and Developmental Models

13

A Neurobiological Perspective on the Work of Berry Brazelton

Allan N. Schore

The current intense interest among all theoretical and applied sciences in the psychobiological relational mechanisms that underlie early human development in large part derives from Brazelton's groundbreaking studies in the last quarter of the twentieth century. In this chapter evidence from developmental neuroscience will be presented which strongly supports three essential concepts that lie at the core of Brazelton's work. This chapter explores the central role of arousal regulation in maternal–infant interactions, the interpersonal neurobiology of mother–infant face-to-face communication, and the experience-dependent maturation of control systems in the infant's right brain. Throughout the focus will be only on optimal development in infancy (for models of disturbed mother–infant interactions, impaired brain maturation, altered developmental trajectories, and psychopathogenesis, see Schore, 2001a, 2002, 2003a, 2003b, 2009).

Central Role of Arousal Regulation in Maternal–Infant Interactions

Over three decades ago Brazelton, Koslowski, and Main (1974) asserted that at the most fundamental level, the attuned caregiver acts to maintain the infant's arousal level. Following this lead, my work offers interdisciplinary evidence which demonstrates that in order to optimize her child's developmental processes the mother must be psychobiologically attuned to the dynamic shifts in her infant's bodily based internal states of central and autonomic arousal. As summarized in a recent contribution, the essential task of the first year of human life is the creation of a secure attachment bond of emotional communication between the infant and his/her primary caregiver (Schore & Schore, 2008). During these affective transactions the psychobiologically attuned caregiver, at levels beneath awareness, appraises nonverbal expressions of the infant's arousal and then regulates these positively and negatively valenced affective states. The attachment relationship mediates the interactive regulation of emotion, whereby the mother co-regulates the infant's postnatally developing central (CNS) and autonomic (ANS) nervous systems.

In pioneering work on these dyadic communications Brazelton et al. (1974) demonstrated that infant–mother gaze is fundamentally a critical regulator of arousal. In these face-to-face affective interactions, the mother sensitively and contingently dispenses her stimulation. Expanding this conceptualization, my interdisciplinary studies indicate that during such bodily based affective communications of mutual gaze, the attuned mother synchronizes the spatiotemporal patterning of her exogenous sensory stimulation with the infant's spontaneous expressions of his endogenous organismic rhythms (Schore, 1994). Through synchronous visual-facial, auditory-prosodic and tactile-gestural communications, caregiver and infant learn "the rhythmic structure of the other and modifying his or her behavior to fit that structure" (Lester, Hoffman, & Brazelton, 1985, p. 24), thereby co-creating a specifically fitted interaction. In order to regulate the infant's state, the crescendos and decrescendos of mother's affective state must be in resonance with similar crescendos and decrescendos of the infant's internal states of positive and negative arousal.

Within this co-created dyadic psychobiological system the mother appraises the nonverbal expressions of her infant's internal arousal and affective states, regulates them, and communicates them back to the infant. In this dialogical process the more the mother contingently tunes her activity level to the infant during periods of social engagement, the more she allows him to recover quietly in periods of disengagement, and the more she attends to his reinitiating cues for reengagement, the more synchronized their interaction. The regulatory processes of affective synchrony that creates states of positive arousal and interactive repair that modulates states of negative arousal are the fundamental building blocks of attachment and its associated emotions, and resilience in the face of stress and novelty is an ultimate indicator of attachment security (Schore, 2000, 2005).

According to Ovtscharoff and Braun, "The dyadic interaction between the newborn and the mother . . . serves as a regulator of the developing individual's internal homeostasis" (2001, p. 33). The evolutionary mechanism of attachment, the interactive regulation of emotion, thus represents the regulation of biological synchronicity between and within organisms (Bradshaw & Schore, 2007). Attachment communications are imprinted into implicit-procedural memory in an internal working model that acts at nonconscious levels. For the rest of the lifespan this internal working model, stored in the right brain, encodes strategies of affect regulation that nonconsciously guide the individual through interpersonal contexts. These adaptive capacities are central to the emergence of the dual processes of self-regulation: interactive regulation, the ability to flexibly regulate psychobiological states of emotions with other humans in interconnected contexts, and autoregulation, which occurs apart from other humans in autonomous contexts.

Interpersonal Neurobiology of Mother–Infant Face-to-Face Communications

Over the last decade a large body of interdisciplinary studies has explored the rapid psychobiological dynamics of mother–infant interactions, with an emphasis on their affective communications. Brazelton and Cramer (1990) observed critical developmental phases when energy is high in the infant and the parent for receptivity to each other's cues and for adapting to each other. Bowlby (1969) contended "facial expression, posture, and tone of voice" are essential vehicles of attachment communications between the emerging self, and Trevarthen (1990) observed how prosodic vocalizations, coordinated visual eye-to-eye messages, and tactile and body gestures serve as channels of communicative signals between infant and mother that induce instant emotional effects. The implicit processing of these nonverbal attachment communications are the product of the operations of the infant's right hemisphere interacting with the mother's right hemisphere (Schore, 2005). Indeed, this interpersonal neurobiology allows for the creation of the "the human social brain," which current neuroscience now locates in the right hemisphere. In a recent major overview Brancucci, Lucci, Mazzatenta, & Tommasi (2009) note, "The neural substrates of the perception of voices, faces, gestures, smells, and pheromones, as evidenced by modern neuroimaging techniques, are characterized by a general pattern of right-hemispheric functional asymmetry" (p. 895).

This model of right-brain-to-right-brain mother–infant transactions fits well with Brazelton's seminal observations. With respect to the previously discussed importance of mutual gaze (Brazelton et al., 1974), current research supports the principle that gaze perception is an important mother–infant communicative skill that has adaptive benefits. Neurobiological studies of this facial-visual communication show that the development of the capacity to efficiently process information from faces requires visual input to the right (and not left) hemisphere during infancy (Le Grand, Mondloch, Maurer, & Brent, 2003). At two months of age infants show right hemispheric activation when exposed to a woman's face (Tzourio-Mazoyer et al., 2002). Four-month-old infants presented with images of a female face gazing directly ahead express enhanced gamma electrical activity over right prefrontal areas (Grossman, Johnson, Farroni, & Csibra, 2007). And very recent near-infrared spectroscopy research reveals that the 5-month-olds' right hemisphere responds to images of adult female faces (Nakato et al., 2009).

As for tactile-gestural communications, Nagy (2006, p. 227) observes, "The early advantage of the right hemisphere (Chiron et al., 1997; Schore, 2000; Trevarthen, 2001) in the first few months of life may affect the lateralized appearance of the first imitative gestures." And with respect to auditory-prosodic communications and the infant's ability to process the emotional tone of the voice (motherese), Homae, Watanabe, Nakano, Asakawa, and Taga (2006) document that prosodic processing in 3-month-old infants is subserved by the right temporoparietal region. On the other side of the right-brain-to-right-brain communication system, researchers describe the mother's processing capacities: "A number of functions located within the right hemisphere work together to aid monitoring of a baby. As well as emotion and face processing, the right hemisphere is also specialized in auditory perception, the perception of intonation, attention, and tactile information" (Bourne & Todd, 2004, pp. 22–23).

In line with earlier proposals that affect-laden, arousal-regulating attachment communications facilitate the experience-dependent maturation of emotion-regulating brain circuits (Schore, 1994), developmental neuroscientists now conclude, "The mother functions as a regulator of the socio-emotional environment during early stages of postnatal development . . . subtle emotional regulatory interactions, which obviously can transiently or permanently alter brain activity levels . . . may play a critical role during the establishment and maintenance of limbic system circuits" (Ziabreva, Poeggel, Schnabel, & Braun, 2003, p. 5334).

It is well established that the human emotion-processing limbic system extensively myelinates in the first year-and-a-half, and that the early-maturing right hemisphere – which is deeply connected into the limbic system – undergoes a growth spurt at this time (Chiron et al., 1997; Gupta et al., 2005; Schore, 2003a; Sun et al., 2005). A recent developmental neuroimaging study reports that cortical and subcortical brain volumes more than double in this time period (Knickmeyer et al., 2008). Howard and Reggia (2007) conclude, "Earlier maturation of the right hemisphere is supported by both anatomical and imaging evidence" (p. 112). These data confirm my earlier proposal that emotional attachment transactions specifically impact the experience-dependent maturation of the right brain, the "emotional brain" (Schore, 1994).

Referring back to my previous comments on autonomic arousal, the right hemisphere has tight connections with the involuntary autonomic nervous system that generates peripheral arousal and controls visceral organs, effectors in the skin, and the cardiovascular system. Affect-regulating attachment experiences thus specifically impact cortical and limbic-autonomic circuits of the developing right cerebral hemisphere (Cozolino, 2002; Schore, 1994; Siegel, 1999). Ongoing research documents that this hemisphere is critically involved in regulating the hypothalamic-pituitary-adrenal (HPA) axis and in activating stress responses (Wittling, 1997), and that growth-facilitating attachment experiences have long-term effects on the developing HPA axis and its central role in the regulation of stress reactivity (Gunnar, 2000).

This right brain developmental model is supported by ongoing studies which observe that right lateralized limbic areas responsible for the regulation of emotional and autonomic functions and higher cognitive processes are involved in the "formation of social bonds" and are "part of the circuitry supporting human social networks," and that the "the strong and consistent predominance for the right hemisphere emerges postnatally" (Allman, Watson, Tetreault, & Hakeem, 2005, p. 367). Schuetze and Reid (2005) conclude, "Although the infant brain was historically reported to be undifferentiated in terms of cerebral lateralisation until 2 years of age, evidence has accumulated indicating that lateralised functions are present much earlier in development" (p. 207).

Confirming this relational neurobiological model, in very recent functional magnetic resonance imaging studies of mother–infant emotional communication, Lenzi et al. (2009) offer data "supporting the theory that the right hemisphere is more involved than the left hemisphere in emotional processing and thus, mothering," and Noriuchi, Kikuchi, & Senoo (2008) report activation of the mother's right orbitofrontal cortex during moments of maternal love triggered by viewing a video of her own infant. Another near-infrared spectroscopy study of infant–mother attachment at 12 months concludes, "Our results are in agreement with that of Schore (2000) who addressed the importance of the right hemisphere in the attachment system" (Minagawa-Kawai et al., 2009, p. 289).

Experience-Dependent Maturation of Right Brain Control Systems

Brazelton and Cramer described stages of mother–infant interaction which are temporally associated with the emergence of more complex control (regulatory) systems in the infant's brain:

> The central nervous system, as it develops, drives infants towards mastery of themselves and their world. As they achieve each level of mastery, they seek a kind of homeostasis, until the nervous system presses them on to their next level. Internal equilibrium is always being upset by a new imbalance created as the nervous system matures. Maturation of the nervous system, accompanied by increasing differentiation of skills, drives infants to reorganize their control systems. (Brazelton and Cramer, 1990, p. 98)

This last statement about control systems gives some clue as to the sequence of specific developing systems involved in the regulation of affective functions appearing over the course of human infancy. Bowlby (1969) speculated that the ontogeny of control systems is influenced by the particular environment in which development occurs. Neurobiological studies reveal that the dramatic onset of function in the first 18 months of life reflects the immense synaptogenesis that occurs during this period of infancy. Indeed the specific period from 7 to 15 months (roughly Bowlby's period for the establishment of attachment patterns) has been shown to be a critical period for the myelination and therefore the maturation of particular rapidly developing limbic and cortical association areas (Kinney, Brody, Kloman, & Gilles, 1988).

My studies integrate neuroscience and research in social and emotional development in order to identify the progression of early developing corticolimbic control systems described by Brazelton and Cramer. It is well established that developing brain systems organize, disorganize, and reorganize over the stages of human infancy (Schore, 1994). The neuroanatomy of the emotion-processing limbic system is now characterized as a hierarchical system of vertically organized circuits within the brain. Authors are referring to the "rostral limbic system," a hierarchical sequence of interconnected limbic areas in orbitofrontal (ventromedial), anterior cingulate, insular cortex, and amygdala. A large body of evidence shows that the orbitofrontal-insula, medial frontal anterior cingulate, and amygdala systems all interconnect with each other and with brain-stem bioaminergic neuromodulatory and neuroendocrine nuclei in the hypothalamus, the "head ganglion" of the autonomic nervous system. Because they are all components of the limbic system, each processes and imprints a positive or negative hedonic charge on current exteroceptive information about changes in the external social environment and then integrates it with interoceptive information about concurrent alterations in internal bodily states (Schore, 2001b, 2003a).

Due to the fact that they each directly interconnect with the ANS and that autonomic activity is controlled by multiple integrative sites within the CNS that are hierarchically organized, all are involved in the regulation of bodily driven affective states. Although all components process exteroceptive and interoceptive information, the later maturing systems in the cortex process this information in a more complex fashion than the earlier subcortical components. The output of the lowest limbic levels has the character of automatic innate reflexes, while higher processing produces more flexible intuitive responses that allow fine adjustment to environmental circumstances.

In optimal socioemotional environments, each limbic level has bidirectional connections with the others, and in this manner information can be forwarded both up and down the limbic axis for further appraisal and hierarchical modulation. The earliest and simplest appraisals of exteroceptive and interoceptive affective stimuli are rapid, nonconscious hedonic and aversive affective core processes in the amygdala, the later and most complex subjective experiences of pleasure and pain in the orbitofrontal areas. These operations are primarily lateralized to the right limbic system, which is preferentially connected downward to the right neurochemical systems associated with emotion and arousal, and upward to the ipsilateral right neocortex.

As applied to the developmental organization of the limbic circuits of the right brain, this conception suggests a three-tiered self-organizing dynamic system. Increased interconnectivity (energy flow) among the three component circuits would allow for information stored at one level to be transferred to the others. The top level that receives feedback from the lower performs an executive function, and this allows for emergent properties, that is, novel combinations of more complex emotional states.

In line with the ontogenetic concept of vertical brain organization and the principle of caudal to rostral brain development, a model of the ontogeny of the limbic system can be offered. Keeping in mind that in humans this development continues postnatally, reversing the sequence of the rostral limbic system (amygdala, anterior cingulate, orbitofrontal) offers specific ideas about how a number of discrete limbic components could come on line in a defined sequence in the first year. Recall Bowlby's speculation that the limbic system is centrally involved in attachment and that the "upgrading of control during individual development from simple to more sophisticated is no doubt in large part a result of the growth of the central nervous system" (1969, p. 156).

In earlier writings Schore (2001a) proposed that areas of the amygdala in the medial temporal lobe, especially the central and medial nuclei, and also the insula are in a critical period of maturation that onsets in the last trimester of pregnancy and continues through the first two months of human life, the earliest period of bonding and the timeframe of the first-to-mature homeostatic control system described by Brazelton that is on line in the first weeks of life. Brazelton and Cramer (1990) also described the emergence in the second quarter of the first year of a second homeostatic control system, one associated with a mutual reciprocal feedback system. Though an advance on the former control system it is still "an immature psychophysiological system." This system can now be identified as a maturing anterior cingulate (medial frontal) cortex, which hierarchically controls the earlier amygdala-dominated limbic configuration.

Ongoing studies in developmental brain research indicate that the orbital prefrontal cortex enters a critical period of growth that spans the last quarter of the first through the middle of the second year, an interval that corresponds with the beginnings of human socialization (Schore, 2003a, 2003b). This ventromedial prefrontal limbic structure is reciprocally interconnected with other limbic areas in the amygdala, insula, anterior cingulate, and represents the hierarchical apex of the right lateralized limbic system. It also forms direct connections with the hypothalamus, the head ganglion of the autonomic nervous system (Barbas, Saha, Rempel-Clower, & Ghashghaei, 2003), as well as bioaminergic neurons in the reticular system that control arousal (Schore, 1994).

For the rest of the life span, this system is centrally involved in "the representation of emotional information and the regulator of emotional processes" (Roberts et al., 2004, p. 307). The dendritic and synaptic maturation of the anterior cingulate and orbitofrontal cortices is specifically influenced by the social environment (Bock, Murmu, Ferdman, Leshem, & Braun, 2008). Referring back to Brazelton and Cramer's conception of the developmental reorganization of control systems, neurobiological studies show that the mature orbitofrontal cortex acts in "the highest level of control of behavior, especially in relation to emotion" (Price, Carmichael, & Drevets, 1996, p. 523), acts to "control autonomic responses associated with emotional events" (Cavada & Schultz, 2000), and is identical to Bowlby's control system of attachment (Schore, 2000). Recent studies show that right orbitofrontal areas of both the mother and 12-month infant are activated in positively valenced emotional attachment communications (Minagawa-Kawai et al., 2009).

Thus, Brazelton's control systems are complex psychological regulatory structures, located in "the right hemispheric specialization in regulating stress – and emotion-related processes" (Sullivan & Dufresne, 2006). Neuroscientists are suggesting that the essential function of the right lateralized system is to "maintain a coherent, continuous, and unified sense of self" (Devinsky, 2000, p. 69), and that "the right hemisphere, particularly the right frontal region . . . plays a crucial role in establishing the appropriate relationship between the self and the world" (Feinberg & Keenan, 2005, p. 15). This right lateralized affect regulatory system is the locus of Brazelton's highest-level control system, and its experience-dependent maturation over the first two years of life is directly related to the relational origin of the self (Schore, 1994, 2003a, 2003b).

References and further reading

Allman, J. M., Watson, K. K., Tetreault, N. A., & Hakeem, A. Y. (2005). Intuition and autism: A possible role for Von Economo neurons. *Trends in Cognitive Sciences, 9*, 367–373.

Barbas, H., Saha, S., Rempel-Clower, N., & Ghashghaei, T. (2003). Serial pathways from primate prefrontal cortex to autonomic areas may influence emotional expression. *BMC Neuroscience, 4*, 25.

Bock, J., Murmu, R. P., Ferdman, N., Leshem, M., & Braun, K. (2008). Refinement of dendritic and synaptic networks in the rodent anterior cingulate and orbitofrontal cortex: critical impact of early and late social experience. *Developmental Neurobiology*, *68*, 695–698.

Bourne, V. J., & Todd, B. K. (2004). When left means right: An explanation of the left cradling bias in terms right hemisphere specializations. *Developmental Science*, *7*, 19–24.

Bowlby, J. (1969). *Attachment and loss. Vol. 1: Attachment*. New York: Basic Books.

Bradshaw, G. A., & Schore, A. N. (2007). How elephants are opening doors: Developmental neuroethology, attachment and social context. *Ethology*, *113*, 426–436.

Brancucci, A., Lucci, G., Mazzatenta, A., & Tommasi, L. (2009). Asymmetries of the human social brain in the visual, auditory and chemical modalities. *Philosophical Transactions of the Royal Society B*, *364*, 895–914.

Brazelton, T. B., & Cramer, B. G. (1990). *The earliest relationship*. Reading: Addison-Wesley.

Brazelton, T. B., Koslowski, B., & Main, M. (1974). The origins of reciprocity: The early mother–infant interaction. In M. Lewis & L. Rosenblum (Eds.), *The effect of the infant on its caregiver* (pp. 49–77). New York: Wiley.

Cavada, C., & Schultz, W. (2000). The mysterious orbitofrontal cortex. Foreword. *Cerebral Cortex*, *10*, 205.

Chiron, C., Jambaque, I., Nabbout, R., Lounes, R., Syrota, A., & Dulac, O. (1997). The right brain hemisphere is dominant in human infants. *Brain*, *120*, 1057–1065.

Cozolino, L. (2002). *The neuroscience of psychotherapy*. Norton: New York.

Devinsky, O. (2000). Right cerebral hemisphere dominance for a sense of corporeal and emotional self. *Epilepsy & Behavior*, *1*, 60–73.

Feinberg, T. E., & Keenan, J. P. (2005). Where in the brain is the self? *Consciousness and Cognition*, *14*, 661–678.

Grossman, T., Johnson, M. H., Farroni, T., & Csibra, G. (2007). Social perception in the infant brain: Gamma oscillatory activity in response to eye gaze. *Social Cognitive and Affective Neuroscience*, *2*, 284–291.

Gunnar, M. R. (2000). Early adversity and the development of stress reactivity and regulation. In C. A. Nelson (Ed.), *The Minnesota Symposium on Child Psychology: Vol. 31: The effects of early adversity on neurobehavioral development* (pp. 163–200). Mahwah, NJ: Erlbaum.

Gupta, R. K., Hasan, K. M., Trivedi, R., Pradhan, M., Das, V., Parikh, N. A., & Narayana, P. A. (2005). Diffusion tensor imaging of the developing human cerebrum. *Journal of Neuroscience Research*, *81*, 172–178.

Homae, F., Watanabe, H., Nakano, T., Asakawa, K., & Taga, G. (2006). The right hemisphere of sleeping infants perceives sentential prosody. *Neuroscience Research*, *54*, 276–280.

Howard, M. F., & Reggia, J. A. (2007). A theory of the visual system biology underlying development of spatial frequency lateralization. *Brain and Cognition*, *64*, 111–123.

Kinney, H. C., Brody, B. A., Kloman, A. S., & Gilles, F. H. (1988). Sequence of central nervous system myelination in human infancy. II. Patterns of myelination in autopsied infants. *Journal of Neuropathology and Experimental Neurology, 47*, 217–234.

Knickmeyer, R. C., Gouttard, S., Kang, C., Evans, D., Wilber, K., Smith, J. K., … Gilmore, J. H. (2008). A structural MRI study of human brain development from birth to 2 years. *Journal of Neuroscience, 28*, 12176–12182.

LeGrand, R., Mondloch, C., Maurer, D., & Brent, H. P. (2003). Expert face processing requires visual input to the right hemisphere during infancy. *Nature Neuroscience, 6*, 1108–1112.

Lenzi, D., Trentini, C., Pantano, P., Macaluso, E., Iacaboni, M., Lenzi, G. I., & Ammaniti, M. (2009). Neural basis of maternal communication and emotional expression processing during infant preverbal stage. *Cerebral Cortex, 19*, 1124–1133.

Lester, B. M., Hoffman, J., & Brazelton, T. B. (1985). The rhythmic structure of mother–infant interaction in term and preterm infants. *Child Development, 56*, 15–27.

Minagawa-Kawai, Y., Matsuoka, S., Dan, I., Naoi, N., Nakamura, K., & Kojima, S. (2009). Prefrontal activation associated with social attachment: Facial-emotion recognition in mothers and infants. *Cerebral Cortex, 19*, 284–292.

Nagy, E. (2006). From imitation to conversation: The first dialogues with human neonates. *Infant and Child Development, 15*, 223–232.

Nakato, E., Otsuka, Y., Kanazawa, S., Yamaguchi, M. K., Watanabe, S., & Kakigi, R. (2009). When do infants differentiate profile face from frontal face? A near-infrared spectroscopic study. *Human Brain Mapping, 30*, 462–472.

Noriuchi, M., Kikuchi, Y., & Senoo, A. (2008). The functional neuroanatomy of maternal love: Mother's response to infant's attachment behaviors. *Biological Psychiatry, 63*, 415–423.

Ovtscharoff, W. Jr., & Braun, K. (2001). Maternal separation and social isolation modulate the postnatal development of synaptic composition in the infralimbic cortex of *octodon degus. Neuroscience, 104*, 33–40.

Price, J. L., Carmichael, S. T., & Drevets, W. C. (1996). Networks related to the orbital and medial prefrontal cortex: A substrate for emotional behavior? *Progress in Brain Research, 107*, 523–536.

Roberts, N. A., Beer, J. S., Werner, K. H., Scabini, D., Levens, S. M., Knight, R. T., & Levenson, R. W. (2004). The impact of orbital prefrontal cortex damage on emotional activation to unanticipated acoustic startle stimuli. *Cognitive, Affective, and Behavioral Neuroscience, 4*, 307–316.

Schore, A. N. (1994). *Affect regulation and the origin of the self.* Mahwah, NJ: Erlbaum.

Schore, A. N. (2000). Attachment and the regulation of the right brain. *Attachment & Human Development, 2*, 23–47.

Schore, A. N. (2001a). The effects of relational trauma on right brain development, affect regulation, and infant mental health. *Infant Mental Health Journal, 22*, 201–269.

Schore, A. N. (2001b). The effects of a secure attachment relationship on right brain development, affect regulation, and infant mental health. *Infant Mental Health Journal, 22*, 7–66.

Schore, A. N. (2002). Dysregulation of the right brain: A fundamental mechanism of traumatic attachment and the psychopathogenesis of posttraumatic stress disorder. *Australian & New Zealand Journal of Psychiatry, 36*, 9–30.

Schore, A. N. (2003a). *Affect regulation and the repair of the self.* New York: W. W. Norton.

Schore, A. N. (2003b). *Affect dysregulation and disorders of the self.* New York: W. W. Norton.

Schore, A. N. (2005). Attachment, affect regulation, and the developing right brain: Linking developmental neuroscience to pediatrics. *Pediatrics in Review, 26*, 204–211.

Schore, A. N. (2009). Relational trauma and the developing right brain: An interface of psychoanalytic self psychology and neuroscience. *Annals of the New York Academy of Sciences, 1159*, 189–203.

Schore, J. R., & Schore, A. N. (2008). Modern attachment theory: The central role of affect regulation in development and treatment. *Clinical Social Work Journal, 36*, 9–20.

Schuetze, P., & Reid, H. M. (2005). Emotional lateralization in the second year of life: Evidence from oral asymmetries. *Laterality, 10*, 207–217.

Siegel, D. J. (1999). Developing mind: Toward a neurobiology of interpersonal experience. New York: W. W. Norton.

Sullivan, R. M., & Dufresne, M. M. (2006). Mesocortical dopamine and HPA axis regulation: Role of laterality and early environment. *Brain Research, 1076*, 49–59.

Sun, T., Patoine, C., Abu-Khalil, A., Visvader, J., Sum, E., Cherry, T. J., Orkin, S. H., Geschwind, D. H., & Walsh, C. A. (2005). Early asymmetry of gene transcription in embryonic human left and right cerebral cortex. *Science, 308*, 1794–1798.

Trevarthen, C. (1990). Growth and education of the hemispheres. In C. Trevarthen (Ed.), *Brain circuits and functions of the mind* (pp. 334–363). Cambridge, UK: Cambridge University Press.

Trevarthen, C. (2001). The neurobiology of early communication: Intersubjective regulations in human brain development. In A. F. Kalverboer, & A. Gramsbergen (Eds.), *Handbook on brain and behavior in human development* (pp. 841–882). Dordrecht, The Netherlands: Kluwer.

Tzourio-Mazoyer, N., De Schonen, S., Crivello, F., Reutter, B., Aujard, Y., & Mazoyer, B. (2002). Neural correlates of woman face processing by 2-month-old infants. *NeuroImage, 15*, 454–461.

Wittling, W. (1997). The right hemisphere and the human stress response. *Acta Physiologica Scandinavica, 640* (suppl.), 55–59.

Ziabreva, I., Poeggel, G., Schnabel, R., & Braun, K. (2003). Separation-induced receptor changes in the hippocampus and amygdala of *Octodon degus*: Influence of maternal vocalizations. *Journal of Neuroscience, 23*, 5329–5336.

14

Hidden Regulators Within the Mother–Infant Interaction

Myron Hofer

Our work that led to the understanding of hidden regulators within the mother–infant interaction has its roots in the mid-1950s, when the customary childbirth practices were to anesthetize the mother fully as soon as labor pains began, and to continue throughout birth. Then, mothers and babies were kept (separately) in the hospital for a week with daily short visits between the two, while the mother became accustomed to the strange "bag of reflexes" that newborns were thought to be, and learned to manage the sterilization procedures for the bottle feedings when finally the time came to go home. But "natural childbirth" was beginning to be imported from Britain and T. Berry Brazelton and a very few developmental psychologists around the country were beginning to discover what newborns (and mothers) could do if studied under natural conditions rather than in the laboratory or a clinical setting. However, natural childbirth was actually part of a more general "enlightenment" making slow progress throughout medicine and embodied in the new field of psychosomatic medicine. Related work on animal models in the 1960s, including the extraordinary impact of Harry Harlow's maternal deprivation studies in monkeys, led to an interest in learning more about the behavior and biology of the early mother–infant relationship.

From Relationship to Interaction

In the early 1970s the parent–infant relationship field was in one of its periods of intense controversy and confusion, with new findings that appeared to call for major changes in medical practice during birth and in the newborn period. Marshall Klaus and John Kennell were convinced from their data that a sensitive period existed in the seconds and minutes after birth when an unusually happy and effective long-term relationship between mother and baby could be established – if only the two could be in skin (and close emotional) contact as immediately as possible after birth. These findings posed the greatest threat to hospital practice in the case of prematurely born infants, for whom isolation in the first postnatal weeks was regarded as a life-saving priority due to the supposed risk of infection.

Brazelton and his colleagues had discovered an essential ingredient of the concept of "relationship" in the reciprocity or dance-like synchrony of movement, facial expression, and vocalization that they found by film analysis of mothers' play interactions with their babies (Brazelton, Koslowski, & Main, 1974) The newly discovered "still-face" effect reported by the Brazelton group (Brazelton, Tronick, Adamson, Als, & Wise, 1975), and the dance-like synchrony being found by other investigators as well, led to the transformation of the term "relationship" into the term "'interaction" to describe research on the mother–infant dyad.

The infant's response, when a face-to-face play interaction was terminated abruptly by the mothers' assuming an immobile, expressionless face, was dramatic, and like the response to maternal separation, demonstrated that something surprisingly important was going on in the previous interaction that we needed to know more about. And indeed in the last 30 years or more of research, the mother–infant play interaction has taught us an enormous amount, as is evidenced by the tremendous growth in this field.

Separation, Loss, and the Regulation of Development

Our work in this area was on the biological and behavioral processes responsible for the infant's response to prolonged separation from its mother – research that could only be done in an animal model. Bowlby, psychoanalysts and even Harlow viewed the process responsible for the mother–infant separation response as inherently psychological and considered it highly unlikely to occur in sub-primate mammalian species such as the laboratory rat. The complex response of primate infants to maternal separation was conceived of as an integrated emotional–physiological response to "rupture" of a psychological attachment "bond" that was part of what Bowlby called "the attachment system." Influenced by the European ethologists, we explored the possibility of studying maternal separation in a simpler organism, such as the infant rat. To our surprise, we found major changes in a number of the pup's physiological and behavioral systems during the 24 hours following the removal of the mother from the litter, 2 weeks after their birth – an age at which they can survive without her but normally remain close and continue nursing. By using an experimental analytic approach, our group has since found a network of simple behavioral and biological processes that underlie the psychological constructs we use to define and understand early attachment.

Experiments in our laboratory have shown that infant rats have complex and lasting responses to maternal separation similar to primates: an acute "protest" stage of intense "calling" (in the ultrasonic range in infant rodents) that is normally responded to rapidly by the mother. This is followed by a longer "despair" phase with much reduced activity levels, loss of body temperature and changes in cardiovascular, hormonal, and sleep–wake organization. This "biphasic" response, however was *not* an integrated emotional-psychophysiological response, as had been supposed, but the result of a novel mechanism. As separation took place, each of the individual behavioral and physiological systems of the infant rat responded to the loss of one or another of the components of the infants' previous interaction with its mother. Providing one of these components to a separated pup, for example maternal warmth, maintained the level of brain biogenic amine function underlying the pups' general activity level (Stone, Bonnet, & Hofer, 1976; Hofer, 1980) but had no effect on other systems, for example, the pups' cardiac rate continued to fall regardless of whether supplemental heat was provided (Hofer, 1971). The heart rate, normally maintained by sympathetic autonomic tone, we found was regulated by provision of milk to neural receptors in the lining of the pup's stomach (Hofer & Weiner, 1975). With loss of the maternal milk supply, sympathetic tone fell and cardiac rate was reduced by 40 percent in 12–18 hours.

By studying a number of additional systems, such as those controlling sleep–wake states (Hofer, 1976), activity level (Hofer, 1975), sucking pattern (Brake, Sager, Sullivan, & Hofer, 1982), and blood pressure, we found different components of the mother–infant interaction, such as olfaction, taste, touch, warmth, and texture, that either up-regulated or down-regulated each of these functions. Thus we concluded that, in maternal separation, all these regulatory components of the mother–infant interaction are withdrawn at once. This widespread loss creates a pattern of increases or decreases in level of function of the infant's systems, depending upon whether the particular system had been up- or down-regulated previously by specific components of the previous mother–infant interaction. We called these components, "hidden regulators" because they were not evident when simply observing the ongoing mother–infant relationship.

Early separation, we found, can elicit widespread behavioral and biological responses through a novel mechanism not dependent on an attachment bond, but instead being a consequence of the simultaneous loss of multiple regulators hidden within the preceding mother–infant interaction, such as touch, warmth or milk letdown, for example. These operate together, forming an extended, maternally based homeostatic regulatory system, maintaining age-specific levels of function prior to separation and creating an assemblage of withdrawal effects following maternal loss. There is good evidence that such "hidden regulators" are functioning within primate (Mason & Berkson, 1975) and human (Field et al., 1986) mother–infant dyads.

Over time, these maternal regulators can shape development through their capacity to increase or decrease the level of function of the infant's behavioral, neuroendocrine, and autonomic systems on an ongoing basis throughout infancy. Different overall patterns or qualities of mother–infant interaction are composed of different relative intensities, rhythms or timing of these regulatory interactions. Different variations in these patterns can exert long-term shaping effects on biological responses of the infant, such as corticosterone stress responses and behavioral fear reactions in adulthood (Cameron et al., 2005). Finally these mother–infant regulatory processes also act on the early precursors of the neural circuitry for maternal behavior, present in daughters as infants, shaping the later development of this circuitry (Champagne, 2008). The adult maternal behaviors of daughters in the next generation are thus shaped by these interactions that took place during their infancy, providing a novel form of biological support for psychological and cultural processes of transgenerational continuity. The early developmental processes found in our animal studies can thus be thought of as underlying components of the psychological concepts that we have formulated to help us think about complex behaviors and mental experiences.

Synchrony and Reciprocity

In the previous section, the *levels* of function in different behavioral and physiologic systems of the infant were found to be regulated by different aspects of the mother–infant interaction. But the mother–infant interaction involves more than levels of supply and stimulation. It consists of a number of interlocking, precisely timed events which underlie the synchrony and reciprocity in the relationship that were so evident in the initial research by Brazelton (Brazelton et al., 1975).

To our initial surprise, the cyclic aspect of time in early development is also beautifully represented in the nursing cycle and in the sleep–wake cycles of the infant and its mother (reviewed in Brake, Shair, & Hofer, 1988). The suckling behaviors of the infant rat and the repeated episodes of milk letdown by its mother are embedded within these longer cycles. Our group (Shair, Brake, & Hofer, 1984) gradually developed the methods needed to study all of these events together in the course of normal nursing cycles. We found to our surprise that pups (with chronically implanted cortical EEG electrodes) were asleep as much of the time when they were attached to the teat and suckling as during the periods between nursing bouts, when their mother had left and they were huddled in the home cage nest with littermates. A second surprise was that pups did a great deal of their sucking (about 45%) while they were asleep. The rate of periodic short sucking bursts was actually higher in slow wave sleep than in the awake state. The lowest rates of sucking occurred during REM sleep. A third surprise was that, although pups were awake 35% of the time while attached to the teat, they were asleep 90% of the time during the minute prior to milk ejection and were *always* asleep in the 15 sec immediately before their characteristic "stretch" response to milk ejection. Pups always awoke when milk ejection occurred, then treadled with their front paws against the dam's ventrum and sucked vigorously in a sustained rhythmic pattern. But half the time they were asleep again within 30 sec. Other investigators (Voloschin & Tramezzani, 1979) have shown that the mother rat also sleeps during nursing bouts and, remarkably, must be in slow wave sleep in order for milk ejection to take place.

This embedding and coordination of sucking patterns within the sleep of the infant, and of milk ejection in the sleep of the mother, appear to carry the physical closeness, intricacy of interaction and mutual advantage that is conveyed by the biological (and psychological) term "symbiosis" (Hofer, 1990). At the level of neurophysiology, we can understand the links between mother and infant in the studies described above in the following way. Oxytocin-releasing cells in the dam's hypothalamus require high levels of afferent stimulation from sensory fibers in her teats and ventrum in order to produce the periodic bursting discharge pattern necessary for release of their stored hormone into the circulation, resulting in contraction of the muscles enveloping the milk storage ducts leading to the teats. The repeated sucking bursts of sleeping pups provide this form of sensory input. The mother also must be in slow wave sleep in order to have a milk ejection, and the bodily inactivity of the pups no doubt facilitates this state in the mother. The times when both pups and dam are simultaneously asleep are those with maximal chance of milk ejection, providing a neurohormonal mechanism for this remarkable synchrony.

Maternal Entrainment of Infant Sleep–Wake State Organization

What effect does a prolonged period of separation have on the sleep–wake states of infants and how are these effects of separation created? Can we learn as much about the long-term regulators of these timed cyclic events within the mother–infant interaction as we did about *levels* of other functions?

We had found that maternal separation reduced the amount of time spent by rat pups in REM sleep, increased their time awake, shortened the average duration of both slow wave and REM sleep periods and increased the frequency of state transitions (Hofer, 1976). These changes occurred in pups whose core temperature was maintained at nest levels. The cycles of awake, REM sleep, and slow wave sleep were altered in a consistent manner by separation, suggesting that they might also be responsive to the withdrawal of some hidden regulators within the mother–pup interaction. We first tried continuous 24h milk infusion (via gastric cannula) that had been so successful in preventing the cardiac response to separation, but this failed to prevent any of the separation-induced changes (Hofer & Shair, 1982). Providing a nonlactating foster mother which spent long periods with infants, but not with normal maternal timing, reduced wakefulness but did not affect the other disruptions of the sleep–wakefulness cycle. A similar partial preventive effect was achieved by periodic stimulation of separated pups based on nursing schedules, forcing them to periodically wake and change position. A novel environment, which elicited prolonged increased motor activity, had no such effect. However, in two experiments with gastric infusion of nutrient on an intermittent schedule, simulating the maternal one, we succeeded in markedly ameliorating the separation-induced fragmentation of sleep–wake state organization. Finally, periodic scheduled infusions of a formula enriched with fat fully prevented all the changes in sleep–wake state organization of separated pups, whereas constant infusions of this enriched formula were much less effective.

Thus we found that the element of rhythmicity (on a timescale of nursing bouts), using nutrient infusion and to a lesser extent tactile stimulation, was an essential ingredient in the prevention or amelioration of separation-induced changes in sleep–wake state organization. From this evidence we inferred that periodic, rhythmic events occurring within the mother–infant interaction act to entrain the cyclic rhythms of sleep–wake state organization in her infants.

Implications

In the Healthy Steps program, Brazelton's novel clinical and research observations are applied to the needs of infants, mothers, and children. The program enabled us to see how basic and clinical research findings can be translated into changes in medical practice and shows the imagination, knowledge, and planning that went into this remarkable and successful enterprise. One person described it this way: "The results of the research you're telling us about help us believe that what we're trying to do is real." It was good to know that all the control experiments, replications, and testing of alternative hypotheses that we carried out in our research gave this kind of support to people who were committing themselves, and considerable resources, to new clinical programs. It was equally true that watching the process of establishing the Healthy Steps program showed that the ideas that came from all of our research were not just interesting to us, but could be of some use to the world.

Our discovery of "hidden regulators" operating within the mother–infant interaction implies that we can understand psychological constructs more fully by looking for underlying component processes operating at the level of simple behaviors and biological events and mechanisms (Hofer, 2005). Loss has new dimensions when we ask more deeply "What was lost"? And the idea that mental representations are made up of remembered physiological events, as well as memories of behavioral interactions at the simplest levels, provides a potential bridge between mental and physical processes that can be useful in understanding the effects of separation and the phenomenon of grief (Hofer, 1984). This way of thinking suggests that we should search for ways to make clinical interventions as early as possible in an infant's development, and at the level of simple sensory, behavioral, and physiological interactions and processes. Further, since the mother may be the best and most constantly available source for so many of such interactions, she should be the "target" of interventions, as much as the infant or child itself. Tiffany Field noted that in her early efforts to use tactile-behavioral therapy with abused infants and children, this intervention did not succeed until massage treatments for the mother were provided first!

The findings described above on the rhythmic timing of sleep, suckling, and nursing interactions in young rats and their dams implies deep evolutionary roots for a hidden world of biological interactions and argues for the concept of "symbiosis" as an apt and useful way of thinking about the early mother–infant relationship (Rosenblum & Moltz, 1983). Symbiosis is being used in the classical nineteenth-century biological sense of organisms living in close proximity, with mutual exchanges and adaptations. These exchanges are usually mutually beneficial, but evolutionary adaptations also involve competition, so that parent–infant conflict is inevitable, particularly during weaning and may be present in other similar periods in development, such as adolescence. The idea of an evolution-based parent–offspring conflict may also be helpful in planning interventions in the chaotic conditions of some disadvantaged mothers and children where our concepts of resilience and vulnerability may have to be reconsidered (Hofer, 2006).

These findings in "simpler" mammals demonstrate the deep evolutionary biological roots that underlie what we see and how we feel about the early relationship of infants with their caretakers. The use of the concept of interaction, that is evident in the pioneering clinical and research studies of Brazelton, has played a major role in the careers of many of us.

References and further reading

Brake, S. C., Sager, D. J., Sullivan, R., & Hofer, M. (1982). The role of intraoral and gastrointestinal cues in the control of sucking and milk consumption in rat pups. *Developmental Psychobiology, 15*(6), 529–541.

Brake, S. C., Shair, H. N., & Hofer, M. A. (1988). Exploiting the nursing niche: Infant's sucking and feeding behavior in the context of the mother–infant interaction. In E. Blass (Ed.), *Developmental Psychobiology and Behavioral Ecology* (Vol. 9, pp. 347–388). New York: Plenum Publishing.

Brazelton, T. B., Koslowski, B., & Main, M. (1974). The origins of reciprocity: The early mother–infant interaction. In M. L. M. Rosenblum (Ed.), *The effect of the infant on its caretaker: The origins of behavior* (pp. 49–76). New York: Wiley.

Brazelton, T. B., Tronick, E., Adamson, L., Als, H., & Wise, S. (1975). Early mother–infant reciprocity. In *Parent–infant interaction* (pp. 137–154). Ciba Foundation Symposium 33. Amsterdam: Elsevier.

Cameron, N., Parent, C., Champagne, F., Fish, E., Kuroda, K., & Meaney, M. (2005). The programming of individual differences in defensive responses and reproductive strategies in the rat through variations inmaternal care. *Neuroscience and Biobehavioral Review, 29*, 843–865.

Champagne, F. A. (2008). Epigenetic mechanisms and the transgenerational effects of maternal care. *Frontiers in Neuroendocrinology, 29*(3), 386–397.

Field, T. M., Schanberg, S. M., Scafidi, F., Bauer, C. R., Vega-Lahr, N., Garcia, R., … Kuhn, C. M. (1986). Tactile/kinesthetic stimulation effects on preterm neonates. *Pediatrics, 77*(5), 654–658.

Hofer, M. A. (1971). Cardiac rate regulated by nutritional factor in young rats. *Science, 172*(987), 1039–1041.

Hofer, M. A. (1975). Studies on how early maternal separation produces behavioral change in young rats. *Psychosomatic Medicine, 37*(3), 245–264.

Hofer, M. A. (1976). The organization of sleep and wakefulness after maternal separation in young rats. *Developmental Psychobiology, 9*(2), 189–205.

Hofer, M. A. (1980). Effects of reserpine and amphetamine on the development of hyperactivity in maternally deprived rat pups. *Psychosomatic Medicine, 42*(5), 513–520.

Hofer, M. A. (1984). Relationships as regulators: A psychobiologic perspective on bereavement. *Psychosomatic Medicine, 46*(3), 183–197.

Hofer, M. A. (1990). Early symbiotic processes: Hard evidence from a soft place. In R. S. Glick & S. Bone (Eds.), *The role of affect in motivation, development and adaptation: Pleasure beyond the pleasure principle* (Vol. 1). New Haven: Yale University Press.

Hofer, M. A. (2005). The psychobiology of early attachment. *Clinical Neuroscience Research 4*, 291–300.

Hofer, M. A. (2006). Evolutionary basis of adaptation in resilience and vulnerability: Response to Cicchetti and Blender. *Annals of the New York Academy of Sciences, 1094*, 259–262.

Hofer, M. A., & Shair, H. (1982). Control of sleep–wake states in the infant rat by features of the mother–infant relationship. *Developmental Psychobiology, 15*(3), 229–243.

Hofer, M. A., & Weiner, H. (1975). Physiological mechanisms for cardiac control by nutritional intake after early maternal separation in the young rat. *Psychosomatic Medicine, 37*(1), 8–24.

Mason, W. A., & Berkson, G. (1975). Effects of maternal mobility on the development of rocking and other behaviors in rhesus monkeys: A study with artificial mothers. *Developmental Psychobiology, 8*(3), 197–211.

Rosenblum, L. A., & Moltz, H. (1983). *Symbiosis in parent–offspring interactions.* New York: Plenum Press.

Shair, H., Brake, S., & Hofer, M. (1984). Suckling in the rat: Evidence for patterned behavior during sleep. *Behavioral Neuroscience, 98*(2), 366–370.

Stone, E. A., Bonnet, K. A., & Hofer, M. A. (1976). Survival and development of maternally deprived rats: Role of body temperature. *Psychosomatic Medicine, 38*(4), 242–249.

Voloschin, L. M., & Tramezzani, J. H. (1979). Milk ejection reflex linked to slow wave sleep in nursing rats. *Endocrinology, 105*(5), 1202–1207.

15

Temperaments as Sets of Preparedness

Jerome Kagan

Each generation contains a small number of prescient minds that refuse to accept the popular and often simplistic conceptualizations that dominate their discipline and insist on accommodating to what they have observed. Berry Brazelton is a special member of this rare category. When developmental psychologists denied that infants possessed any biologically based biases for emotional or behavioral reactions, Brazelton's rich experience with infants led him to suggest that each infant brought into the world a set of dispositions that prepared her or him to develop, with ease or difficulty, particular personality profiles. But he insisted that the profiles that emerged over the years depended on the family and other environmental settings. These social contexts selected from a potential envelope of many profiles inherent in the infants' temperamental biases a most likely pattern of traits. The initial biases do not determine a particular psychological profile in later childhood; they only limit the range of profiles that might occur. Psychologists, pediatricians, and psychiatrists who resisted this idea initially have recently become more receptive to its validity.

The reintroduction of the idea of temperamental biases a half century after their exile by behaviorists and psychoanalysts is one of the most important scientific advances of the past four decades. Although we are still far from being able to describe all the human temperaments, and have not invented the procedures to quantify them, scientists have begun this task. My colleagues and I have been studying only two of the large number of possible temperaments and this paper summarizes what we have learned over the past 30 years.

What is Temperament?

Temperamental biases are biologically based foundations for patterns of feelings and actions that appear during infancy or early childhood and are sculpted by environments into a large but limited number of profiles that define the large set of personality categories. It is assumed, but not yet proven, that the biological foundations for most, but certainly not all, human temperaments are heritable neurochemical profiles. This hypothesis was present in an early form in the writings of the ancient Greeks, who posited melancholic, sanguine, choleric, and phlegmatic temperaments derived from the balance of the four humors of blood, bile, phlegm, and black bile (Kagan, 1994).

Nonheritable alterations in brain chemistry may also account for some neurochemical profiles that influence temperament. For example, a female fetus lying next to a fraternal twin brother is affected by the androgen secreted by the latter and is likely as an older child to have a higher pain threshold (Morley-Fletcher, Palanza, Parolaro, Vigaero, & Laviola, 2003). A second example is the modest association between season of conception and behaviors and moods that seem to be derivatives of a temperament. Early Fall conceptions in the Northern Hemisphere (conceptions in February through April in the Southern Hemisphere) are associated with extreme levels of shyness in children (Gortmaker, Kagan, Caspi, & Silva, 1997), and affective disorder (Pjrek et al., 2004), and differential dopamine turnover in the brain (Chotai & Adolfsson, 2002). Melatonin, secreted by the pineal gland, is a likely basis for these associations because all humans secrete large amounts of melatonin when the hours of daylight are decreasing and inhibit its secretion when the light is increasing. Hence, it is not surprising that 8-week-old infants who had been conceived in October had the highest concentration of melatonin metabolites in their urine (Sivan, Laudon, Tauman, & Zisapel, 2001). A pregnant mother's secretion of melatonin can affect fetal brain development in diverse ways. This molecule binds to receptors in many sites, including the hypothalamus, contributes to cell death, and suppresses both dopamine release and cortisol production (Ciesla, 2001; Torres-Farton et al., 2004; Zisapel, 2001).

Recent research by biologists provides some preliminary scaffolding for speculations regarding the possible neurochemical biases for human temperaments. There are at present at least 150 different molecules that, along with the density and location of their receptors, have the potential to influence the feelings and behaviors that define human temperaments. These molecules include norepinephrine, dopamine, epinephrine, serotonin, corticotropin-releasing hormone, glutamate, gamma aminobutryic acid, opioids, vasopressin, oxytocin, prolactin, monoamine oxidase, neuropeptide S, and, of course, the sex hormones androgen and estrogen (Hartl & Jones, 2005). Some frequently studied polymorphisms that appear to be significant to human temperaments include: (1) the short (s) and long (1) variants in the promoter region of the gene for the serotonin transporter molecule; (2) presence of the base adenine or guanine in codon 158 of the gene for the enzyme catechol-o-methyltransferase (COMT); (3) the number of repeats in the 48 base pair sequence in the exon of the gene for the dopamine D4 receptor (DRD4); (4) variation in the DRD4 promoter region; and (5) variation in the promoter region of the genes for MAO (A or B) associated with differential degradation of serotonin, norepinephrine, epinephrine in the synapse (Hariri & Brown, 2006; Surtees et al., 2006; Hartl & Jones, 2005). Because brain states are the products of reciprocal interactions among many molecules, most psychological phenotypes should be the products of combinations of polymorphisms. For example, one year olds who showed extreme levels of avoidant behavior to a stranger possessed both the two short alleles of the serotonin transporter as well as the 7-repeat polymorphisms of DRD4, whereas the least avoidant children combined the two long forms of the serotonin transporter gene with the 7 repeat polymorphism (Lakatos et al., 2003).

If each gene, consisting of exons, introns, enhancers, and promoters, capable of influencing brain chemistry had an average of five polymorphisms, there would be 3^{750} possible neurochemical combinations that could become the foundation of a temperamental bias. Even if a majority of these profiles had no relevance for temperaments, the large number of patterns that remain implies that scientists will discover many temperaments that have not yet been characterized.

High- and Low-Reactive Infants

My colleagues and I have been studying a large longitudinal cohort of middle-class, Caucasian infants born to intact, middle-class families who were first observed at 16 weeks of age in order to discover early profiles that might predict the inhibited and uninhibited behavioral patterns that appear first in the second year. Inhibited children show a restrained, cautious, avoidant reaction to unfamiliar persons, objects, events, and places while uninhibited children show a spontaneous approach (Kagan & Snidman, 2004). The behaviors that define inhibited and uninhibited children were moderately stable from the second to the fifth year and modestly associated with peripheral biological measurements that were in theoretical accord with the presumed physiological bases for the two temperaments.

The major hypothesis behind the infant assessments designed to detect the anlage of inhibited and uninhibited profiles was that variation in the excitability of the amygdala and its projections to other brain regions should be an important basis for the development of inhibited or uninhibited behaviors. A primary function of the amygdala is to respond to unfamiliar or unexpected events; therefore, young infants with an excitable amygdala should be more likely than others to become shy, vigilant, and inhibited several years later.

We posited the categories of high- and low-reactive infants after examining the motor and crying behavior of a large group of infants following presentation of unfamiliar visual, auditory, and olfactory stimuli that were nonthreatening but unexpected. The 20% of infants who showed vigorous motor behavior and frequent crying were called high-reactive and were expected to become inhibited. The 40% who showed minimal motor behavior and no crying were called low-reactive and were expected to become uninhibited. Follow-up assessments with one and two year olds revealed that those who had been high-reactive were more fearful than low-reactives when exposed to unfamiliar events. At 7 years of age, high-reactives were more likely than low-reactives to display anxious symptoms and, at 11 years of age, high-reactives were quieter, emotionally subdued, and showed two or three biological signs that are regarded as indirect indices of an excitable amygdala. For example, the resting EEGs of the high-reactives displayed greater activation in the right, compared with the left, hemisphere. Greater activation in the left frontal area, more characteristic of low-reactives, is likely when individuals are in a happy, relaxed state. High-reactives also showed a larger brain-stem auditory evoked response (BAER) from the inferior colliculus at 11 years of age, called wave five. Because the amygdala primes the inferior colliculus, this result implies that high-reactives possess a more excitable amygdala. High-reactives also showed larger ERP waveforms at about 400 msec. to unexpected, discrepant visual scenes (for example, a baby's head on an animal's body) and greater sympathetic rather than parasympathetic tone in the cardiovascular system (Kagan & Snidman, 2004).

The 15 year olds were first interviewed at home. The adolescents who had been high-reactive at 4 months smiled less often and showed more restless motor activity during the interview. The low-reactives, by contrast, showed little muscle tension in their trunk or limbs throughout the three-hour interview and described themselves as relaxed and happy. More important, high-reactives were more likely than low-reactives to worry over unrealistic events, such as encounters with unfamiliar people, places, or situations, and felt uncertain when they did not know what might happen in the future. Some excerpts from the interviews illustrate these concerns, "In a crowd I feel isolated, left out; I don't know what to pay attention to because it is all so ambiguous"; "I worry about the future, over not knowing what will happen next"; "I wanted to be a doctor but decided against it because I felt it would be too much of a strain"; "I like being alone and, therefore, horses are my hobby. I don't have to worry about fitting in with others when I'm with my horses"; "I get nervous before every vacation because I don't know what will happen". Statements with this content were rare among the low-reactive 15 year olds (Kagan, Snidman, Kahn, & Towsley, 2007).

Youths in contemporary America are trying to establish their personal philosophy at a time when there is little consensus on the meaning of life or its origin. This state of affairs creates uncertainty in many adolescents. Hence, those who have a temperamental bias that renders them vulnerable to worry about the moral standards they believe deserve unquestioned loyalty should try to find a belief system that might mute their private angst. A religious commitment is one effective strategy because it provides a partial answer to these questions and assures each individual of his or her essential virtue when disappointments, failures, and frustrations occur. Forty-five percent of the adolescents who had been high-reactive said that they were very religious compared with only 25 percent of the low-reactives.

High-reactives worry about their inability to control the future because they are more susceptible to the sensations that follow unexpected visceral feedback from targets of the autonomic nervous system. When these sensations pierce consciousness, they create uncertainty because their origin is ambiguous. This psychological state resembles the one evoked when, as children, they encountered unfamiliar objects, people, or situations. The state created by detection of unexpected visceral feedback can provoke uncertainty because the child or adolescent does not understand its cause.

We believe that the biology associated with maleness and the different biology that is the foundation of low-reactivity combine to produce a unique psychological pattern in about one of every four low-reactive boys. Our results are remarkably similar to those reported by Fox and his colleagues (Fox, Henderson, Marshall, Nichols, & Ghera, 2005) who followed similar temperamental groups initially classified at four months with a battery similar to the one that we administered. Our evidence is also in accord with the data of a longitudinal study conducted at the University of Wisconsin which affirmed that the probability of an inhibited child becoming uninhibited, or an uninhibited child becoming inhibited, is very low (Pfeifer, Goldsmith, Davidson, & Rickman, 2002).

However, it is important to note that only about one-fourth of the children in the high- or the low-reactive groups actualized both the behavioral and physiological profiles that were in accord with expectation. But it was rare for any member of either the high- or low-reactive group to develop the profile of the other group. Thus, the most accurate summary is that an early temperamental bias for high- or low-reactivity prevents the development of the contrasting profile. That is, an infant's temperament is more effective in constraining the development of some profiles than in determining a particular one.

The principle that a temperamental bias eliminates many more possibilities than it determines applies to environmental conditions as well. If the only knowledge investigators had about a sample of children was that they were born to economically secure, well-educated, nurturant parents, it would be easier to predict what they will not become – criminals, school dropouts, psychotics, drug addicts – than to predict what they will become. Thus, a temperamental bias can be likened to the basic form of the song of a particular bird species. The bird's genome constrains the basic form of a song but does not determine all of its variations because the variations depend on exposure to the songs of other birds and the opportunity to hear its own vocal sounds. A bird that is deafened early in life develops an abnormal song. Thus, knowing that a bird is a finch rather than a meadow lark allows one to predict with great confidence the songs it will not sing, but does not allow a prediction of the particular songs it will sing (Brainard & Doupe, 2002).

Most of the 15 year olds who had been high-reactive were not unusually shy, but their feeling tone was characterized by greater vigilance and tension. That is why we suggest that each person's usual feeling tone, not their level of shyness or sociability, is the most important property that differentiates the adolescents who belong to each of the two temperamental groups. The dysphoric quality in the poetry of T. S. Eliot and Sylvia Plath is easily distinguished from the celebration of life and love in the poems of E. E. Cummings and Robert Graves. Temperament makes a more substantial contribution to feeling tone than to public behavior during adolescence and adulthood. In order to predict the emotions that a particular individual will experience, one has to know three facts which, at the moment, remain a mystery: (1) the dominant neurophysiological profile that describes the usual brain state when an incentive occurs; (2) the history of the individual, which determines the likely reaction to an incentive; and (3) the class of incentive. Obviously, the social context in which the individual lives influences which incentives are more and which less probable. Each of these three factors has many subfactors. Hence, scientists confront a matrix that contains a very large number of cells, most of which remain unfilled.

Finally, it is worthwhile noting that the genes that contribute to temperamental biases vary across reproductively isolated human groups. There are substantial differences among Asians, Africans, and Europeans in alleles located in the promoter regions of many genes. The most consistent evidence comes from comparisons of Asian and European-Caucasians who were reproductively isolated for close to 30,000 years, or about 1,000 generations. Asian and Caucasian adults differ in the length of the DNA segment in the promoter region of the gene responsible for the serotonin transporter molecule, as well as in an allele that affects gastrin-releasing peptide (Marui et al., 2004). The latter molecule affects activity in the basolateral nucleus of the amygdala by enhancing GABA activity.

It may not be a coincidence that a high-reactive temperament is far more frequent among Caucasian than among Chinese 4-month-old infants (Kagan et al., 1994). Moreover, Japanese, compared with Caucasian-American, infants are less easily aroused, less likely to cry during an inoculation, and less distressed by restraint of their arms (Caudill & Weinstein, 1969; Lewis, Ramsey, & Kawakami, 1993). Anthropologists report that the ancient Japanese celebrated the feeling of *kami* (translated as surprise). This state might be more salient among those who normally show low levels of cortical and autonomic arousal.

These facts and others invite a speculation on the possible reasons for the differential appeal of Christianity versus Buddhism to Europeans and Asians. Martin Luther and John Calvin (the latter was a chronic melancholic) believed that anxiety and guilt were endemic to the human condition. Hence, the most desirable psychological state was to be free of anxiety or guilt. Buddhist philosophy, which was more attractive to Asians, made the attainment of serenity, rather than the absence of anxiety or guilt, the primary goal in life. The Buddhist imperative urges the elimination of all desires for material and sensory pleasures because frustrated wishes are the primary cause of suffering. However, the unpleasant feeling of sadness or anger that accompanies the inability to gain a desired goal differs from the anxiety, guilt, or shame that accompanies criticism, failure, or self-reproach. Sadness and anxiety are distinct feeling states. If large numbers of European adults experienced high levels of cortical and autonomic arousal and interpreted these feelings as guilt, fear, or anxiety, a philosophy that urged serenity of mind would have met resistance because the idealized state would have seemed unattainable. By contrast, a philosophy that accepted anxiety and guilt as definitive of the human condition would seem less valid to those whose temperament permitted so many moments of serenity. Attaining a state that was free of this suffering might seem a real possibility. It is tempting to speculate, therefore, that temperamental differences, based on the neurochemistry of Asians and Europeans, made a small contribution to the differential attractiveness of these two religious philosophies.

Although temperaments have a biological component, it is important not to exaggerate their importance. I am skeptical of the claim that most variation in personality and mental illness is due primarily to genes. This bias is seen in papers that report that among English-speaking respondents of 18 years and older, the lifetime prevalence for anxiety disorders was 28 percent and for mood disorders 20 percent (Kessler, Berglund, Demler, Jin, & Walters, 2005). This claim implies, without stating so explicitly, that the pathophysiological bases for anxiety and mood disorders lie primarily within the patients, rather than in profound interactions between their biology, which appears to be measurable, and the person's past histories and current social settings which are more difficult to quantify. Rather than report a national prevalence of 20 percent for anxiety disorders, it would be wiser to present the prevalence rates for groups defined by their social class, ethnicity, and even region of the country, for depression is, and has always been, more common among the urban poor and the rural rich (Weich, Twigg, & Lewis, 2006). Although the current biological perspective has value, it has two disadvantages. The emphasis on biological causation diverts attention from the personal contributions to a patient's symptoms by those who interact with them. Second, it motivates the singleminded approach to finding new drug treatments directed only at patients rather than urging clinicians to combine these treatments with strategies that might alter the social context. Each river is capable of becoming polluted and losing its capacity to sustain life. However, ecologists do not attribute an inherited flaw to a river that has become polluted. Rather, they urge changes in the practices of industry and agriculture that were root causes of the pollution. Psychiatrists and psychologists should think about adopting a similar strategy when they study anxiety and mood disorders.

My colleagues and I were surprised by the length of the shadows cast by the high- and low-reactive profiles detected at 16 weeks of age. We were lucky that we assessed the infants when they were four months old. There is a maturational transition at 2–3 months which permits four month olds to relate events to acquired knowledge, even though they are not mature enough to modulate their behavior. Had we observed the infants at one week or one year, we might not have found as persuasive evidence for the derivatives of the high- and low-reactive profiles. Nature occasionally opens her door for a moment to reveal some of the exotic secrets she is hiding inside. If the scientist happens to be turned the other way, her inner sanctum will remain a mystery.

References and further reading

Brainard, M. S., & Doupe, A. J. (2002). Do songbirds teach us about learning? *Nature, 417*, 351–358.

Caudill, W., & Weinstein, H. (1969). Maternal care and infant behavior in Japan and America. *Psychiatry, 32*, 12–43.

Chotai, J., & Adolfsson, R. (2002). Converging evidence suggests that monoamine neurotransmitter turnover in human adults is associated with their season of birth. *European Archives of Psychiatry and Clinical Neuroscience, 252*, 130–134.

Ciesla, W. (2001). Can melatonin regulate the expression of prohormone convertase 1 and 2 gene via monomeric and dimeric forms of RZR/ROR nuclear receptor, and can melatonin influence the processes of embryogenesis or carcinogenesis by disturbing the proportion of cAMP and cGMP concentrations? *Medical Hypotheses, 56*, 181–193.

Fox, N. A., Henderson, H. A., Marshall, T. J., Nichols, K. E., & Ghera, M. N. (2005). Behavioral inhibition: Linking biology and behavior within a developmental framework. In S. T. Fiske, A. E. Kazdin, & D. L. Schacter (Eds.), *Annual Review of Psychology* (Vol. 56, pp. 235–262). Palo Alto, CA.

Gortmaker, S. L., Kagan, J., Caspi, A., & Silva, P. A. (1997). Daylength during pregnancy and shyness in children. *Developmental Psychology, 31*, 107–114.

Hariri, A. R., & Brown, S. M. (2006). Serotonin. *The American Journal of Psychiatry, 163*, 12.

Hartl, D., & Jones, E. W. (2005). *Genetics* (6th ed.). Boston: Jones & Bartlett.

Kagan, J. (1994). *Galen's prophecy*. New York: Basic Books.

Kagan, J., & Snidman, N. (2004). *The long shadow of temperament*. Cambridge, MA: Harvard University Press.

Kagan, J., Arcus, D., Snidman, N., Feng, W. U., Hendler, J., & Greene, S. (1994). Reactivity in infants: A cross-national comparison. *Developmental Psychology, 30*, 342–345.

Kagan, J., Snidman, N., Kahn, V., & Towsley, S. (2007). The preservation of two infant temperaments into adolescence. *Monographs of the Society of Research in Child Development,* Serial No. 287, *72*, 1–75.

Kessler, R. C., Berglund, P., Demler, O., Jin, R., & Walters, E. E. (2005). Lifetime prevalence and age-of-onset distribution of DSM-IV disorders in the National Cormobidity Survey replication. *Archives of General Psychiatry, 62*, 593–602.

Lakatos, K., Nemoda, Z., Birkas, E., Ronai, Z., Kovacs, E., Ney, K., … Gervai, J. (2003). Association of D4 dopamine receptor gene and serotonin transporter promoter polymorphism and infants' response to novelty. *Molecular Psychiatry, 8*, 90–98.

Lewis, M. M., Ramsey, D. S., & Kawakami, K. (1993). Differences between Japanese infants and Caucasian-American infants in behavioral and cortisol response to inoculation. *Child Development, 64*, 1722–1731.

Marui, T., Hashimoto, O., Namba, E., Kato, C., & Tochiji, M., Umekage, T., Kato, N., & Sasaki, T. (2004). Gastrin-releasing peptide receptor locus in Japanese subjects with autism. *Brain and Development, 26*, 5–7.

Morley-Fletcher, S. S., Palanza, P., Parolaro, B., Vigaero, D., & Laviola, G. (2003). Intra-uterine position has long-term influences on brain mu opioid receptor densities in behavior in mice. *Psychoneuroendocrinology, 28*, 386–400.

Pfeifer, M., Goldsmith, H. H., Davidson, R. J., & Rickman, M. (2002). Continuity and change in inhibited and uninhibited children. *Child Development, 73*, 1474–1485.

Pjrek, E., Winkler, D., Heiden, A., Praschak-Rieder, N., Willeit, M., Konstantinidis, A., Statny, J., & Kasper, S. (2004). Seasonality of birth in seasonal affective disorder. *Journal of Clinical Psychiatry, 65*, 1389–1393.

Sivan, Y., Laudon, M., Tauman, R., & Zisapel, N. (2001). Melatonin production in healthy infants: Evidence for seasonal variations. *Pediatric Research, 49*, 63–68.

Surtees, P. G., Wainwright, N. W. J., Willis-Owen, S. A. G., Luben, R., Day, N. E., & Flint, J. (2006). Social adversity, the serotonin transporter (5-HTTLPR): Polymorphism and major depressive disorder. *Biological Psychiatry, 59*, 224–229.

Torres-Farton, C., Richter, H. G., Germain, A. M., Valenzuela, G. J., Campino, C., Rojas-Garcia, P., … Seron-Ferre, M. (2004). Maternal melatonin selectively inhibits cortisol production in the primate fetal adrenal gland. *The Journal of Physiology, 554*, 841–856.

Weich, S., Twigg, L., & Lewis, G. (2006). Rural/non-rural differences in rates of common mental disorders in Britain. *The British Journal of Psychiatry, 188*, 51–57.

Zisapel, N. (2001). Melatonin-dopamine interactions: From basic neurochemistry to a clinical setting. *Cell Molecular Neurobiology, 21*, 605–616.

Part II

From Theory to Practice

Innovations in Clinical Intervention

Section I

Preventive Interventions
Home Visitation

16

Touchpoints in a Nurse Home Visiting Program

Kristie Brandt
and J. Michael Murphy

Introduction

The beneficial effects of nurse home visits to young children and their mothers are among the best documented in the medical/social science literature (Department of Health and Human Services, 2000; Gomby, Culross, & Behrman, 1999; Gomby, 2005; Sweet & Appelbaum, 2004). Nurse home visits to high-risk pregnant women and mothers of infants and toddlers have been associated with a reduction in child abuse and neglect (Eckenrode et al., 2000; Olds, 1997), child healthcare visits for ingestion and injury (Kitzman et al., 2000), welfare dependence (Olds et al., 2004), involvement with the child and adult justice system, and child antisocial behaviors (Olds et al., 1998) up to fifteen years post-intervention.

The frequency, intention, and education of the home visitor and the home-visit content can have a significant impact on outcomes (Korfmacher, O'Brien, Hiatt, & Olds, 1999; Olds, 2002; Olds et al., 2002; Olds, Hill, O'Brien, Racine, & Moritz, 2003). Home visitors' and healthcare providers' capacity to form strong, respectful relationships with families, and their impact on brief and long-term health promotion and treatment outcomes, has drawn growing attention (Barnard & Morisset, 1995; Brazelton, 1994;

Gomby, 2005; Kalmanson & Seligman, 1992; Lieberman & Pawl, 1993; Weston, Ivins, Heffron, & Sweet, 1997). The parent–provider relationship has been identified as a decisive variable in the efficacy of health-related services (Safran, Miller, & Beckman, 2006; Suchman, 2006; Zuckerman & Brazelton, 1994).

Brazelton (1975) posited that establishing a supportive relationship with parents and respecting parental strengths could promote their attachment to and nurturance of their children, enhancing children's developmental potential. This became a central concept of the neurodevelopmental, neurorelational Touchpoints Model (Brazelton, 1992) for pediatric encounters as opportunities for providers and parents to develop a shared understanding of the unique capacities and development of child and family (Brazelton, 1975, 1992, 1994; Brazelton, O'Brien, & Brandt, 1997; Zuckerman & Brazelton, 1994).

The critical role of relationships and the skills required to achieve them are rarely addressed in the training of child/family professionals, while objectivity, avoidance of over-involvement, and rigid professional boundaries are often stressed (Edelman, 2004; Epstein, 1999; Lussier & Richard, 2007; Wissow, Larson, Anderson, & Hadjiisky, 2005). Professional education emphasizes "teaching" rather than listening and collaboration, and is aimed at securing patient compliance rather than genuine participation. The Touchpoints (TP) Model has become the basis for training physicians, nurses, social workers, educators, and others working with children and families to understand and value the parent–provider relationship and appreciate the potential of this relationship for optimal development of the child and family (Hornstein, O'Brien, & Stadtler, 1997).

Touchpoints are predictable points in development when children temporarily regress prior to a developmental burst (Brazelton, 1992), causing disruption in the family system, parental anxiety, and concern. The parent may feel that their child is ill, failing, or needs more disciplinary structure (Zuckerman & Brazelton, 1994) and may call or visit the healthcare provider or emergency room. Parental understanding of these regressions as part of typical development can lead to greater confidence, skill, and satisfaction in parenting. Without this understanding, parents may become stressed and react inappropriately to these cycles, including extreme responses such as child abuse or neglect, resulting in developmental derailment. With anticipatory guidance about touchpoints, providers can join the family system, enhancing parents' success and confidence and, in turn, children's development (Brazelton, 1992, 1994; Brazelton et al., 1997).

The study described in this chapter examined whether a Touchpoints-based approach for public health nurse (PHN) home visits was associated with better six-month outcomes for high-risk dyads than a traditional nurse home visit model or no home visits at all. Examining the efficacy of home visiting models has relevance for families' health and wellbeing and for public health practice and policy (Foege, 1998). For the complete study report, see Brandt et al. (2001).

Methods

The study was conducted in Napa County, California by the Napa County Health & Human Services Agency (NCHHSA) with the cooperation of several community organizations and programs. Home visitors were PHNs employed by NCHHSA and IRB approval was obtained for the study.

Participants were drawn from the community's Comprehensive Perinatal Services Program (CPSP), providing expanded services for pregnant women on Medi-Cal. In addition to prenatal care, CPSPs provide nutritional and psychosocial screening and counseling, perinatal education, assistance in reducing barriers to care (e.g., transportation, translation, childcare, etc.), and referrals for other needs (e.g., housing, WIC, social services, etc.). CPSP enrollees were screened for a variety of psychosocial, medical, and nutritional (PSMN) risks and given a total risk score with classifications of high, medium, or low risk on a state-approved screening form (Department of Health Services, Maternal & Child Health Branch, 1997, 1999).

The study was based on two separate data collections over a year. First was a retrospective sample to obtain both an untreated community baseline group without PHN home visits (HVs) and a group who received home visits from non-TP-trained PHNs. This sample consisted of all CPSP clients determined to be high PSMN risk who delivered babies within a specific 4-month period. At 20 weeks post-partum, 33 eligible women were contacted and agreed to participate. One did not come to the assessment, and the final two were not used once the desired sample size of 30 was achieved. In this and subsequent phases of the study, data collectors were unaware of the home visit variable.

Eight of the subjects in this group had received perinatal PHN HVs as a part of usual care for high-risk families. PHNs conducting these HVs were not TP-trained at the time, so these eight dyads were assigned to the non-Touchpoints HV group in the Combined Sample. This design provided a control group that received PHN HVs before the experimental introduction of TP.

Four months after this phase, a second sample using prospective random assignment was obtained to explore parent–infant outcomes associated with HVs by TP-trained PHNs. All CPSP-enrolled women with high PSMN risk were informed of the study at 28–36 weeks gestation. Forty-four were invited to participate to achieve the desired sample size of 40 and potential participants were randomly assigned to a treatment and a comparison group by a coin toss. From the group of 44 women referred for participation, one declined due to relocation, one elected not to participate with no reason noted, and the last two were not used as the desired sample size had been attained.

At the time of the study, all CPSP-enrolled women with high PSMN risk were referred to Public Health for PHN HVs – but, for logistical and other reasons, only about one-third received them. Due to high PSMN risk status, some control subjects would therefore receive PHN HVs as part of usual community practice. Because withholding PHN services altogether from referred clients would have been unethical, referrals during the course of the study of pregnant women or children from birth to 26 weeks were assigned to non-TP-trained PHNs. This research protocol was blind to PHNs and seven women in the comparison group did receive perinatal PHN home visits.

Design and implementation of the Home Visitation Program

Those PHNs to be trained in TP received standard 3-day TP training and were asked to apply the model in their work with families. All PHNs were blind to their referrals' study participation status. TP-trained PHNs were assigned to TP-trained clinical supervisors and monthly reflective mentoring with members of their training cohort. Non-TP-trained PHNs had only regular staff meetings. In both groups, and in keeping with standard practice for PHNs in the agency at that time, PHNs used professional judgment to determine home visit frequency and intervals.

Measures

A 2-hour assessment was conducted when infants were 22–26 weeks adjusted age using the following measures administered by personnel unaware of subjects' group assignment:

1 Child's developmental status: Ages & Stages 6-Month Questionnaire (ASQ) (Bricker, Squires, Kaminski, & Mounts, 1988; Bricker, Squires, Nickel, & Mounts, 1990).
2 Caregiver sensitivity to cues, response to distress, social-emotional growth fostering, cognitive growth fostering, child's clarity of cues and responsiveness to caregiver: NCAST Teaching Scale (Barnard et al., 1989; Sumner & Spietz, 1994).
3 Post-partum depression symptoms screen: Edinburgh Depression Scale (Cox, Holden, & Sagovksy, 1987).
4 Maternal mental health symptoms and difficulties in daily functioning: Behavior and Symptom Identification Scale (BASIS-32®) (Eisen, Dill, & Grob, 1994).
5 Parental satisfaction with community providers: Perinatal-Child & Adolescent Services Assessment (P-CASA), a perinatal version of the "Relationship with Providers" CASA subscale (Farmer, Angold, Burns, & Costello, 1994).[1]

Participants consented to researcher review of prenatal, delivery, newborn, pediatric healthcare records, local hospital emergency department, and inpatient records. Record reviewers were unaware of subjects' group assignment. Demographic data collected included partner status, parity, maternal age, income, infant feeding, ethnicity and educational level.

Statistical methods

Prospective and Retrospective samples were compared on five background variables using t-tests for continuous variables and chi square tests for categorical variables. Within the Prospective sample, differences between Touchpoints (TP) treatment versus control groups were tested using t-tests and chi square. Given the lack of differences between the retrospective sample and the prospective sample (except for home visits), the retrospective sample was divided into two groups, home-visited (non-TPs PHN) and non-home-visited. Within the prospective randomly assigned sample, the group designated for no home visits was divided into two groups: non-home-visited and home-visited by a non-TPs PHN. The retrospective non-home-visited group was combined with the prospective non-home-visited group to create the Baseline group, and the retrospective home-visited group was combined with the prospective subjects that ultimately received home visits to create the Comparison group in order to compare the impact of no home visits at all to PHN home visiting with and without TP. This allowed for a full analysis of the 70 mothers and 70 infants, and a secondary analysis of just the prospective sample to compare the impact of TPs. One-way Analysis of Variance tested differences in means for three groups: dyads that had received TP-trained PHNs HVs versus dyads that received non-TP-trained PHNs HVs versus dyads that were not home visited. Post hoc pairwise comparisons used Tukey HSD statistics to explore the relative impact of TP-trained PHNs HVs versus standard PHN HVs. In the final set of analyses, main effect linear regression models were created to test the hypothesis that TP-trained PHNs HVs were associated with significantly better outcomes after controlling for all background factors (number of HVs, risk level, maternal age, education, income, and Latina ethnicity).

Results

Demographics

There were no significant differences between Retrospective and Prospective samples in maternal age, percent Hispanic, risk status, or income. The two samples were not significantly different in the number of HVs with the Prospective sample receiving 4.2 versus 2.0 for the Retrospective.

Given the similarities within the samples and the need to control for the impact of PHN HVs in the Retrospective and Control groups, data from the two samples were combined for all subsequent analyses, producing three analytic groups:

1 *Baseline* (n=35): no PHN HVs;
2 *Comparison* (n=15): PHN HVs, without TP;
3 *Treatment* (n=20): PHN TP HVs.

Demographic data for the three groups in the combined analytic sample showed, as might be expected, that for the group that eventually received PHN HVs based on community referrals, the Comparison group was significantly more likely to be at high or very high risk (73%) on the psychosocial portion of the PSMN risk, while 35% of the Treatment and 23% of the Baseline groups had been rated at high or very high risk on this portion of the risk screen. This difference in risk levels may have been a design artifact, since higher risk women may have been more likely to have been assigned a PHN (non-TPs-trained) by virtue of their higher risk status, though no policies were in place at the time that specified this.

Given the analytic sample's composition, there were statistically significant group differences in the number of HVs. By definition, the Baseline group received no HVs and by design the Treatment group received HVs from TP-trained PHNs. The Comparison group received an average of 5.3 HVs, while the Treatment group averaged 7.3 HVs. There were also significant differences in maternal education among the three analytic groups with education higher in the Baseline group than in the Comparison and Treatment groups.

Treatment group infants had statistically significantly fewer hospital emergency room visits than the Comparison and Baseline groups, and statistically significantly more well-child visits than the Comparison or Baseline groups. Treatment group infants had statistically significantly fewer sick-child office visits than infants in the Comparison or Baseline groups. Differences between the Comparison groups and Baseline groups were not statistically significant.

The Treatment group's infants were breastfed significantly longer than infants in the Comparison or Baseline groups. In the Treatment group, a substantial number of dyads were still breastfeeding at 24 weeks while more infants in the Comparison and Baseline groups had been weaned or never breastfed.

Infant functioning

The Treatment group had significantly better subscale and total scores on the ASQ. The scores on all five of the ASQ subscales showed the same pattern: statistically significantly higher in the Treatment group than the Comparison and Baseline groups. On three subscale scores, the Comparison group also did significantly better than the Baseline group. Although the Treatment group had a higher mean score on all five subscales and the ASQ total score than the Comparison group, none of these differences attained statistical significance in post hoc analyses. On the NCAST Teach total score, the Treatment group did statistically significantly better than both Comparison and Baseline groups.

Parent functioning

On the BASIS 32, the Treatment group showed the smallest mean number of symptoms and problems in daily functioning and had statistically significantly better functioning than the Baseline group and the Comparison group on this measure. There was also a marginally significant trend for groups to differ on the Edinburgh post-partum depression scale, where lower scores are better, with scores in the treatment group lower than the comparison and baseline groups.

Satisfaction with services

Parental satisfaction with perinatal services in the county was assessed using the P-CASA. Treatment group parents were significantly more satisfied with services than were Comparison and Baseline groups.

Regression modeling

Given the need to control for HVs number, maternal education, and psychosocial risk level for each outcome variable, we conducted multivariable analysis to determine the effects of Touchpoints exposure controlling for the effects of each of these factors plus the demographic variables of maternal age, family income, and Latina (versus not Latina). *For all of the outcomes, Touchpoints was associated with significantly or marginally better outcomes, even controlling for the six background factors.* For three variables (weeks of breastfeeding, ASQ gross motor, and NCAST Total score) number of years of maternal education was also a significant predictor of better outcome, and for the BASIS 32, the number of PHN HVs also significantly predicted better outcome. *But in all of these instances, PHN HVs with TP was the strongest predictor of better outcomes.*

Following "intention-to-treat" recommendations (Fisher et al., 1990), a secondary analysis was conducted using the prospective, randomly assigned experimental design with Group A (20 Touchpoints home-visited subjects) and Group B (20 subjects without home visits). Within Group B, 13 dyads did not receive home visits, as planned, and 7 ultimately were visited by a non-TP-trained PHN. The two groups did not differ significantly from each other in terms of age, income, risk level, or percent Latina. Dyads in Group A (TP-home-visited) showed statistically significantly lower numbers of ER and sick-child visits, more well-child visits, and statistically significantly better functioning on the ASQ total score, ASQ problem solving subscale, NCAST, BASIS 32, P-CASA, and breastfeeding at 6 months post-partum. As in the combined group, there was a trend of fewer hospitalizations in the TP HV group that was not statistically significant. As in the larger sample, there was no statistically significant difference in the Edinburgh. Virtually all of the findings were consistent with those in the larger sample (that included the Retrospective sample) with the exception of four of the ASQ subscales (communication, fine motor, gross motor, and personal-social) that showed no statistically significant difference despite the ASQ total score, while the problem-solving subscale continued to be statistically significantly higher in the prospectively randomly assigned TP HV group.

Discussion

By 6 months post-partum, results show improved health and developmental outcomes and maternal mental health indicators, better maternal–infant interaction, longer breastfeeding duration, and greater satisfaction with care providers with PHN TP HVs as compared with no HVs. At-risk dyads who received PHN HVs without TP as part of usual care showed better outcomes than those receiving no HVs on two outcome measures, but on the same two measures and on ten additional measures, dyads who received PHN TP HVs did better than the group with no HVs. These results strongly suggest that home visits using a Touchpoints approach contribute to the health and wellbeing of infants and mothers, favorably impact the health-care delivery system, and improve scores on measures that correlate with later child developmental and cognitive outcomes (Morisset, 1994; Sweet & Appelbaum, 2004; Weiss & Wagner, 1998).

Limitations of this study include previously noted differences in the groups, small sample size, and the small number of PHNs. The study subjects were exclusively women initially determined to be at high psychosocial, medical and/or nutritional risk, drawn from a single geographic area. It is unknown if similar results would occur with women of low–moderate risk, or in other populations. One portion of this study mixed retrospective and prospective data which could have confounded, enhanced, or diminished results for the related findings.

The Comparison group was more likely to be at high psychosocial risk, less educated, and have fewer home visits, possibly accounting for some observed differences. For this reason, the relationship between TP-based HVs and outcomes was assessed through a series of regression equations controlling for these confounding factors. In all cases, having a TP-trained PHN was the most powerful and statistically significant predictor of better outcome.

These results are consistent with studies showing statistically significantly better family outcomes with nurse HVs, and a relationally based intervention approach. The strength of these results in a small sample may suggest a substantial effect-size associated with the Touchpoints approach in perinatal HVs. For example, in this study there was a .44 hospital emergency room visit reduction rate between the Baseline group and the Treatment group. If a visit-rate reduction of 0.44/child age 0–24 weeks were sustained in a larger project, it would constitute 440 fewer emergency visits per 1,000 infants in the first 6 months of life, and the 1.4/child reduction in the rate of sick-child visits would translate to 1,400 fewer sick visits per 1,000 children in this same period. The potential cost savings of these findings warrant additional study.

HV duration was 30–60 minutes and a post-research data review showed that the Treatment group's visits were not significantly longer than those of the Comparison group. Anecdotal data from the TPs trained PHNs showed that their visits were more focused on the parent–PHN relationship and infant development, and were more affectively charged. Client satisfaction was evidenced by a 9% "no-show" rate, as compared with the 48% agency no-show rate, similar to the Comparison group.

PHNs involved in the Touchpoints intervention reported greater job satisfaction and charting efficiency, and that mothers called when infants reached developmental milestones and to confirm appointments. There were no such reports from the non-TP PHNs.

Conclusion

In addition to other positive findings, this study provides evidence that home visits based on the Touchpoints Model are associated with longer breastfeeding and increased well-child care treatment adherence. A positive parent–child relationship is strongly associated with future child and adult health and wellbeing, and related indicators (Anda et al., 1999; Brandt, Andrews, & Kvale, 1998; Brown, Cohen, Johnson & Smailes, 1999; Dallam, 2001; Felitti et al., 1998; Heim, Ehlert, & Hellhammer, 2000; Weiss & Wagner, 1998). Such improvements enhance not only the individual health and wellbeing of the infant but the overall health of the community and have relevance beyond nursing for pediatric providers, hospitals, health economists, public health officials, and other professionals and programs working with very young children and their families. From these broader perspectives, a home-visiting program using the neurodevelopmental, neurorelational Touchpoints Model is an evidence-based intervention with preventive impacts on the individual, family, community, and healthcare system.

Acknowledgment

The authors acknowledge and thank Sharrie Pitman, RN, BSN, Laura Keller, NP, BSN, PHN, and Terry Longoria, MA for their contributions, dedication, support, and encouragement during the planning, implementation, and data intake portions of this project. In addition, we thank the Napa County Public Health staff, Napa community agencies, and the participating families for contributing to this work.

Note

1 This measure modified with permission of the CASA authors to assess health and social service providers within a community.

Primary reference

Brandt, K. A., Brazelton, T. B., Keller, L., Longoria, T., Murphy, J. M., & Pitman, S. (2001). Touchpoints in prenatal home visiting: The impact on health and wellness indicators for mother and baby at six months postpartum. *Project Report*. Napa, CA: Napa County Health & Human Services.

Secondary references and further reading

Anda, R. F., Croft, J. B., Felitti, V. J., Nordenberg, D., Giles, W. H., Williamson, D. F., & Giovino, D. A. (1999). Adverse childhood experiences and smoking during adolescence and adulthood. *Journal of the American Medical Association, 282*(17), 1652–1658.

Barnard, K. E., & Morisset, C. E. (1995). Preventive health and developmental care for children: Relationship as a primary factor in service delivery with at risk populations. In H. Fitzgerald, B. Lester, & B. Zuckerman (Eds.), *Children of poverty: Research, health and policy issues* (pp. 167–195). New York: Garland Publishing.

Barnard, K. E., Hammond, M. A., Booth, C. L., Bee, H. L., Mitchell, S. K., & Spieker, S. J. (1989). Measurement and meaning of parent–child interaction. In F. J. Morrison, C. E. Lord, & D. P. Keating (Eds.), *Applied developmental psychology* (Vol. 3). New York: Academic Press.

Brandt, K. A., Andrews, C. M., & Kvale, J. (1998). Mother–infant interaction and breastfeeding outcome 6 weeks after birth. *Journal of Obstetric, Gynecologic & Neonatal Nursing, 27*(2), 169–174.

Brazelton, T. B. (1975). Anticipatory guidance. *Pediatric clinics of North America, 22*(3), 533–544.

Brazelton, T. B. (1992). *Touchpoints: Your child's emotional and behavioral development, birth to 3: The essential reference for the early years.* Reading, MA: Addison-Wesley.

Brazelton, T. B. (1994). Touchpoints: Opportunities for preventing problems in the parent–child relationship. *ACTA Pediatrics Supplemental, 394*, 35–39.

Brazelton, T. B., O'Brien, M., & Brandt, K. (1997). Combining relationships and development: Applying Touchpoints to individual and community practices. *Infants & Young Children, 10*(1), 74–84.

Bricker, D., Squires, J., Kaminski, T., & Mounts, L. (1988).The validity, reliability and cost of a parent-completed questionnaire system to evaluate at-risk infants. *Journal of Pediatric Psychology, 13*(1), 55–68.

Bricker, D., Squires, J., Nickel, R., & Mounts, L. (1990). *Infant child monitoring questionnaires.* Eugene, OR: Center on Human Development, University of Oregon.

Brown, J., Cohen, P., Johnson, J. G., & Smailes, E. M. (1999). Childhood abuse and neglect: Specificity of effects on adolescent and young adult depression and suicidality. *Journal of American Academy of Child & Adolescent Psychiatry, 38*, 1490–1496.

Cox, J. L., Holden, J. M., & Sagovksy, R. (1987). Detection of postnatal depression: Development of the 10-item Edinburgh postnatal depression scale. *British Journal of Psychiatry, 150*, 782–786.

Dallam, S. J. (2001). The long-term medical consequences of childhood trauma. In K. Franey, R. Geffner, & R. Falconer (Eds.), *The cost of child maltreatment: Who pays? We all do* (pp. 1–14). San Diego, CA: FVSAI Publications.

Department of Health and Human Services (2000). *Report of the Surgeon General's conference on children's mental health: A national action agenda.* Washington, DC: U.S. Public Health Service.

Department of Health Services, Maternal & Child Health Branch (1997). *Steps to take: First steps.* Sacramento, CA: State of California.

Department of Health Services, Maternal & Child Health Branch (1999). *Comprehensive perinatal services program: Provider handbook.* Sacramento, CA: State of California.

Eckenrode, J., Ganzel, B., Henderson, C. R., Smith, E., Olds, D., Powers, J., … Sidora, K. (2000). Preventing child abuse and neglect with a program of nurse home visitation: The limiting effects of domestic violence. *Journal of the American Medical Association, 284,* 1385–1391.

Edelman, L. (2004). A relationship-based approach to early intervention. *Resources and Connections, 3*(2), 2–10.

Eisen, S. V., Dill, D. L., & Grob, M. C. (1994). Reliability and validity of a brief patient-report instrument for psychiatric outcome evaluation. *Hospital and Community Psychiatry, 45*(3), 242–247.

Epstein, R. (1999). Mindful practice. *Journal of the American Medical Association, 282,* 833–839.

Farmer, E. M. Z., Angold, A., Burns, B. J., & Costello, E. J. (1994). Reliability of self-reported service use: Test-retest consistency of children's responses to the Child and Adolescent Services Assessment (CASA). *Journal of Child and Family Studies, 3,* 307–325.

Felitti, V. J., Anda, R. F., Nordenberg, D., Williamson, D. F., Spitz, A. M., Edwards, V., et al. (1998). The relationship of adult health status to childhood abuse and household dysfunction. *American Journal of Preventive Medicine, 14,* 245–258.

Fisher L. D., Dixon, D. O., Herson, J., Frankowski, R. K., Hearon, M. S., & Pearce, K. E. (1990). Intention to treat in clinical trials. In K. E. Pearce (Ed.), *Statistical issues in drug research and development* (pp. 331–350). New York: Marcel Dekker.

Foege, W. H. (1998). Adverse childhood experiences: A public health perspective (editorial). *American Journal of Preventive Medicine, 14,* 354–355.

Gomby, D. (2005). Home visitation in 2005: Outcomes for children and parents. *Invest in Kids Working Paper No. 7.*

Gomby, D. S., Culross, P. L., & Behrman, R. E. (1999). Home visiting: Recent program evaluations. *The Future of Children, 9*(1), 4–26.

Heim, C., Ehlert, U., & Hellhammer, D. H. (2000). The potential role of hypocortisolism in the pathophysiology of stress-related bodily disorders. *Psychoneuroendocrinology, 25,* 1–35.

Hornstein, J., O'Brien, M., & Stadtler, A. (1997). Touchpoints practice: Lessons learned from training and implementation. *Zero to Three, 17*(6), 26–33.

Kalmanson, B., & Seligman, S. (1992). Family-provider relationships: The basis of all interventions. *Infants & Young Children, 4*(4), 46–52.

Kitzman, H., Olds, D., Sidora, K., Henderson, C. R., Hanks, C., Cole, R., … Glazner, J. (2000). Enduring effects of nurse home visitation on maternal life course: A 3-year follow-up of a randomized trial. *Journal of the American Medical Association, 283*(12), 1983–1989.

Korfmacher, J., O'Brien, R., Hiatt, R., & Olds, D. (1999). Differences in program implementation between nurses and paraprofessionals in prenatal and infancy home visitation: A randomized trial. *American Journal of Public Health, 89*(12), 1847–1851.

Lieberman, A. F., & Pawl, J. H. (1993). Infant–parent psychotherapy. In C. Zeanah (Ed.), *Handbook of infant mental health* (pp. 477–484). New York: The Guilford Press.

Lussier, M., & Richard, C. (2007). Feeling understood: Expression of empathy during medical consultations. *Canadian Family Physician, 53*(5), 640–641.

Morisset, C. (1994). What the teaching scale measures. In G. Sumner and A. Spietz (Eds.), *NCAST caregiver–child interaction teaching manuals* (pp. 102–130). Seattle: NCAST Publications, University of Washington.

Olds, D. (1997). The prenatal early infancy project: Preventing child abuse and neglect in the context of promoting maternal and child health. In D. A. Wolfe, R. J. McMahon, & R. D. V. Peters (Eds.), *Child abuse: New directions in prevention and treatment across the lifespan* (pp. 130–154). Thousand Oaks, CA: Sage Publications.

Olds, D. (2002). Prenatal and infancy home visiting by nurses: From randomized trials to community replication. *Prevention Science, 3*(3), 153–172.

Olds, D., Henderson, C. Jr., Cole, R., Eckenrode, J., Kitzman, H., & Luckey, D. (1998). Long-term effects of nurse home visitation on children's criminal and antisocial behavior: 15–year follow up of a randomized trial. *Journal of the American Medical Association, 280*(14), 1238–1244.

Olds, D., Hill, P. L., O'Brien, R., Racine, D., & Moritz, P. (2003). Taking preventive intervention to scale: The nurse–family partnership. *Cognitive & Behavioral Practice, 10*(4), 278–290.

Olds, D. L., Kitzman, H., Cole, R., Robinson, J., Sidora, K., Luckey, D. W., et al. (2004). Effects of nurse home-visiting on maternal life course and child development: Age 6 follow-up results of a randomized trial. *Pediatrics, 114*(6), 1550–1559.

Olds, D., Robinson, J., O'Brien, R., Luckey, D. W., Pettitt, L. M., Henderson, C. R., et al. (2002). Home visiting by nurses and by paraprofessionals: A randomized, controlled trial. *Pediatrics, 110*(3), 486–496.

Safran, D. G., Miller, W., & Beckman, H. (2006). Organizational dimensions of relationship-centered care: Theory, evidence and practice. *Journal of General Internal Medicine, 21*(1), 9–15.

Suchman, A. (2006). A new theoretical foundation for relationship-centered care complex responsive process of relating. *Journal of General Internal Medicine, 21*, 540–545.

Sumner, G., & Spietz, A. (Eds.) (1994). *NCAST caregiver/parent–child feeding manual.* Seattle: NCAST Publications, University of Washington.

Sweet, M. A., & Appelbaum, M. I. (2004). Is home visiting an effective strategy? A meta-analytic review of home visiting programs for families with young children. *Child Development, 75*(5), 1435–1456.

Weiss, J., & Wagner, S. H. (1998). What explains the negative consequences of adverse childhood experiences on adult health? Insights from cognitive and neuroscience research (Editorial). *American Journal of Preventive Medicine, 14,* 356–360.

Weston, D., Ivins, B., Heffron, M., & Sweet, N. (1997). Formulating the centrality of relationships in early intervention: An organizational perspective. *Infants & Young Children, 9*(3), 1–12.

Wissow, L., Larson, S., Anderson, J., & Hadjiisky, E. (2005). Pediatric residents' responses that discourage discussion of psychosocial problems in primary care. *Pediatrics, 115,* 1569–1578.

Zuckerman, B., & Brazelton, T. B. (1994). Strategies for a family-supportive child health care system. In S. L. Kagan, & B. Weissbourd, B. (Eds.), *Putting families first: America's family support movement and the challenge of change* (pp. 114–132). San Francisco: Jossey-Bass.

17

The Nurse–Family Partnership

David L. Olds

Pregnancy and the early years of children's lives are an opportune time to prevent a host of adverse maternal and child outcomes that are important in their own right, but that also have significant implications for the development and prevention of maladaptive behaviors, including crime. Over the past 30 years, our team of investigators has been involved in developing and testing a program of prenatal and infancy home visiting by nurses aimed at improving the health of mothers and children and their future life prospects, known as the Nurse–Family Partnership (NFP).

Theory-driven

The NFP is grounded in theories of human ecology (Bronfenbrenner, 1979, 1995), self-efficacy (Bandura, 1977), and human attachment (Bowlby, 1969). These theories emphasize the importance of families' social context and individuals' beliefs, motivations, emotions, and internal representations of their experience in explaining development. In attachment theory, infants are biologically predisposed to seek proximity to specific caregivers in times of stress, illness, or fatigue in order to promote survival (Bowlby, 1969). Children's trust in the world and their later capacity for empathy and responsiveness to their own children is influenced by the degree to which they formed an attachment with a caring, responsive, and sensitive adult when they were growing up. This affects both their internal representations of themselves and their relationships with others (Main, Kaplan, & Cassidy, 1985).

In designing the parenting component of the program, we relied significantly on the wisdom and brilliant insights of T. Berry Brazelton and followed his advice to help parents anticipate and tune into their babies' temperamental characteristics and competencies as a way of helping

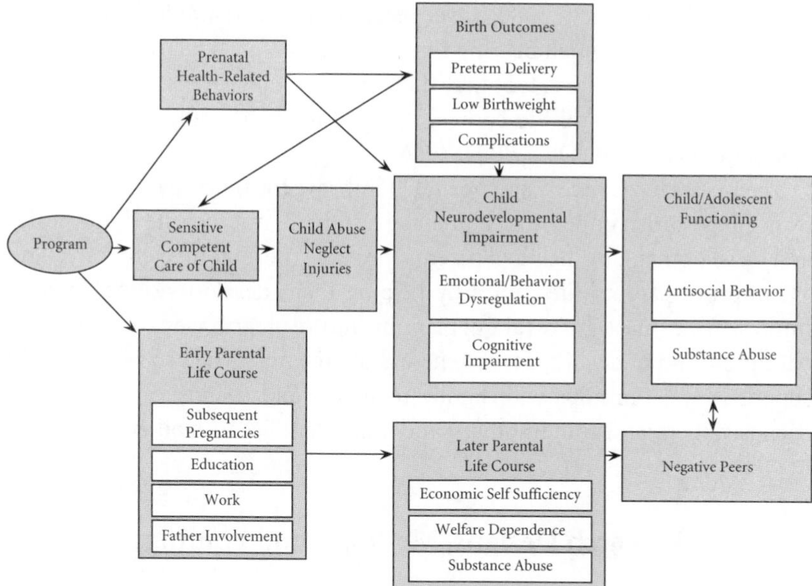

Figure 17.1 General conceptual model of Nurse–Family Partnership Program influences on maternal and child health and development

them engage with and tune into their babies' communicative signaling (Brazelton, 1969). We used the Brazelton Neonatal Behavioral Assessment Scale to help parents develop a sense of joy in observing their newborns' competencies. These parenting behaviors at the very earliest stages of development were expected to help infants develop trust that their parents would meet their needs, increasing the infants' security of attachment.

To help set the stage for parents' accurately reading and responding sensitively to their babies communications, the nurses encourage mothers and other caregivers to review their own child-rearing histories and make decisions about how they wish to care for their children in light of the way they were cared for as children. Finally, the visitors seek to develop an empathic and trusting relationship with the mother and other family members because experience in such a relationship is expected to help women eventually trust others and to promote more sensitive, empathic care of their children (Figure 17.1).

Nurses enroll low-income mothers having their first births, including adolescent and unmarried women. They have higher rates of the problems the program was designed to address (e.g., poor birth outcomes, child abuse and neglect, and diminished parental economic self-sufficiency)

(Elster & McAnarney, 1980; Overpeck, Brenner, Trumble, Trifiletti, & Berendes, 1998). Women bearing first children are particularly receptive to this service and, to the extent that they improve their prenatal health, care of their firstborns, and life-course, they are likely to apply those skills to subsequent children (Olds, 2002, 2006).

The nurses have three major goals: (1) improve the outcomes of pregnancy by helping women improve their prenatal health; (2) improve the child's health and development by helping parents provide more competent care; and (3) improve parents' life-course by helping them develop visions for their futures, make smart choices about planning future pregnancies, complete their education, and find work. Toward these goals, the nurses helped women build supportive relationships with family members and friends, especially boyfriends, fathers, and grandmothers; and linked families with other services.

Research Designs, Methods, and Findings

We conducted three trials in which women were randomized to receive either home visitation services or comparison services. While the nature of the home-visitation services was essentially the same in each trial, the comparison services were slightly different. The Elmira sample (n=400) was primarily white. The Memphis sample (n=1138 for pregnancy and 743 for the infancy phase) was primarily black. The Denver trial (n=735) was primarily Hispanic and examined the impact of the program when delivered by paraprofessionals (who shared many of the social characteristics of the families they served) and by nurses. Unless otherwise stated, all findings reported below were statistically significant ($p \leq .05$).

Elmira Results

Prenatal health behaviors

During pregnancy, nurse-visited women improved the quality of their diets to a greater extent, and those identified as smokers smoked 25 percent fewer cigarettes by the 34th week of pregnancy than controls (Olds, Henderson, Tatelbaum, & Chamberlin, 1986). By the end of pregnancy, nurse-visited women experienced greater informal social support and made better use of formal community services.

Pregnancy and birth outcomes

By the end of pregnancy, nurse-visited women had fewer kidney infections, and among women who smoked those who were nurse-visited had 75 percent fewer preterm deliveries, while among very young adolescents (aged 14–16), those who were nurse-visited had babies who were 395 grams heavier than controls (Olds, Henderson, Tatelbaum, & Chamberlin, 1986).

Sensitive, competent care of child

At child age 10 and 22 months, nurse-visited poor, unmarried teens, exhibited less punishment and restriction of their infants and provided more appropriate play materials than controls (Olds, Henderson, Chamberlin, & Tatelbaum, 1986). At 34 and 46 months of the babies' lives, nurse-visited mothers provided home environments that were more conducive to their children's emotional and cognitive development and that were safer (Olds, Henderson, & Kitzman, 1994).

Child abuse, neglect, and injuries

At child age 2, nurse-visited children born to low-income, unmarried teens had fewer verified cases of child abuse and neglect than controls (1 case or 4% of the nurse-visited teens, versus 8 cases or 19% of controls, p=.07). Nurse-visited children were also seen in the emergency department 32% fewer times, due in part to a 56% reduction in visits for injuries and ingestions. These effects of the program on child abuse and neglect and emergency department encounters were greatest among children whose mothers had little belief in their control over their lives when they registered for the program. These findings deepened our conviction that the nurses' emphasis on supporting women's development of self-efficacy was crucial.

Two years after the program ended, its impact on healthcare encounters for injuries endured: irrespective of risk, children of nurse-visited women were less likely than controls to receive emergency room treatment and visit a physician for injuries and ingestions (Olds, Henderson, & Kitzman, 1994). The impact of the program on state-verified cases of child abuse and neglect disappeared during that time (Olds, Henderson, & Kitzman, 1994), probably because of increased detection of child abuse and neglect in nurse-visited families and nurses' linkage of families with needed services (Olds, Henderson, Kitzman, & Cole, 1995).

A 15-year follow-up of the Elmira sample (Olds et al., 1997) showed that the group differences in rates of state-verified reports of child abuse and neglect grew between the child age 4 and 15. Compared to controls, those visited by nurses during pregnancy and infancy were identified as perpetrators of child abuse and neglect in an average of 0.29 versus 0.54 verified reports per program participant, an effect that was greater for women who were poor and unmarried (Olds et al., 1997).

Early parental life-course

By four years, nurse-visited low-income, unmarried women had fewer subsequent pregnancies, longer intervals between births of first and second children, and greater participation in the work force than controls (Olds et al., 1988).

Later parental life-course

At the 15-year follow-up, poor, unmarried women visited by nurses had fewer pregnancies, fewer births, longer intervals between the birth of their first and second children, fewer months on welfare or receiving food stamps, fewer behavioral problems due to substance abuse, and fewer arrests than controls (Olds et al., 1997).

Child/adolescent functioning

Fifteen-year-old children visited by nurses had fewer arrests and adjudications as Persons in Need of Supervision. These effects were greater for children born to mothers who were poor and unmarried. Nurse-visited children also reported fewer sexual partners and fewer convictions and violations of probation.

Memphis Results

Prenatal health behaviors

By the 36th week of pregnancy, nurse-visited women were more likely to use other community services than were controls.

Pregnancy and birth outcomes

Nurse-visited women had fewer instances of pregnancy-induced hypertension and nurse-visited cases were less serious than controls (Kitzman et al., 1997).

Sensitive, competent care of child

Nurse-visited mothers attempted breastfeeding more frequently than controls. By child age 24 months, nurse-visited women held fewer beliefs about child rearing associated with child abuse and neglect than controls. Moreover, the homes of nurse-visited women were rated as more conducive to children's development. Children born to nurse-visited mothers with low levels of psychological resources were more communicative and responsive toward their mothers than controls (Kitzman et al., 1997).

Child abuse, neglect, injuries, and death

The rate of child abuse and neglect in the two-year-old, low-income children in Memphis was too low (3–4%) to serve as a valid indicator of child maltreatment. During their first two years, compared to controls, nurse-visited children had 23% fewer healthcare encounters for injuries and ingestions and were hospitalized for 79% fewer days with injuries and/or ingestions, effects that were more pronounced for children born to mothers with few psychological resources. Nurse-visited children were older when hospitalized and had less severe conditions. Reasons for hospitalizations suggest that many of the comparison-group children suffered from more seriously deficient care than children visited by nurses. We (Olds et al., 2007) also found that by child age 9 nurse-visited children were less likely to have died than controls (p=.08). The rates of death were 4.5 times higher in the control group than in the group visited by nurses.

Child neurodevelopmental impairment

By age 6, compared to controls, children visited by nurses had higher intellectual functioning and receptive vocabulary scores and fewer behavior problems. Nurse-visited children born to mothers with low psychological resources had higher arithmetic achievement test scores and expressed less aggression and incoherence in response to stories. By age 9, nurse-visited children born to mothers with low psychological resources had higher grade point averages in reading and math than controls (Olds et al., 2007).

Early parental life-course

At child age 2, nurse-visited women reported fewer second pregnancies and fewer subsequent live births than controls. Nurse-visited women and their firstborn children relied upon welfare for fewer months than controls (Kitzman et al., 1997).

Later parental life-course

At child age 4½, compared to controls, women visited by nurses had fewer subsequent pregnancies, fewer therapeutic abortions, and longer durations between the birth of the first and second child; fewer total person-months using welfare and food stamps; higher rates of living with a partner and living with the biological father of the child; and partners who had been employed for longer durations (Kitzman et al., 2000). By child age 6, women visited by nurses continued to have fewer subsequent pregnancies and births; longer intervals between births of first and second children; longer relationships with current partners; and, since last follow-up at 4½, fewer months using welfare and food stamps. They also were more likely to register their children in formal out-of-home care between age 2 and 4½ (Olds, Kitzman, et al., 2004). At child age 9, nurse-visited women continued to have longer intervals between the births of first and second children, fewer cumulative subsequent births, and longer relationships with their partners. Nurse-visited women continued to use welfare and food stamps for fewer months (Olds et al., 2007).

Denver Results

In the Denver trial, we were unable to use the women's or children's medical records to assess their health. Moreover, the rate of state-verified reports of child abuse and neglect was too low to use Child Protective Service records to assess the impact of the program on child maltreatment.

Denver Results for Paraprofessionals

There were no paraprofessional effects on women's prenatal health behavior (use of tobacco), maternal life-course, or child development, although at 24 months, paraprofessional-visited mother–child pairs in which the mother had low psychological resources interacted more responsively than controls. While paraprofessional-visited women did not have statistically significant reductions in the rates of subsequent pregnancy, the reductions observed were clinically significant (Olds et al., 2002). By child age 4, mothers and children visited by paraprofessionals, compared to controls, displayed greater sensitivity and responsiveness toward one another and, in those cases in which the mothers had low psychological resources, home environments were more supportive of children's early learning. Children of low-resource women visited by paraprofessionals had better behavioral adaptation during testing than their control-group counterparts (Olds, Robinson, et al., 2004).

Denver Results for Nurses

Prenatal health behaviors

Nurse-visited smokers had greater reductions in urine cotinine (the major nicotine metabolite) from intake to the end of pregnancy than controls (Olds et al., 2002).

Sensitive, competent care of child

By child age 2, nurse-visited mother–infant dyads interacted more responsively than control dyads, an effect concentrated in the low-resource group. As trends, nurse-visited mothers provided home environments that were more supportive of children's early learning (Olds et al., 2002).

Child neurodevelopmental impairment

At child age 6 months, nurse-visited infants were less likely to exhibit emotional vulnerability in response to fear stimuli than controls and those born to women with low psychological resources were less likely to display low emotional vitality in response to joy and anger stimuli. At 21 months, nurse-visited children were less likely to exhibit language delays than controls, an effect again concentrated among children born to mothers with low psychological resources. Nurse-visited children born to women with low psychological resources also had superior language and mental development (Olds et al., 2002). At child age 4, nurse-visited children whose mothers had low psychological resources had more advanced language, superior executive functioning, and better behavioral adaptation during testing (Olds, Robinson, et al., 2004).

Early maternal life-course

By 24 months after delivery, nurse-visited women, compared to controls, had fewer subsequent pregnancies and birth with longer intervals between the birth of the first child and the next conception. Women visited by nurses were employed longer during the second year following the birth of their first child than controls (Olds et al., 2002). By child age 4, nurse-visited women continued to have greater intervals between the birth of their first and second children, less domestic violence, and enrolled their children less frequently in either preschool, Head Start, or licensed day care than controls (Olds, Robinson, et al., 2004).

Cost Savings

The Washington State Institute for Public Policy conducted an economic analysis of prevention programs from the standpoint of their impact on crime, substance abuse, educational outcomes, teen pregnancy, suicide, child abuse and neglect, and domestic violence (Aos, Lieb, Mayfield, Miller, & Pennucci, 2004). This report sums the findings across all three trials of the NFP and estimates that it saves $17,000 per family. This estimate is consistent with a subsequent analysis produced by the Rand Corporation (Karoly, Kilburn, & Cannon, 2005).

Policy Implications and Program Replication

One of the clearest messages from this research is that the functional and economic benefits of the NFP are greatest for families at greater risk. For this reason, we recommend that these precious resources be focused on those populations living in concentrated social disadvantage. Since 1996, the NFP national office has helped new communities develop the program outside of traditional research contexts so that today the program is operating in 380 counties in the United States, serving over 186,000 families per day. State and local governments are securing financial support for the NFP (about $11,000 per family for 2½ years of services, in 2008 dollars) out of existing sources of funds, such as Temporary Assistance to Needy Families, Medicaid, the Maternal and Child Health Block-Grant, and child-abuse and crime-prevention dollars.

Each site choosing to implement the NFP needs certain capacities to operate and sustain the program with high quality. These capacities include having an organization and community that are fully knowledgeable and supportive of the program; a staff that is well trained and supported in the conduct of the program model; and real-time information on implementation of the program and its achievement of benchmarks to guide efforts in continuous quality improvement. Staff members at the NFP National Service Office are organized to help create these state and local capacities.

Our approach to international replication of the program is to make no assumptions about its possible benefits in societies that have different health and human service delivery systems and cultures than those in which the program was tested in the United States. Given this, our team has taken the position that the program ought to be adapted and tested in other societies before it is offered for public investment. We currently are working with partners in England, Holland, Germany, Australia, and Canada to adapt the program with disadvantaged populations in those societies and to support the planning of randomized controlled trials of the program conducted by independent evaluators.

References

Aos, S., Lieb, R., Mayfield, J., Miller, M., & Pennucci, A. (2004). *Benefits and costs of prevention and early intervention programs for youth*. Olympia, WA: Washington State Institute for Public Policy.

Bandura, A. (1977). Self-efficacy: Toward a unifying theory of behavioral change. *Psychological Review, 84*, 191–215.

Bowlby, J. (1969). *Attachment and loss: Attachment* (Vol. 1). New York: Basic Books.

Brazelton, T. B. (1969). *Infants and mothers: Differences in development*. New York: Dell Publishing.

Bronfenbrenner, U. (1979). *The ecology of human development: Experiments by nature and design*. Cambridge, MA: Harvard University Press.

Bronfenbrenner, U. (1995). Developmental ecology through space and time: A future perspective. In P. Moen, G. H. J. Elder, & K. Luscher (Eds.), *Examining lives in context*. Washington, DC: American Psychological Association.

Elster, A. B., & McAnarney, E. R. (1980). Medical and psychosocial risks of pregnancy and childbearing during adolescence. *Pediatric Annals, 9*, 89–94.

Karoly, L. A., Kilburn, M. R., & Cannon, J. S. (2005). *Early childhood interventions: Proven results, future promise*. Santa Monica, CA: Rand.

Kitzman, H., Olds, D. L., Henderson, C. R. Jr., Hanks, C., Cole, R., Tatelbaum, R., … Barnard, K. (1997). Effect of prenatal and infancy home visitation by nurses on pregnancy outcomes, childhood injuries, and repeated childbearing: A randomized controlled trial. *Journal of the American Medical Association, 278*, 644–652.

Kitzman, H., Olds, D. L., Sidora, K., Henderson C. R. Jr., Hanks, C., Cole, R., … Glazner, J. (2000). Enduring effects of nurse home visitation on maternal life course: A 3-year follow-up of a randomized trial. *Journal of the American Medical Association, 283*, 1983–1989.

Main, M., Kaplan, N., & Cassidy, J. (1985). Security in infancy, childhood, and adulthood: A move to the level of representation. *Monographs of the Society for Research in Child Development, 50*, 66–104.

Olds, D. L. (2002). Prenatal and infancy home visiting by nurses: From randomized trials to community replication. *Prevention Science, 3*, 153–172.

Olds, D. L. (2006). The Nurse–Family Partnership: An evidence-based preventive intervention. *Infant Mental Health Journal, 27*, 5–25.

Olds, D. L., Eckenrode, J., Henderson, C. R. Jr., Kitzman, H., Powers, J., Cole, R., … Luckey, D. (1997). Long-term effects of home visitation on maternal life course and child abuse and neglect: Fifteen-year follow-up of a randomized trial. *Journal of the American Medical Association, 278*, 637–643.

Olds, D. L, Henderson, C. R. Jr., Chamberlin, R., & Tatelbaum, R. (1986). Preventing child abuse and neglect: A randomized trial of nurse home visitation. *Pediatrics, 78*, 65–78.

Olds, D. L., Henderson, C. R. Jr., & Kitzman, H. (1994). Does prenatal and infancy nurse home visitation have enduring effects on qualities of parental caregiving and child health at 25 to 50 months of life? *Pediatrics, 93*, 89–98.

Olds, D., Henderson, C., Kitzman, H., & Cole, R. (1995). Effects of prenatal and infancy nurse home visitation on surveillance of child maltreatment. *Pediatrics, 95*, 365–372.

Olds, D. L., Henderson, C. R. Jr., Tatelbaum, R., & Chamberlin, R. (1986). Improving the delivery of prenatal care and outcomes of pregnancy: A randomized trial of nurse home visitation. *Pediatrics, 77*, 16–28.

Olds, D. L., Henderson, C. R. J., Tatelbaum, R., & Chamberlin, R. (1988). Improving the life-course development of socially disadvantaged mothers: a randomized trial of nurse home visitation. *American Journal of Public Health, 78*, 1436–1445.

Olds, D. L., Kitzman, H., Cole, R., Robinson, J., Sidora, K., Luckey, D., … Holmberg, J. (2004). Effects of nurse home visiting on maternal life-course and child development: age-six follow-up of a randomized trial. *Pediatrics, 114*, 1550–1559.

Olds, D. L., Kitzman, H., Hanks, C., Cole, R., Anson, E., Sidora-Arcoleo, K., … Bondy, J. (2007). Effects of nurse home visiting on maternal and child functioning: Age-9 follow-up of a randomized trial. *Pediatrics, 120*, e832–845.

Olds, D. L., Robinson J., O'Brien, R., Luckey, D. W., Pettitt, L. M., Henderson C. R. Jr., … Talmi, A. (2002). Home visiting by paraprofessionals and by nurses: a randomized, controlled trial. *Pediatrics, 110*, 486–496.

Olds, D. L., Robinson, J., Pettitt, L., Luckey, D. W., Holmberg, J., Ng, R. K., Isacks, K., & Sheff, K. (2004). Effects of home visits by paraprofessionals and by nurses: Age-four follow-up of a randomized trial. *Pediatrics, 114*, 1560–1568.

Overpeck, M. D., Brenner, R. A., Trumble, A. C., Trifiletti L. B., Berendes, H. W. (1998). Risk factors for infant homicide in the United States. *New England Journal of Medicine, 339*, 1211–1216.

Section II

Early Interventions
The Care of Infants Born Preterm

18

Advances in the Understanding and Care of the Preterm Infant

Heidelise Als

"Paradigm changes cause scientists to see the world differently. . . . After a revolution scientists are responding to a different world." (Kuhn, 1970)

Introduction

T. Berry Brazelton has inspired several generations of scientists to ask new and different questions about infants, parents, their relationship to one another, and their place in the world. His revolutionary approach to understanding newborn behavior has uncovered urgent questions and exciting potential for the care of preterm infants.

About 13 million preterm deliveries occur worldwide annually, while survival rates have dramatically increased for very low and extremely low birth weight infants. More than 95% of infants born before 28 weeks gestation, 12 weeks too early, and under 1250 g, survive. Previously it was believed that in the absence of major complications these children would "catch up." Recent research suggests, however, that preterm-born infants remain and often become increasingly disadvantaged on many measures of neuro-integrative functioning. They show difficulties in terms of academic achievement, behavior regulation, social and emotional adaptation, and visual-motor integration.

This chapter presents a neurodevelopmental framework for understanding preterm infants' individual development, and the effects of individualized developmentally supportive care on their outcomes, as well as implications for system change and staff training and support that derive from these new insights. Building on Brazelton's newborn research, developmental psychology studies have shown that very immature infants are complex, responsive, active and goal-oriented in eliciting social and sensory stimulation, and in their attempts to regulate their own thresholds of reaction and response. Expanding the reach of Brazelton's Neonatal Behavioral Assessment Scale (Brazelton, 1973), innovative specialized assessments such as the Assessment of Preterm Infants' Behavior (APIB) (Als, Lester, Tronick, & Brazelton, 1982a, 1982b) help identify even very preterm-born newborns' strengths, vulnerabilities, and goals, and contribute to individualized, developmental care plans for them.

The Preterm Infant, a Displaced Fetus

Neurodevelopmental framework

Preterm infants are fetuses who develop in extrauterine settings during a period when their brains are growing more rapidly than at any other time. They require care that is available only in the specialized, medical technological environments of modern newborn intensive care units (NICU) and special care nurseries (SCN). Yet, in these environments, procedures that assure their survival put preterm infants at risk for significant organ damage, including bronchopulmonary dysplasia (BPD), intraventricular hemorrhage (IVH), retinopathy of prematurity (ROP), and necrotizing enterocolitis (NEC). The mismatch of the fetal brain and the characteristics of the intensive care nursery pose significant challenges for the immature infant's development, significantly altering neurostructural, neurophysiological, and neuropsychological development.

Fetal infants expect to experience continual sensory and kinesthetic input from the amniotic fluid and the continuously reactive amniotic sac which provide for appropriate intrauterine tactile, olfactory, gustatory and motor system development. They expect maternal diurnal and hormonal rhythms, which provide appropriate state differentiation and regulation. Sensory experiences that were expected to occur in a scaffolded timeline have been abruptly removed. Parental development is also suddenly disrupted. These challenges lead to increased developmental difficulties later on, including learning disabilities, lowered intelligence quotients, executive function and attention deficit disorders, lower thresholds to fatigue, visual motor impairments, spatial and computational processing disturbances, language comprehension and speech problems, emotional vulnerabilities, and difficulties with self-regulation and self-esteem. These result in significant school performance deficits in more than 50 percent of preterm-born children (Hack et al., 2005; Saigal et al., 2006). Improving conditions in neonatal intensive care units for the brain development of these fragile infants becomes a critical endeavor.

The importance of brain–environment interaction

Each of the millions of cerebral cortex neurons originates in the germinal lining of the ventricular system and migrates in waves through the entire thickness of cortex. Migrational waves begin at around eight postovulatory weeks and tail off around 24 weeks of pregnancy, when neuronal maturation increases dramatically and continues to burgeon for preterm infants in the interaction with the extrauterine rather than intrauterine environment. Each of the estimated total 100 billion neurons, once migrated to their respective locations, develops dendritic and axonal interconnections with an average of 100 other cells, beginning as early as 7 weeks. A marked increase in the number of gyri occurs at the end of the second trimester, when fetal behavior becomes increasingly complex with increased sucking on fingers and hands, grasping, extension, and flexion rotations, increasingly discernible sleep and wake periods, and reactions to sound.

Special cells, oligodendrocytes, grow and deposit myelin, a fatty sheath around the axons that allows for fast conduction, accommodating growing neuronal tracks and speeding up processing time. Myelination occurs with peak activity around fullterm birth. Concurrent with the processes of cell differentiation and myelination, neurobehavioral differentiation and neurochemical development occur. The sensitivities and densities of neurotransmitter receptors vary widely from brain region to region, changing over time, influenced by experience.

Structural and functional development of brain and sensory organs are interactive and interdependent. Animal models have provided substantial evidence for the fine-tuned specificity of environmental inputs necessary for normal cortical ontogenesis in the course of sensitive periods of brain development. Differential cell death and other regressive events, which begin around 24 weeks gestation, are also of key importance in sculpting developing cortex. The developmental timeline of these regressive events causes them to be directly affected by premature birth. The frontal cortex subplate neuron layer, strongly involved in cerebral cortical organization, reaches its peak at 32–34 weeks of gestation, when preterm infants experience unexpected sensory inputs, which reach primary cortical areas. Preterm infants' still fused or closed eyelids are very thin and highly light permeable, and do not protect visual cortex from light stimulation. Somatosensory and auditory cortices receive inputs that are modified considerably from those that would have been received in the womb.

The NICU environment, despite its advances, continues to be a grossly inadequate substitute for the well-functioning human womb. The NICU involves massive sensory overload in modalities including touch, smell, taste, sound, and light, yet lacks regulatory input that the fetal brain relies on, such as the fluid environment, the amniotic sac wall, and maternal hormonal inputs. The NICU is mismatched to the developing nervous system's expectations. Messages transmitted from primary cortical regions to other cortical areas, including prefrontal cortex, are probably quite different for the preterm infant in the NICU than for the fetus in the womb. It is likely that subplate neuron activity and regressive events (cell death) are modified when the fetal brain finds itself in unusual sensory circumstances, such as occur outside the womb; cells may be preserved that otherwise would be eliminated, and cells may be eliminated that would otherwise be preserved. Monkeys experimentally delivered prematurely show significantly different cortical synapse formations in terms of size, type, and laminar distribution as compared with fullterm monkeys tested at comparable postterm ages. The extent of difference correlates with the degree of prematurity. While some events influence neuronal migration per se, other events, including differences in sensory input, appear to alter cortico-cortical connectivities and lead to unique cyto- and chemo-architectures of cerebral cortex. This supports the finding that preterm infants show brain-based differences in neurofunctional performance due to difference in experience. Premature activation of cortical pathways appears to inhibit later differentiations and to interfere with appropriate development and sculpting, especially of cross-modal and prefrontal connection systems implicated in complex mental processing, as well as attention processes and self-regulation.

Differences between preterm and fullterm infants

Differences between preterm-born and fullterm infants are manifest in all aspects of neurodevelopment, such as neurobehavior, neurophysiology, and neurostructure.

Neurobehavioral differences From the very beginning of extrauterine life, the newborn is launched onto the species, specific, interactive, collaborative, and communicative track, which is supported and affectively rewarded by the caregiver. Newborn interactive attention appears to be of high species value. Parents are keen to elicit and support their newborn infant's alertness. Yet preterm infants tend to be too immature to reciprocate the preterm parents' intuitive expectations for social interaction.

Infants born early often show great reluctance to come into alertness. They may demonstrate hypertonic, defensive high guard arm positions with fisted hands, become pale, breathe rapidly and unsteadily, and show pained, drawn facial expressions. With slow, calm support they may gradually open their eyes. At the same time the defensive posture may shift abruptly into flaccidity and tuning out. The infant may pale, and breathe slowly and unsteadily. The attention will likely be glassy-eyed, strained, and barely focused. The pattern of poor subsystem differentiation exemplifies the overall cost for even a small accomplishment, such as eye opening. Measurement of subsystem involvement in specific performances is important in understanding an infant's current competence and developmental trajectory.

The APIB is a comprehensive newborn behavioral assessment that grew out of the Brazelton Neonatal Behavioral Assessment Scale. Numerous studies have demonstrated the APIB's sensitivity in differentiating subgroups of infants of varying gestational ages and risk degree status. The APIB also detects developmental differences between medically low-risk infants born at varying gestational ages, and it provides significant information for clinical care and support.

EEG measures validate APIB results, as do magnetic resonance imaging (MRI) findings (Als et al., 2004; Duffy, Als, & McAnulty, 2003). Preterm and fullterm infants differ in unmyelinated as well as myelinated white matter at term. The investigators also report preterm reduction in myelination and gray-white matter differentiation as well as poorer performance on six out of six APIB system scores when compared to fullterms (Hüppi et al., 1996). Fetal growth restricted (FGR) preterm infants at term compared to appropriately grown (AGA) preterm infants at term (Zimine, Lazeyras, Henry, Borradori-Tolsa, & Hüppi, 2002) displayed poorer MRI-based neurostructural and poorer APIB neurofunctional measures.

The brain differences between preterm and fullterm infants continue into school age. Brain imaging studies show generalized thinning of *corpus callosum* in association with word production difficulties and clumsiness (Peterson et al., 2000). Significant volume reduction has also been observed in basal ganglia, amygdala, and hippocampus, and found to correlate with reduction in Full-Scale IQ. A volumetric comparison study of very preterm- and fullterm-born adolescents identified significant cerebellar volume reduction for the preterm-born children (Constable et al., 2008). Cognitive test scores showed strong association with cerebellar volume reduction, likely due to the many reciprocal connections between the cerebellum and other brain areas.

Improving the future for infants born preterm Given the significant differences between preterm and fullterm infants at comparable post-menstrual ages, the challenge is to reduce the discrepancy of the NICU experience and the immature brain's expectation.

Behavior: reliable route to understanding the infant

Infant behavior is the always observable route to understanding infant well-being and brain function. Underlying the developing nervous system's striving for integration is the tension between two basic antagonists of behavior, the exploratory and the avoiding (Denny-Brown, 1962). When the two dimensions are released simultaneously they are in conflict with one another. If a threshold of organization-appropriate stimulation is surpassed, one dimension may abruptly switch into the other. The two dimensions are basic to all functioning, as basic as the cellular level. For instance, upon stimulation, complex single cells in somatosensory cortex produce total body-toward or total body-avoidance movements. The principle of dual antagonist integration is helpful when assessing preterm infants' behavioral thresholds from integration to stress. In the well-integrated performance, the two antagonists of toward and away modulate one another and bring about an adaptive response. When an input is compelling, the infant will approach the input, seek it out, and become sensitized to and receptive for it. When the input overloads the infant's neuronal network, the infant will defend against it, actively avoid the input, and withdraw from it. The response patterns mutually modulate one another. For instance, the animated face of the interacting caregiver will draw in the fullterm newborn. As the infant's attention intensifies, the infant's eyes may widen, the eyebrows rise, and the mouth shape toward the interactor. The infant's fingers may open and close softly. If dampening processes are poorly developed, as in preterm infants, the whole head may move forward, and arms, legs, fingers, and toes may extend toward the interactor; the mouth may tightly shape forward. With poor subsystem differentiation, the wide-eyed gaze may trigger the visceral system, and the infant may hiccough or vomit. The response, which a fullterm infant will largely confine to face and hands, may generalize to the preterm infant's entire body.

Premature newborns appear to struggle with the differential activation and inhibition of autonomic function, including respiration, heart rate, temperature control, digestion, and elimination, and the autonomic system's integration with the functioning of the motor and state system. Preterm infants' motor systems expect cutaneous input from the amniotic fluid and sac wall, which *in utero* support the development and differentiation of increasing flexor-extensor balance. Preterm infants' state organization, furthermore, expects gating by maternal sleep–wake, rest–activity, and hormonal and nutritional cycles.

The model for the observation and assessment of behavioral subsystem differentiation, termed synactive (Figure 18.1), highlights the simultaneity of the behavioral subsystems in negotiation with one another and with the current environment. The behavioral subsystems continually transform to new levels of more differentiated integration. To paraphrase E. Erikson, self-actualization is participation with the world and interaction with another with a "minimum of defensive maneuvers and a maximum of activation, a minimum of idiosyncratic distortion and a maximum of joint validation" (Erikson, 1962).

The Synactive Theory of Behavioral Organization (Als, 1982) takes into account the dynamic nature of all development as a process of continuous differentiation, integration, and modulation of the interrelationships of behaviorally observable subsystems of function. At each stage of development, various subsystems of functioning exist simultaneously, while they mutually influence one another. Often their functioning is truly interactive. At other times, interactively supportive holding patterns provide a steady multisystem base for one of the subsystem's current further differentiation. The subsystems addressed, as mentioned, include the autonomic, motor, state organization, and attention and interaction subsystems, as

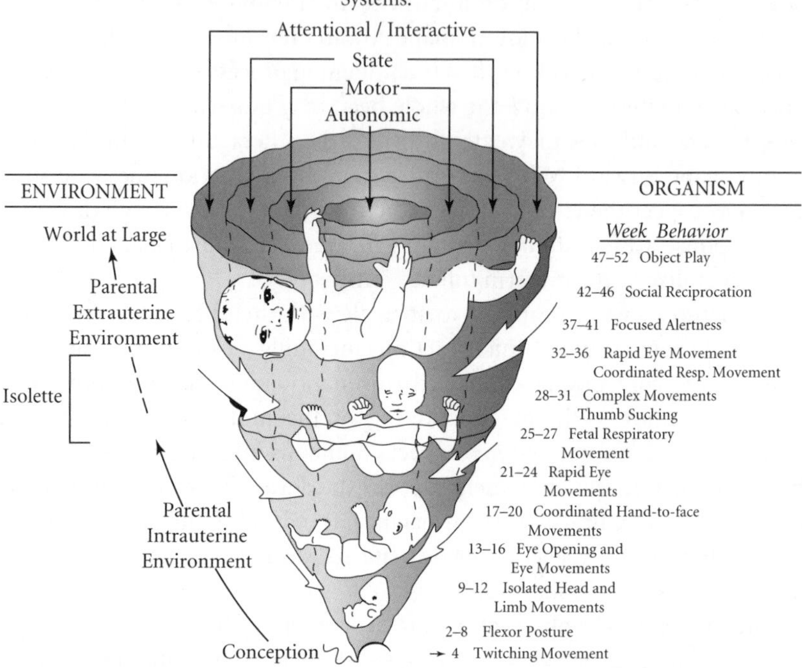

Figure 18.1 Model of Synactive Theory
Source: From H. Als (1982) Toward a synactive theory of development: Promise for the assessment of infant individuality. *Infant Mental Health Journal, 3*, 229–243. Reproduced by permission of The Michigan Association of Infant Mental Health

well as the self-regulation subsystem. A further "system" addressed is the physical and social environment and its role in an infant's successful subsystem reorganization.

Observation of preterm infants' behavior provides a way to infer the infant's current developmental goals and functional competence. Even very early-born infants display reliably observable behaviors along the lines of the three main subsystems, the autonomic, motor, and state systems. The autonomic system's behavioral communication signals include breathing patterns, color fluctuations, and visceral responses such as spitting up, gagging, hiccoughing, bowel movement strains, and actual defecation, among others. The motor system's signals include muscle tone of trunk, extremities, and face with modulation, flaccidity, or hypertonicity; as well as postures and movement patterns, such as finger splays, arching, grimacing, grasping, among others. The state system's signals include the infant's range of states such as sleeping, wakefulness, and aroused upset; the patterns of transition from state to state; and the robustness and modulation of each of the states. Alertness and attention are the further differentiation of the waking state. The self-regulation system's signals are the efforts and successes of the basic systems' interplay in reaching balance and restfulness at the next level of differentiation. These reliably observable behavioral communications provide valuable information for the clinician and caregiver on how to structure and adapt care and interaction to enhance the infant's own competence and strength and to prevent or diminish the infant's signals of stress, discomfort, and/or pain.

The Newborn Individualized Developmental Care and Assessment Program

The Newborn Individualized Developmental Care and Assessment Program (NIDCAP) is an approach to physical and social environmental support and care that is based on continuously reading and adapting to each preterm infant's behavioral cues. Cue reading leads to the formulation of a care plan to enhance and build upon the infant's strengths and support the infant in areas of sensitivity and vulnerability. Typically, the infant is observed for about 20 minutes before a caregiver interacts with the infant, throughout the duration of the caregiving interaction, such as the assessment of the infant's vital signs, suctioning, diaper change, feeding, etc., and for at least 20 minutes after the caregiving interaction as the infant returns to a restful state. These observations, especially when systematically repeated over time, yield much information regarding the infant's robustness and development, current sensitivities and thresholds to stress, and self-regulation. The observations lead to written reports describing infant strengths and efforts (Als, 1999).

Assuring parents' roles as the primary nurturers is crucial to infant developmental outcomes. Parents and infants seek respectful, supportive, professional and consistently nurturing environments in the NICU that help them grow in their roles as competent parents and infants and become well-functioning mutually supportive and trusting families. This requires informed NICU leadership and a well-differentiated communication system assuring privacy yet appropriate collaboration and support for the family in nurturing and caring for their infant and themselves.

The transitions and transformations of the NICU setting necessitated by developmentally supportive care involve systems transformation from a protocol-based to a relationship-based framework of care. Staff must let go of well-practiced conceptualizations and routines and become open to learning and practicing in new ways. The key concept within relationship-based, individualized, developmental care is co-regulation, based in an evolutionary neurobiological understanding of the social, interconnected nature of humans. Implementation of a theory-guided rather than procedurally driven approach is especially challenging in an intensive care setting, oriented toward standards, protocols, strictly enforced rules, and caregiving routines. A co-regulatory framework of care requires that caregivers are mindful of one another, mindful of the personhood of each infant and family member, and of their own actions and ways of being, while functioning effectively in an acute care setting. Reflection as a framework of practice at first may appear foreign and almost subversive to those used to action-driven, intensive, technologically focused care. NIDCAP implementation transforms such care, with time, support, and guidance, into reflective, self-aware practice, coupling superb relational and technical skill.

Empirical evidence for the effectiveness of the NIDCAP

Seven randomized controlled trials (Als et al., 1994, 2003, 2004; Buehler, Als, Duffy, McAnulty, & Liederman, 1995; Fleisher et al., 1995; Maguire et al., 2009; Westrup, Kleberg, von Eichwald, Stjernqvist, & Lagercrantz, 2000) have investigated the NIDCAP model's effectiveness. With exception of one inconclusive trial (Maguire et al., 2009), the studies' results provide consistent evidence of improved lung function, feeding behavior, and growth, reduced length of hospitalization, improved neurobehavioral and neurophysiological functioning and, for infants 28 ≥ 33 weeks gestational age at birth, enhanced brain fiber tract development in frontal lobe and internal capsule. Lower parental stress, enhanced parental competence, and higher infant individualization also have been documented. Several studies have demonstrated significantly better Bayley Mental and Psychomotor Developmental Indices at three, five (Parker, Zahr, Cole, & Brecht, 1992) and nine months (Als et al., 1994) corrected age, along with improved attention, interaction, cognitive planning, affect regulation, fine and gross motor modulation, as well as improved communication. Other results include at three years (Kleberg, Westrup, & Stjernqvist, 2000) better auditory processing and speech, fewer behavior symptoms and better mother–child communication; at six years (Westrup, Böhm, Lagercrantz, & Stjernqvist, 2003), higher survival rates without mental retardation and attention deficits; and at eight years (McAnulty et al., in press), better visual spatial abilities in the respective trials' NIDCAP groups.

System-wide NIDCAP implementation

The NIDCAP approach saves significantly on medical and educational costs, and assures significantly better quality of life for infants and families. NIDCAP training requires up-front financial and time investment that is highly cost- effective in the long run. Documented U.S. care cost reductions range from U.S. $4,000–$12,000 per NIDCAP infant. Infants are released from the intensive (Level-3) care to lower intensity (Level-2) care in significantly fewer days, saving on hospital costs (Fleisher et al., 1995; Petryshen, Stevens, Hawkins, & Stewart, 1997).

Introduction of NIDCAP into a nursery involves system-wide investment not only in education and physical changes but also in transformation of all practice and relationships. Considerable staff education and professional, technical, and emotional support are required. Research has shown that in order to effect reliable behavior change in caregivers, it is critical to provide onsite one-on-one coaching, collaboration, and guidance.

In keeping with and in continuation of Dr. Brazelton's revolutionary approach to understanding newborn, infant, child and family development, NIDCAP emphasizes the preterm infant's behavior as meaningful communication and moves traditional newborn intensive care into a collaborative, relationship-based, neurodevelopmental framework. It leads to respect for infants and families as mutually attuned and invested in one another and as active structurers of their own developments. It sees infants, parents, and professional caregivers engaged in continuous co-regulation with one another, and in turn with their social and physical environments. The approach emphasizes from early on the infant's own strengths and developmental goals and institutes support for the infant's self-regulatory competence and achievement of these goals.

All NICU work involves human interaction at many levels and at the complex interface of physical and emotional vulnerability. At the core is the tiny, immature, fully dependent, highly sensitive, and rapidly developing fetal infant and this infant's hopeful, open, and vulnerable parents, who count on and trust the caregivers' attention and investment. This realization constitutes the challenge and the opportunity of NIDCAP.

References and further reading

Als, H. (1982). Toward a synactive theory of development: Promise for the assessment of infant individuality. *Infant Mental Health Journal, 3*, 229–243.

Als, H. (1999). Reading the premature infant. In E. Goldson (Ed.), *Developmental interventions in the neonatal intensive care nursery* (pp. 18–85). New York: Oxford University Press.

Als, H., Duffy, F. H., McAnulty, G. B., Rivkin, M. J., Vajapeyam, S., Mulkern, R. V., … Eichenwald, E. C. (2004). Early experience alters brain function and structure. *Pediatrics, 113*(4), 846–857.

Als, H., Gilkerson, L., Duffy, F. H., McAnulty, G. B., Buehler, D. M., VandenBerg, K. A., … Jones, K. G. (2003). A three-center randomized controlled trial of individualized developmental care for very low birth weight preterm infants: Medical, neurodevelopmental, parenting and caregiving effects. *Journal of Developmental Behavioral Pediatrics, 24*(6), 399–408.

Als, H., Lawhon, G., Duffy, F. H., McAnulty, G. B., Gibes-Grossman, R., & Blickman, J. G. (1994). Individualized developmental care for the very low birthweight preterm infant: Medical and neurofunctional effects. *Journal of the American Medical Association, 272*, 853–858.

Als, H., Lester, B. M., Tronick, E. Z., & Brazelton, T. B. (1982a). Manual for the assessment of preterm infants' behavior (APIB). In H. E. Fitzgerald, B. M. Lester, & M. W. Yogman (Eds.), *Theory and research in behavioral pediatrics* (Vol. 1, pp. 65–132). New York: Plenum Press.

Als, H., Lester, B. M., Tronick, E. Z., & Brazelton, T. B. (1982b). Towards a research instrument for the assessment of preterm infants' behavior. In H. E. Fitzgerald, B. M. Lester, & M. W. Yogman (Eds.), *Theory and research in behavioral pediatrics* (Vol. 1, pp. 35–63). New York: Plenum Press.

Brazelton, T. B. (1973). *Neonatal Behavioral Assessment Scale*. London: Heinemann.

Buehler, D. M., Als, H., Duffy, F. H., McAnulty, G. B., & Liederman, J. (1995). Effectiveness of individualized developmental care for low-risk preterm infants: Behavioral and electrophysiological evidence. *Pediatrics, 96*, 923–932.

Constable, R. T., Ment, L. R., Vohr, B., Kesler, S. R., Fulbright, R. K., Lacadie, C., … Reiss, A. R. (2008). Prematurely born children demonstrate white matter miscrostructural differences at 12 years of age, relative to term control subjects: An investigation of group and gender effects. *Pediatrics, 121*(2), 306–316.

Denny-Brown, D. (1962). *The basal ganglia and their relation to disorders of movement*. Oxford: Oxford University Press.

Duffy, F. H., Als, H., & McAnulty, G. B. (2003). Infant EEG spectral coherence data during quiet sleep: Unrestricted principal components analysis – Relation of factors to gestational age, medical risk, and neurobehavioral status. *Clinical EEG (Electroencephalography), 34*(2), 54–69.

Erikson, E. H. (1962). Reality and actualization. *Journal of the American Psychoanalytic Association, 10*, 451–475.

Fleisher, B. F., VandenBerg, K. A., Constantinou, J., Heller, C., Benitz, W. E., Johnson, A., … Stevenson, D. K. (1995). Individualized developmental care for very-low-birth-weight premature infants. *Clinical Pediatrics, 34*, 523–529.

Hack, M., Taylor, H. G., Drotar, D., Schluchter, M., Cartar, L., Andreias, L., et al. (2005). Chronic conditions, functional limitations, and special health care needs of school-aged children born with extremely low-birth-weight in the 1990s. *Journal of the American Medical Association, 294*(3), 318–325.

Hüppi, P. S., Schuknecht, B., Boesch, C., Bossi, E., Felblinger, J., Fusch, C., & Herschkowitz, N. (1996). Structural and neurobehavioral delay in postnatal brain development of preterm infants. *Pediatric Research, 39*(5), 895–901.

Kleberg, A., Westrup, B., & Stjernqvist, K. (2000). Developmental outcome, child behavior and mother–child interaction at 3 years of age following Newborn Individualized Developmental Care and Intervention Program (NIDCAP) intervention. *Early Human Development, 60*, 123–135.

Kuhn, T. (1970). *The structure of scientific revolutions*. Chicago: University of Chicago Press.

Maguire, C. M., Walther, F. J., Van Zwieten, P. H. T., Le Cessie, S., Wit, J. M., & Veen, S., (2009). Follow-up outcomes at 1 and 2 years of infants born less than 32 weeks after Newborn Individualized Developmental Care and Assessment Program. *Pediatrics, 123*(4), 1081–1087.

McAnulty, G., Duffy, F., Butler, S., Bernstein, J., Zurakowski, D., & Als, H. (in press). Effects of the Newborn Individualized Developmental Care and Assessment Program (NIDCAP) at age eight years: Preliminary data. *Clinical Pediatrics.*

Parker, S. J., Zahr, L. K., Cole, J. G., & Brecht, M. (1992). Outcome after developmental intervention in the neonatal intensive care unit for mothers of preterm infants with low socioeconomic status. *Journal of Pediatrics, 120*, 780–785.

Peterson, B. S., Vohr, B., Staib, L. H., Cannistraci, C. J., Dolberg, A., Schneider, K. C., … Ment, R. L. (2000). Regional brain volume abnormalities and long-term cognitive outcome in preterm infants. *Journal of the American Medical Association, 284*, 1939–1947.

Petryshen, P., Stevens, B., Hawkins, J., & Stewart, M. (1997). Comparing nursing costs for preterm infants receiving conventional vs. developmental care. *Nursing Economics, 15*, 138–150.

Saigal, S., Stoskopf, B., Streiner, D., Boyle, M., Pinelli, J., Paneth, N., & Goddeeris, J. (2006). Transition of extremely low-birth-weight infants from adolescence to young adulthood: Comparison with normal birth-weight controls. *Journal of the American Medical Association, 295*(6), 667–675.

Westrup, B., Böhm, B., Lagercrantz, H., & Stjernqvist, K. (2003). Preschool outcome in children born very prematurely and cared for according to the Newborn Individualized Development Care and Assessment Program (NIDCAP). In *Developmentally supportive neonatal care: A study of the Newborn Individualized*

Developmental Care and Assessment Program (NIDCAP) in Swedish settings (Vol. 1, pp. 1–2). Stockholm: Repro Print AB.

Westrup, B., Kleberg, A., von Eichwald, K., Stjernqvist, K., & Lagercrantz, H. (2000). A randomized controlled trial to evaluate the effects of the Newborn Individualized Developmental Care and Assessment Program in a Swedish setting. *Pediatrics, 105*(1), 66–72.

Zimine, S., Lazeyras, F., Henry, F., Borradori-Tolsa, C., & Hüppi, P. (2002). Study of brain development by diffusion tensor imaging: evidence of altered brain development in newborn babies with intrauterine growth restriction. *Proceedings of the International Society for Magnetic Resonance in Medicine, 10.*

19

Fueling Development by Enhancing Infant–Caregiver Relationships

Transformation in the Developmental Therapies

Rosemarie Bigsby

Advances in the care of newborn infants, both healthy and sick, reflect a greater focus on family participation in infant care, an increased emphasis on infant mental health, and a broader systems approach to service delivery. The notion that developmental processes are impacted not only by individual characteristics of the child but by a "transaction" between those characteristics and the environmental context is no longer new (Sameroff & Chandler, 1975). However, translating that concept into a public policy that supports families' nurturing of child behavior and development has been over 30 years in the making. During that time, developmental programs and the provision of therapy services for infants and young children have been transformed. The prevailing direct service model, in which parents observed while individual therapies were administered, has been replaced by a relationship-based model that acknowledges the inherent complexity of developmental processes, and the primacy of the family in the infant's life. This evidence-based model demands that clinicians acquire a broader skill-set, shared across disciplines (Klein, Holloway, Myck-Wayne, Salcedo, & Snell, 2008), including strategies for active engagement of the family and for supporting the family psychosocially.

Regression in Normal Development

Dips and surges in developmental progress are a frequently expressed concern of families with infants and small children. Temporary regressions are particularly evident when skills in another area are emerging (Brazelton,

1969), and are hypothesized to clear the way for the next phase in development. These periods, termed "phase shifts," offer opportunities for dynamic aspects of a particular movement or task to be reorganized in preparation for the next, more complex step (Thelen & Fogel, 1989). Dynamical systems theory provides a useful framework for study of typical infant motor development, dovetails well with transactional theory, and can be incorporated into approaches to developmental intervention with infants at risk for delays.

As systems models have been translated into practice, additional useful constructs have emerged. An example is infant/caregiver *coping* (Zeitlin & Williamson, 1994) in which management of the behavioral challenges that go along with learning and growing are viewed in terms of the adaptability of both the infant and the caregiver. Brazelton (1992) refers to these periods of instability as "Touchpoints," emphasizing that they represent not only hurdles to be overcome but opportunities to intervene in ways that may strengthen the infant–caregiver relationship. Anticipatory guidance (Brazelton, 1975) around expected dips and surges in development brings developmental systems theory into the practical realm for families. Learning that regression and inconsistency are expected, and may represent the advent of new skills, can be reassuring, particularly for parents of infants at risk. Incorporating shared observation of infant behavior with anticipatory guidance enables developmental therapists to assist parent and child through these trouble spots.

The Power of Shared Observation

The Neonatal Behavioral Assessment Scale (NBAS) has provided a useful format for identifying strengths and documenting individual differences among newborn infants. Beyond those intended functions, the NBAS has demonstrated that engaging parents in structured observations of their infant's developmental abilities enhances appreciation of their infant as a competent individual, improves understanding of their baby's needs, and enhances infant–caregiver attachment, even among infants at risk for developmental delay. This dyad-specific strength-based approach to assessment is considered to be best practice in neonatal and early infant intervention programs (Lowman, Stone, & Cole, 2006).

Parents' participation in their baby's assessment is one of the earliest developmental interventions for an infant at risk. The assessment demonstrates infant competencies and highlights individual preferences for handling, touch, movement, and social interaction, all of which influence the ways in which parents provide care. Neonatal assessment opens the dialogue between infant and caregiver – an opportunity for the infant to communicate temperamental differences, while giving caregivers tools they need to create an optimal environment for development. Consistent with transactional systems theory, infant behavior is recognized as having the potential to shape parents' responses, and vice versa.

"Talk to Me!" – The Communicative Infant–Caregiver Dance

Reciprocity in communication between infants and caregivers can be a positive force for infant–caregiver attachment (Brazelton & Cramer, 1990). Qualitative aspects of this early communication have been codified (Lester, Hoffman & Brazelton, 1985), generating such questions as: Is there a critical element of timing that needs to be established for optimal engagement between infant and caregiver? Are infants with significant health problems less likely to be able to communicate clearly? What are the ramifications for emotional attachment of the dyad . . . for infant cognition and development of language and motor skills . . . for establishment of healthy interactive caregiving routines?

Of the methods used to tease out answers to these questions, the Face-to-Face/Still-Face Paradigm (Tronick, Als, Adamson, Wise, & Brazelton, 1978) is perhaps the best known. Initially conceived to simulate maternal depression, the paradigm has since been used as an imposed stressor – a break in the flow of interaction which reveals infants' and caregivers' response to stress. Within this context, healthy infants and caregivers each are able to make efforts to restore communication, or to "repair" the mismatch between the infant's expectation and the mother's unexpected behavior (Weinberg & Tronick, 1998).

In contrast, early-born infants, those with intrauterine growth restriction, or who experience significant illness during the neonatal period display particular sensitivities that may be missed by parents, resulting in a poor fit between infant temperament and caregiver interaction style (Garcia-Coll, Halpern, Vohr, Seifer, & Oh, 1992). This mismatch has the potential to jeopardize the infant–parent attachment relationship.

What are the characteristics of high-risk preterm infants that contribute to parents' difficulty in reading their behavioral cues? Gorski, Davison, & Brazelton (1979) used a hierarchical model to describe behavioral organization of the early preterm infant. In the initial stage, "in-turning," the infant is predominantly in a sleep state, and is entirely focused on maintaining physiologic stability. The next stage, "coming-out," refers to a time when the infant is able to respond briefly to caregiving without a loss of physiologic stability. At this stage, the infant is still highly susceptible to stress, and motor behaviors are likely to reflect both stress and CNS immaturity. In the final stage, "active reciprocity," the infant is able to self-arouse and to self-soothe, reducing the energy needed to interact with caregivers in a mutually satisfying way. A related model by Als, Lester & Brazelton (1979), synactive theory, takes into account maturation of physiologic, motor, and arousal subsystems within the context of availability of environmental support in determining the infant's ability to become an active participant in care and social interaction. Individual behavioral and physiologic responses of the infant are the focus of observation, forming the basis for a unique plan for developmental support, which optimizes opportunities for "balanced behavioral function" and, potentially, improved relationships between infant and caregiver (Als & Gilkerson, 1997).

Preterm infants who have prolonged NICU stays (i.e., "sick preterms") display behavior that is poorly organized and cues that may be difficult for a parent to read. Goldberg demonstrated that parents of sick preterms were less likely to engage in face-to-face social interaction with their infants, including smiling and touching, than parents of healthy infants, and went on to demonstrate associated disturbances in parent–infant behavior at preschool age (Goldberg, Corter, Lojkasek, & Minde, 1990). Bigsby, LaGasse and Lester (1996) tested the notion that infants who display poor physiologic regulation (respiratory sinus arrhythmia) during interactive challenges (NBAS) at 1 month of age would be less likely to engage in self-regulatory/coping behaviors (still-face procedure and temperament assessment) at 3 months corrected age, among 82 term and preterm infants. We demonstrated that the ability to self-soothe via thumbsucking, or to use active strategies such as gaze aversion to withdraw from social interaction before it is perceived as too intense, can be related to social responsiveness and attention.

The relationship between physiologic and behavioral regulation among early-born preterm infants continues to be of interest, particularly with regard to reduction of pain and stress in the NICU. Due to their CNS immaturity, preterm infants may not reliably demonstrate behavioral responses to pain until after 30 weeks (Lucas-Thompson et al., 2008). Yet, behavioral indicators correlate with increases in HR and decreases in oxygen saturation in response to painful procedures (Holsti, Grunau, Oberlander, & Osiovich, 2008), suggesting that both physiologic and behavioral indicators contribute to pain assessment.

The most potent behavioral indicators of pain among preterm infants are facial expressions (Gibbins et al., 2008), which correspond with hemodynamic changes in the cortex during painful stimuli (Slater, Cantarella, Franck, Meek, & Fitzgerald, 2008). Ballistic movements of the extremities (i.e., arm and leg extensions, finger splaying) (Holsti et al., 2008), arching, yawning and fisting (Gibbins et al., 2008) also correspond with painful procedures. The behavior of preterm infants while in the NICU has taken on greater importance as these relationships have come to light. There has been a corresponding increase in the utilization of developmental support personnel in the NICU setting to assist caregivers in interpreting infant behavior and modifying care to enhance self-regulation and energy conservation.

Parental Involvement in Infant Care

A primary focus of this kind of support is parental involvement in infant care and enhancement of the relationship between infants and family members. Although parents may participate with NICU staff in providing basic supportive care (e.g., gentle containment, facilitated tucking during procedures [Hill, Engle, Jorgensene, Kralik, & Whitman, 2005] according to the infant's tolerance), some of the most effective components of developmentally supportive care are those that can be provided *only by a parent.* Skin-to-skin (Kangaroo) care, improves a mother's milk production, enhances breastfeeding outcomes (Hake-Brooks & Anderson, 2008) and has the potential to reduce stress for both members of the dyad (Morelius, Theodorsson, & Nelson, 2005). Kangaroo care also reduces negative behavioral and physiologic responses to routine painful procedures, including suctioning and heel-lance (Johnston et al., 2008).

Gentle infant massage shows increasing potential as a positive intervention in the NICU and in early intervention – one that is best provided by parents. Positive effects of parent-administered movement and massage include improved infant growth and bone mineralization (Moyer-Mileur, Ball, Brunstetter, & Chan, 2008) and a significant reduction in postnatal depression among mothers who massaged their term infants during the first year of life (O'Higgins, St. James Roberts, & Glover, 2008).

As Brazelton and colleagues originally conceptualized, all aspects of developmental intervention require careful attention to infants' physiologic stability, and to regulation of states of arousal and behavior, in order to provide optimal circumstances for growth. This does not imply the absence of stress or challenge in the infant's life. In order to move development forward, infants need to be "active seekers of solutions" (Thelen & Smith, p. 146) to a variety of experiences, some more challenging than others. From these experiences, infants learn strategies for regulating their own behavior and for engaging with their world. The challenge in providing optimal developmental support for high-risk infants in the NICU and during the transition home is not in offering total protection, but in discerning, on an individual basis, experiences that will encourage organized, acquisitive behaviors.

Honoring Individual Sensory Thresholds

When the comfort and pleasure of each member of the infant–caregiver dyad are attended to, positive caregiving interactions will be sustained and will be more likely to be repeated in the future (McCollum & Bair, 1994). Goodness of fit (Thomas, Chess, & Birch, 1968) between a child and his or her environment has an important place in early intervention. Assisting caregivers in modifying their approach to the infant helps them to arrive at a better "fit" between individual tolerances of the infant and sensory aspects of the caregiving environment. The infant is likely to be contented and the caregiver thus rewarded. Alternatively, when an infant's thresholds for stimulation are violated, he or she is less likely to maintain the quiet alert state necessary for optimal social interaction. The infant may engage in motor behavior which signals distress, or may fuss, cry, or simply go to sleep. The behavior of infants with a poor "fit" makes interaction less pleasurable and sustainable for parents, and limits opportunities to progress the infant's learning. Such infants may begin to show signs of social disengagement, as compared with those who are engaged in enjoyable interactions that are contingent on the infant's behavior (Greenspan et al., 2008). This contextual approach demands flexibility on the part of professionals, including openness to take their model for service delivery outside the traditional direct-service format.

The contextual model keeps the child, his or her caregivers, and their needs in the forefront of the intervention plan by identifying strengths as well as factors that are limiting developmental progress. This service model may be most effective when delivered by a single member of the team who possesses skills that cross traditional disciplinary boundaries. Guralnick (2000) describes an effective approach to assessment and intervention as one in which personnel acknowledge the particular expertise represented on their team and defer to other team members in the service of optimal intervention with families.

Common in current approaches to early intervention, whether in the NICU setting or the home, is the principle that interactions between infants and caregivers should be pleasurable for all involved. Starting intervention where the infant and parent are most comfortable and able to cope sounds deceptively simple. Yet, these approaches require extensive, supervised observation for the developmental therapist to learn how to interpret the behavior of infants and caregivers and to guide them toward success. The NICU Network Neurobehavioral Scale (NNNS) (Lester & Tronick, 2004), an expansion of the NBAS initially designed for research with infants at risk, provides a framework for assessment of infant strengths and vulnerabilities that also can be used clinically as a foundation for developmental support in the NICU. An evidence-based pathway for developmental support provides additional structure that guides infant–parent participation as the infant matures. Figure 19.1 represents the collaborative efforts of parents and staff at Women & Infants' Hospital in preparation for the move from open-bays to a single-room model of NICU care. The goal of the pathway is to enhance opportunities for parent participation, in addition to improving infant outcomes, by linking assessment information to the care the infant is receiving. Shared observation of the infant using the NNNS is the initial step in a developmental support process that is practical in implementation, grounded in behavioral and developmental science, and tempered by the belief that what babies and families are telling us should be valued. By using shared observation within the context of the infant's daily routines, and a relationship-based approach to intervention (Lieberman & Zeanah, 1999), infants and caregivers can be engaged in active, gratifying interaction.

Your Baby's Developmental Progress in the NICU

NICU Family Centered Care & NICU Family Advisory Council

	< 26 weeks	27 & 28 weeks	29 & 30 weeks
Overall goals of Developmental Support	Encourage family participation in baby's care Increase rest/sleep/energy conservation for baby Keep baby at comfortable temperature, heart rate & breathing rate during care Support baby's developmental progress	Recognize baby's cues & needs Become more comfortable assisting in infant care	
Helping Baby to Stay Rested & Calm	Plan activity with baby around nursing care schedule to encourage rest/sleep/growth Reduce activity/sound levels at bedside Nest, swaddle and/or use snuggle-up to keep baby comfortable Position baby with good posture support (head toward midline; shoulders forward; use props as needed)		
Helping Baby to Stay Comfortable During Care	Change baby's position slowly to reduce stress Keep baby calm by offering a pacifier/finger-hold or nesting with your hands during care Learn to recognize baby's signs of stress (finger splaying, crying, startling) or contentment (calm face, relaxed body)		Help nurse to give baby a sponge bath
Age Appropriate Developmental Experiences	Keep baby calm with minimal activity/handling (hand on baby rather than stroking) Keep voices low; avoid loud noises at bedside Silence Cell phones Protect baby's eyes from bright lighting Use pacifier for soothing and sucking/swallowing practice while awake	Keep bedside lighting appropriate to the time of day when possible (softly lit bed space during the day & dim lighting for naps and at night) Speak softly before touching baby or changing position Provide baby with a finger to hold Practice nurturing touch when possible (nesting with your hands; Kangaroo Care) Encourage non-nutritive sucking on own hand/pacifier when awake or during baby's feedings Talk/read/sing softly to baby	
Family Participation	Begin Kangaroo Care (skin-to-skin holding on your chest) when baby's medical team gives the OK Keep a journal or care notebook Create baby's Care-Pages Website Attend NICU Parent Hours		
Support of Breast/Bottle Feeding	Begin pumping early & often (within 6 hours of delivery and at bedside, if possible) Keep weekly breastfeeding log	Allow baby to nuzzle at mother's nipple during Kangaroo Care Begin non-nutritive comfort sucking on the breast/own hand/pacifier when Ask about gavage feedings at the breast	

Figure 19.1 Your baby's developmental progress in NICU
Source: NICU Developmental and Family Centered Care Committees, Women & Infants Hospital, Providence, RI, 2009

Women & Infants
New England's premier hospital for women and newborns

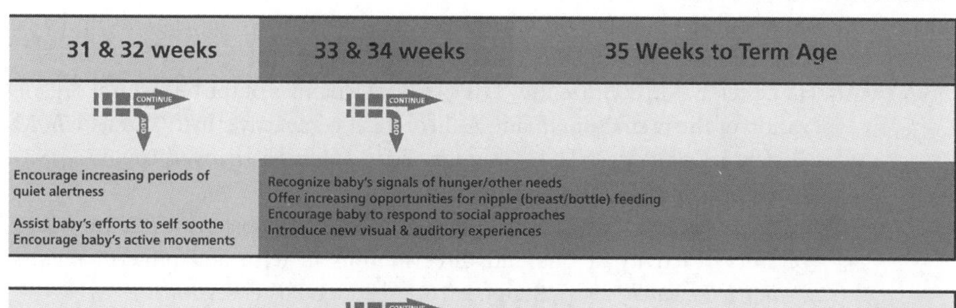

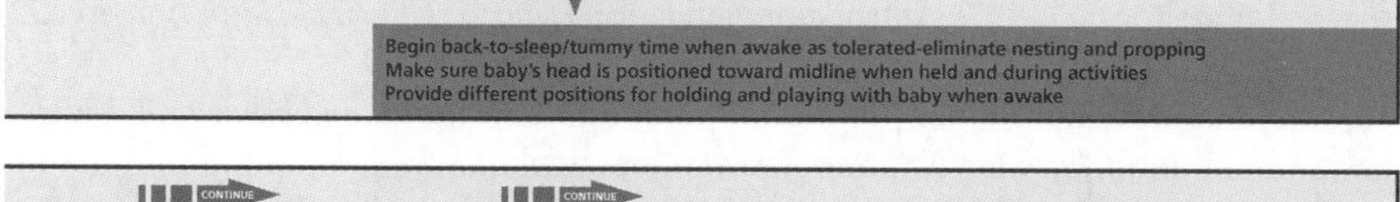

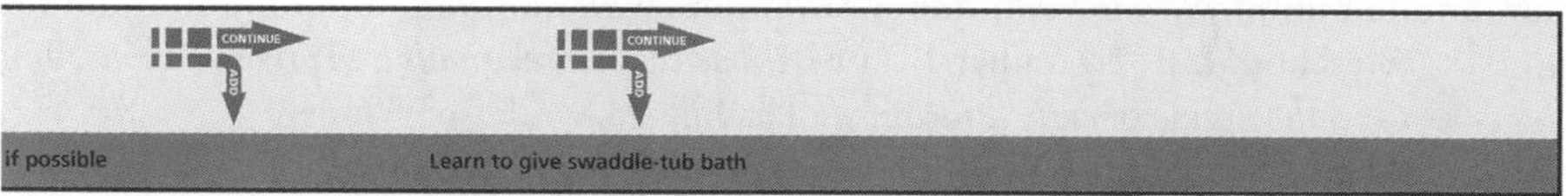

31 & 32 weeks	33 & 34 weeks	35 Weeks to Term Age
Hold on chest (Continue Kangaroo Care) Hold baby so he/she can see parent and surroundings Use one form of play at a time (read, stuffed toy, music) Introduce soft music/pleasant sounds for brief periods of time, especially when its time to go to sleep Gentle rocking in arms or upright holding at shoulder as tolerated Encourage hand to mouth/face; sucking on hand/pacifier	Encourage social responsiveness to your face and voice Encourage baby to focus on faces/mirror/mobile Begin to establish back-to-sleep bedtime routine; read to baby; musical toys/soft sounds (e.g., music player/aquarium) as baby is falling asleep	
Learn gentle positive touch/infant massage if appropriate for your baby	Sign up to go to CPR class Learn all infant care	Attend discharge class Bring in car seat for car seat challenge Review "Parent Readiness Checklist" with nurses to ensure that you are comfortable giving all care, including medications
	Discuss readiness for nipple feeding with team (breast and/or bottle) Offer breast or bottle when baby is stable, alert and responsive Begin nutritive breast/bottle feeding when baby is ready/gavage remainder Stop/slow down feeding when baby seems stressed/fatigued	
medical team gives the OK		Continue to transition toward full nipple (breast/bottle) feeding according to baby's cues and abilities

References and further reading

Als, H., & Gilkerson, L. (1997). Change from protocol-based to relationship-based care. *Seminars in Perinatology, 21*(3), 178–189.

Als, H., Lester, B. M., & Brazelton, T. B. (1979). Dynamics of the behavioral organization of the premature infant: A theoretical perspective. In T. M. Field, A. M. Sostek, S. Goldberg, & H. H. Shuman (Eds.), *Infants born at risk* (pp. 173–193). New York: Spectrum Publications.

Bigsby, R., LaGasse, L., & Lester, B. (1996). Self-regulatory behavior and cardiorespiratory reactivity at one and three months in term and preterm infants. *Pediatric Research, 39*(4), Suppl. 2, 16. (Abstract: Poster session).

Brazelton, T. B. (1969). *Infants and mothers.* New York: Delacorte.

Brazelton, T. (1975). Anticipatory guidance. *Pediatric Clinics of North America, 22,* 533–544.

Brazelton, T. B. (1992). *Touchpoints: Your child's emotional and behavioral development, birth to three.* New York: Perseus Books.

Brazelton, T. B., & Cramer, B. (1990). *The earliest relationship: Parents, infants, and the drama of early attachment.* Reading, MA: Addison-Wesley.

Chen, D. (2008). *Early intervention in action: Working across disciplines to support infants with multiple disabilities and their families.* Baltimore, MD: Brookes.

Garcia-Coll, C. T., Halpern, L., Vohr, B. R., Seifer, R., & Oh, W. (1992). Stability and correlates of change of early temperament in preterm and full-term infants. *Infant Behavior and Development, 15,* 137–153.

Gibbins, S., Stevens, B., Beyene, J., Chan, P. C., Bagg, M., & Asztalos, E. (2008). Pain behaviours in extremely low gestational age infants. *Early Human Development, 84*(7), 451–458.

Goldberg, S., Corter, C., Lojkasek, M., & Minde, K. (1990). Prediction of behavior problems in four-year-olds born prematurely. *Development and Psychopathology, 2,* 15–30.

Gorski, P., Davison, M. F., & Brazelton, T. B. (1979). Stages of behavioral organization in the high-risk neonate: Theoretical and clinical considerations. *Seminars in Perinatology, 3,* 61–72.

Greenspan, S., Brazelton, T. B., Cordero, J., Solomon, R., Bauman, M. L., Robinson, R., Shanker, S., & Breinbauer, C. (2008). Guidelines for early identification, screening, and clinical management of children with autism spectrum disorders. *Pediatrics, 121*(4), 828–830.

Guralnick, M. J. (2000). Interdisciplinary team assessment for young children: Purposes and processes. In M. J. Guralnick (Ed.), *Interdisciplinary clinical assessment of young children with developmental disabilities* (pp. 3–15). Baltimore, MD: Brookes.

Hake-Brooks, S. J., & Anderson, G. C. (2008). Kangaroo care and breastfeeding of mother–preterm infant dyads 0–18 months: A randomized, controlled trial. *Neonatal Network, 27*(3), 151–159.

Core Features of Infant Mental Health

Despite the breadth of infant mental health, there are core features that are important across a range of settings and activities.

Strengths perspective

From its inception, infant mental health is a strengths-based discipline. This means that clinicians work to identify strengths from which to build competence and address problems. Brazelton has always been a major proponent of the strengths perspective, believing that mobilizing parents' strengths is more productive than focusing on their deficits. In addition, the Neonatal Behavioral Assessment Scale (Brazelton, 1973) is designed to captivate parents with the strengths (special capacities) of their newborns. This perspective has influenced specific infant mental health interventions that explicitly focus on strengths (McDonough, 2000) but more broadly is a characteristic of most interventions in infant mental health. However, being strengths-based does not mean ignoring liabilities (Zeanah, 1998). Clinicians must identify problems in young children and in their parents without minimizing them in order to address them effectively. Further, there is often a complex interrelationship between strengths and weaknesses, so that strengths may be obscured by weaknesses but also may be mobilized to ameliorate weaknesses. Moreover, intervention efforts always involve prevention. This means there is a simultaneous focus on relieving suffering here and now, as well as attending to future development, all through attention to primary caregiving relationships (Zeanah, Stafford, Nagle, & Rice, 2005a; Zeanah, Stafford, & Zeanah, 2005b; Zeanah, Gleason & Zeanah, 2008; Zeanah & Zeanah, 2009).

Child in context

In the 1980s, infant mental health preventive interventions changed in focus from the child as an individual to the child in context. Environmental characteristics are typically far more stable than the child's own characteristics, especially in early childhood. Although the effects of child and environment are unquestionably bidirectional, environments are more likely to change children than the other way round (Sameroff, 2009). Young children develop within interrelated contexts of biological/genetic characteristics, family, culture, social class, and historical epochs. These contexts exert their influences both from within the infant and from the environmental context in which the infant is reared. They determine both the types of experiences an infant has and how that infant perceives those experiences (Zeanah & Zeanah, 2009). For young children, infant–caregiver relationships are the most important experience-near context for infant development and are the distinctive focus of infant mental health.

Relational Focus

The relational focus of infant mental health has been the sine qua non of this field from the beginning. It is not the infant who is the target of intervention but rather the infant–parent relationship. This is not only because infants are so dependent upon their caregivers but also because infant competence may vary widely in different relationships. This has been reported in clinical case reports (Zeanah, Mammen, & Lieberman, 1993) but also demonstrated in attachment research, in which the infant may have qualitatively different kinds of attachment relations with different parents (Steele, Steele & Fonagy, 1996).

Considering the relationship to be the patient, of course, has important implications for how assessments and treatments are conducted, as well as for how psychopathology is conceptualized. Instead of the problem or disturbance being understood as within the child or within the parent, the problem may be understood as between child and caregiver (Sameroff & Emde, 1989).

Value of observing interactions

Careful attention to behavior has been an important focus of developmental research on infants and young children, and this emphasis is maintained in clinical work in infant mental health. Patterns of interactive behavior enacted over time between child and caregiver are an important index of the infant caregiver relationship (Zeanah, Larrieu, Valliere, & Heller, 2000). Distinctive patterns of interaction between an infant and his/her parents are demonstrable in the earliest months of life. Changes in interactive patterns over time and context are coherent within a given relationship – that is, the specific behaviors may change, but the way that the behaviors are organized is maintained (Sroufe & Fleeson, 1986). A common strategy in

Gaynes, B. N., Gavin, N., Meltzer-Brody, S., Lohr, K. N., Swinson, T., Gartlehner, G., Brody, S. & Miller, W. C. (February, 2005). Perinatal depression: Prevalence, screening accuracy, and screening outcomes. Summary, Evidence Report/ Technology Assessment: Number 119. AHRQ Publication Number 05-E006-1, Agency for Healthcare Research and Quality, Rockville, MD.

Ghera, M., Marshall, P. J., Fox, N. A., Zeanah, C. H., & Nelson, C. A. (2009). The effect of early intervention on young children's attention and expression of positive affect. *Journal of Child Psychology, Psychiatry and Allied Disciplines, 50,* 246–253.

Hagan, J. F., Shaw, J. S., & Duncan, P. (2008). *Bright futures: Guidelines for health supervision of infants, children, and adolescents* (3rd ed.). Elk Grove Village, IL: American Academy of Pediatrics.

Johnston, K., & Brinamen, C. (2009). Mental health consultation: A transactional approach in childcare. In C. H. Zeanah (Ed.), *Handbook of infant mental health,* (3rd ed., pp. 564–577). New York: Guilford Press.

Kreppner, J., Rutter, M., Beckett, C., Castle, J., Colvert, E., Groothues, C., … Sonuga-Barke, E. J. S. (2007). Normality and impairment following profound early institutional deprivation: A longitudinal follow-up into early adolescence. *Developmental Psychology, 43,* 931–946.

Larrieu, J. A., & Zeanah, C. H. (2003). Treating infant–parent relationships in the context of maltreatment: An integrated, systems approach. In A. Sameroff, S. McDonough, & K. Rosenblum (Eds.), *Treatment of infant–parent relationship disturbances* (pp. 243–264). New York: Guilford Press.

LeMare, L., & Audet, K. (2006). A longitudinal study of the physical growth and health of postinstitutionalized Romanian adoptees. *Pediatric Child Health, 11,* 85–91.

MacKenzie, M. J., & McDonough, S. C. (2009). Transactions between perception and reality: Maternal beliefs and infant regulatory behavior. In A. J. Sameroff (Ed.), *The transactional model of development: How children and contexts shape each other* (pp. 35–54). Washington, DC: American Psychological Association.

Marshall, P. J., & Kenney, J. W. (2009). Biological perspectives on the effects of early psychosocial experiences. *Developmental Review, 29,* 96–119.

McDonough, S. (2000). Interaction guidance: An approach for difficult to engage families. In C. H. Zeanah (Ed.), *Handbook of infant mental health* (2nd ed., pp. 485–493). New York: Guilford Press.

Miron, D., Lewis, M., & Zeanah, C. H. (2009). Clinical use of observational procedures in early childhood relationship assessment. In C. H. Zeanah (Ed.), *Handbook of infant mental health* (3rd ed., pp. 252–265). New York: Guilford Press.

Nelson, C. A., Zeanah, C. H., Fox, N. A., Marshall, P. J., Smyke, A., & Guthrie, D. (2007). Cognitive recovery in socially deprived young children: The Bucharest Early Intervention Project. *Science, 318,* 1937–1940.

NICHD Early Child Care Research Network (2006). Childcare effect sizes for the NICHD study of early child care and youth development. *American Psychologist, 61*, 99–116.

Olds, D. L., Sadler, L., & Kitzman, H. (2007). Programs for parents of infants and toddlers: Recent evidence from randomized trials. *Journal of Child Psychology and Psychiatry, 48*, 355–391.

Oppenheim, D., & Koren-Karie, N. (2009). Infant–parent relationship assessment: parents' insightfulness regarding their young children's internal worlds. In C. H. Zeanah (Ed.), *Handbook of infant mental health* (3rd ed., pp. 266–280). New York: Guilford Press.

Oppenheim, D., Koren-Karie, N., Dolev, S., & Yirmiya, N. (2009). Maternal insightfulness and resolution of the diagnosis are associated with secure attachment in preschoolers with autism spectrum disorders. *Child Development, 80*, 517–529.

Powell, B., Cooper, G., Hoffman, K., & Marvin, R. (2009). The circle of security. In C. H. Zeanah (Ed.), *Handbook of infant mental health* (3rd ed., pp. 450–467). New York: Guilford Press.

Rusconi-Serpa, S., Rossignol, A. S., & McDonough, S. C. (2009). Video feedback in parent–infant treatments. In D. Schechter & M. M. Gleason (Eds.), *Infant and early childhood mental health, child and adolescent psychiatric clinics of North Carolina* 18 (pp. 735–751). Philadelphia: Saunders.

Sameroff, A. J. (2009). The transactional model. In A. J. Sameroff (Ed.), *The transactional model of development* (pp. 3–21). Washington, DC: American Psychological Association.

Sameroff, A. J., & Emde, R. N. (Eds.) (1989). *Relationship disturbances in early childhood.* New York: Basic Books.

Smyke, A. T., Zeanah, C. H., Fox, N. A., Nelson, C. A., & Guthrie, D. (2010). Placement in foster care enhances attachment among young children in institutions. *Child Development, 81*, 212–223.

Sroufe, L. A., & Fleeson, J. (1986). Attachment and the construction of relationships. In W. W. Hartup, and Z. Rubin (Eds.), *The nature and development of relationships.* Hillsdale, NJ: Lawrence Erlbaum.

Steele, H., Steele, M., & Fonagy, P. (1996). Associations among attachment classifications of mothers, fathers and their infants. *Child Development, 67*, 541–555.

Suchman, N., DeCoste, C., & Mayes, L. (2009). The mothers and toddlers program: An attachment-based intervention for mothers in substance abuse treatment. In C. H. Zeanah (Ed.), *Handbook of infant mental health* (3rd ed., 485–499). New York: Guilford Press.

Zeanah, C. H. (1998). Reflections on the strengths perspective. *The Signal, 6*, 12–13.

Zeanah, C. H. (2008). Observational procedures and psychopathology in young children. *Journal of the American Academy of Child and Adolescent Psychiatry, 47*, 611–613.

Zeanah, C. H., Aoki, Y., Heller, S. S., & Larrieu, J. A. (1999, March). Relationship specificity in maltreated toddlers and their birth and foster parents. Presented at the biennial meeting of the Society for Research in Child Development. Albuquerque, NM.

Zeanah, C. H., & Benoit, D. (1995). Clinical applications of a parent perception interview. In K. Minde (Ed.), *Infant psychiatry, child psychiatric clinics of North America* (pp. 539–554). Philadelphia: W. B. Saunders,

Zeanah, C. H., Egger, H., Smyke, A. T., Nelson, C., Fox, N., Marshall, P., & Guthrie, D. (2009). Institutional rearing and psychiatric disorders in Romanian preschool children. *American Journal of Psychiatry, 166*, 777–785.

Zeanah, C. H., Larrieu, J. A., Valliere, J., & Heller, S. S. (2000). Infant–parent relationship assessment. In C. H. Zeanah (Ed.), *Handbook of infant mental health* (2nd ed., pp. 222–235), New York: Guilford Press.

Zeanah, C. H., Mammen, O., & Lieberman, A. (1993). Disorders of attachment. In C. H. Zeanah (Ed.), *Handbook of infant mental health* (pp. 332–349). New York: Guilford Press.

Zeanah, C. H., & Zeanah, P. D. (2009). The scope of infant mental health. In C. H. Zeanah (Ed.), *Handbook of infant mental health* (3rd ed., pp. 5–21). New York: Guilford Press.

Zeanah, P. D., Bailey, L. O., & Berry, S. (2009). Infant mental health in the real world: Opportunities for interface and impact. In D. Schechter, & M. M. Gleason (Eds.), *Infant and early childhood mental health, child and adolescent psychiatric clinics of North Carolina*, 18 (pp. 773–787). Philadelphia: Saunders.

Zeanah, P. D., & Gleason, M. M. (2009). Infant mental health in primary health care. In C. H. Zeanah (Ed.), *Handbook of infant mental health* (3rd ed., pp. 549–563). New York: Guilford Press.

Zeanah, P. D., Gleason, M. M., & Zeanah, C. H. (2008). Infant mental health. In M. M. Haith, & J. B. Benson (Eds.), *Encyclopedia of infant and early childhood development* (pp. 301–311). New York: Elsevier Publishing.

Zeanah, P. D., Stafford, B., Nagle, G., & Rice, T. (2005a). Addressing social emotional development and infant mental health: Building state early childhood comprehensive systems series (Vol. 12), Los Angeles, CA: National Center for Infant and Early Childhood Health Policy.

Zeanah, P. D., Stafford, B., & Zeanah, C. H. (2005b). Clinical interventions in infant mental health: A selective review. Building state early childhood comprehensive systems series (Vol. 13). Los Angeles, CA: National Center for Infant and Early Childhood Health Policy.

Zero to Three (2001). *Definition of infant mental health.* Zero to Three Infant Mental Health Steering Committee.

21

Ghosts and Angels in the Nursery
Conflict and Hope in Raising Babies

Alicia F. Lieberman
and William W. Harris

Health – physical and emotional – is not an expectable state or a biological given but rather a cultural as well as a personal achievement: the blessed convergence of biology, psychology, human relationships, environmental factors and social supports working in synchrony to protect and foster the wellbeing of the individual in his or her community. The higher rates of asthma, elevated lead levels, diabetes, cardiovascular disease, depression, and traumatic stress in poor neighborhoods, co-occurring with violence, toxic environmental conditions, and scarcity of basic resources, attest to the public health consequences of seemingly unrelated policy decisions – the unnatural social causes of ostensibly physical conditions. Illness is often sociological as much as biological (World Health Organization, 2007). Berry Brazelton's work involves the conscious and conscientious cultivation of health in all its facets by attending to the myriad factors that bring it about. He understood the influence of the group's ecological niche in shaping childrearing practices long before the term "cultural sensitivity" became a mantra in our fields, and his observations, for example, of Mayan childrearing practices in rural Mexico still stand as a model of developmental ethnography. From his earliest subtle observations of each baby's unique individuality and the reciprocity of parent–infant interactions to more recent work describing the touchpoints of children's development in the context of family and social expectations, Brazelton is a persuasive champion for the child's and parent's momentum towards health and the duty of adults and society to provide the conditions needed to bring that momentum to fruition.

To this end, there is still a regrettable lack of collaboration between the fields of infant mental health and developmental pediatrics in spite of their fundamental need for each other. Brazelton has endeavored for decades to remedy this situation by connecting the two disciplines. He forged a unified approach to infant health with pediatricians who had become child psychoanalysts and helped found Zero to Three, the first organization to make developmental and emotional health in the first three years of life the focus of its mission. It was in learning to administer the groundbreaking Neonatal Behavioral Assessment Scale (NBAS) (Brazelton & Nugent, 1995) that one of the authors (Lieberman) first understood the implications of Brazelton's work for helping beleaguered parents experience love and protectiveness for their babies.

Until this instrument became widely adopted by researchers and practitioners, infant observation had often been guided by attachment theory and the "ghosts in the nursery" paradigm, which interpreted a baby's responses primarily as indicators of secure versus anxious expectations about the mother's availability and responsiveness. The field of infancy began coming into its own in the 1970s when Brazelton expanded its range of knowledge, identifying individual differences in babies' self-regulation and responsiveness to stimuli and the multitude of responses that these unique behaviors evoked in their mothers. Brazelton was the first and most forceful spokesman for babies' autonomous agency in co-creating relationships with their mothers. Through his contributions, the field of infant mental health incorporated a more comprehensive approach to the mutuality inherent in mother–infant interaction and acquired a powerful new lens to aid in prevention and intervention with attachment disorders.

Simultaneously, Selma Fraiberg was exploring what mothers bring to their relationships with their babies, and how their unresolved childhood conflicts interfere with giving and deriving pleasure from their babies. Fraiberg's metaphor of "ghosts in the nursery" (Fraiberg, Adelson, & Shapiro, 1975) became an iconic expression of parents' enduring conflicts that can prevent optimal development for baby and mother. Brazelton's contributions were a balance to Fraiberg's focus on mothers and led babies to be recognized as powerful partners in the developing dyadic relationship.

Brazelton observed, Fraiberg observed – and both intervened, each at a different segment of the health–pathology spectrum. Brazelton promoted awe, pleasure, and competence in parents who often were seeing the wondrous capacities of their babies for the first time. Through their babies' responses to them, parents developed a reinforcing sense of self-efficacy, a sense that they were indeed up to the parenting task. Fraiberg focused on parents whose capacity to connect to the unique individuality of their baby was thwarted by their negative attributions, rooted in their own childhood experiences of having felt unprotected and unloved. Brazelton was working through a lens of optimism, using the baby's competence to help parents discover their own; Fraiberg was focusing on the mother's psychopathology, using the baby's potential to help the mother escape from entrapment in her own past. Together, they created a chiaroscuro that honors the complexity of what Daniel Stern calls "the first relationship" (2002).

Brazelton's and Fraiberg's discoveries led inevitably to a new focus for intervention – not just the baby or the mother, but the dyad. The insights into the mind of the baby and the mother converged to lead to novel forms of treatment that focused on their relationship. Most of these integrated developmental guidance with insight-oriented psychodynamic strategies as in infant–parent psychotherapy, the relationship-based treatment, created by Selma Fraiberg, now adapted and practiced by infant mental health programs across the USA.

A new development occurred in the 1990s, after clinicians and researchers had begun to ponder the role of trauma in the etiology of illness. Back in 1962, Henry Kempe and his colleagues had reported the discovery of the battered child syndrome and concluded that only a few hundred children were affected (Kempe, Silverman, Steele, Droegemueller, & Silver, 1962). Early researchers usually worked within their own circumscribed areas of expertise, assessing exposure to only one type of maltreatment. Since then, there have been many painstaking efforts to elucidate the prevalence and impact of child maltreatment. It has taken our fields too long to identify and address the toll that interpersonal violence takes on young children's physical and psychological integrity, both directly and through its impact on parents and their relationships with their children. We have come a long way, but not far enough since Kempe's simultaneous identification and underestimation of child maltreatment as a form of trauma.

The field of traumatic stress, which had begun with studies of war's impact on combatants, slowly extended to include women, through the work of Herman, and children, through the seminal contributions of Terr, van der Kolk, Cohen, Pynoos, Cicchetti, and others (Cicchetti & Cohen, 1995; Herman, 1992; Pynoos, 1990; Spinazzola, Blaustein, & van der Kolk, 2005; Terr, 1991; van der Kolk, 2005). Research gradually evolved to encompass different forms of violence exposure, their overlap, and the exponential consequences of cumulative exposure, and to link different databases to gauge the true scope of exposure. We now know from clinical and epidemiological data that violence is a virus that makes its way from people to systems and from systems to people, so that there are significant overlaps linking war, community and domestic violence, child physical and sexual abuse, and violence against the self in the form of suicide. Exposure to violence, far from affecting a few hundred children every year, is an urgent public health problem that has many overlapping facets and affects millions of children and their families (Harris, Putnam, & Fairbank, 2006; van der Kolk, 2005).

The health consequences are staggering. In the words of Steven Sharfstein, the former president of the American Psychiatric Association, "interpersonal violence, especially violence experienced by children, is the largest single preventable cause of mental illness. What cigarette smoking is to the rest of medicine, early childhood violence is to psychiatry" (2006). Indeed, the Adverse Childhood Experiences (ACE) study conducted by Felitti and Anda with about 18,000 Kaiser-Permanente members shows that childhood maltreatment and exposure to domestic violence predict the leading causes of morbidity and early mortality decades later, with the mediators for this prediction consisting of self-destructive behaviors such as smoking, substance abuse, and reckless sexuality that are used as coping mechanisms to fend off depression, hopelessness, and anxiety (Felitti et al., 1998).

Remarkably, but also predictably, infants, toddlers and preschoolers have been largely absent from epidemiological studies of children's exposure to domestic and community violence. The youngest children surveyed are usually of school age because preverbal children cannot articulate their experience, which is dismissed as unimportant by adults for whom language is the primary vehicle for communication. Yet Cicchetti, Osofsky, Zeanah and others have demonstrated the destructive impact of violence in infancy and early childhood on social, emotional, and cognitive functioning (Cicchetti & Lynch, 1993; Osofsky, 1995; Zeanah & Scheeringa, 1997).

As understanding of how trauma affects babies and young children sharpened and expanded, the logical next question was: how does it affect their earliest interactions? How can a trauma lens elucidate component parts of the dyadic relationship and suggest opportunities for intervention? The search for answers led to the creation of the UCSF Child Trauma Research Program, where Patricia Van Horn and I (AFL) introduced the assessment and treatment of traumatic stress in the parent–child dyad as the focus for child–parent psychotherapy with children aged birth to five (Lieberman & Van Horn, 2005, 2008). Present-day trauma became for us the next frontier in understanding and treating the etiology of disorders in the parent–child relationship. Building on Brazelton's and Fraiberg's work, child–parent psychotherapy incorporates sustained attention not only to the baby's individuality and the mother's enactment with the baby of internalized conflicts from her past, but also to the shattering impact that domestic and community violence and child maltreatment can have on the child's and parent's perceptions of each other.

We have come to believe that assessing for traumatic stressors in the parent–child relationship is a clinical duty because of their high prevalence, despite the widespread professional reluctance to openly inquire about them. Learning to probe for traumatic events is essential to helping parents and children overcome their shame and fear to disclose them. Without this information, it would be impossible to make a differential diagnosis, for example, between post-traumatic stress disorder (PTSD) and ADHD and to provide appropriate treatment because symptoms such as inability to concentrate, hyperarousal, hypervigilance, constriction of affect, and excessive reactivity are key criteria for both conditions.

For each diagnosis, the child's relationship with the parents needs to be addressed differently. When there is family violence, our data show a significant relationship between the child's traumatic experiences and the mother's symptoms of post-traumatic stress disorder. This finding complements the findings by Scheeringa and Zeanah (1995) that young children showed more symptoms of PTSD when they witnessed their mothers being abused than when the children were abuse victims. These two sets of findings suggest that mother and child are each deeply traumatized by the trauma of the other. This is the dark side of the exquisite mutuality between mother and child that Brazelton so masterfully describes.

Hope is intricately embedded even into this bleak picture. In our sample of preschoolers referred for witnessing domestic violence to their mothers, significant clinical improvement in the child and mother and in their relationship occurred when battered mothers and their children processed their traumatic experience together by using play with dolls and animals to enact the trauma and give it a safe ending, and talked with each other about it, dispelling the terrible taboo – associated with unspeakable events of family violence – against putting terror into words. On follow-up six months after child–parent treatment termination, mothers continued to improve in symptoms of global psychiatric distress when compared with the comparison group in which about 70 percent of mothers received individual psychotherapy (Lieberman, Ghosh Ippen, & Van Horn, 2006). Children's improvement at treatment's end serves as an ongoing source of wellbeing and increased self-esteem for mothers, an antidote to maternal depression, anxiety, and traumatic stress. An unpublished analysis of our outcome data shows that child–parent psychotherapy is particularly effective in repairing the parent–child relationship for children subjected to multiple traumas, e.g., physical abuse and witnessing domestic violence.

Addressing trauma directly is necessary, but focusing only on trauma can be traumatizing and derail the clinical process. This is where "angels in the nursery" become allies in our work. "Angels in the nursery" is a term coined by one of the authors (Harris) and represents the intersection of Fraiberg's focus on childhood experiences that haunt parents and Brazelton's positive focus. During the initial assessment we ask mothers about past and present trauma, but also about memories of times when they felt unconditionally loved and protected as they were growing up. Their early and current experiences are marked by poverty, violence, and cultural marginalization and dislocation, including ethnic discrimination and immigration from countries at war or civil strife. Sadly, 50 percent of the women cannot retrieve any memories of being unconditionally loved. For these women, our explicit message is that child–parent psychotherapy can offer an opportunity to create these loving memories for the first time in their relationship with their child. As the remaining 50 percent tell us about tender memories with their mother, father, a grandmother or aunt, they often seem to rediscover an experience of themselves that had long been forgotten under the burden of present adversities. We then ask them how their loving memories might apply to what they want to create for their child. These memories become our guide, linking what is best in the mothers' past to what they hope for in their relationship with their children.

Energized by our successful outcomes, and the fact that 50 percent of mothers reported domestic violence starting during pregnancy, we expanded our protocol to include pregnant women battered by their partners, continuing treatment after delivery. The intervention model involves collaboration with our hospital's OB-GYN and Pediatrics departments to coordinate emotional and physical care of mother and baby. Our experience to date confirms Brazelton's wisdom in designating pregnancy as the first touchpoint of development.

The effects of domestic violence on pregnant women's health are equal to or greater than routinely monitored complications (e.g., gestational diabetes, preeclampsia), and include low weight gain, hemorrhage, infections, anemia, predelivery hospitalization, Cesarean sections, and complications from delayed medical care from fear of abuse disclosure (Gazmararian et al., 1996). Fetal exposure to domestic violence is linked to prematurity and low birth weight (Gazmararian et al., 1996) and behavioral outcomes like excessive crying and feeding and sleeping problems (Regalado & Halfon,

2002). Battered women have greater difficulty bonding with their infants and show higher rates of punitive childrearing practices and child abuse (Osofsky, 1995). Brazelton's emphasis on the affective loop between baby and mother appears to be in play.

When a traumatized mother's baby is not responsive to her care, blaming the baby for making her feel inadequate can lead to the predictable next link in a cycle of violence that is transmitted from battering father to battered mother to battered child. Our program's clinicians report that psychotherapy with battered pregnant women and their babies is the most emotionally demanding aspect of their work because of their acute sense of responsibility for the pregnant woman, her fetus, and later, the newborn. It is particularly rewarding that our intervention leads to dramatic improvements beyond treatment's end, when the baby is six months old. Comparisons of the spread of scores for maternal depression, PTSD, and parenting stress before and after treatment show no overlap at all between the pretreatment and the posttreatment scores – which we attribute to this relationship-focused intervention during pregnancy and babies' first months of life.

One of Brazelton's most persistent themes is the importance of involving fathers in every aspect of intervention on children's behalf and from the beginning, asking mothers to bring fathers for pediatric prenatal visits. We strive to meet Brazelton's stringent standards for paternal inclusion, but encounter formidable obstacles. One is the sobering instability of marriages and partnerships. In our sample of battered pregnant women, only 47 percent are still with the baby's father in the second or third trimester of their pregnancies, when they are referred for treatment. It is very difficult to engage fathers on behalf of their babies when parental relationships have ended – particularly when mothers want to maintain distance from them.

Another obstacle to paternal participation in this context is safety – for the mother, child, and therapist. There is a very high overlap between the incidence of domestic violence and of child abuse, ranging from 30–70 percent depending on the sample (Kitzmann, Gaylord, Holt, & Kenny, 2003). Many of the women we work with report harrowing histories of child-witnessed domestic violence. Stalking and threats of violence after separation are common. The father's denial of his aggression in spite of medical evidence and police reports jeopardizes the hope for his successful participation in our treatment, in which an explicit examination of traumatic events and their emotional impact is an integral component.

A third obstacle is the relative leniency of the courts in child custody disputes with allegations of domestic violence. Judges are often skeptical about maternal disclosures of domestic violence. They may order treatment as a condition for shared custody or visits with the child, but often fail to ask at the next hearing whether the father enrolled in or completed the program. Without court involvement to assure accountability, offending partners lack external incentives for treatment and therapists lack the institutional protection they need to provide treatment to these men.

Children are best served by meaningful relationships with loving and protective mothers and fathers. Mindful of the obstacles, we created a co-parenting model for child–parent psychotherapy with parents who committed acts of domestic violence. To nurture the violent parent's safe relationship with the child, safe cooperation between estranged parents with regard to their child is required. Prerequisites for treatment of court-referred parents locked in child custody disputes include continued court oversight of the violent parent's compliance with court decisions and specialized community programs or individual psychotherapy. The assessment with each parent addresses the violent partner's lethality, recognition of the aggression, remorse, and motivation to change, and requires the violent parent to make a commitment to refrain from aggressive behavior as a prerequisite to continue evaluation for treatment. Only when the clinician feels that he or she can work safely with both parents is treatment proposed. Both parents must sign information release consents for all institutions and service providers involved and agree to information sharing with the other parent.

Within this protective framework, the treatment format involves separate mother–child and father–child sessions with the same therapist. This single co-parenting therapist model enables the child to build a much-needed continuity of experience while going back and forth between the mother and the father. It also helps clinicians balance perspectives so that neither parent is demonized or idealized – a common pitfall when listening only to one parent's viewpoint. The child is our best information source. When the child engages with the parent without apprehension or fear, we feel more confident of the potential for treatment success. When the child remains guarded and hesitant after several sessions with one or both parents, this signals that the danger risk remains high. If joint sessions with each parent are not informative, individual sessions with the child are prescribed to offer a setting where frightening experiences can be safely disclosed.

We are cautiously extending this co-parenting model beyond parents engaged in child custody disputes to parents living together. The violent parent's commitment to refrain from aggression is again a prerequisite for treatment. We can't emphasize enough how shaky the ground feels in working with perpetrators of violence. The work calls for faith in the possibility of meaningful change combined with an unsentimental realism about the elements conspiring against change and a hard-headed determination to stop treatment if necessary and file reports that may lead to parental custody or rights termination. We cannot afford complacency when treating perpetrators of violence and their children. Not all clinicians are equipped for this work but, when they are and when parents cooperate, the results can be truly astounding as parents overcome lifelong patterns of interpersonal violence for their children's sake.

Treatment can repair the shattering effects of violence and related adversities on the parent–child relationship and the child's emotional health. Five randomized studies, two of them by our team at UCSF (Lieberman et al. 2006) and three of them from the University of Rochester Mount Hope Family Center (Cicchetti, Rogosch, & Toth, 2000, 2006; Toth, Maughan, Manly, Spagnola, & Cicchetti, 2002; Toth, Rogosch, Manly, & Cicchetti, 2006), show that child–parent psychotherapy is effective.

Clinical programs need highly specialized knowledge and work intensively with a relatively small number of families. They are not likely, given current funding policies and priorities, to be scaled to reach all the young children and families traumatized by violence. Most of these children never receive care from the mental health system, so knowledge about early trauma must be brought to the systems of care most likely to serve them. Within the SAMHSA-funded National Child Traumatic Stress Network (NCTSN), we direct the Early Trauma Treatment Network (ETTN), a consortium of four programs devoted to increasing access to services and raising the standard of care for traumatized young children and their families. The ETTN programs learn from each other and teach others how to transpose the core principles of trauma-focused early intervention to primary healthcare, childcare, law enforcement, child protective services, and the judicial system. Manuals and DVDs have been developed to enhance treatment and train trainers and service providers in these systems. As a way of building capacity in the field for trauma-focused treatment of children in the first five years of life, we are providing long-distance training to clinicians in about twenty-five states on child–parent psychotherapy. Our goal is to act as a prosocial virus that contains and repairs the damage caused by the virus of violence much as the angels in the nursery push back against the onslaught of the ghosts.

Irving Harris said that "there is nothing as practical as a good theory." All of our efforts are guided by the power of observation and reframing parent–child conflict to bring to the surface the benevolent motives under the alienation and rage, to support and celebrate the capacity of infant and parent to grow together and surmount adversity. We thank Berry Brazelton for showing us the way.

References and further reading

Brazelton, T. B., & Nugent, J. K. (1995). *Neonatal behavioral assessment scale (NBAS)* (3rd ed.). London: Mac Keith Press.

Cicchetti, D., & Cohen, D. J. (Eds.). (1995). *Developmental psychopathology* (Vol. 2). *Risk, disorder, and adaptation*. New York: Wiley.

Cicchetti, D., & Lynch, M. (1993). Toward an ecological/transactional model of community violence and child maltreatment: Consequences for children's development. *Psychiatry: Interpersonal and Biological Processes, 56*(1), 96–118.

Cicchetti, D., Rogosch, F. A., & Toth, S. L. (2000). The efficacy of toddler–parent psychotherapy for fostering cognitive development in offspring of depressed mothers. *Journal of Abnormal Child Psychology, 28*, 135–148.

Cicchetti, D., Rogosch, F. A., & Toth, S. L. (2006). Fostering secure attachment in infants in maltreating families through preventive interventions. *Development and Psychopathology, 18*, 623–649.

Felitti, V. J., Anda, R. F., Nordenberg, D., Williamson, D. F., Spitz, A. M., & Edwards, V. (1998). Relationship of childhood abuse and household dysfunction to many of the leading causes of death in adults: The adverse childhood experiences study. *American Journal of Preventive Medicine, 14*, 245–258.

Fraiberg, S., Adelson, E., & Shapiro, V. (1975). Ghosts in the nursery: A psychoanalytic approach to the problems of impaired mother–infant relationships. *Journal of the American Academy of Child and Adolescent Psychiatry, 14*, 387–422.

Gazmararian, J. A., Lazorick, S., Spitz, A. M., Ballard, T. J., Saltzman, L. E., & Marks, J. S. (1996). Prevalence of violence against pregnant women. *Journal of the American Medical Association, 275*, 1915–1920.

Harris, W. W., Putnam, F. W., & Fairbank, J. A. (2006). Mobilizing trauma resources for children. In A. F. Lieberman, & R. DeMartino (Eds.), *Interventions for children exposed to violence* (pp. 311–340). New Brunswick, NJ: Johnson & Johnson Pediatric Institute.

Herman, J. (1992). *Trauma and recovery: The aftermath of violence – From domestic violence to political terror*. New York: Basic Books.

Kempe, C. H., Silverman, F. N., Steele, B. F., Droegemueller, W., & Silver, H. K. (1962). The battered-child syndrome. *Journal of the American Medical Association, 181*, 17–24.

Kitzmann, K. M., Gaylord, N. K., Holt, A. R., & Kenny, E. D. (2003). Child witnesses to domestic violence: A meta-analytic review. *Journal of Consulting and Clinical Psychology, 71,* 339–352.

Lieberman, A. F., Ghosh Ippen, C., & Van Horn, P. (2006). Child–parent psychotherapy: Six month follow-up of a randomized control trail. *Journal of the American Academy of Child and Adolescent Psychiatry, 45,* 913–918.

Lieberman, A. F., & Van Horn, P. (2005). *Don't hit my mommy! A manual for child–parent psychotherapy with young witnesses of family violence.* Washington, DC: Zero to Three Press.

Lieberman, A. F., & Van Horn, P. (2008). *Psychotherapy with infants and young children: Repairing the effects of stress and trauma on early attachment.* New York: Guilford.

Osofsky, J. D. (1995). The effects of exposure to violence on young children. *American Psychologist, 50,* 782–788.

Pynoos, R. S. (1990). Post-traumatic stress in children and adolescents. In B. Garfinkel, G. Carlson, & E. Weller (Eds.), *Psychiatric disorders in children and adolescents* (pp. 48–63). Philadelphia: Saunders.

Regalado, M., & Halfon, N. (2002). Primary care services promoting optimal child development from birth to age 3 years: Review of the literature. *Archives of Pediatrics & Adolescent Medicine, 155,* 1311–1322.

Scheeringa, M. S., & Zeanah, C. (1995). Symptom expression and trauma variables in children under 48 months of age. *Infant Mental Health Journal, 16,* 259–270.

Sharfstein, S. (2006). New task force will address early childhood violence. *Psychiatric News, 41,* 3.

Spinazzola, J., Blaustein, M., & van der Kolk, B. A. (2005). Posttraumatic stress disorder treatment outcome research: The study of unrepresentative samples? *Journal of Traumatic Stress, 18,* 425–436.

Stern, D. (2002). *The first relationship: Infant and mother.* Cambridge, MA: Harvard University Press.

Terr, L. C. (1991). Childhood traumas: An outline and overview. *American Journal of Psychiatry, 148,* 10–20.

Toth, S. L., Maughan, A., Manly, J. T., Spagnola, M., & Cicchetti, D. (2002). The relative efficacy of two interventions in altering maltreated preschool children's representational models: Implications for attachment theory. *Development and Psychopathology, 14,* 877–908.

Toth, S. L., Rogosch, F. A., Manly, J. T., & Cicchetti, D. (2006). The efficacy of toddler–parent psychotherapy to reorganize attachment in the young offspring of mothers with major depressive disorder: A randomized preventive trial. *Journal of Consulting and Clinical Psychology, 74,* 1006–1016.

van der Kolk, B. A. (2005). Developmental trauma disorder: Towards a rational diagnosis for children with complex trauma histories. *Psychiatric Annals, 35,* 401–408.

World Health Organization, Commission on Social Determinants of Health (2007). *Achieving health equity: from root causes to fair outcomes.* Retrieved June 11, 2009, from: www.who.int/social_determinants/en/

Zeanah, C. H., & Scheeringa, M. S. (1997). The experience and effects of violence in infancy. In J. D. Osofsky (Ed.), *Children in a violent society* (pp. 97–123). New York: Guilford Press.

22

Understanding and Helping Traumatized Infants and Families

Joy D. Osofsky and Howard J. Osofsky

T. Berry Brazelton has been a model for all of us in recognizing the power of infancy and the crucial role of prevention and early intervention that has characterized much of our work. In this chapter, we focus on two areas of our work which have been profoundly influenced by Brazelton's teachings about the importance of infancy and early childhood. These are: (1) work with traumatized, abused, and neglected young children, and prevention and early intervention to minimize risk and increase potential; and (2) work with young children and their families after their traumatic exposure to Hurricane Katrina and the complex and uneven recovery – work that has allowed us to offer prevention, intervention, and resilience-building interventions. We conclude by describing some lessons learned through our work, reflective of Brazelton's approach.

The Problem of Abuse and Neglect

Every year, approximately one million cases of child abuse and neglect are substantiated in the United States (U.S. Department of Health and Human Services, Administration on Children, Youth, and Families, Children's Bureau, 2008). It is likely that the actual rate of abuse and neglect is considerably higher than the numbers in official records. Forty-five percent of these children are under the age of five, comprising the largest percentage of maltreated children. In 2006, more than 100,000 children under the age of three entered the child welfare system in the United States (State of Child Welfare in America, 2009); infants under the age of one are the largest cohort to enter care. Not only do infants and toddlers make up one third of all admissions into the child welfare system but, once they are in care, young children remain longer and are more likely to be abused and neglected (Wulczyn,

Hislop, & Harden, 2002). Recent data indicates, alarmingly, that each change in social worker reduces the chances of permanency by 52 percent (National Clearing House on Child Abuse and Neglect, April 2005). Further, there is greater vulnerability for young children with those under age four accounting for 79 percent of child fatalities, and children under age one accounting for 44 percent (U.S. Department of Health and Human Services, 2005).

It has been well established that abuse and neglect impact children negatively, affecting their physical, cognitive, social, and emotional development. Developmental delays are four to five times greater for abused than nonabused children, and they have a much higher incidence of behavioral problems and risk for mental health problems (Dore, 2005; Leslie et al., 2005). The high prevalence of mental health problems among these children is a major focus of concern, with one in five having a diagnosable mental health disorder (Mills et al, 2006). As they grow older, these children are at higher risk than nonabused children for problems in school and behavioral problems with at least half of all children who are maltreated experiencing such problems. In addition to behavioral difficulties, risk for truancy, delinquency, and risk-taking behaviors such as substance abuse and sexual promiscuity are common (Widom & Maxfield, 2001). There is increasing evidence that multiple traumas such as maltreatment combined with exposure to other types of violence, such as domestic violence, can affect children even more negatively, including lowering a child's IQ (Knitzer, Hirokazu, Cauthen, & Aber, 2000; Koenen, Moffitt, Caspi, & Taylor, 2003). The social and educational consequences of maltreatment start early in childhood and continue into later development. Maltreatment not only leads to increases in behavioral problems, especially aggression, but also depression and other deviant social behaviors such as school dropout. Just as important, it needs to be recognized that the personal costs and financial obligations for society are very significant.

Work that the first author has done in juvenile courts with abused and neglected children and their families provides the opportunity for intervention and systems change with the objective of breaking intergenerational cycles of abuse and neglect affecting maltreated infants and young children (Lederman & Osofsky, 2008; Lederman, Osofsky, & Katz, 2001; Osofsky & Lederman, 2004; Osofsky, Kronenberg et al., 2007). Many of the parents whose children have been adjudicated dependent related to abuse and/or neglect have become parents at a young age, often without having received nurturance and guidance from their own parents. Frequently they repeat the neglectful and abusive patterns that they grew up with, which results in their children being taken into the foster care system, at times, shortly after they are born. The Miami Court Team Project, a collaborative effort between Judge Cindy Lederman, Dr. Joy Osofsky, and Dr. Lynne Katz, has provided an opportunity for establishing an effective, evidence-based early intervention program. The project, which has been extended to other jurisdictions nationally, adds the essential component of science to the decisions that judges make about children in their courts. This approach provides judges in juvenile and family courts with additional information, evaluations, and services to further their efforts to break the intergenerational cycle of trauma that these children experience and give both the parents and the children a chance for a healthy, safe, nurturing future. The program provides information about the developmental needs of infants and toddlers in order for judges to incorporate this knowledge in taking the most appropriate actions and in making the best decisions related to the best interests of young children. The project involves coordination of the different systems and agencies that impact on children adjudicated dependent with the leadership and convening power of the judge. Finally, the program includes intensive evidence-based training for mental health and outreach providers and implementation of clinical and parenting components.

A key component to the success of the program is the ability to work with judges who recognize the benefit to the court of having more information, knowledge, and training about the science of early childhood development to aid them in making more developmentally informed decisions. This knowledge needs to be available to all who interface and make decisions related to children and families in court, including judges, lawyers, child welfare, Child Appointed Special Advocates, and others with whom children will come in contact. Outcome data and clinical reports from the program demonstrate a significant decrease in future abuse, increase in successful reunifications and permanency for the children, improved functioning of parents, enhanced developmental outcomes, and satisfaction with parenting. Clearly significant improvements result if the different components of a quality system are implemented collaboratively in a court system (Lederman & Osofsky, 2004, 2008; Lederman, Osofsky, & Katz, 2001; Osofsky & Lederman, 2006; Osofsky, Osofsky, & Harris, 2007). As anticipated, positive outcomes are more likely if the parents referred to the program are able to comply with their case plan goals with the support of a coordinated provider response. For such a program to be successful, it is crucial to build capacity both through collaborative effort with the courts and through training professionals to help them gain expertise in infant and early childhood mental health, health, early intervention, child welfare, and early childhood education.

An Example of Trauma, Intervention, and Recovery

Children and Disasters

Unique opportunities have emerged in Louisiana in the past three years related to young children and trauma. In the aftermath of Hurricane Katrina, the authors and LSU Health Sciences Center Trauma Team have not only been able to respond to and help support communities following a major natural and man-made disaster, but also to take a leadership role in keeping a perspective on young children and families and their needs in a postdisaster and recovery environment. In the New Orleans Metropolitan Area, we are now 3½ years post Hurricane Katrina and yet mental health problems remain as the recovery continues. As one sensitive school administrator commented recently, it is as if some people are now "becoming unraveled." Once families are resettled in their homes and communities, they are coming to the realization that their life is not and will never be the same as it was before Hurricane Katrina. Their neighborhood and community is different, their extended family and close friends are no longer there, and their life is different. The LSU Health Sciences Center Departments of Psychiatry and Pediatrics in New Orleans are continuing to provide multidisciplinary training, research, consultations, evaluations, and clinical services, as well as play a key role in supporting the behavioral health recovery of young children and their families in Louisiana and throughout the Gulf Region.

Young children are particularly vulnerable during and after disasters because they are totally dependent on caregivers and others to take care of them – and they do not have a clear way to express their needs. Further, disasters also traumatize caregivers so that they are often less emotionally available and sensitive to the needs of young children. Many caregivers and responders do not recognize that developmentally specific responses to trauma and disasters vary for children of different ages. In fact, disaster response often does not take into account the needs of our youngest children for safety, consistency, nurturance, places to play, and ways to be children.

In considering the response of Louisiana to young children following Hurricane Katrina, it is important to note that Louisiana ranks 49th in the nation in a recent state-by-state study on the wellbeing of America's children (KIDS COUNT Data Book, 2008) and 50th in percentage of population lacking access to quality health and mental healthcare (*Congressional Quarterly*, March 2008, "Health Care State Rankings 2008"; "Health Care Across America," *The Advocate*, March 27, 2008). The city of New Orleans has a tradition of being a community with much history and character but also a legacy of racism and continuing poverty. When Hurricane Katrina devastated New Orleans in August 2005, the reported poverty level was 23.2%, almost twice the national average of 12.7%. Thirty-eight percent of New Orleans children live in poverty (Fass & Cauthen, 2005), and two-thirds of families living below the poverty level are headed by a single mother. Unfortunately, children who live in poor families often experience more trauma than children whose families are more advantaged, placing them at risk for mental health problems. Children who are exposed to multiple traumas are at greater risk of mental health problems, and also less likely to receive mental health services that can prevent more serious problems over time.

Separation from family members as a consequence of disaster is one of the most disturbing issues facing young children. Hurricane Katrina was particularly hard on children; within one week after the hurricane made landfall, the National Center for Missing and Exploited Children received calls regarding 4,909 children who were missing or dislocated from their families (Broughton, Allen, Hanneman, & Petrikin, 2006). In addition to separation from family, young survivors of Hurricane Katrina lost their homes, their toys, stability from caregivers, relatives and surroundings, all of which are so important for children's healthy development.

Trauma Symptoms in Young Children

The manifestation of trauma in young children is a function of age and developmental phase and is strongly influenced by the child's limited perceptual, cognitive, and linguistic abilities (Kronenberg et al., in press; Lubit, Rovine, Defrancisci, & Eth, 2003; Osofsky & Lederman, 2004). Posttraumatic stress disorder, including re-experiencing, avoidance, and hyperarousal, has been shown to occur in young children in varying degrees and forms, with manifestations that are somewhat different from those of older children (Blank, 2007; De Bellis & Van Dillen, 2005; Lieberman & Knorr, 2007; Zero to Three, 2005). For example, young children re-experience the traumatic event, but are more likely to show their reactions through changes in play, new fears, regressive behaviors, and frightening nightmares. Young children are also more likely to engage in avoidant behaviors similar to older children.

Young children can become withdrawn, emotionally restricted, and numb, and lose interest in play. Regression may include the loss of previously acquired self-care, language, or motor skills; young children may demonstrate regression reverting to behaviors from an earlier developmental stage such as thumbsucking and clinging (Lieberman & Knorr, 2007). Symptoms of increased arousal may be manifested through exaggerated startle responses, irritability, hypervigilance, and physiologic deregulation (Blank, 2007). Following a trauma, preschoolers are more likely to engage in irritable, impulsive, and aggressive behaviors.

A limited number of studies have documented the chronicity of PTSD symptoms in young children. Lubit et al. (2003) found that while half of the traumatized children in their study were able to address and deal with their PTSD symptoms within three months, a substantial number continued to exhibit PTSD symptoms for a year or more. Based on maternal reports, Swenson et al. (1996) found that 33% of young children demonstrated emotional and behavioral problems three months after Hurricane Hugo, 16% showed them six months after the storm, and 9% still had problems seven to nine months after the storm. In our work (Kronenberg et al., in press; Osofsky, Osofsky, & Harris, 2007; Osofsky, Osofsky, Kronenberg, & Cross 2009), in the most heavily devastated areas immediately following Hurricane Katrina to four years after the storm, we are finding that young children demonstrate increased dysregulation and aggressive or withdrawn behaviors. The most common symptoms for young children include clingy behavior and worries about separation, worries about what might happen, especially during hurricane season, a hard time concentrating and behavior problems. Their parents reported that 93% were displaced, 81% lost their homes and personal property, 75% were unemployed, 69% of their children were transferred to a new school, 31% were separated from their pets, 17% were separated from caregivers, and 16% had experienced prior loss or trauma contributing to greater risk. Of this group of young children, 8% reported family or friends were killed. Perhaps, not unexpectedly, 34% of the parents requested counseling for their young children.

Conclusions and Lessons Learned

For prevention and early intervention, it is essential to raise awareness by providing immediate and ongoing education and training about trauma and the effects on infants and young children to service providers across systems that serve young children and their families. We have found these precepts to be crucial in a wide variety of settings, exemplified here both in work with young children in court settings who have been traumatized by abuse and neglect, and young children who have been traumatized by an overwhelming disaster impacting on them, their caregivers, and the community. The goal is to work toward the development of a coordinated system that focuses on social, emotional, and behavioral wellbeing for children under 6 years of age. From a preventive mental health perspective, child and family mental health needs are a crucial component of child-serving systems. At present, children under age 6 are seldom identified by primary care providers or childcare providers as needing mental health services, with a concomitant scarcity of referrals to mental health programs. The stigma associated with mental health problems and the fear of "labeling" children at such a young age are powerful reasons for this situation, as is limited knowledge about the developmentally grounded mental health needs of infants and young children. These obstacles can be addressed by providing more accessible consultation, assessment, prevention, and therapeutic services in ecologically acceptable settings, including homes, childcare centers, Head Start and Early Head Start Centers, schools, family resource centers, and community centers. Accessible services of this type have been crucial during the crisis and slow recovery following Hurricane Katrina. Services should also be extended to other sites such as court settings for vulnerable abused and neglected infants and young children in assessing and assisting them with their care and recovery, leading to reunification or permanency placement.

It is also crucial to recognize that intervention and services will be most effective by addressing the parent–child relationship. Focus must be placed both on the young child's symptoms, behaviors, or regulatory problems and the parent or caregiver so that the relationship, which is so crucial for healthy development, will be strengthened. We have found in our work with traumatized young children that it is crucial to emphasize resilience and the strengths in the relationship rather than just weaknesses and problems (Masten, 2001; Masten & Obradovic, 2008). This approach is consistent with Brazelton's ability to bring to responsiveness even the most fragile or at-risk baby. By emphasizing resilience in development, we can also take advantage of the perspective of Selma Fraiberg who has influenced our thinking with her wonderful statement, "working with young children is a little bit like having God on your side!" The Brazelton approach has helped us in our work with high-risk infants and families to always focus on the positive side of development.

Finally, we have learned from Brazelton that prevention is of the utmost importance. It is essential to learn ways to prevent difficulties by intervening as early as possible, during the prenatal period when risk is identified, in newborn nurseries with nurses and hospital visits, and through active, consistent home visiting programs. Pediatricians and healthcare providers need to be educated on "red flag" behaviors to note in pediatric clinics and emergency rooms to refer young children who may be traumatized or need mental health evaluation and services. By focusing on the needs of our most vulnerable citizens, our youngest children, we can prevent human tragedy and also save immeasurable human and financial costs for the repair and rehabilitation that may be needed later in their lives.

References and further reading

Blank, M. (2007). Posttraumatic stress disorder in infants, toddlers, and preschoolers. *BC Medical Journal, 49*(3), 133–138.

Broughton, D. D., Allen, E. E., Hannemann, R. E., & Petrikin, J. E. (2006). Getting 5,000 families back together: Reuniting fractured families after a disaster: The role of the National Center for Missing and Exploited Children. *Pediatrics, 117*(5), S442–S445.

De Bellis, M. D., & Van Dillen, T. (2005). Childhood post-traumatic stress disorder: An overview. *Child and Adolescent Psychiatric Clinics of North America, 14,* 745–772.

Dore, M. (2005). Child and adolescent mental health. In G. Malon and P. Hess (Eds.), *Child welfare for the twenty-first century: A handbook of practices, policies, and programs* (pp. 148–172). New York: Columbia University Press.

Fass, S., & Cauthen, N. J. (2005). *Child poverty in states hit by Hurricane Katrina.* National Center for Children in Poverty, Fact Sheet 1 (Sept).

KIDS COUNT (2008). *Data book online.* Baltimore, MD: Annie Casey Foundation.

Knitzer, J., Hirokazu Y., Cauthen, N. K., & Aber, J. L. (2000). Welfare reform, family support, and child development perspectives from policy analysis and developmental psychopathology. *Development and Psychopathology, 12,* 619–632.

Koenen, K. C., Moffitt, T. E., Caspi, A., & Taylor, S. (2003). Domestic violence is associated with suppression of IQ in young children. *Development and Psychopathology, 15,* 297–311.

Kronenberg, M. E., Hansel, T. C., Brennan, A. M., Lawrason, B., Osofsky, H. J., & Osofsky, J. D. (in press). Children of Katrina: Lessons learned about post-disaster resilience and recovery patterns. *Child Development.*

Lederman, C. S., & Osofsky, J. D. (2008). A judicial-mental health partnership to heal young children in juvenile court. *Infant Mental Health Journal, 29,* 36–47.

Lederman, C. S., Osofsky, J. D., & Katz, L. (2001). When the bough breaks the cradle will fall: Promoting the health and well being of infants and toddlers in juvenile court. *Juvenile and Family Court Journal, 52*, 33–38.

Leslie, L., Gordon, J. N., Lambros, K., Premji, K., Peoples, J., & Gist, K. (2005). Addressing the developmental and mental health needs of young children in foster care. *Developmental and Behavioral Pediatrics, 26*(2), 140–151.

Lieberman, A., & Knorr, K. (2007). The impact of trauma: A developmental framework for infancy and early childhood. *Psych Annals* (June), 416–422.

Lubit, R., Rovine, D., Defrancisci, L., & Eth, S. (2003). Impact of trauma on children. *Journal of Psychiatric Practice, 9*(2), 128–138.

Masten, A. S. (2001). Ordinary magic: Resilience processes in development. *American Psychologist, 56*(3), 227–238.

Masten, A. S., & Obradovic J. (2008). Disaster preparation and recovery: Lessons from research on resilience in human development. *Ecology and Society, 13*(1). Retrieved March 22, 2009 from www.ecologyandsociety.org/vol13/iss1/art9/.

Mills, C., Stephan, S. H., Moore, E., Weist, M. D., Daly, B. P., & Edwards, M. (2006). The president's new freedom commission: Capitalizing on opportunities to advance school-based mental health services. *Clinical Child and Family Psychology Review, 9*, 149–161.

National Clearinghouse on Child Abuse and Neglect, Washington, DC (April, 2005). In J. D. Osofsky (Ed.), *Young children and trauma: Intervention and treatment*. New York: Guilford Publishers.

Osofsky, J. D., Kronenberg, M., Hammer, J. H., Lederman, C. S., Katz, L., Adams, S., Graham, M., & Hogan, A. (2007). The development and evaluation of the intervention model for the Florida infant mental health pilot program. *Infant Mental Health Journal, 28*, 259–280.

Osofsky, J. D., & Lederman, C. (2004). Healing the child in juvenile court. In J. D. Osofsky (Ed.), *Young children and trauma: Intervention and treatment* (pp. 221–241). New York: Guilford Publishers.

Osofsky, J. D., & Lederman, C. S. (2006). Mental health and judicial partnerships: Collaborating to reduce the effects of abuse on infants and families. In A. F. Lieberman & R. DeMartino (Eds.), *Interventions for children exposed to violence* (pp. 89–110). United States: Johnson and Johnson Pediatric Institute, LLC.

Osofsky, J. D., Osofsky, H. J., & Harris, W. W. (2007). Katrina's children: Social policy for children in disasters. *Social Policy Reports, Society for Research in Child Development, 21*, 1–20.

Osofsky, J. D., Osofsky, H. J., Kronenberg, M., & Cross, T. (2009). The aftermath of Hurricane Katrina: Mental health considerations and lessons learned. In R. Kilmer, V. Gil-Rivas, R. Tedeschi, & L. Calhoun (Eds.), *Meeting the needs of children, families, and communities post-disaster: Lessons learned from Hurricane Katrina and its aftermath*. American Psychological Association Press.

State of Child Welfare in America (2009). Center for Family Policy and Research. Accessed March 31, 2009 at http://mucenter.missouri.edu/statechildwelfare09.pdf

Swenson, C. C., Saylor, C., Powell, P., Stokes, S., Foster, K., & Belter, R. W. (1996). Impact of a natural disaster on preschool children: Adjustment 14 months after a hurricane. *American Journal of Orthopsychiatry*, *66*(1), 122–130.

U.S. Department of Health and Human Services, Administration on Children, Youth and Families, Children's Bureau. (2008). Child Maltreatment 2008. Available from www.acf.hhs.gov/programs/cb/stats_research/index.htm#can.

Widom, C., & Maxfield, M. (2001). An update on the cycle of violence. Research in Brief, Washington, DC: U.S. Department of Justice, National Institute of Justice.

Wulczyn, F., Hislop, K., & Harden, B. (2002). The placement of children in foster care. *Infant Mental Health Journal, 23,* 454–475.

Zero to Three (2005). *Diagnostic classification: 0-3R. Diagnostic classification of mental health and developmental disorders of infancy and early childhood.* Washington, DC: Zero to Three: National Center for Infants, Toddlers and Families.

23

Child Maltreatment

The Research Imperative and the Exportation of Results to Clinical Contexts

Dante Cicchetti and Sheree L. Toth

Child maltreatment illustrates how negative caregiving experiences pose substantial risk for adversely affecting biological and psychological development across a broad range of domains of functioning. The importance of parenting, particularly during the early years of a child's life, has long been recognized and continues to be the hallmark of many resources for parents (Brazelton & Sparrow, 2006). Consequently, research on child maltreatment has an urgency characteristic of all problems that are of profound concern for society. Moreover, given the alarming epidemiological rates of maltreatment, which most likely underestimate the actual incidence and prevalence of the problem (Cicchetti & Toth, 2003; Sedlak, 1997), it is especially important that researchers who study developmental pathways to maladaptation, psychopathology, and resilience in maltreated children export their findings into the practice arena.

The importance of conducting empirical research on the developmental sequelae of child maltreatment was underscored by Aber and Cicchetti (1984). They argued that such investigations had great potential for enhancing the quality of clinical, legal, and policy-making decisions for abused and neglected children, including the development of specific interventions to meet the psychological needs of maltreated children, and the evaluation of services. In the absence of methodologically rigorous research on the effects of child maltreatment, myth would be put forward in place of knowledge as a guide to social action.

The biological and psychological sequelae associated with maltreatment initiate a path for maltreated children that is characterized by an increased likelihood of failure and disruption of the successful resolution of major issues of development (Cicchetti & Toth, 1995; Cicchetti & Valentino, 2006). Repeated developmental disruptions create a profile of enduring vulnerability that increases the likelihood of maladaptation and psychopathology as negative transactions between abused and neglected children and their social and caregiving environments are perpetuated over time (Cicchetti & Lynch, 1995). Despite this seemingly dire portrayal, a history of maltreatment does not doom all children to negative outcomes. In fact, resilience can develop even in the context of seemingly overwhelming adverse circumstances (Cicchetti & Rogosch, 1997; Luthar, Cicchetti, & Becker, 2000).

Increased fiscal constraints demand that service providers document the effectiveness of their prevention and intervention efforts. Basic scientific investigations in the area of child abuse and neglect are well positioned to contribute to the type of research required to justify service dollars. Likewise, these empirical findings can be utilized to modify existing ineffective intervention programs or policies so that the needs of maltreated children and their families can be better served (Toth & Cicchetti, 1993, 1999).

Translating Research on the Developmental Sequelae of Child Maltreatment into Preventive Interventions

Illustration from Investigations on Attachment Organization and Representational Processes

Prevention efforts for child maltreatment have emanated from public health, epidemiology, and community psychology, initiated by the 1974 Child Abuse Treatment and Prevention Act. Although these early efforts were important from a public health perspective, a paucity of developmental research was present in the conceptualization, implementation, or evaluation of these initiatives (Toth & Cicchetti, 1993, 1999; Toth & Valentino, 2008). Moreover, these initiatives typically targeted parents, with little attention directed toward maltreated children. Given their salience during infancy and early childhood and their continued importance across the life span, we focus on attachment and representational processes.

Attachment Organization

Throughout his pediatric practice, T. Berry Brazelton recognized the importance of rhythmic and cyclical mother–infant interactions during the early weeks of life. During observations of dyads, Brazelton and his colleagues noted that the synchrony of mother–infant rhythms appeared to be at the root of their communication and attachment (Brazelton, Koslowski, & Main,

1974). This perspective was extremely influential on decades of work that followed on mother–infant attachment. Although maltreated children do form attachments to their caregivers, the main issue in our research has been the quality of these attachments and their influence on the internal representational models of attachment figures and the self. Attachments that maltreated children form with their caregivers are highly likely to be insecure. Percentages of attachment insecurity in maltreated children have been found to be between 70% and 100% (Cicchetti & Valentino, 2006). Unlike children with more typical "organized" patterns of secure (Type B) and insecure (Type A and Type C) attachments (Ainsworth, Blehar, Waters, & Wall, 1978), maltreated children often lack organized strategies for dealing with their caregivers. Main and Solomon (1990) described this pattern of attachment as "disorganized/disoriented" (Type D). Children with disorganized attachments often exhibit fear toward the caregiver upon reunion from brief laboratory separations. They display a number of bizarre symptoms in the presence of the caregiver, including dazing, stilling, and freezing behaviors, and affect expressions that are "over-bright." These disorganized attachments may be the result of frightened and/or frightening parental behavior (Hesse & Main, 2006) and may initiate a cascade of difficulties with future relationships partners.

Representations of Caregivers and of Self

Children form representational models based on their relationship history with their primary caregiver (Bowlby, 1969/1982) and they carry these mental models into subsequent relationships. The poor-quality representational models of attachment figures that accompany these insecure attachments, with their complementary mental models of self in relation to other, could lead to negative expectations of how others will behave and how successful the self will be in relation to others (Bowlby, 1969/1982; Sroufe & Fleeson, 1988).

Our work on maltreated children's representations of their caregivers and of themselves has utilized the MacArthur Story Stem Battery (MSSB; Bretherton, Oppenheim, Buchsbaum, Emde, & the MacArthur Narrative Group, 1990) which contains story beginnings that describe a range of emotionally laden interactions among family members. Each story stem involves a combination of family dolls, including a mother, a father, and two same-sex children (detailed in Emde, Wolf, & Oppenheim, 2003). The MSSB coding yields measures of positive and negative maternal representations, positive and negative self-representations, mother–child relationship expectations, control, and relationship with the examiner.

Toth, Cicchetti, Macfie, and Emde (1997) utilized the MSSB to examine maternal and self-representations in neglected, physically abused, sexually abused, and nonmaltreated preschool children. The narratives of the maltreated youngsters contained more negative maternal representations and more negative self-representations than did the narratives of nonmaltreated children. Maltreated preschoolers also were more controlling with and less responsive to the examiner. Physically abused children evidenced the most negative maternal representations; they also had more negative self-representations than did nonmaltreated children. Sexually abused youngsters manifested more positive self-representations than did the neglected children. Despite the differences in maternal and self-representations, physically and sexually abused preschoolers both were found to be more controlling and less responsive to the examiner than were the neglected and nonmaltreated children.

Finding that sexually abused children had a high level of positive self-representations raises the possibility that these representations are not genuine but are more consistent with a "false self," wherein individuals present as overly positive to guard against their psychic pain (Calverley, Fischer, & Ayoub, 1994; Crittenden & DiLalla, 1988). Whereas physically abused children had high levels of negative self-representations, the neglected children had low levels of positive self-representation. The fact that neglected children had restricted positive self-representations is consistent with the reality of these children's lives, in which they most likely receive minimal attention to their basic needs. Conversely, physically abused children, although also confronted with parenting dysfunction, may experience periods during which they are responded to, possibly even positively, by their physically abusive parents. It may be that physically abused children are more likely to develop some sense of self as positive, whereas neglected children have fewer opportunities to do so. Additionally, the tendency for neglect to be a more ongoing, chronic condition involving parental acts of omission, whereas physical abuse may involve intermittent acts of commission, may be influencing the differences between these groups of children. Because physically abused children also seem to accurately perceive the negativity of their caregiving environments, as evidenced by their elevated negative maternal representations, this may be a strength. It may be more realistic to help children move beyond a history of maltreatment if they are in touch with its negativity than if they are prone to deny the realities that confront them.

Toth, Cicchetti, Macfie, Maughan, and VanMeenan (2000) conducted a longitudinal investigation of the narrative representations of parents and of self, as well as of child behavior, using the MSSB in maltreated and nonmaltreated youngsters. At age 4 the only significant difference was that the maltreated preschoolers evidenced fewer positive representations of parents and of self. However, one year later, maltreated children showed more negative representations of parent and of self as well as more negative behavior with the examiner. Thus, during this period noted for developmental transformations in the self, the representational models of maltreated children become increasingly more negative.

Translating Maltreatment Research into Practice

The Implementation of Randomized Control Trials to Improve Attachment Insecurity and Negative Representational Models of Self and Other in Maltreated Youngsters

Guided by research documenting that maltreated youngsters manifest impairments in attachment organization and representational models of self and caregiver, we implemented two RCTs for maltreated children. Because there is a high probability that these children will develop insecure disorganized attachments and unsuccessfully resolve subsequent developmental issues (Cicchetti & Toth, 2005) we reasoned that preventive interventions to promote the attainment of secure attachment organization in maltreated infants were essential.

We implemented two intervention models to foster attachment security and increase positive developmental outcomes in maltreated infants (Cicchetti, Rogosch, & Toth, 2006). The first model, child–parent psychotherapy (CPP), consisted of dyadic infant–mother therapy to improve infant–mother attachment relationships by altering the influence of negative maternal representational models of attachment on mother–infant relations. The second model, psycho-educational parenting intervention (PPI), provided mothers with didactic training in child development, parenting skills, coping strategies for managing stress, and assistance in developing social support networks (detailed in Cicchetti et al., 2006).

Baseline (pre-) and postintervention attachment relationships of mothers and infants in both CPP and PPI interventions were compared with the functioning of mothers and infants in maltreating families who received services typically available when a child had been maltreated – the community standard (CS) group. A fourth nonmaltreated comparison (NC) group, composed of infants and mothers who were demographically comparable to the three maltreatment groups, was included to compare normative developmental changes in infants who had not experienced maltreatment, but who had similar environmental stressors, with those who had been identified by the DHS for child abuse and/or neglect. All infants in maltreating families and their mothers were randomly assigned to either the CPP, PPI, or the CS group. Nonmaltreating (NC) families were chosen randomly from a list of recipients of Temporary Assistance to Needy Families. Both the CPP and PPI interventions were manualized, and were provided on a weekly basis by trained Master's level therapists, continued for 12 months, and were home-based.

Assessments of quality of attachment, utilizing the Strange Situation (Ainsworth et al., 1978), were conducted at baseline (infant age 13 months) and at the conclusion of the intervention (infant age 26 months). Videotapes of the Strange Situations were coded independently by individuals who were unaware of maltreatment status or intervention treatment conditions. At baseline, there were no differences among the three maltreatment groups (CPP, PPI, and CS) in the percentage of infants who were securely attached to their mothers. Notably, 3.6% of the infants in the CPP and 0% of the babies in the PPI and CS groups were securely attached (Cicchetti et al., 2006). Although a significantly greater percentage of infants in the nonmaltreated group were securely attached than were infants in any of the three maltreatment groups, the rate of security among the comparisons (33%) underscores that these families are a very high-risk group. In addition, at baseline, the three groups of maltreated infants each displayed extremely high rates of attachment disorganization (86% CPP; 82% PPI; 91% CS). These percentages of disorganized attachment did not significantly differ among the three maltreatment groups. In contrast, the rate of Type D attachment in the NC group was 20%.

Postintervention findings showed that maltreated infants in the CS group had a 1.9% attachment security rate, a nonsignificant improvement over their 0% baseline rate of security. The maltreated infants in each of the two interventions exhibited large increases in attachment security from baseline to postintervention (CPP: 3.6% to 60.7%; PPI: 0% to 54.5%). Both the CPP and PPI interventions were equally successful in modifying attachment insecurity. The percentage of attachment security remained at 39% in the infants in the NC group. Also, at the conclusion of the intervention, the percentage of Type D attachment declined from 86% to 32% for the CPP group and from 82% to 46% for the PPI group. Conversely, the infants in the CS group continued to exhibit high rates of disorganization (78%); the percentages of Type D attachment in the NC group at baseline and postintervention were virtually identical (20% and 19%).

This RCT demonstrates that both attachment theory and psycho-educationally based interventions were successful in altering the predominantly insecure and disorganized attachment organizations of maltreated infants. We believe these therapeutic models were effective for several reasons. All therapists received extensive training before implementing the interventions, they were familiar with the intervention modality and with the theory from which the interventions were derived, and they had considerable experience working with low-income maltreating families. Both models were manualized, weekly individual and group supervision was provided, therapists' adherence to their model was monitored for each case and caseloads were lower than is typical of outpatient mental health settings. The positive outcome of this investigation supports the importance of investing in more costly interventions, including allowing therapists sufficient time for training and supervision.

Clearly, the early insecure, generally disorganized attachments displayed by maltreated infants do not doom these youngsters to have poor-quality relationship expectations and negative self-representations throughout development. Attachment organization is modifiable, even if a high percentage of Type D attachment is initially characteristic of the sample.

Early Intervention for Maltreated Preschoolers

The second RCT was designed to modify maladaptive representational development in maltreated preschoolers. In this RCT, participants were again recruited through DHS. Maltreating mothers and their preschoolers were randomly assigned to one of three intervention groups: Child Parent Psychotherapy (CPP), Psycho-educational Parenting Intervention (PPI), and Community Standard (CS). The CPP and PPI interventions were similar to those described above (Toth & Cicchetti, 1999).

At baseline and at postintervention, the MSSB (Bretherton et al., 1990) was administered to child participants. Maternal representations, child representations, and mother–child relationship expectations were coded from the children's narratives (see Toth, Maughan, Manly, Spagnola, & Cicchetti, 2002).

Following the interventions, preschool-age children in the CPP intervention evidenced a greater decline in maladaptive maternal representations than did preschoolers in the PPI and CS interventions. In addition, children who took part in the CPP intervention displayed a greater decrease in negative self-representations than children in the PPI, CS, and NC groups. Additionally, the mother–child relationship expectations of children receiving CPP became more positive over the course of the intervention as compared with children in the PPI, CS, and NC groups. These results suggest that a model of intervention informed by attachment theory (CPP) is more efficacious at fostering positive representations than a psycho-educational model. Rather than assuming that "sensitive" periods exist during infancy and that the attachment relationship becomes less amenable to change over the course of development, our findings suggest that, at least during the preschool years, the internalized mother–child relationship continues to evolve and remains open to reorganization. The improvements in self-representations found in the children in the CPP intervention are a positive sign that resilient self-strivings may have been initiated in these youngsters (cf. Cicchetti & Rogosch, 1997). The developments that occurred in self-system processes may prove to serve a protective function in future years. Moreover, the positive changes in the maltreated preschoolers who received the CPP intervention may bode well for these children's future relationships with peers and other relationship partners.

From Research to Practice

Finding that attachment insecurity, including its most disorganized form, and negative representations of self and other are modifiable in extremely dysfunctional mother–child dyads offers significant hope for maltreated children and their families. In addition, costlier interventions such as foster care placement, special education services, residential treatment, and incarceration can be averted. The optimism engendered by our results also highlights the harsh reality of the ineffectiveness of services being provided to maltreated children in many communities. The lack of positive results emanating from treatment as usual are particularly distressing, as this may lead to even fewer resources being directed toward this problem. It is essential that clinicians, government officials, social policy advocates, and mental health insurers recognize the criticality of investing in the delivery of evidence-based interventions.

Government funders are increasingly committed to fostering the translation of evidence-based prevention and intervention strategies into the broader community. One such initiative, Building Healthy Children (BHC), has been launched in Rochester, New York. BHC utilizes a service pyramid, with broad universal outreach at its base and with evidence-based services, including CPP, at its peak (detailed in Toth, Manly, & Nilsen, 2008) to provide services to disadvantaged mothers who had their first child prior to age 18. The recognition of the importance of incorporating empirically supported treatments into a primary prevention program and committing financial resources toward evaluating the model represents a true sea change in the synergy that can occur when governmental bodies join with university- and community-based organizations. The implementation of such models also holds considerable hope for increasing the translation of empirically supported treatments to the children and families most in need. The implications of efforts such as these for reducing the overall burden of mental illness in society are compelling. As findings on effective outcomes emerge, it is hoped that the seeds of these pioneering initiatives will inspire others to forge similar partnerships on behalf of vulnerable children and families.

References

Aber, J. L., & Cicchetti, D. (1984). Socioemotional development in maltreated children: An empirical and theoretical analysis. In H. Fitzgerald, B. Lester & M. Yogman (Eds.), *Theory and research in behavioral pediatrics* (Vol. 2, pp. 147–205). New York: Plenum press.

Ainsworth, M. D. S., Blehar, M. C., Waters, E., & Wall, S. (1978). *Patterns of attachment: A psychological study of the Strange Situation.* Hillsdale, NJ: Lawrence Erlbaum Associates.

Bowlby, J. (1969/1982). *Attachment and loss* (Vol. 1). New York: Basic Books.

Brazelton, T. B., Koslowski, B., & Main, M. (1974). The origins of reciprocity: The early mother–infant interaction. In M. Lewis & L. A. Rosenblum (Eds.), *The effect of the infant on its caregiver* (pp. 49–76). New York: John Wiley.

Brazelton, T. B., & Sparrow, J. D. (2006). *Touchpoints Birth to 3: Your Child's Emotional and Behavioral Development* (2nd ed.). Cambridge, ME: Da Capo Press.

Bretherton, I., Oppenheim, D., Buchsbaum, H., & Emde, R. N. (1990). *MacArthur Story Stem Battery.* (Available from the authors).

Calverley, R. M., Fischer, K. W., & Ayoub, C. (1994). Complex splitting of self-representations in sexually abused adolescent girls. *Development and Psychopathology, 6*, 195–213.

Cicchetti, D., & Lynch, M. (1995). Failures in the expectable environment and their impact on individual development: The case of child maltreatment. In D. Cicchetti, & D. J. Cohen (Eds.), *Developmental psychopathology: Risk, disorder, and adaptation* (Vol. 2, pp. 32–71). New York: John Wiley & Sons.

Cicchetti, D., & Rogosch, F. A. (1997). The role of self-organization in the promotion of resilience in maltreated children. *Development and Psychopathology, 9,* 799–817.

Cicchetti, D., Rogosch, F. A., & Toth, S. L. (2006). Fostering secure attachment in infants in maltreating families through preventive interventions. *Development and Psychopathology, 18*(3), 623–650.

Cicchetti, D., & Toth, S. L. (1995). A developmental psychopathology perspective on child abuse and neglect. *Journal of the American Academy of Child and Adolescent Psychiatry, 34,* 541–565.

Cicchetti, D., & Toth, S. L. (2003). Child maltreatment: A research and policy agent for the dawn of the millennium. In R. P. Weissberg, L. H. Weiss, O. Reyes, & H. J. Walberg (Eds.), *Trends in the well-being of children and youth* (Vol. 2, pp. 181–206). Washington, DC: CWLA Press.

Cicchetti, D., & Toth, S. L. (2005). Child maltreatment. *Annual Review of Clinical Psychology, 1,* 409–438.

Cicchetti, D., & Valentino, K. (2006). An ecological transactional perspective on child maltreatment: Failure of the average expectable environment and its influence upon child development. In D. Cicchetti, & D. J. Cohen (Eds.), *Developmental Psychopathology* (2nd ed., Vol. 3: Risk, Disorder, and Adaptation, pp. 129–201). New York: Wiley.

Crittenden, P. M., & DiLalla, D. (1988). Compulsive compliance: The development of an inhibitory coping strategy in infancy. *Journal of Abnormal Child Psychology, 16,* 585–599.

Emde, R. N., Wolf, D. P., & Oppenheim, D. (2003). *Revealing the inner worlds of young children: The MacArthur Story Stem Battery and parent–child narratives.* Oxford University Press. New York.

Hesse, E., & Main, M. (2006). Frightened, threatening, and dissociative parental behavior in low-risk samples: Description, discussion, and interpretations. *Development and Psychopathology, 18,* 309–343.

Luthar, S. S., Cicchetti, D., & Becker, B. (2000). The construct of resilience: A critical evaluation and guidelines for future work. *Child Development, 71,* 543–562.

Main, M., & Solomon, J. (1990). Procedures for identifying infants as disorganized/disoriented during the Ainsworth Strange Situation. In M. Greenberg, D. Cicchetti, & E. M. Cummings (Eds.), *Attachment in the preschool years* (pp. 121–160). Chicago: University of Chicago Press.

Sedlak, A. J. (1997). Risk factors for the occurrence of child abuse and neglect. *Journal of Aggression, Maltreatment, and Trauma, 1,* 149–187.

Sroufe, L. A., & Fleeson, J. (1988). The coherence of family relationships. In R. A. Hinde, & J. Stevenson–Hinde (Eds.), *Relationships within families: Mutual influences* (pp. 27–47). Oxford, UK: Oxford University Press.

Toth, S. L., & Cicchetti, D. (1993). Child maltreatment: Where do we go from here in our treatment of victims? In D. Cicchetti, & S. L. Toth (Eds.), *Child abuse, child development, and social policy* (pp. 399–438). Norwood, NJ: Ablex.

Toth, S. L., & Cicchetti, D. (1999). Developmental psychopathology and child psychotherapy. In S. Russ, & T. Ollendick (Eds.), *Handbook of psychotherapies with children and families* (pp. 15–44). New York: Plenum Press.

Toth, S. L., Cicchetti, D., Macfie, J., & Emde, R. N. (1997). Representations of self and other in the narratives of neglected, physically abused, and sexually abused preschoolers. *Development and Psychopathology, 9*, 781–796.

Toth, S. L., Cicchetti, D., Macfie, J., Maughan, A., & VanMeenen, K. (2000). Narrative representations of caregivers and self in maltreated preschoolers. *Attachment and Human Development, 2*, 271–305.

Toth, S. L., Manly, J. T., & Nilsen, W. (2008). From research to practice: Lessons learned. *Journal of Applied Developmental Psychology, 29*, 317–325.

Toth, S. L., Maughan, A., Manly, J. T., Spagnola, M., & Cicchetti, D. (2002). The relative efficacy of two interventions in altering maltreated preschool children's representational models: Implications for attachment theory. *Development and Psychopathology, 14*, 777–808.

Toth, S. L., & Valentino, K. (2008). Translating research on children's memory and trauma into practice: Clinical and forensic implications. In M. Howe, G. Goodman, & D. Cicchetti (Eds.), *Children's memory and trauma: Cognitive, neuropsychological, and clinical perspectives* (pp. 363–399). New York: Oxford University Press.

Part III

Translational Science

Implications for Professional Development, Systems of Care, and Policy

Section I

Changing Practice and Improving Care through Professional Development

24

Developing the Infant Mental Health Workforce

Opportunities, Challenges, and Strengths for Translating Research to Professional Development and Practice

Libby Zimmerman

The responsibility for fostering nurturing relationships and repairing disruptions during infancy and early childhood is not just the province of mental health professionals. A pediatrician who helps a mother notice her baby's engaging smile can mitigate that mother's anxiety and help her see her baby more clearly. A caring, consistent, childcare teacher can ease the pain of a toddler and parent struggling to understand each other. A physical therapist trained to help a father accurately interpret his baby's looking away as a request for a break – rather than a sign of annoyance with the father – increases the father's pleasure and the baby's sense of competence.

Through his observations, research, and clinical wisdom, T. Berry Brazelton first supported infants' relationships with their mothers and later fathers and elaborated concepts that are at the heart of infant mental health.

In 1969 he published *Infants and Mothers: Differences in Development*, a book with what were then radical messages: each baby brings a unique self to relationships; mothers have the capacity to accurately respond to the unique person in their care. Summarizing a study of identical twin boys in which four physicians, including himself, observed the babies for 30 hours and the mother recorded her impression of each baby after she had held him for twenty minutes, Brazelton notes:

> Not only was her impression of each boy after twenty minutes more accurate, more clear-cut than ours, she also saw them as potential human beings. We were impressed with the accuracy and depth of insight that is a mother's intuitions. This kind of intuition influences a mother's relationship to her infant in the first hours she spends with him or her. Her own capacity to relate to his or her individual qualities is predetermined by her past experiences, but each baby becomes a specific experience to a mother. There are potentials for change and adjustment not only in the baby but also in the mother (Brazelton, 1969, p. 1).

What were later to become infant mental health principles are highlighted in Brazelton's early writing: the relationship between mother and baby is central; each baby is unique; he or she exerts influence on the mother; mothers are fundamentally accurate observers whose capacity to read cues is influenced by past relationship experiences; and both partners are capable of change. These ideas attracted a group of researchers and clinicians of various backgrounds and training.

Over the course of more than thirty years, Brazelton's observations on infants' rapidly unfolding development, the unique nature of each child and family, the importance of finding strengths in parents and in the "give and take" of relationships were echoed in the research and clinical analysis of "baby watchers" (Fraiberg, Adelson, & Shapiro, 1975; Stern, 1985; Trevarthen, 1980) and policy advisers drawing from research on brain development (Shonkoff & Phillips, 2000). More recently in psychotherapy, the emphasis has shifted from traumatized parents uncovering and releasing past hurts experienced in childhood relationships (Fraiberg et al., 1975) to embracing the importance of uncovering "angels" – loving, care-receiving experiences – in childhood (Lieberman, Padron, Van Horn, & Harris, 2005). Clinical research suggests that a traumatized parent who is encouraged to draw on experiences of intense positive emotional exchanges when she or he felt "nearly understood, accepted, and loved" can help break the cycle of transmission of abuse. In addition, the research lens has opened beyond mothers to other caregivers (Hossain et al., 1994; Pelaez-Nogueras, Field, Cigales, Gonzales, & Clasky, 1994; Zimmerman & Fassler, 2003) to suggest that infants and young children who grow up in challenging family and community environments can be protected from emotional disorders by stable relationships with nurturing caregivers – within and beyond the family.

There is little debate that relationships are the "center of the universe" for infants and young children. But how slowly research evidence moves into professional development and frontline practice, even in communities where many influential researchers have conducted their work (for example, Massachusetts, home to Brazelton and other leading infant researchers and clinicians)! Despite the research evidence, most practitioners were and are still trained to focus on individual development, without the benefit of a paradigm shift that places relationships at the center of professional awareness and intervention. What helps a busy pediatrician look beyond the infant in the exam room to the interactions with that infant's mother and father? What helps an Early Intervention (EI) practitioner working in the "natural environment" (Individuals with Disabilities Education Improvement Act, 2004) of the home stay focused on working with parent and baby together when the overwhelmed, isolated parent wants to go off to do the laundry or appears to have no energy to sit on the floor and participate in physical therapy or play?

Brazelton and a team of mental health researchers and practitioners provided leadership in creating Touchpoints (Brazelton & Sparrow, 2003), a developmental and relational professional development model for physicians, nurses, childcare providers, and EI and other practitioners working with parents and very young children. It emphasizes supporting parent–child relationships by predicting that development is not continuous and then helping parents as they identify and nurture their children's own unique way of going forward and backward in the course of their rapid development in the first six years of life. Identifying and nurturing the strengths of parents and children is at the core of this approach. Touchpoints training has enriched practitioners in many communities in the USA and abroad. The model has much in common with infant mental health. Practitioners who work within this model are following basic infant mental health principles, integrating reflective practice and focusing on the behavior of the child as the language for communication with parents.

What Competencies are Needed? What Programs and Policies Will Ensure that These Are Acquired?

As of this writing, nine U.S. states have developed infant mental health competencies (Michigan, Arizona, California, New Mexico, Oklahoma, Vermont, Florida, Indiana, and Connecticut) – an attempt to establish standards and training content for providers who work with children from birth to three or birth to five. In a recent review of six state systems, Jon Korfmacher and Aimee Hilardo (2008) found differences of opinion about areas of knowledge and skill but agreement on the importance of relationships. The meaning of the term "relationships" was broad, however, and open to different interpretations. They found that the term referred to the interdependent web of relationships a child develops, yet often was applied only to the importance of the parent–child relationship without also including the young child's relationship with childcare providers. In addition, five systems focus training on the ability of practitioners to form relationships with families.

Training content alone is not powerful enough to ensure change in practice. When frontline staff attend an infant mental health training and return to their agency, inspired to focus on relationships, change is unlikely to take place unless the agency's leaders and mentors provide support for it (Knapp-Philo, Hindman, Stice, & Turbiville, 2006). Best practice suggests training leaders, supervisors, and direct practice people together. When people speak the same "language" and see the world through the same lens, new ideas can ripple through the system. One of Brazelton's observations elaborated in Touchpoints is the importance of valuing "passion" – going where the energy is – in working with parents. Achieving systems change requires the same attention to pockets of interest and activity.

The scope of the work is daunting. How do we deliver professional development and set priorities for professional development for practitioners interacting with children aged birth to five, their parents, and other significant caregivers, around the country and across the globe? Efforts to date in Massachusetts, where in 2004 there were approximately 400,000 children age 5 and under (U.S. Census Bureau, 2004), while still fledgling, exemplify some of the opportunities, challenges, and strategies for improving and expanding the infant mental health workforce. In 2006, spurred in part by escalating expulsions of four- and five-year-old children from preschool classrooms, United Way of Mass Bay and Merrimack Valley (UWMB&MV) released a request for proposals for training efforts that would help infant and early childhood mental health consultants and clinicians to address and prevent such behavioral problems. As a result, Connected Beginnings was founded as a training institute to promote awareness of the central importance of relationships in the lives of infants and young children. The goals of the organization are to provide, evaluate, and support infant and early childhood mental health professional development throughout Massachusetts for frontline professionals, the people who are in a position to nurture the developing relationships between infants/toddlers, their parents, and other significant caregivers.

Connected Beginnings identified two communities of professionals who work with very young children and are ideally positioned to nurture relationships and make a significant difference: EI, with approximately sixty EI programs that interact with children from birth to three at risk for or experiencing developmental challenges (29,000); and the childcare community, with 2,124 early care and education centers and 7,789 family childcare homes that respond to children from birth to five (173,000) (Bartlett, Waddoups, & Zimmerman, 2007).

Beginning in 2002, an EI agency in Massachusetts reached out to the infant mental health community, requesting professional development in infant mental health – not to help EI practitioners become infant mental health clinicians but to achieve competence in intervening to promote the social and emotional wellbeing of children receiving EI intervention. Thom Child and Family Services, an EI agency, wrote and received a grant to provide infant mental health training to EI practitioners in one region of the state. Over the course of the past four years, the author worked with Thom to develop and evaluate IN-TIME, a 36-hour infant mental health professional development curriculum, and to train 75 practitioners in three cohorts. Process evaluations and one qualitative follow-up study of IN-TIME suggested that practitioners increased their knowledge of infant mental health and their confidence in focusing on relationships (Leutz & Zimmerman, 2008). Participants describe the increased energy and interest that comes from focusing on relationships – even revitalizing practitioners who had been feeling depleted.

What Helps Practitioners Shift Their Perspective? What Convinces Practitioners that Relationships Are Key?

The following section describes some of the elements of this interactive training that help EI practitioners shift their focus of attention from individuals to relationship dynamics and helps the practitioner appreciate their influence on those dynamics.

To promote sustaining change within agencies, IN-TIME requires that each participating agency send a leader, a supervisor, and a frontline staff to the training. A follow-up qualitative evaluation suggested that this continuity of staff presence helps participants to maintain and enhance their focus on infant mental health and to work within a relationship paradigm.

The seminar integrates a variety of modalities to reach experienced adult learners: reflection on beliefs and values; reading and writing; mini-lectures accompanied by PowerPoint handouts; experiential exercises, e.g., role plays; observations in the field and in the seminar using videotapes; and small and large group discussions of observations. In addition there are a minimum of six hours of facilitated peer supervision in groups of no more than nine participants.

Before a seminar begins, participants are asked to think about what brings them the most joy in their work and to identify their favorite infant mental health researchers-theorists. Brazelton is mentioned by more than half of the participants. Asking about favorite theorists establishes the participants as professionals who are likely to come with knowledge and expertise. Participants describe experiencing joy in many ways, including promoting give and take in relationships, observing development unfold, and helping parents become more confident.

To bring into awareness the influence of culture and past experience on the participants' view of relationships, participants are asked to write down their family of origin's beliefs about newborn competencies and then to share their experiences within small groups. The groups discuss the ways their beliefs may influence their acceptance or rejection of various research studies. To ground the seminar in research and participant observations of behavior, video clips are shown, for example, Trevarthen's study, aired by the BBC, of two fullterm infants conversing with parents and one premature baby with an intravenous tube who is skin-to-skin with his father. Participants record and share their observations of the give and take, observing what the father does (vocalize, leave a space, provide skin-to-skin contact) and what the infant does (vocalize, leave a space, grasp his father's finger). The participants are trained in many different disciplines and bring their own unique perspectives to these observations. The observation process is repeated throughout the 30-hour seminar and the six hours of follow-up facilitated peer supervision.

To illustrate the relationship dynamics that influence the social and emotional wellbeing of infants, toddlers, their parents, and other significant caregivers, a model broadly adapted from Dan Stern (1985) is used

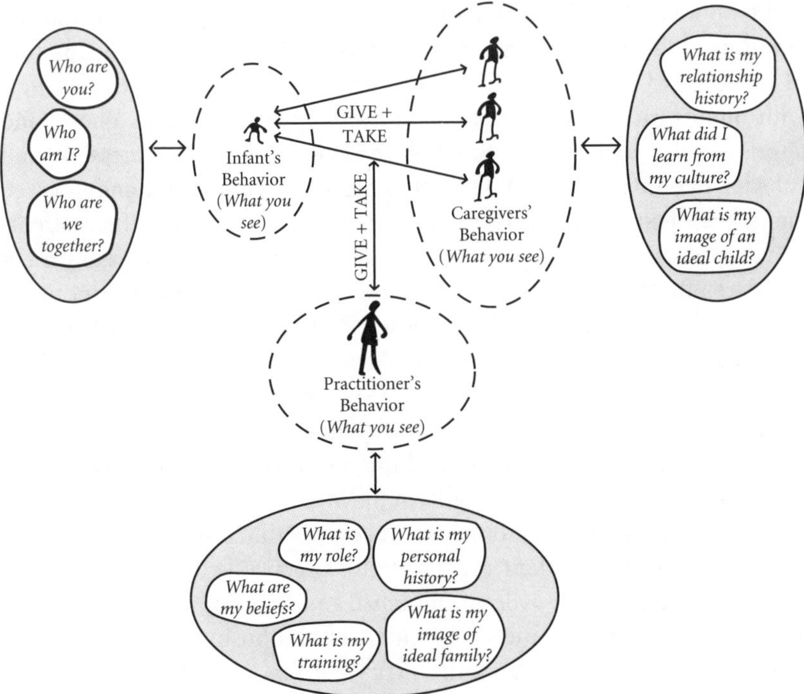

Figure 24.1 An illustration of the relationship dynamics that influence the social and emotional wellbeing of infants, toddlers, their parents, and other significant caregivers
Source: Broadly adapted from Dan Stern (1985)

(Figure 24.1). The diagram provides a visual guide that helps maintain a focus on the give and take within an infant's network of social relationships, focusing on both behavior that is observable in the exchanges and the inner subjective world that guides and is changed by those behaviors.

The diagram presents the essential elements of infant mental health theory: behavior that is observable in the give and take among adults and infants/toddlers; the internal experience of each caregiver that influences behavior and is hopefully influenced by the "real" baby; the developing internal world of the infant that develops from his/her interactions; and the internal experience that guides the practitioners' observable behavior.

The content of the seminar follows the diagram and is divided into four modules: (1) introduction and framework for infant mental health; (2) what infants bring to relationships including sensitive periods of social and emotional development, temperament, and the capacity of acquiring emotional self-regulation in conjunction with the patience and adaptation of caregivers; (3) what parents and caregivers bring to their relationships with infants including the process of becoming a parent, the ghosts and angels of the past, and emotional challenges such as depression and substance abuse that can influence the ability to accurately see and interact; and (4) understanding the give and take between infants and their parents and other significant caregiver. In the child and parent modules, assessment tools are integrated, e.g., Ages and Stages Questionnaire-Social-Emotional (infants and toddlers) (Squires, Bricker, & Twombley, 2002), Edinburgh Postnatal Depression Scale (Cox, Holden, & Sagovsky, 1987), and Two Question Depression Screen (parents) (MacArthur Foundation, 2002).

Throughout the seminar, the multidisciplinary participants (social workers, physical therapists, occupational therapists, speech therapists, nurses) are encouraged to look for strengths in the infant, the adult, and their interactions, as they keep in mind the vulnerabilities that brought the family to EI. A key strategy of infant mental health practice is to identify what is already working well in order to mobilize and enhance the resources that are present in the infant, the adult, and their relationships.

To help practitioners overcome their reluctance to identify strengths, participants are asked to reflect on and document their own experience: receiving positive feedback in their family, school, and work place; how they feel when they receive positive feedback; and how often they give feedback about strengths to families, coworkers, supervisees, and supervisors. What emerges is the realization that most people do not have extensive experience hearing what they did well. For some, there are even cultural prohibitions against saying anything positive, e.g., the danger of inviting the "evil eye." This exercise affirms that it takes conscious thought to give the kind of positive feedback that is energizing and helpful to families and even supervisees.

Careful observation is a critical skill for practitioners. Detailed, behaviorally specific observations can inform feedback and open up dialogue between practitioners and parents. For example, when a father shares his anxiety about being a good father with a practitioner, the practitioner who observes carefully can describe to that father how he soothed his crying daughter by holding her securely next to his chest and rocking her back and forth, and help the father see how his daughter found her fist and gently sucked on it while he held her. Or the practitioner can ask the father what he thought worked to calm his daughter and be ready to agree or supplement the father's observations. One homework assignment is to describe a positive interaction in two different situations – one in a family the practitioner finds easy to work with and the other in a family the practitioner finds hard to work with. In both instances the participants are able to see that positive exchanges do occur although it is sometimes harder to find them when a family presents challenges to the practitioner – and those challenges will be different for each practitioner. Role play is then used to help practitioners practice engaging caregivers in observation and providing feedback in ways that caregivers can hear.

Future Challenges – Scaling Relationship-based Infant Mental Health Workforce Development

Given the size of the EI work force, expansion of training potential is critical. In Massachusetts, policy changes supported such an expansion effort. Although the original provisions of the Education for all Handicapped Children Act Amendments of 1986 (Congressional Record, 1986) mandated services to address social and emotional challenges as well as problems in language, cognition and motor development, the social and emotional aspects of development were not recognized as essential. However, in 2006, the Federal Office of Special Education Programs (U.S. Department of Education, 2008) mandated that all states provide summary information from EI on infants' and toddlers' positive social-emotional skills in social relationships and their use of appropriate behavior to meet their own needs, i.e. the capacity for self-regulation.

In the fall of 2008, the Massachusetts Inter-Agency Coordinating Council that provides guidance to EI programs unanimously approved a Vision Statement and Draft Recommendations to present to the Massachusetts Department of Public Health, affirming the importance of providing professional development and reflective supervision for EI practitioners to ensure integration of a relationship-based approach to practice. That year, the Department of Public Health provided financial support to Connected Beginnings to provide a train-the-trainer seminar on IN-TIME for 19 people. Connected Beginnings also facilitates peer consultation among IN-TIME trainers and provides support for implementation across the state.

IN-TIME is only one effort at integrating a relationship-based, developmental, culturally sensitive model into the practice of frontline professionals who work with infants, toddlers and their families. Questions about the long- and short-term effectiveness of this and other professional development efforts are significant. A pre- and post-survey evaluation of this training provides outcome data of modest reliability and validity.

Yet there is great hope for system-wide change in promoting relationship-focused professional development based on encouraging early successes from model programs and initiatives in a number of the United States, as well as a new federal commitment to early childhood. Changing the paradigm across systems, along with corresponding changes in policies, procedures, protocols, and professional practice, requires combining resources and overcoming the challenges of working across institutions and systems. We need to follow the wisdom of Berry Brazelton in looking for strengths and passion within these systems, just as we do with parents and children. What keeps practitioners going is the intimate knowledge that caring about parent and child makes a profound difference. It is this passion that will inspire meaningful and lasting change across systems of care and within them at all levels.

References and further reading

Bartlett, J. D., Waddoups, A. B., & Zimmerman, L. (2007). *Training professionals to support the mental health of young children and their families: Lessons for Massachusetts from the national landscape*. Boston, MA: Connected Beginnings Training Institute.

Brazelton, T. B. (1969). *Infants and young mothers: Differences in development*. New York: Dell Publishing.

Brazelton, T. B., & Sparrow, J. (2003). *The Touchpoints™ model of development*. Boston, MA: Brazelton Touchpoints Center, Children's Hospital, Boston.

Congressional Record (1986). *The education for the handicapped act (EHA)* (P.L. 94–142), Amendments (P.L. 99-457). Washington, DC Preschool and Infant/Toddler Programs.

Cox, J. L., Holden, J. M., & Sagovsky, R. (1987). Edinburgh Postnatal Depression Scale (EPDS). *British Journal of Psychiatry, 150*, 782–786.

Fraiberg, S., Adelson, E., & Shapiro, V. (1975). Ghosts in the nursery: A psychoanalytic approach to the problems of impaired infant–mother relationships. *Journal of the American Academy of Child Psychiatry, 14*(3), 387–421.

Hossain, Z., Field, T., Gomzales, J., Malphurs, J., Dell Valle, C., & Pickens, J. (1994). Infants of "depressed" mothers interact better with their nondepressed fathers. *Infant Mental Health Journal, 15*(4), 348–357.

Individuals with Disabilities Education Improvement Act (2004). U.S. Code §635(a)(16) (A-B). Washington, DC: U.S. Government Printing Office.

Knapp-Philo, J., Hindman, J., Stice, K., & Turbiville, V. (2006). Professional development that changes practices and programs: Six successful strategies. *Zero to Three, 26*(3), 43–49.

Korfmacher, J. & Hilado, A. (2008). *Creating a workforce in early childhood mental health: Defining the competent specialist* (Research Report, 2008, No. 1). Retrieved from the Herr Research Center for Children and Social Policy at Erikson Institute Web Site, June 16, 2009: http://www.erikson.edu/hrc/publications/pubstopic.aspx.

Leutz, B., & Zimmerman, L. (2008, Dec. 5). *Strengthening relationship-based practice in early intervention: A field-tested professional development model.* Presentation to the 23rd National Training Institute, Los Angeles, CA.

Lieberman, A. F., Padron, E., Van Horn, P., & Harris, W. W. (2005). Angels in the nursery: The intergenerational transmission of benevolent parental influences. *Infant Mental Health Journal, 26*(6), 504–520.

MacArthur Foundation Initiative on Depression and Primary Care (2002). *Depression management tool kit: Two question screen.* Retrieved February 2010 from http://depression-primarycare.org/clinicians/toolkits/.

Pelaez-Nogueras, M., Field, R., Cigales, M., Gonzales, A., & Clasky, S. (1994). Infants of depressed mothers show less "depressed" behavior with their nursery teachers. *Infant Mental Health Journal, 15*(4), 358–367.

Shonkoff, J. P., & Phillips, D. (2000). *From neurons to neighborhoods: The science of early childhood development.* Washington, DC: National Academies Press.

Squires, J., Bricker, D., and Twombley, E. (2002). *Ages and stages questionnaire: Social emotional.* Baltimore, MD: Paul H. Brooks.

Stern, D. N. (1985). *The interpersonal world of the infant.* New York: Basic Books.

Trevarthen, C. (1980). The foundations of intersubjectivity: Development of interpersonal and cooperative understanding in infants. In D. Olson (Ed.), *The social foundations of language and thought* (pp. 242–316). New York: W. W. Norton.

U.S. Census Bureau (2004). *Statistical abstract of the United States.* Washington, DC: U.S. Government Printing Office.

U.S. Department of Education's Office of Special Education and Rehabilitative Services (2008). *U.S. Department of Education Determination Letters on State Implementation of the IDEA for Part B and Part C for Fiscal Year 2006.* Retrieved February 2010 from www.ed.gov/policy/speced/guid/idea/monitor/factsheet.html

Zimmerman, L., & Fassler, I. (2003). The dynamic of emotional availability in childcare: How infants involve and respond to their teen mothers and childcare teachers. *Infants and Young Children, 16*(3), 258–269.

25

The Touchpoints Approach for Early Childhood Care and Education Providers

Jayne Singer and John Hornstein

T. Berry Brazelton has had a profound influence upon the early childhood care and education (ECCE) profession. His pioneering research on infants' and young children's competence (Brazelton, 1987) has led to a reassessment of how children are understood by all disciplines. Public policy for quality childcare for working parents (Brazelton & Greenspan, 2001) has been driven by his eloquent advocacy for several decades. His popular books for parents have expanded their knowledge and their influence in interactions with caregivers. Brazelton's Touchpoints Approach to understanding development and building stronger partnerships with parents has inspired a unique professional development program, the subject of this chapter, to improve the quality of early childhood care and education.

Grounded in Dr. Brazelton's research and pediatric practice, Touchpoints proposes that developmental processes are discontinuous rather than linear, unfolding across multiple dimensions and within relationships. This new approach to development was first articulated for parents in *Touchpoints, The Essential Reference* (1992). In the mid-1990s, the Touchpoints Approach was developed into a professional development program for all disciplines serving young children and their families (Stadtler, O'Brien, & Hornstein, 1995) to provide professionals with tools to reflect upon and improve their practice. It has since been adapted to address specific areas of concern to the ECCE field: young children's social and emotional development, parent–child interactions, and parent–provider partnerships. A lag-phase-matched comparison group trial of this adaptation, comparing centers with and without providers trained in Touchpoints, found statistically significant outcome differences, including stabilized parental stress, enhanced developmental knowledge of providers, and improved parent–provider relationships (Easterbrooks & Jacobs, 2007).

ECCE and the Touchpoints Approach

Perhaps the most important contribution teachers make to quality ECCE environments is predictable nurturance that builds children's emotional competence. Teachers accomplish this in part by sensitively responding to children's bids for their involvement, facilitating children's social interactions, and using their relationships with children to promote learning (Baker & Manfredi-Petitt, 2004; Hyson, 1994; Leavitt, 1994). A quality childcare environment enhances children's emotional security and freedom to build new relationships, and to use this to explore learning opportunities.

Teachers who have "specific foundational knowledge of the development of children's social and affective behavior, thinking, and language" (Bowman, Donovan, & Burns, 2000, p. 330) exhibit the highest quality teaching. "If there is a single critical component to quality, it rests in the relationship between the child and the teacher/caregiver, and in the ability of the adult to be responsive to the child. This responsiveness extends in many directions: to the child's cognitive, social, emotional, and physical characteristics and development" (p. 341). A strong, stable child–teacher relationship has been found to enhance child social competence with adults and peers (Churchill, 2003), predict better adaptation to childcare (Sroufe, 1983), and improve cognitive performance (Pianta & Stuhlman, 2004). From the beginning of the progressive education movement, children's curiosity for the learning process has been seen as embedded in relationships with teachers that support both children's self-esteem and the resulting risk-taking necessary for learning (Biber, 1984). Howes and colleagues found that, of three main domains regarding quality of care, the quality of child–caregiver interactions best predicted child outcomes (Howes, Whitebook, & Phillips, 1992). The Early Child Care Research Network (National Institute of Child Health and Human Development [NICHD], 2002), in their broadly publicized study of early childcare centers nationwide, found that higher quality childcare was positively related to better cognitive and language abilities, and also predictive of higher social and emotional competence.

Children's families are typically their first relational environment and have powerful effects on later functioning (Bowlby, 1980; Bradley et al., 1989; Brazelton & Cramer, 1990; Zigler, Finn-Stevenson, & Hall, 2002), not only influencing emotional wellbeing (Davies & Forman, 2002; Dawson & Ashman, 2000), basic coping and problem-solving abilities (Bowlby, 1988), and future capacity for relationships (Lerner & Castellino, 2002; Main,

Kaplan, & Cassidy, 1985), but also actually performing a regulatory role in cognition and brain architecture as well (Trevarthen, 2001). The effect of first relationships on brain development is strong and well documented by the National Scientific Council on the Developing Child (2004).

Best child outcomes are associated with consistency and sensitive responsiveness in relationships between children and their primary attachments, usually within their families. Positive outcomes across all developmental domains are associated with self-regulation and emotional competency elaborated in a child's first relationships. A child's capacity for self-regulation is gaining recognition as essential to learning readiness and early achievement (Blair & Razza, 2009). Increasingly, rigorous research is finding children's capacity for self-regulation to be strongly associated with outcome measures in the areas of mental health, behavior, academic achievement, and social competence (Buckner, Mezzacappa, & Beardslee, 2009). In earliest childhood, cognitive development and emotional functioning are inseparable (Bell & Wolfe, 2004; Greenspan & Lewis, 2000). "The growth of self-regulation is a cornerstone of early childhood development that cuts across all domains of behavior . . . relationships, and the effects of relationships on relationships, are the building blocks of healthy development" (Shonkoff & Phillips, 2000, p. 3).

Fostering children's development means supporting these relationships within families. Bronfenbrenner (2002), in his "ecological" approach to the system of relationships promoting young children's development, strongly recommended that primary caregivers have at least one other caregiver adult who "encourages and expresses admiration and affection for the person caring for and engaging in joint activity with the child." ECCE providers have an important role to play here. Owen and colleagues (2000) suggested that a "child's quality of experience in each environment may be enhanced when parent and childcare provider bridge the distance between the two social worlds of childcare and home and work together as partners in the child's care" (p. 426). They found that more partnership behavior between parent and provider predicted interactions with the child that were more sensitive, supportive, and stimulating. These characteristics of early child–parent and child–teacher interactions support the development of self-regulatory capacities essential to learning. Shpancer (2002) documents the link between parent–teacher interactions and parent–child interactions. As a result of findings like these, there is a growing emphasis within quality ECCE settings on becoming more truly "family-centered" by providing support to whole families (Baker & Manfredi-Petitt, 2004; Keyser, 2006).

The Touchpoints Approach for ECCE settings strengthens these caregiving relationships to withstand the predictable stresses of development and of sharing the care of young children. It is designed to reinforce ECCE providers' sense of competence and professionalism, while valuing parents' primary relationship with and intimate knowledge of their children. Children are understood developmentally, and honored for their individual learning pace, style, and temperament.

Touchpoints, observed by Brazelton in his pediatric practice, are periods during which a burst forward in one developmental area is often preceded or accompanied by regression in another, or in a child's behavior (Brazelton, 1992). Periods of temporary, predictable regression in typical development have also been identified in several research studies (Lindahl, Heimann, & Ullstadius, 2003; van de Rijt-Plooij & Plooij, 1992). They can create frustration and self-doubt for parents and teachers, and strain their relationships as they struggle to understand the child's behavior and needs, and to coordinate caregiving techniques.

Touchpoints can be particularly disorganizing for parents and providers when natural feelings of "gatekeeping" arise. Gatekeeping – Brazelton's term – predictably occurs among "all adults who care about a baby (who) will naturally be in competition for that baby" and serves as "energy for attachment to the child" (Brazelton, 1992, p. 4). Gatekeeping is common among members of a family system, and can also emerge between parents and ECCE caregivers. Sharing their child with someone else can stir up strong emotions for parents. Parents so often feel, "If I share her, will she love someone else more?" (Brazelton, 1992, p. 368). Added to the ambivalent feelings of 'giving up' one's child to childcare, parents often feel that they must 'give up' their baby to the past with each new developmental advance.

Research indicates that strong attachments between children and ECCE providers arise and are correlated with positive child outcomes (Howes et al., 1992). However, the intensity of child–teacher relationships, and parents' and children's experience of separating from each other for the ECCE setting, inevitably stresses parent–teacher relationships. The Touchpoints Approach to ECCE has been founded upon an understanding of the powerful emotional relationships that children form with their caregivers and of the passionate feelings between parents and teachers that result.

Vulnerabilities inherent in the process of development can become opportunities for teachers to "touch" into the family system, helping parents anticipate and respond positively to times of disorganization; these are opportunities for parents and teachers to build their collaboration, support, and appreciation for each other. Caregivers also benefit from this understanding of development's vicissitudes since children's behavior and caregiving routines such as feeding and sleeping also become disorganized in the ECCE setting. Children become more deeply understood and appreciated when a regression is recognized as part of the process of expanding competencies. Teachers join with parents in identifying children's strengths, even when behavior and caregiving routines can be challenging, and credit the parents' relationship with the child for those strengths.

By supporting parents through difficult periods and predicting the progress foreshadowed by these regressions, teachers can assist parents in co-regulating their own behavior and interactions with their children. Parents' resulting appreciation for their child and their child's ECCE provider are essential ingredients in the caregiving cycle of nurturance and partnership and helps mutualize the respect that parents and providers need and deserve from each other (Singer, 2005). This, in turn, optimizes children's development by establishing trusting relationships in their environment within which self-regulation is most effectively modeled and scaffolded. The Touchpoints Approach promotes children's emotional competence through professional development for ECCE caregivers that strengthens their relationships with parents, children, and each other.

Training and Reflective Practice for ECCE Providers

Constructivist and Therapeutic Perspectives

Benner's (1984) classic description of a novice-to-expert progression informed the initial process of distilling the Touchpoints professional development program from Brazelton's approach. She describes experts in any field, in part, as people who invent their own language for their work. Brazelton is this kind of expert, innovating new ways of working with families and a new language, based upon both scientific inquiry and decades of clinical practice. A group of his colleagues assembled to extract generalizable principles from his practice and research that could be broadly applied in all of the disciplines serving infants, young children, and their families. This group process, centering on the understanding and articulation of one expert's practice through those principles, is replicated in the Touchpoints professional development program for ECCE providers.

Progressive educational theory and therapeutic models of self-discovery and change have influenced the transposition of Touchpoints developmental and relational theory to professional development and practice improvement. Both are consistent with the Touchpoints Approach to families of young children, and inform Touchpoints relational strategies for training adult learners. Bruner describes effective education as involving agency and collaboration. "We do not learn a way of life and ways of deploying mind unassisted, unscaffolded ... The agentive mind is not only active in nature, but it seeks out dialogue and discourse with other active minds" (Bruner, 1996, p. 93). Learning is a social process in which people co-construct knowledge together, whether it is about how to feed a baby, learn from a book, or teach others how to apply the Touchpoints Guiding Principles. In Touchpoints training, early childhood educators actively construct new understandings in an intellectually stimulating and emotionally supportive context.

Therapeutic models of change entail a safe and facilitated process of reflection, emotional perspective-taking and self-discovery that prepares for mastery of new skills (Weiner & Bornstein, 2009) and knowledge embedded within a new professional stance. In the learning process, according to Rogoff (2003), "Communication and coordination during participation in shared endeavors are key aspects of how people develop. Participants adjust among themselves (with varying, complementary, or even competing roles) to stretch their common understanding to fit new perspectives" (p. 285). Touchpoints professional development activities involve guided participation in a process at once emotional and cognitive of new understanding and mastery. Trainers lead a conversation about work with children and families. Participants scaffold each other as they apply the elements of the approach to practice with both real and imagined families. Dissent and questions are welcomed as opportunities to advance understanding. Training in the Touchpoints Approach provides an emotional process of mastery as well as shifts in cognitive understanding. Trainers do not function as didactic repositories of knowledge, but instead establish relationships and facilitate discovery to supports learners' mastery. Collaboration, a sense of agency, and relationships that encourage dialogue and shared reflection offer participants a parallel process in which they experience the key elements for maturation and learning, for themselves, and also for parents and children.

The training begins with the needs and opinions of the participants. Providers are first asked to reflect on the motivation, energy, or personal contributions they bring to their work. Their passion can then be reflected back to them, instilling a sense of shared respect, and enhancing their own internal sense of self-worth – both often compromised in this traditionally low-status field. After this affirmation, a shift to discussion about challenges at work allows providers to offer their opinions on the barriers to establishing productive working relationships with families. The challenges to professional identity development faced by ECCE providers in a society where their work is undervalued can be a potential source of gatekeeping between parents and providers. Providers understandably have difficulty affirming parents' expertise when their own is so often belittled. Often they see themselves less as authors of their own work than as relatively powerless participants in a system that requires their labor (Leavitt, 1994). Training techniques aim at empowering providers to recognize the importance of their own passion for children and families. Through this process they find their own way to perspectives that expand their professional identities. Touchpoints training cultivates a sense of agency, efficacy, and responsibility in ECCE providers. Those who learn to view themselves as developmental consultants to parents take on valuable roles well beyond the conventions provided either in their professional preparation or by their employers.

Trainers actively establish a relational context in which participants can challenge their existing notions about development and relationships, deepen their understanding of whole families' developmental processes, and appreciate the vital role they play in assisting families in regulating their own responses to developmental disruptions in children's behavior and routines. Early in the training, for example, providers are asked to use this developmental and relational approach to imagine first a child's "touchpoints" through the first four months, and then a parent's emotional experience of placing that child in someone else's care. Participants experience a shift in their perspective on the challenge of parent–child separations in ECCE settings, and on the emotional importance to children of their relationships with teachers. They develop a new appreciation of the powerful developmental and relational forces affecting parent–teacher relationships and of their potential to influence them positively.

Cumulative training exercises integrate emotional and cognitive experiences, building towards a shift in self-reflection and perspective-taking ability. Through the exercises focusing on providers' needs and concerns, their own perspective and that of parents is more deeply understood. Participants discover their own desire for respect and communication as they recognize parents' wish for the same. Instead of being taught this by trainers, participants lead their own empathic shift in perspective towards the parents' point of view.

Although learning is, in part, a process of encoding information into memory, rote memorization is insufficient (National Research Council, 2000). The object of Touchpoints professional development is to expand knowledge and to build skills, but also to enhance empathic understanding and the capacity for emotional availability to the whole family. Training exercises that build on this are designed for learners to internalize specific strategies for caregiving and communication challenges. This is consistent with a constructivist approach to education in which learning is seen to be the acquisition of processes that allow learners to integrate new knowledge and, more importantly, apply their learning to new situations (National Research Council, 2000). Real world ECCE settings offer opportunities for experiential learning through practice. New strategies based on new understandings are used, for example, when working with a parent who mistreats a child, or managing biting in a classroom of toddlers, or supporting a parent whose 9-month-old infant stops sleeping through the night.

In addition to therapeutic reflection techniques, a central training method is the use of Touchpoints Guiding Principles and Parent Assumptions as tools of the mind, metacognitive strategies applied in reflective practice. They guide practitioners' reflection on and choice of strategies for interaction with children, parents, and peers. The Parent Assumptions provide a strengths-based, parent-empowering paradigm from which relationship-enhancing attitudes and stances emerge. The Touchpoints Approach also offers unique relational strategies based on the predictable bursts and regressions of development and the meanings of a child's behavior to parents. These can be used by ECCE providers to support and enhance parent–child interactions.

Touchpoints training presentations, exercises, demonstrations, and group reflections constitute a reflective exploration about best practices. Trainers rely on a variety of linguistic maneuvers during conversations about both theory and practice to advance the understanding of participants. They pose carefully constructed questions, paraphrase, summarize, empathize, reflect, refocus, and actively listen, looking for opportunities to support the process of mastering this approach. They lead the conversation in a way that allows group members to value their own contributions while at the same time learning from others, using the Touchpoints framework as a guide, and modeling the Touchpoints Approach as it applies to work with families.

Future Steps

Currently, the majority of roughly 100 Touchpoints community sites in the USA are training ECCE professionals in the Touchpoints Approach. As this network of sites continues to expand, it is fulfilling its promise as a learning community for the collaborative sharing of best practices and innovations through annual forums, electronic media, and other organized and informal means. Future research and evaluation will be needed to replicate initial findings and assess child outcomes. Additional professional development components and applications are being adapted for bilingual and multicultural settings, for the increasing number of Pre-K programs around the country, and to address the mounting demand for workforce development in this field.

The field of early childhood education is dynamic and expanding. Research on brain development and greater awareness of cultural variation among families has led to significant changes in how early childhood educators view their work with children and their relationships with families. The Touchpoints Approach is consistent with both of these trends with its emphasis on a dynamic and contextualized model of development and deeper and more purposeful partnerships with families. As public policy makers and society as a whole attend more to the genuine needs of young children, Touchpoints will serve an important role in guiding those who care for other people's children.

References and further reading

Baker, A. C., & Manfredi-Pettit, L. A. (2004). *Relationships, the heart of quality care: Creating community among adults in early care settings.* Washington, DC: NAEYC.

Bell, M. A., & Wolfe, C. D. (2004). Emotion and cognition: An intricately bound developmental process. *Child Development. 75*(2), 366–370.

Benner, P. (1984). *From novice to expert: Excellence and power in clinical nursing practice.* Menlo Park, CA: Addison-Wesley.

Biber, B. (1984). *Early education and psychological development.* New Haven, CT: Yale University Press.

Blair, C., & Razza, R. P. (2009). Relating effortful control, executive function, and false belief understanding to emerging math and literacy ability in kindergarten. *Child Development, 78*(2), 647–663.

Bowlby, J. (1980). *Attachment and loss. Loss, sadness, and depression* (Vol. III). London, UK: The Hogarth Press and the Institute of Psychoanalysis.

Bowlby, J. (1988). *A secure base.* New York, NY: Basic Books.

Bowman, B. T., Donovan, M. S., & Burns, M. S. (2000). *Eager to learn: Educating our preschoolers.* Washington, DC: National Academies Press.

Bradley, R. H., Caldwell, B. M., Rock, S. L., Ramey, C. T., Gray, C., Hammond, M. A., ... Johnson, D. L. (1989). Home environment and cognitive development in the first three years of life: A collaborative study involving six sites and three ethnic groups in North America. *Developmental Psychology, 23*, 217–255.

Brazelton, T. B. (1987). Behavioral competence in the newborn infant. In G. B. Avery (Ed.), *Neonatology: Pathophysiology and management of the newborn* (pp. 379–399). Philadelphia: Lippincott.

Brazelton, T. B. (1992). *Touchpoints: The essential reference.* Reading, MA: Perseus Books.

Brazelton, T. B., & Cramer, B. (1990). *The first relationship.* New York, NY: Addison Wesley.

Brazelton, T., & Greenspan, S. (2001). *Irreducible needs of children: What every child must have to grow learn and flourish.* Jackson, TN: DaCapo Press.

Bronfenbrenner, U. (2002). Preparing a world for the infant in the twenty-first century: The research challenge. In J. Gomes-Pedro, J. K. Nugent, J. G. Young, & T. B. Brazelton (Eds.), *The infant and family in the twenty-first century* (pp. 45–52). New York, NY: Brunner-Routledge.

Bruner, J. (1996). *The culture of education.* Cambridge, MA: Harvard University Press.

Buckner, J. C., Mezzacappa, E., & Beardslee, W. (2009). Self-regulation and its relations to adaptive functioning in low-income youth. *American Journal of Orthopsychiatry, 79*(1), 19.

Churchill, S. L. (2003). Goodness-of-fit in early childhood settings. *Early Childhood Education Journal, 31*(2), 113–118.

Davies, P. T., & Forman, E. M. (2002). Children's patterns of preserving emotional security in the interparental subsystem. *Child Development, 73*, 1880–1903.

Dawson, G., & Ashman, D. B. (2000). On the origins of a vulnerability to depression: The influence of the early social environment on the development of psychobiological systems related to risk of affective disorder. In C. A. Nelson (Ed.), *The effects of early adversity on neurobehavioral development. Minnesota Symposia on Child Psychology*, (Vol. 31, pp. 245–279). Mahwah, NJ: Erlbaum.

Easterbrooks, M. A., & Jacobs, F. (2007). *Touchpoints early child care and education initiative final evaluation report.* Medford, MA: Tufts University.

Greenspan, S. I., & Lewis, N. B. (1997). *Building healthy minds.* Cambridge, MA: Merloyd Lawrence.

Greenspan, S. I., & Lewis, N. B. (2000). *Building healthy minds.* Cambridge, MA: Da Capo Press.

Howes, C., Whitebook, M., & Phillips, D. (1992). Teacher characteristics and effective teaching in child care: Findings from the National Child Care Staffing Study. *Child & Youth Care Forum, 21*(6), 399–414.

Hyson, M. C. (1994). *The emotional development of young children: Building an emotion-centered curriculum.* New York: Teachers College Columbia University.

Keyser, J. (2006). *From parents to partners: Building a family-centered early childhood program.* St. Paul, MN: Redleaf Press.

Leavitt, R. (1994). *Power and emotion in infant toddler care.* Albany: State University of New York Press.

Lerner, R. M., & Castellino, D. R. (2002). Contemporary developmental theory and adolescence: Developmental systems and applied developmental science. *Journal of Adolescent Health, 31*, 122–135.

Lindahl L. B., Heimann, M., & Ullstadius, E. (2003). Occurrence of regressive periods in the normal development of Swedish infants. In M. Heimann and F. X. Plooij (Eds.), *Regression periods in human infancy* (pp. 34–47). Mahwah, NJ: Erlbaum.

Main, M., Kaplan, N., & Cassidy, J. (1985). Security in infancy, childhood, and adulthood: A move to the level of representation. In I. Bretherton & E. Waters (Eds.), *Growing points of attachment theory and research. Monographs of the Society for Research in Child Development, 50*(1–2), 233–256.

National Research Council (2000). *How people learn: Brain, mind, experience, and school.* J. Bransford, A. Brown, and R. Cocking (Eds.). Washington, DC: The National Academy Press.

National Scientific Council on the Developing Child (2004). *Young children develop in an environment of relationships,* Working Paper No. 1. Retrieved 2004, from www.developingchild.net/reports.shtml.

NICHD Early Child Care Research Network (2002). Early child care and children's development prior to school entry: Results from the NICHD Study of Early Child Care. *American Educational Research Journal, 39*, 133–164.

Owen, M. T., Ware, A. M., & Barfoot, B. (2000). Caregiver–mother partnership behavior and the quality of caregiver–child and mother–child interactions. *Early Childhood Research Quarterly, 15*(3), 413–428.

Pianta, R. C., & Stuhlman, M. W. (2004). Teacher–child relationships and children's success in the first years of school. *School Psychology Review, 33*(3), 444–458.

Rogoff, B. (2003). *The cultural nature of human development.* New York: Oxford University Press.

Shonkoff, J. P., & Phillips, D. (Eds.) (2000). *From neurons to neighborhoods: The science of early childhood development.* Committee on Integrating the Science of Early Childhood Development. Washington, DC: National Academy Press.

Shpancer, N. (2002). The home-daycare link: Mapping children's new world order. *Early Childhood Research Quarterly, 17*, 374–392.

Singer, J. (2005). Using the Touchpoints in early care and education. Reference guide. In *Brazelton Touchpoints Center®, Touchpoints™ in Early Care and Education Reference Guide and Participant Training Materials* (pp. 5–13). Boston, MA: Brazelton Touchpoints Center®.

Sroufe, L. A. (1983). Infant–caregiver attachment and patterns of adaptation in preschool: The roots of maladaptation and competence. In M. Perlmutter (Ed.), *Minnesota Symposium on Child Psychology, 16* (pp. 41–81). Hillsdale, NJ: Erlbaum.

Stadtler, A., O'Brien, M., & Hornstein, J. (1995, Aug./Sept.). The Touchpoints model: Building supportive alliances between parents and professionals. *Zero to Three, 1*(16), 24–28.

Trevarthen, C. (2001). Intrinsic motives for companionship in understanding: Their origin, development and significance for infant mental health. *International Journal of Infant Mental Health, 11*(1–2), 95–131.

van de Rijt-Plooij, H., & Plooij, F. (1992). Infantile regressions: Disorganization and the onset of transition periods. *Journal of Reproductive and Infant Psychology, 10*, 129–149.

Weiner, I., & Bornstein, R. (2009). *Principles of psychotherapy: Promoting evidence-based psychodynamic practice*. Malden, MA: Wiley.

Zigler, E., Finn-Stevenson, M., & Hall, N. W. (2002). *The first three years and beyond: Brain development and social policy*. New Haven, CT: Yale University Press.

26

Early Innovations in Behavioral/ Developmental Pediatric Fellowship Training

A Fresh Approach to Medical Professional Development

Constance H. Keefer

Introduction

By 1972, pediatrics as a discipline was on the cusp of subspecialization. Developmental behavioral pediatrics (DBP) was not identified as a field or discipline. The dimensions and content had not yet been defined. Within pediatric residency training, development and behavior issues included mainly developmental disabilities (DD) and mental retardation (MR). Much of that teaching was done through neurology rotations. There was also fellowship training in MR and DD. Addressing behavior problems was left to psychiatry, often with little connection to pediatrics. There were certainly no divisions of DBP in hospitals, and residents were left with little more than an understanding of milestones and introduction to DD and MR.

Interest was rising, however, as definitions of development and behavior within pediatrics broadened. The concept of the "new morbidities," for example, attention deficit hyperactivity disorder (ADHD), was defined to include functional disorders of high frequency, low intensity but with serious effects on children and families. Along with the broadening of interest in behavior and development, and as important, was the foresight and leadership of individuals and institutions in recognizing the imperative for pediatric responsibility for these issues and the need they would engender for training, research, and expansion of clinical approaches. Charles Janeway and Julius Richmond stood out, as did the Carnegie and Robert Wood Johnson Foundations, in encouraging and supporting Brazelton in establishing the Child Development Unit at Children's Hospital, Boston.

Brazelton not only rose but leapt to the challenge, bringing the same deep insight to fellowship training that he brought to the creation of the Neonatal Behavioral Assessment Scale (NBAS) (Brazelton, 1973). This includes insistence on a strengths-based model, the whole range of developmental behaviors from normal to disturbed, adapting assessment to the condition of the child, eliciting best, not average, performance, and an awareness of the experience of the examiner.

This chapter presents a glimpse into the strikingly unique and innovative training program that emerged under Brazelton's direction, affecting every aspect of the fellowship: the content based in the science of developmental psychology and biology and theories of developmental process and behavior; the training structure of interdisciplinary faculty and learners, including experiential learning and learner-centered methods of teaching; and, above all, the whole imbued with a strengths-based approach to teaching and clinical work.

We start with a vignette from 1973 that took place at the Boston Children's Hospital Infant Inpatient Unit with Brazelton and first year Fellows Peter Paladin, Winnie Parker, and the author, in the second year of Brazelton's Child Development Fellowship.

Peter paused outside the four-crib room where he was leading Dr. Brazelton, Winnie Parker, and the author to discuss a baby whom he had evaluated for behavior and development. The infant was nine months of age, and had been in the hospital since birth because of a congenital defect in his abdominal wall which caused significant damage to his small intestine, preventing normal digestion and absorption of food. The baby was receiving Total Parenteral Nutrition (TPN), i.e., he was being fed through an intravenous line. Peter had been asked to evaluate and offer advice on ways to mitigate the effects of the long hospitalization on the baby's behavior and development.

"Let's talk about the baby out here," Peter said, "because the one-month-old baby in the next crib, just inside the door here, has the very same problem, and I am afraid that our discussion of my patient will be disturbing to her mother, hearing about what her own baby might have to endure."

("Wow," I thought to myself, "how wonderful to see a pediatrician be sensitive to the emotional state of a parent." Peter, Winnie, and I had just finished pediatric residencies, and Peter's attitude was very different from the sort of physician behavior we often witnessed for the past three years, and, indeed, for the two years before that in medical school.)

Peter told us about his assessment of the baby and about the concerns the parents had expressed to him, and then entered the room, heading for his patient's crib. Winnie and I followed, but Dr. Brazelton stopped at the crib of the one-month-old baby, approached the mother, and gently asked: "I understand that your baby has the same problem as our patient in the next bed." The mother nodded in assent, maintaining a wary and worried expression. "I wonder," Dr. Brazelton continued, "if you don't have concerns about how your baby will do?" The mother's face relaxed as she looked down at her baby, stroked her head, and looked up to Dr. Brazelton with a sigh of relief. "Oh yes," she said, "I wish someone could tell me what will happen to her. Do you think she will be OK?"

Dr. Brazelton moved closer to look at the baby on the mother's lap, touched the mother's shoulder, and said: "Well, I would like very much to come back tomorrow and hear about her and examine her with you, and then we can think together about your concerns for her."

This was one of the first of many moments of profound learning from Dr. Brazelton for me. What was I learning, as my thoughts tumbled forward?

1 "Of course, that's what we are here for as pediatricians, to hear parents' concerns, not to avoid them or deny them, nor to offer false reassurance but, just for a start, to hear them."
2 "Of course, a mother will have all sorts of concerns; the pediatrician's asking about the concerns is not causing them; the asking is done to allow, share, and address the concerns; a mother left with unspoken concerns may feel guilty." This was one of the many facets of "the positive model," a term to which Dr. Brazelton introduced us in the very beginning of our Fellowship, though this was my first experiential learning of it. We Fellows would struggle for many years to understand the term and the phenomenon, to define and clarify them.

Dr. Brazelton, of course, demonstrated the term in the many encounters that we observed of him with families; it was central in his approach to parents and students and colleagues. But we struggled to find the words to define it as we extricated ourselves from the grip of medicine's need to search for pathology, to frame all encounters in a negative model.

3 This particular incident presented a counterintuitive construction I was to gradually incorporate, a first step in understanding the positive model. It goes like this: "Oh, saying 'yes' to (allowing, discovering, bringing to

light) the mother's 'negative' experience (her worry, sadness, anger) was the positive model at work; with it we are saying to the mother, 'yes', I am interested in your baby's problems, and your concerns are quite expectable and acceptable to me, just as I will be interested in your baby's strengths and your expertise as we work together to understand and tend to his problem".

In July 1972, Dr. Brazelton accepted the first two graduating pediatric residents to the two-year Child Development Fellowship at Children's Hospital, Boston. In 1988, the last of the 46 Fellows graduated from the program. During those 16 years, 2–4 pediatric trainees entered the Fellowship each year. Initial faculty included Ed Tronick, PhD directing research, Elizabeth Fox (now Maury), PhD facilitating academic learning, and Robert McCarter, MD providing psychiatric supervision of the Fellows' clinical work with parents and young children. Others eventually filled these roles and, within a few years, one of the graduating Fellows filled an additional faculty position.

The goal of the Fellowship was to prepare pediatricians for clinical behavioral developmental pediatrics and, equally, to prepare them for research in child development and behavior in order for them to join academic pediatric faculties. The training focused on younger children and was based on a model of typical child development.

More than half of the graduates established themselves in pediatric departments and, since 2001 when the American Board of Pediatrics granted subspecialty status to Developmental-Behavioral Pediatrics, they became directors and faculty of DBP divisions. Many of the other 21 graduates provide clinical teaching in DBP in pediatric settings.

These were among the first pediatric residents trained in DBP and, even before the establishment of the formal subspecialty, they were training residents to pursue developmental pediatrics in academic settings. For example, Brazelton trained Barry Zuckerman who trained Marilyn Augustyn, who has now trained several generations in developmental pediatrics (Grandfellows of Brazelton).

The program was unique, different, and innovative. It was unique because there was no other fellowship in development and behavior by a pediatrician in a pediatric department of a children's hospital. There were other programs but they were not pediatric nor centered on typical development. Brazelton informed his Child Development Fellowship with his experience in primary care, rather than disabilities or neurological disorders. He based it on observation of real behavior, teaching us to observe before describing, to describe before explaining, and to explain before interpreting. He helped students to learn to look in new places for their observations – from the finest of infant finger movements to the inner experience of being with a family and child.

Implanting behavior and development training within pediatrics is no longer unique, but extricating DBP from child neurology and developmental disabilities subspecialties was a struggle of some years and much time and effort. Of course, today's DBP subspecialty and the Society of Developmental and Behavioral Pediatricians (SDBP) are the products of many earnest, authentic, and talented developmental and behavioral pediatricians. Some of Dr. Brazelton's Fellows are among them, e.g., Suzanne Dixon, Heidi Feldman, Debbie Frank, Alex Geertsma, Peter Gorski, Susan Gottlieb, Barbara Howard, Chet Johnson, Daniel Kessler, John McCarthy, Richard Olsen, Steven Parker, David Snyder, and Barry Zuckerman.

Steven Parker, a Fellow who went on to make major contributions to teaching DBP, passed away while still in the midst of these efforts in May of 2009. The Society for Developmental Behavioral Pediatrics lost a compassionate teacher, clinician, and colleague. Many residents, medical students, and Fellows at Boston Medical Center and in the Boston Combined Residency in Pediatrics have benefited from his skills and sensitivity and will carry his work on in their own.

Brazelton's Fellowship was different. It was rooted in developmental psychology. He brought dynamic and process-oriented theoretical models. Other programs at that time, and many of those that have developed since then, are focused on a disease or dysfunctional system or outcome (e.g., ADHD, sleep disturbance, obesity). Basing the program on developmental psychology meant that a major and grounding focus of the Fellowship was the study and application of developmental processes afforded by this basic (behavioral) science.

In Brazelton's clinic for young children with behavior problems, e.g., crying, sleeping, discipline, we came to understand that the problems were rooted in disturbances in the development of the parent–child relationship, and not solely in the child's functional system. Today we call this Infant Mental Health. By focusing on the relationship, rather than only on the specific behavior, we were much better able to help the parent and child undo the behavioral disturbance. The target of our assessment and intervention was not, for example, hair-pulling, per se, but a mother's depression following the death of her own mother; not sleep, per se, but the web of family dynamics when a father traveled frequently for work; not hyperactivity, per se, but a mother's reliving her own childhood experience, abused for the same behaviors she now saw in her son.

Another dynamic and process-oriented model that Brazelton brought to the Fellowship was psychoanalytic theories and clinical methods. Yet the application of these theories and methods in our clinical work did not consist of psychoanalysis or psychotherapy. The applications were to ourselves, using our feelings and responses to patients and clinical situations in order to better our role as pediatricians interested in behavior and development: we learned to listen, and to tolerate silences in conversation with families and becoming aware of their unspoken but powerful thoughts and feelings.

Brazelton's teaching methods were informed by his innovative approach to clinical practice, and based on his observations of how parents and professionals learn, grow, and change. Teaching was not telling, rather, it was guided learning; his methods were experiential and reflective and relational. He challenged, but contained the challenge within the relationship between himself and students/learners. Clinical methods were also relational, and inclusive of parents. They relied on narrative as much as report. Since then, these methods have been discovered by others and validated in principles of care (e.g., family-centered care and the medical home provide structures within which these methods can be applied); and in medical education (e.g., New Pathway in Medical Education at Harvard Medical School and the Macy Program for Medical Educators at Harvard Medical International). Brazelton was a true leader in this field, way ahead of his times.

Organization of the Fellowship

Beginning in the first summer of the Fellowship, the fellows were exposed to innovative methods for learning. During the initial two months of the program, we met weekly to discuss our experiences in two unfamiliar settings, an obstetrical clinic and a childcare center. In the obstetrical clinic at the Boston Hospital for Women, Lying-in Division, we met and spoke individually with expectant mothers in the last weeks of their pregnancies. In the Hawthorne House Day Care Center in Roxbury and in the Children's Center child care in Brookline, we worked twice weekly as child care workers, not as pediatricians. We did not observe from the sidelines or consult as pediatricians. We did not teach the teachers about child development.

Rather, we followed the teacher's instructions. We were down on the floor with the children: struggling to get them to sleep at naptime, supervising their behavior at mealtime, playing with them at the water table. This was experiential learning at its best, and most enjoyable.

Weekly seminars with Liz Fox anchored the rest of our first year. The topics were from developmental psychology and we read primary sources as well as textbooks. We chose an area of research and, guided by Ed Tronick, many brought projects to fruition and all learned a cautious respect for the process and results of research. Eventually, the interdisciplinary mode made its way to collaboration between clinical fellows and research students. For example, Tronick and his colleagues provided a seminar in research methods for fellows; we, in turn, provided a seminar in the basic philosophy of medicine and pediatrics and a review of basic disorders and orientations to them. For both clinical and research purposes, we became reliable in the NBAS.

Our clinical experience started by consulting to the house staff on the infant inpatient services, and providing a weekly patient discussion. The second clinical activity was in the Early Childhood Program Clinic. This was a clinic for families of young children with behavior and development problems. Another truly interdisciplinary experience – nurses, psychologists, psychiatrists, social workers, pediatricians – in which clinical observations influenced research and research informed clinical approaches, and again, far ahead of the times.

Out of that clinic emerged our unique understanding and approach to behavior problems in young children. We learned that these problems are often primarily relational problems, problems in the parent–child relationship due to several intersecting areas: on the child's side – temperament, developmental stage or agenda, developmental deviation; and on the parent's side – young, uninformed, situational stress, trauma and other holdovers from childhood abuse and loss, or psychologically challenged from common neuroses to personality disorders to major psychiatric illness.

Conclusion

We described the Child Development Fellowship that Brazelton created, designed, and developed, highlighting the unique and innovative features of one of the very first programs for pediatric postresidency training in developmental behavioral pediatrics offered even before it was defined as such. In summary, the program situated training in development and behavior within pediatrics, an early seed leading eventually to the fruition of both the DBP subspecialty and the interdisciplinary collaboration of faculty, trainees, combining research and clinical in a way that allowed each to influence the other. The program started from a theoretical and philosophical base in developmental psychology and biology, psychoanalysis, and a positive strengths-based model. The teaching methods were learner-centered, experiential, and relational and far ahead of their time. Content included clinicians' relationships with parents as well as parent–child relationships. Clinical methods paralleled teaching methods: the patient-centered approach drew on narrative rather than report as first source. This program gave fellows a solid and dynamic foundation for clinical, educational, and research careers, and to become leaders in shaping the future of Developmental Behavioral Pediatrics.

References and further reading

Barr, R. G. (2004). From infant crying to political action: What is the basic science of developmental-behavioral pediatrics? *Journal of Developmental &Behavioral Pediatrics*, *25*(2) (Apr.), 123–130.

Brazelton, T. B. (1973). *Neonatal Behavioral Assessment Scale.* Clinics in Developmental Medicine, No. 50. London: Heinemann Medical.

Fox, E. M., & Yogman, M. (1976). Intervention in early childhood problems: A non-pathological developmental model. Paper presented at the First Annual Interdisciplinary Convention of Human Service Associations, March 18–20.

Keefer, C. H., Buttenwieser, C. F., Demos, V., & Brazelton, T. B. (1982). Behavior problems in infants and young children: Follow-up study of care given in a pediatric clinic. Paper presented at Tenth International Congress of the Association for Child and Adolescent Psychiatry and Allied Professions, 25–30 July. Dublin, Ireland.

Section II

Innovating Change in Service Delivery, Systems of Care, and Policy

27

The Birth of Child Life
Creating a Child-Friendly, Developmental Hospital Environment

Myra D. Fox

> "*. . . it is possible for the hospital situation to become excessively impersonal with a great deal of attention being paid to the child's illness and too little to his feelings.*" (Robbins, 1962, p. v)

In the early 1960s, at Harvard Medical School's premier pediatric center where many pioneering pediatricians practiced, parents could not visit for extended periods of time and they certainly could not stay overnight. Everyone at Children's Hospital Boston still wore white coats. House officers wore white uniforms. Nurses wore them with white caps representing their various schools of nursing. Children's Hospital nursing students wore white aprons and bibs starched so stiff they looked like cardboard, along with black stockings and black shoes. The hospital environment had a completely sterile feeling.

Parents sensed this, and that it could not fully address their children's needs. In those days, a nurse would come to a mother to begin the admissions procedures and ask her to hand her baby over. One young mother was lovingly holding her baby, who had a cleft palate. The mother looked at me – the "Child Activity Specialist" better known as "The Play Lady." "Do they *really* know how to take care of babies here?" she asked.

Back then, children were admitted to the hospital for diagnostic tests days prior to an elective surgery and hospitalized for weeks following surgeries that are performed on an ambulatory basis today. Infants and children were hospitalized for a range of medical illnesses also frequently treated on an outpatient basis today. Most of the children admitted to the hospital were very young. This was their first time away from home. Yet at Children's Hospital, it was not until the late 1970s that the pre-admission preparation program was established in recognition that preparation of the child begins prior to hospitalization.

The medical and nursing staff at Children's Hospital Boston were dedicated and highly intelligent. Before Dr. Brazelton's arrival at Children's, the growing science of pediatrics and clinical care innovations were the primary drivers for the organization of care in clinical settings. The diversity of families, sibling issues, preparation for procedures and surgery, and a repertoire of distraction techniques to use during procedures were not part of the staff's frame of reference in those days. Clinicians believed that mere explanations regarding surgery or procedures were adequate. Yet children need to assimilate information through activities that will enable them to return to it on their own terms and time (Plank, 1962, p. 14).

Hospitalization imposed many challenges to a child's development. For very young children without family support, this was a frightening, confusing experience, leaving them without control over the environment. Many had just transferred from a crib to a transitional bed and now, in the hospital, were back in a crib again. Children recently toilet trained were now told to use the bedpan, in bed. In those days, parents often would say: "If you don't eat you'll go to the hospital." In the hospital, children were told *not* to eat prior to and after surgery because they would get sick. All of these medical interventions were necessary, but parents were not present at the bedside to help children understand and adjust to what was considered just a temporary change in the structure of their day.

Before the 1960s, clinicians did not fully understand that, unlike adults who can resume life activities after hospitalization, a child's hospitalization interrupts the child's development (Plank, 1962, p. 1). In her groundbreaking publication, Emma Plank cited the "threat of illness, surgery and the possible nearness of death" as factors that interfere with the child's ability to resume his "rhythm of life and growth" after the hospital experience (Plank, 1962, p. 1).

Not only was preparation for surgery very limited, children were going to surgery in the same operating room (OR) suite as children returning from the OR and recovering from surgery, creating sights, smells, and sounds frightening to the children awaiting surgery. Early attempts to change this led to another less than ideal practice – patients going for surgery would wait in the corridor until their names were called. With very few exceptions, parents were not allowed into the induction room.

Children spent much time in bed and opportunities for play were not a priority (Fig 27.1). Meals were served in bed. The portions were so huge that there was little opportunity for a child to have the satisfaction of finishing the meal. Children with croup or other respiratory problems would frequently be cared for in steam rooms with tiled walls. Staff needed to wear plastic raincoats when entering the room. These children were typically confined to cribs, their vision altered by the mist and fog, almost always without the reassuring presence of their parents.

The child had no supports to master the hospital setting. The hospital environment wasn't fun even when it could be. Children rarely got dressed, remaining in their "johnnies" for most of the day. The summer days were hot and humid, with no air conditioning. Play and school, important elements of a child's day at home, barely existed in the hospital unless initiated by the "play ladies." Not until the late 1970s was The School Program initiated by the Child Life Department to help children keep up with schoolwork, with teaching provided by certified teachers.

While medical care and interventions were of great benefit to the physical recovery of children, they were also invasive. In those days, they were often performed in the child's hospital crib or bed, bringing pain and immeasurable fright without warning and little, if any, preparation. During that era, doctors and nurses cared deeply about the children, but they didn't know enough about the harmful effects of hospitalization and separation from parents.

Understanding the psychological impact of hospitalization on children lagged well behind scientific and technological advancements. Pioneering work on effects of parental separation and hospitalization of infants and young children was conducted by notables such as Robertson (1958) and Ainsworth and Bowlby (1965) in London in the 1950s, but it was several years before clinicians on this side of the Atlantic developed awareness of the devastating aspects of hospitalization for children. It was not until after 1969 that the landmark work of Bowlby (1969) on attachment and loss was gradually incorporated into the curriculum of professionals in disciplines concerned with care of children. Many years passed before child-friendly changes based on this new knowledge were incorporated into the care of children in hospitals.

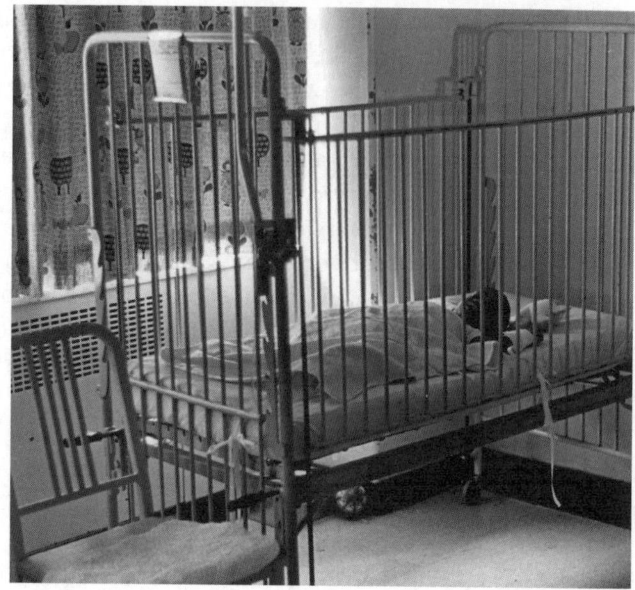

Figure 27.1 Photo of child in crib. Children spent long hours in their cribs. Parents could visit only for limited times and there were few opportunities for patients to interact with each other. Play barely existed in the hospital
Source: Photo courtesy of Children's Hospital Boston Archives, Boston, Massachusetts

Not only did clinicians not fully understand the importance of considering the "whole child and family," but the concept of partnering with parents during children's hospitalizations remained a radical departure from reigning authoritarian belief systems. There were control issues evident throughout an organization that conveyed an authoritarian aura. Clinicians cited various reasons why parents should not be present during a child's hospitalization: parents would interfere with care, they would create "crowding" by taking up space and "most certainly parents at the bedside would probably lead to cross-infection." Only in cases where a child was very ill were exceptions made to allow parents at the bedside outside regular visiting hours. One leading physician kept parents separated from children after surgery because he feared that they would cry. Of course, the children were crying anyway without their parents. During one patient care round, one of the attending MDs displayed pre-Brazelton thinking about a very young patient with asthma, recommending a "parent-*ectomy*." The child would be sent to Colorado for fresh air – without the parent!

Establishing developmental play programs throughout the hospital and encouraging family participation became a critical new goal. It was not generally understood that nearly all types of play can be transplanted to the hospital setting, at the bedside and in the playroom, or that opportunities for play experiences should not stop in the hospital. Play is how children learn, explore, communicate, make sense of, and master the medical trauma they have endured. In response to the hospital environment, children are drawn to becoming play-nurses and play-doctors. As they play hospital, children gain a sense of control of the environment. As Plank (1962) described, "[children] need the opportunity for repetition, in dramatic play and in words, to allow them to go over the events that troubled them" (p. 23). Understanding the experience brings the child peace of mind, release from anxiety, and assurance that the hospital world in which they find themselves is safe.

Already well established as a pediatrician in his private practice and in several leading academic medical centers, Dr. T. Berry Brazelton was extremely concerned about restrictive visiting for families and that parents could not stay overnight with their children. Before his arrival at Children's Hospital in 1967, he spoke to Dr. Leonard Cronkhite, Children's Hospital President, about his concerns, informing him that many families from his pediatric practice preferred to have their children go to less restrictive pediatric centers. Brazelton was appointed by Dr. Charles Janeway, then Physician-in-Chief, to a new medical services position entitled Coordinator of Patient Care. Fortunately for the children and the professional staff, things were never quite the same again. He started laying the foundation for changing care at Children's Hospital almost immediately. The focus had been strictly medical, and the challenge was to make the transition from doctor/nurse-centered care to child- and family-centered care, to humanize pediatrics.

As Coordinator of Patient Care, Brazelton took charge of Patient Care Rounds. The interns, residents, nurses, social workers, play ladies, now referred to as Child Life Specialists, and the senior visit physician were expected to attend. Brazelton's Patient Care Rounds expanded the boundaries of traditional definitions of pediatrics. Dr. Brazelton carefully involved the multidisciplinary team to understand the whole child and family, gently weaving in child development and parenting issues. These were new and foreign concepts for young physicians and nurses. In the beginning, residents did not want to attend the rounds and would arrange to be paged so that they could step out and not return.

Figure 27.2 Children at mealtime. The introduction of sharing meals with other patients helped to normalize the hospital experience for children. Use of child-size chairs and table and the socialization with other patients promoted mastery in a strange environment

Source: Photo courtesy of Myra Fox.

One simple but important early change in care was for children to share mealtimes with their peers at child-size tables whenever bed rest was not required. Portions and menu options were adjusted to meet both the developmental and nutritional needs of the child (Figure 27.2). Dr. Brazelton worked together with Child Life Specialists and nurses to support parents' participation in their children's care, including encouraging parents to stay overnight with them. In addition, they worked to provide supports for patients and families during the stress of long hospitalizations, extensive treatments, and surgery. Another critical change was to create a safe haven in the playroom. No medical treatments or procedures were allowed. Children need to have a place in the hospital where they know they will not experience any medical procedures. Doctors and nurses are not banned from playrooms, but they may not take a child's vital signs, remove a bandage, or do anything else related to the child's care there.

Neither Child Life nor any department alone could make these and other necessary child-friendly environmental changes in the hospital without the support and commitment of nursing leadership, and fortunately a partnership between Child Life and Nursing was developed. Anne Black came to Children's Hospital in 1976 from Indiana University Medical Center, where she had been Associate Professor of Nursing and Assistant Director for Nursing, to assume the position of Director of Nursing at the same time that the author was promoted to the position of Director of Child Life. She was keenly interested in the growing involvement of parents in their children's care and the developing sensitivity of the nursing staff to caring for the whole family. With her leadership, institutional commitment grew to encourage family involvement, and resources were mobilized to assist this movement. The emphasis on the psychosocial ramifications of illness is centrally important in nursing. Helping patients and families assume responsibility for their care requires that health professionals be sensitive to and knowledgeable about the full range of educational and supportive processes available to families to foster that responsibility.

Anne Black introduced primary nursing to Children's. In this care model, a nurse carries the lead responsibility for a number of patients, acting as the primary planner and coordinator for nursing care during the entire hospital stay and, in some instances, participating in care after discharge. When primary nursing was introduced, Child Life Specialists felt threatened, fearing that nurses would take over their responsibilities until a shared understanding emerged of the need for collaboration of the two professions to integrate the best of both into children's care.

During the 1980s Dr. Brazelton established what was referred to as "Brazelton Rounds," promoting multidisciplinary collaboration, furthering the Nursing–Child Life partnership. These weekly rounds focused on an individual patient, usually a very young patient on one of the medical units. The child's mother often participated, including her as a team member too – unprecedented at this time. Dr. Brazelton became an enormous resource for and influence on Child Life Specialist practice. The rounds frequently took place in the activity/playrooms, and were extraordinary opportunities for Dr. Brazelton to model interactions with young children and their families for the bedside team (Figure 27.3). He focused on family dynamics and on the strengths and skills young mothers displayed as they parented their children in a very challenging hospital setting. Suzanne Graca and Maureen Abramson were two Child Life Specialists who vividly remember organizing and participating in the rounds:

> Dr. Brazelton was familiar with the role of Child Life Specialists and was quick to point out to a visiting colleague from the Netherlands that Child Life Specialists were the "soul of the hospital." During Developmental Rounds,

Figure 27.3 Brazelton with children. "Brazelton Rounds" allowed Dr. Brazelton to demonstrate how to interact with infants and young children. He effectively used these opportunities to teach both parents and professional staff
Source: Photo courtesy of Children's Hospital Boston Archives, Boston, Massachusetts

> Dr. Brazelton would highlight the most positive developmental characteristics of each patient. These patients were quite often children with significant health issues – issues impacting their development considerably. Yet the infant was always shown in the most positive light, not only to benefit the anxious, often over-tired mother, but also for the rest of the health care staff. It was the impact of these interactions, these moments of assisting the mother to connect with her child that left an indelible impression on all the staff. In the process of interacting with the child and the parent, Dr. Brazelton was able to draw out the most positive characteristics of the family, whatever the family's circumstances may have been. This, in turn, truly appeared to have an equally positive impact on how the staff viewed the patient and parent. This enabled the bedside staff to build on the child's and family's strengths. (Suzanne M. Graca, MS, CCLS, Child Life Specialist III)
>
> Dr. Brazelton modeled how to look at the whole child and not only the illness. His advocacy for parents enabled them to be a voice for their child in the health care setting. (Maureen Abramson, MS, CCLS, Child Life Specialist II)

At the same time that Dr. Brazelton first began developing his role as Patient Care Coordinator and mentoring residents, he co-founded the

Association for the Care of Children in Hospitals (ACCH). Still in its infancy, ACCH was attempting to define the role of what was to become the Child Life Specialist. On its board of directors from 1967 to 1970, and one of the greatest influences on the advancement of the Child Life profession, Brazelton was committed to enhancing the environment for patients and families. He introduced a new awareness of typical growth and development of children into the clinical setting.

The Association for the Care of Children in Hospitals grew quickly. It was clear to Dr. Brazelton and the other founders that there were many other disciplines, like nursing and social work, that wanted to promote interdisciplinary pediatric practice. Before long, the organization changed its name to The Association for the Care of Children's Health (ACCH). During the same period, the Child Life profession was developing and desperately wanted to set standards for itself. In 1986 a new organization, The Child Life Council, was formed.

The Child Life Council developed educational and practice standards, guidelines for evidenced-based practice, and a credentialing exam for Child Life Specialist certification. Over the years, graduate and undergraduate programs in Child Life developed in several colleges and universities. A variety of internship experiences in hospital and alternative settings were established. Over the years, Child Life Specialists were integrated into many more hospital settings across the country, although funding for many programs was tenuous, and highly vulnerable to hospital budgetary constraints.

A major change occurred in 1991 when the Director of Child Life Services became accountable to Eileen Sporing who, with extensive pediatric nursing background and progressive leadership in pediatric nursing, was appointed Senior Vice President for Patient Services, Chief Nurse at Children's Hospital, in July, 1989. She introduced a whole new interdisciplinary approach to providing patient care services, called the Integrated Model. This model organized the various patient care disciplines in each patient care unit under the leadership of the unit's Nursing/Patient Services Director. Although all departments retained their leadership structure, the professionals of the various disciplines assigned to that unit also had a reporting responsibility to the Nursing/Patient Services Director.

A consistent concern of many Child Life program leaders over the years was that the Child Life Program would need to endure budgetary and staff cuts. Reporting directly to the Vice President of Nursing/Patient Services was a blessing. The new Integrated Model brought strength to the

Child Life Department and improved the care of children and families. Multidisciplinary collaboration of nursing staff and Child Life staff continually improved the child-friendly environment. The new model was a catalyst for the development of a seamless interprofessional relationship and partnership between Child Life and Nursing.

Eileen Sporing understood the importance of the integration of Child Life in the patient care effort. She valued the work of the Child Life Department in new ways and there were no budget cuts for the Child Life Department, even during several financially lean years at Children's Hospital. A testament to the integration of Child Life in Patient Services is that all new Child Life Specialists positions have been added under nursing leadership. Over the years, improvements to the hospital environment for children were accomplished by enlightened hospital administrators, nurses, physicians, parents, and the influence of accrediting bodies.

This progress is illustrated by the comments of a young patient to a Child Life Specialist in the Emergency Department. These highlight the important role Child Life Specialists fulfill by incorporating distraction into pain management at Children's Hospital Boston. At age five or six, a boy named J. needed twenty-one stitches. The Child Life Specialist gathered books and bubbles. The child cried when the Novocain was injected, but he was distracted the whole time by the Child Life Specialist. When the sutures were completed, the child asked the Child Life Specialist: "Are you a nurse or a doctor?"

She said, "No, I'm a Child Life Specialist."

"Oh," he said.

The Child Life Specialist asked him, "Do you know what that is?"

He replied, "Well, Kelly, I think you are here to keep kids calm – and let me tell you something – it worked for me!"

This child's spontaneous testimony is one example of our success in creating a child-friendly environment, of the positive impact of integrating Child Life into the healthcare services provided to all hospitalized children. Children's Hospital Boston has implemented so many of the visions that Dr. Brazelton and I could only dream about in the early years. A partial list of the many elements that have created a child-friendly environment at Children's Hospital Boston appears in Box 27.1.

T. B. Brazelton's contributions to establishing the Child Life field and the critical role of these specialists in the care of children are immeasurable. Together he and they helped to transform pediatric hospitals by aligning their practices with the advances in child development research that he

Box 27.1 Child-friendly hospital elements

Children's Hospital Boston
Child-Friendly Hospital Elements

- 24-hour parent presence including the operating room during anesthesia induction
- Pre-Admission Program
- School Program
- Surgical Liaison Program
- Sensitivity to diversity of cultures, healthcare beliefs and practices, religious faiths, ethnic backgrounds, foods
- Center for Families: multilingual, multidisciplinary resources and support for parents and children
- Parent and Teen Advisory Committees
- Child Life Specialists and Patient Activity Rooms on all inpatient units and many ambulatory and ancillary services
- Clown Care Unit
- Pawprints Program

Source:

propelled for half a century. Like earlier progress of the 1960s and 1970s, twenty-first century technological change has the potential to make hospitals impersonal. The focus on efficiently treating the child's illness can still absorb much of professionals' attention, leaving little for the child's feelings and the family's needs. Yet the absence of interventions to bridge the gap between home and hospital, such as parent participation and support, and preparation for procedures and surgery, can trigger serious reactions of the child to the hospital and delay healing. We now know so much more about the negative physiological effects of severe stress on the immune system, cardiovascular functioning, healing, and health. It is imperative that alongside the medical advances of today and tomorrow we continue to focus on the child and family to improve on what has already been accomplished. Efforts will not be successful without the integration and collaboration of all healthcare disciplines, and their respectful partnerships with each family and the whole child.

References and further reading

Ainsworth, M., & Bowlby, J. (1965). *Child care and the growth of love.* London: Penguin Books.

Bowlby, J. (1969). *Attachment and loss: Attachment* (Vol. 1). London: Hogarth Press & The Institute of Psycho-Analysis.

Plank, E. N. (1962). *Working with children in hospitals: A guide for the professional team.* Cleveland: Press of Western Reserve University.

Robbins, F. C. (1962). Foreword. In E. N. Plank (Ed.), *Working with children in hospitals: A guide for the professional team* (pp. v–vi). Cleveland: Press of Western Reserve University.

Robertson, J. (1958). *Young children in hospital.* London: Tavistock Child Development Unit.

28

Improving Healthcare Service Delivery Systems and Outcomes with Relationship-based Nursing Practices

Ann C. Stadtler, Julie C. Novak, and Joshua D. Sparrow

Before the dawn of the twenty-first century, T. Berry Brazelton had already pronounced the American healthcare system broken, provocatively recommending that it be "scrapped" altogether. Yet during this period, practice and service delivery models have emerged with promise for greater effectiveness and efficiency. Among these are preventive, developmental, relational, strengths-based, holistic, and family- and child-centered approaches that have been espoused in the field of nursing, and resonate with Brazelton's philosophy.

Brazelton's newborn research, developmental model, and relationship-based approach to families have clearly influenced and will continue to influence nursing practice. Yet he would be the first to emphasize that many early adopters and champions of his and related approaches have been nurses and nurse practitioners. Many among them had also independently found their way to paradigms for care consistent with his. While different practitioners within the same discipline often subscribe to a range of practice models, earlier developments within the nursing field had readied many nurses for Brazelton's relational model of care. Compatible family-centered approaches had arisen simultaneously within nursing during times that were ripe for change.

A few years after the first edition of *Touchpoints* (Brazelton, 1992) was published, and just a year before the publication of the third edition of the Neonatal Behavioral Assessment Scale (NBAS) (Brazelton & Nugent, 1995) that contained a family-based adaptation, the Family Administration of Neonatal Activities (FANA), several articles appeared in the nursing literature proposing family-centered models (Ahmann, 1994; Shelton & Stepanek, 1994) and affirming views voiced by others in the discipline far earlier:

> The emphasis on the parent–child–nurse relationship [of the Touchpoints Approach] is similar to that described by the proponents of caring and humanistic nursing (Lenninger, 1984; Patterson & Zderad, 1976; Watson, 1985). Using the Touchpoints approach, nurses join with parents in an authentic, intersubjective, transpersonal process. Humanistic, caring nursing transcends personal boundaries and enables the moment-to-moment human care process in which the nurse is truly being with the parent and child (Watson, 1985). (Percy, Stadtler, & Sands, 2002).

Along with such independent and parallel efforts were numerous occasions for cross-fertilization. As early as the 1970s, Barnard's (Barnard & Kelly, 1989) collaboration with Brazelton was one early instance of such mutual influence. The creation of the pediatric nurse practitioner (PNP) role in 1965 by nursing dean Dr. Loretta Ford and pediatrician Dr. Henry Silver at the University of Colorado afforded many other opportunities. Created for the provision of well-childcare in the wake of a physician shortage, by 1973 several hundred PNPs were providing primary care across the United States (Novak, 2006). Through the National Association of Pediatric Nurse Associates and Practitioners (NAPNAP), PNPs joined with Brazelton, a supporter of the PNP role and the organization, and a frequent participant in NAPNAP conferences, to actively seek out opportunities to advance knowledge and practice together. (Long before it was broadly supported, Brazelton understood the value of interdisciplinary collaboration and was one of its early advocates.) There were few primary care role models for PNPs and Brazelton's practice was considered a model to be emulated. His focus on a systems approach to primary care that considered the family and influences that impacted the family resonated with nurses.

The 2008 joint scope of practice statement by the National Association of Pediatric Nurse Associates and Practitioners, Society of Pediatric Nurses and American Nurses Association states: "Pediatric nursing is the protection, promotion and optimization of health and abilities for children . . . using a family-centered care approach." One PNP (Karl, 1999), who also acknowledges Brazelton's role in establishing the family-centered approach, describes it in the context of the NBAS-based interactive newborn bath as follows: "The driving assumption of family-centered care is that the family is the constant in a child's life, and that care should focus on supporting the family as a dynamic and functional whole. Expanding the traditional instructional format into an interactive approach transforms the newborn bath into a family-centered intervention" (Karl, 1999).

By 2008 the number of PNP training programs exceeded 95 and the number of NAPNAP members exceeded 7,000. Over its 45-year history, NAPNAP members and PNP educational programs have espoused Brazelton's teachings, research, methods, textbooks and, more recently, the Touchpoints Approach, which has been adapted to the challenges of their practice.

Among such adaptations are Toilet School (Stadtler & Burke, 1998; Stadtler, Gorski, & Brazelton, 1999) and Touchpoints Asthma Parent Child Groups (Stadtler, Tronick, & Brazelton, 2001), both developed by multidisciplinary teams that included one of the authors (AS), a nurse practitioner, who had previously participated in the development of the original Touchpoints curriculum (Hornstein, O'Brien, & Stadtler, 1997; Stadtler & Hornstein, 2009). A number of others in nursing have published on their efforts to adapt the NBAS and Touchpoints to perinatal practice (Amy, 2001; Karl, 2004; Karl & O'Hare, 2006; Tedder, 1991), well-childcare visits (Karl, Limbo, & Ricker, 1998; Percy, Stadtler, & Sands, 2002), home visiting (Brandt et al., 2001), parent and parent–child groups (Percy & McIntyre, 2001), prevention and health promotion (Tyler & Horner, 2008a), and chronic obesity treatment (Tyler & Horner, 2008b).

Challenges Addressed by Developmental, Relationship-based Nursing Practices

Health promotion, prevention of illness and developmental derailments, coordination of care and communication, treatment adherence, and healthcare resource utilization are all in need of overhaul if costs are to be contained while quality is improved within the U.S. healthcare system. All of these have been the focus of Brazelton-inspired or Brazelton-related service delivery model innovations. Particularly well suited for the applications of these models are prenatal and postpartum care, parents' understanding of infant behavior and their own development, attachment, breastfeeding, well-child health and development, and chronic illness: all present opportunities for improvements in health and developmental outcomes. While some involve reconfigurations of service delivery, such as Neonatal Intensive Care Unit (NICU) developmental care (Als, 1986 [2008]), or of staffing patterns, for example, to provide continuity from the maternity ward to well-childcare visits, or both, as in home visitation and group care (parent groups and parent–child groups), a reconceptualization of the nursing role and nurse–patient relationship have been at the heart of all of them.

Healthcare provider relationships with families of young children can be an important antidote to the increasing isolation of and stress on families (Barnard & Morriset, 1995) – among the threats to health of the twenty-first century. The Touchpoints approach urges a paradigm shift in the quality of these relationships, from prescriptive to collaborative, from objective to empathic. Karl and O'Hare, in their article on reconceptualizing nursing roles in which Brazelton, the NBAS, and Touchpoints are cited, describe a shift from the traditional nursing roles of "doer" and "teacher" in the postpartum period to "attacher":

> Traditionally, during the newborn period, nursing largely viewed the needs of mothers separately from those of their babies. The nurse who worked with the mother functioned as a "teacher," meeting well-researched maternal learning needs of mothers separately from those of their babies. The nurse who focused on newborn needs was a "doer," providing task-by-task care for the infants during the times the mother was unable to do so. Although "teaching" and "doing" are both extraordinarily important tasks, seeing them as endpoints stops short of the real goal. Focusing on task completion without a theoretical framework undermines the true potential of quality nursing care and produces tedious repetition for the nurse. Ultimately, even with good intentions and caring, an approach lacking dedication to viewing mothers and their newborns as a single entity fails to intervene at the point of this dyad's most essential need . . . attachment. (Karl & O'Hare, 2006)

The nursing role is redefined to attend to the mother–infant relationship, as well as the nurse's relationships with them, as opposed to attending to specific tasks, or to individual family members in isolation. The focus or object of nursing practice becomes the relationship, rather than a single individual. Also noteworthy here is the brief mention of an oft-repeated theme in the nursing literature on the effect of NBAS or Touchpoints adaptations on clinical relationships: the practice of nursing becomes less tedious, less draining, and more deeply rewarding (Amy, 2001; Karl, Limbo, & Ricker, 1998; Percy, Stadtler, & Sands, 2002). Another benefit of this emotionally invested relationship of nurse with mother and infant in the newborn period is its impact on future treatment adherence.

Continuity of relationship-based care for prevention, health promotion, and treatment adherence

As the therapeutic advantages of relationship-based care are recognized, service delivery must be reconfigured to permit the continuity of nurse–family relationships. In a pilot undertaken at Children's Hospital, Boston and Brigham and Women's Hospital called Healthy Connections (HC), and informed both by the NBAS and Touchpoints, nurse practitioners using these relational approaches on the maternity ward were assigned to continue work with the same families for perinatal well-childcare visits. Karl, Limbo, and Ricker refer here to a shift from the nursing roles of "teacher" and "doer" to that of "a collaborator with mothers and . . . facilitator of positive mother–infant interaction. At the heart of Healthy Connections is a relational process in which HC nurses use the care and behavior of the infant to create a nurse–mother relationship and in turn use that relationship to facilitate positive interaction between mother and infant" (Karl, Limbo & Ricker, 1998).

It has been proposed that this plays a particularly important role in promoting attachment with their infants in mothers who are isolated and may not have experienced this kind of nurturing themselves as young children:

> As a parallel to the mother–child attachment bond itself, the nurse–mother relationship models for mothers' ways to relate to their infants. The mother who feels the caring approach of the nurse may internalize this feeling and use it as a standard for interacting with her newborn. Especially for socially-at-risk mothers who lack healthy mothering models, this relationship may serve as a kind of surrogate "attachment" that they have with the nurse and can then replicate in their relationship with their babies. (Karl & O'Hare, 2006)

Initially designed in order to improve continuity of care and clinical communication across settings, HCs' redesign of service delivery to provide continuity in the nurse–family relationship led to the kind of "seamlessness" that Brazelton has long urged across medical specialties, healthcare disciplines, and treatment settings. It also led to increased participation of families in well-childcare visits through infants' fourth month, decreasing unnecessary emergency room use in the same period (Karl, Limbo, & Ricker, 1998).

Nurse home visitation programs also represent an innovative service delivery mechanism that allows for sustained relationships, provided that nurses also possess the skills to sustain them. Those conducted in Napa, California for Medi-Cal-eligible families by nurses trained in Touchpoints, and in East Harlem by nurses trained in both Touchpoints and the Newborn Behavioral Observation (NBO), independently observed far lower "no-show" rates and greater satisfaction than with home visitation conducted by nurses unequipped with these tools (Brandt et al., 2001; personal communication, Sara Mullen, RN/nurse home visitor, Little Sisters of the Assumption, East Harlem, 2007). The Napa Touchpoints-trained nurses also found that their relational approach improved breastfeeding, maternal mental health, and child development outcomes, as compared to non-Touchpoints-trained nurses visiting similar families. As with HC, this home visitation service also led to improved attendance at well-childcare visits, and less frequent and more appropriate emergency room use.

The repositioning of nurses in a "connected" (Morse, 1991) "relationship [in which] the nurse views the mother as a person first and patient second" (Karl, Limbo, & Ricker, 1998) is thought to be a critical ingredient in bringing families back, visit after visit. Almost paradoxically, it also allows nurses to communicate information and guidance – to function as "teachers" – more effectively, because within these relationships mothers are more ready to listen. Within these relationships, nurses are well positioned to offer *anticipatory guidance*, a term used by Brazelton to describe collaborative, empathic communication about upcoming challenges for parents predicted by his Touchpoints model of development.

When parents are prepared for their children's temporary regressions – for example in the areas of feeding, sleep, toilet training, or behavioral control – as harbingers of new advances in their development, these predictable developmental crises, or touchpoints, are less likely to jeopardize parents' sense of competence and effectiveness. Parents are less likely to overreact, putting their children's development at risk for more long-lasting derailment. When anticipatory guidance is offered in the context of ongoing relationship-based services such as these, parents will feel less alone, and "braced" for whatever challenges their children's development may present.

Numerous nursing publications also report the positive impact of Brazelton-informed or Brazelton-related approaches on attachment and breastfeeding. In addition to nurses' attachment-promoting "mothering the mother" relationships (Karl & O'Hare, 2006), a behavioral-developmental mechanism is also at work here. Nurses share observations and understandings of newborn behavior, including state organization, with mothers. Mothers' attention is drawn to their infants' attachment behaviors, to cues demonstrating early signs of readiness for feeding, the need for supports – e.g., soothing from crying, arousing from drowsiness for feeding, and infant contentment and pleasure with feeding. As a result, mothers feel more competent in understanding their babies, more successful at breastfeeding, and more rewarded by both, increasing the likelihood of longer breastfeeding duration (Brandt, Andrews, & Kvale, 1998; Karl & O'Hare, 2006).

Group care to address challenges to mother–infant relationships and infant/child development

Touchpoints-informed relational approaches to optimizing mother–infant interactions have also been applied to adolescent mothers, where the process of attachment may face multiple threats, including very young mothers' isolation, needs for nurturance and heightened sense of inadequacy in the parental role. In a pilot study of a small convenience sample, this approach was used in a group setting to "promote parental self-competence in low-income, minority, pregnant and parenting teen mothers" (Percy & McIntyre, 2001). Although interpretations of the studies' results are limited by its design, participants' scores on the *Parent Sense of Competence Scale* increased from before to after the intervention, with the most marked improvement on the item, "Considering how long I've been a mother, I feel thoroughly familiar with this role." Not only was group attendance better than expected, but participants asked for evenings groups so that the babies' fathers who worked during the day could attend as well.

Group care is another innovative service delivery mechanism structured to facilitate relationships. Not only are parent groups less labor-intensive than individual care, but they add relationships among parents to healthcare provider–parent relationships to counter parental isolation, correlated with increased risk for parental depression and child abuse. Centering Pregnancy, for example, is a nurse midwife-designed program that has helped nurses and other practitioners across the U.S. shift from individual to relationship-based group prenatal care. It has demonstrated positive impact on birth weight, breastfeeding initiation, as well as with prenatal care participation and gestational duration for adolescent mother participants (Ickovics et al., 2007; Schindler Rising, Powell Kennedy, & Klima, 2004).

Parent–child groups can build on the principles of family-centered care. As designed by one of the authors (AS) and colleagues, Toilet School (Stadtler & Burke, 1998; Stadtler, Gorski, & Brazelton, 1999) has operated since 1994 at Children's Hospital, Boston, and Touchpoints Parent–Child Asthma Groups (Stadtler, Tronick, & Brazelton, 2001) have been piloted and adapted in several clinics, private practices, and hospitals across the US. Both specify separate meetings first for parents and children, after which parents and children join in a single group. Consistent with a central strategy of the Touchpoints Approach, the children's behavior – stimulated by their participation in developmentally designed groups – is then described to parents. Through these observations, parents develop a new understanding of their children's struggles and strengths, and are ready for a new repertoire of responses to their children's challenges. Through the groups both parents' and children's mastery are supported.

Professional Development Supporting Change in Practice and Systems of Care

In recent decades, efforts to improve healthcare quality, outcomes, and efficiency have largely ignored the potency of relationship-based care. Nonetheless, nursing programs across the country are realigning their curricula with these new models for practice and service delivery. The majority of pediatric nursing textbooks cite the NBO or NBAS and many now cite Touchpoints. Several schools of nursing are integrating the Touchpoints Approach. Clemson University has developed an online system of reflective practice using the principles and practice of the Touchpoints Approach, while at Purdue University Touchpoints has provided a framework for the integration of education, practice, and research in a nurse-managed clinic setting. At the University of Texas at Austin School of Nursing (UTASON), the Touchpoints Approach is foundational to graduate and undergraduate programs, and is divided into five levels: (1) relationships in the care of children and families; (2) development as a dynamic process characterized by regressions, bursts, and pauses; (3) child's behavior as the nurse's language for entering the parent–child relationship (Stadtler, 1999); (4) parents' past experience as an influence on parenting; (5) markers of relationships with families and integration of the entire approach in practice (Percy, Stadtler, & Sands, 2002). In response to the need for ongoing support for the integration of the Approach, a nurse practitioner-managed health clinic was also instituted at UTASON. Here, students are mentored in reflective practice using the Touchpoints Approach. Touchpoints has also been selected as the framework for an academic–community partnership among the University of Texas Health Science Center San Antonio (UTHSCSA) School of Nursing, UTHSCSA Community Pediatrics, Bexar County Public Health Department, and Head Start.

Future Challenges

Nurses are the largest cadre of healthcare professionals in the United States and are critical to improving existing systems and designing new ones. With its emphasis on prevention and health promotion, and with the efficiencies and effectiveness of relationship-based, family-centered care it espouses, the nursing profession has an opportunity to be a major part of the American healthcare solution. Whether supporting the attachment of newborns and their parents in the hospital by using the NBO or NBAS, providing a relational bridge from obstetrical to pediatric primary care, visiting families in their homes during pregnancy and after birth to support their adjustment to the new baby, or adding another layer of relationships through group care, nurses have already done much to change service delivery models to improve systems of care. A critical challenge they face is to effectively communicate the advantages of relationship-based, family-centered care to their colleagues in other disciplines and specialties, to policy makers and healthcare industry leaders. Perhaps a relationship-based approach will be effective in reaching them as well.

References and further reading

Ahmann, E. (1994). Family-centered care: Shifting orientation. *Pediatric Nursing 20*(2), 1113–1117.

Als, H. (1986 [2008]). Program guide – Newborn Individualized Developmental Care and Assessment Program (NIDCAP): An education and training program for health care professionals. Boston: NIDCAP Federation International.

Amy, E. (2001). Reflections on the interactive newborn bath demonstration. *American Journal of Maternal/Child Nursing, 26*(6), 320–322.

Barnard, K. E., & Kelly, J. F. (1989). Assessment of parent–child interaction. In S. J. Meisels & J. P. Shonkoff (Eds.), *Handbook of Early Childhood Intervention*. New York: Cambridge University Press.

Barnard, K. E., & Morisset, C. E. (1995). Preventive health and developmental care for children: Relationship as a primary factor in service delivery with at risk populations. In H. Fitzgerald, B. Lester, & B. Zuckerman (Eds.), *Children of poverty: Research, health and policy issues* (pp. 167–195). New York: Garland Publishing.

Brandt, K. A., Andrews, C. M., & Kvale, J. (1998). Mother–infant interactions and breastfeeding outcomes 8 weeks after birth. *Journal of Obstetric, Gynecologic, and Neonatal Nursing, 27*(2), 169–174.

Brandt, K. A., Brazelton, T. B., Keller, L., Longoria, T., Murphy, J. M., & Pitman, S. (2001). Touchpoints in prenatal home visiting: The impact on health and wellness indicators for mother and baby at six months postpartum. *Project Report*. Napa, CA: Napa County Health & Human Services.

Brazelton, T. B. (1992). *Touchpoints: Your Child's Emotional and Behavioral Development*. Reading, MA: Addison-Wesley.

Brazelton, T. B., & Nugent, J. K. (1995). Neonatal Behavioral Assessment Scale (3rd ed.). London: MacKeith Press.

Hornstein, J., O'Brien, M., & Stadtler, A. C. (1997). Touchpoints practice: Lessons learned from training and implementation. *Zero to Three, 17*(6), 26–33.

Ickovics, J. R., Kershaw, T. S., Westdahl, C., Magriples, U., Massey, Z., Reynolds, H., & Schindler Rising, S. (2007). Group prenatal care and perinatal outcomes: A randomized controlled trial. *Obstetrics and Gynecology, 110*(2), 330–338.

Karl, D. J. (1999). The interactive newborn bath: Using infant neurobehavior to connect parents and newborns. *American Journal of Maternal/Child Nursing, 24*(6), 280–286.

Karl, D. J. (2004). Using principles of newborn behavioral state organization to facilitate breastfeeding. *American Journal of Maternal/Child Nursing, 29*(5), 292–298.

Karl, D. J., Limbo, D., & Ricker, V. J. (1998). Healthy connections: A relational model to extend primary care into the perinatal period. *Journal of Pediatric Health Care, 12*, 176–182.

Karl, D. J., & O'Hare, C. M. (2006). Reconceptualizing the nurse's role in the newborn period as an attacher. *American Journal of Maternal/Child Nursing, 31*(4), 257–262.

Lenninger, M. M. (1984). Care: The essence of nursing and health care. In M. M. Lenninger (Ed.), *Care: The essence of nursing and health care*. Thorofare, NJ: Slack.

Morse, J. (1991). Negotiating commitment and involvement in the nurse–patient relationship. *Journal of Advanced Nursing, 16*, 455–468.

Novak, J. (2006). Evolution of the pediatric nurse practitioner role. In N. Ryan-Wenger (Ed.), *Core curriculum for primary care pediatric nurse practitioners*. Philadelphia: Elsevier.

Patterson, J., & Zderad, L. (1976). *Humanistic nursing*. New York: Wiley Biomedical Publications.

Percy, M. S., & McIntyre, S. (2001). Using Touchpoints to promote parental self-confidence in low income, minority, pregnant and parenting teen mothers. *Journal of Pediatric Nursing, 16*, 180–186.

Percy, M., Stadtler, A. C., & Sands, D. (2002). Touchpoints: Changing the face of pediatric nurse practitioner education. *American Journal of Maternal Child Nursing, 27*(4), 222–228.

Schindler Rising, S., Powell Kennedy, H., & Klima, C. S. (2004). Redesigning prenatal care through CenteringPregnancy. *Journal of Midwifery and Women's Health, 49*(5), 398–404.

Shelton, T. L., & Stepanek, J. S. (1994). Family-centered care for children needing specialized health and developmental services. Bethesda, MD: Association for the Care of Children's Health.

Stadtler, A. C. (1999). Using the language of the child's behavior in your work with families. *Journal of Pediatric Health Care, 13*(3), S13–S16.

Stadtler, A. C., & Burke, P. (1998). A group treatment approach to failure to toilet train: The case of Max. *Clinical Excellence for Nurse Practitioners, 2*(2), 83–87.

Stadtler, A. C., Gorski, P. A., & Brazelton, T. B. (1999). Toilet training methods, clinical interventions and recommendations. *Pediatrics, 103*, 1359–1361.

Stadtler, A. C., & Hornstein, J. (2009). The Touchpoints Approach: United States. In J. K. Nugent, B. J. Petrauskas, and T. Berry Brazelton, *The newborn as a person: Enabling healthy infant development worldwide.* Hoboken, NJ: John Wiley & Sons.

Stadtler, A. C., Tronick, E. Z., & Brazelton, T. B. (2001). The Touchpoints pediatric asthma program. *Pediatric Nursing, 27*(5), 459–461.

Tedder, J. (1991). Using the NBAS to facilitate the parent–infant relationship in primary care settings. *Nurse Practitioner, 16*(35), 26–30.

Tyler, D. O., & Horner, S. D. (2008a). Family-centered collaborative negotiation: A model for facilitating behavior change in primary care. *Journal of the American Academy of Nurse Practitioners, 20*(4), 194–203.

Tyler, D. O., & Horner, S. D. (2008b). Collaborating with low-income families and their overweight children to improve weight-related behaviors: An intervention process evaluation. *Pediatric Nursing, 13*(4), 263–274.

Watson, J. (1985). *Nursing: Human science and human care.* Norwalk, CT: Appleton Century Crofts.

29

Translating the Science of Early Childhood Development into Policy and Practice

Daniel Pedersen and Jack P. Shonkoff

In 2007, the Buffett Early Childhood Fund became one of America's three largest early childhood philanthropies, targeting more than $19 million in grants to advance an argument Brazelton had been making his entire professional life – that more resources (public, private, and parental) should be invested in our most vulnerable citizens from birth. That's no accident. The decision to invest those fresh millions in early childhood was made by Warren Buffett's oldest child, Susie, who created the Fund at the turn of the new millennium.

Susie Buffett's willingness to make the beginning of life the focus of her foundation began with "America's pediatrician." Like millions of parents across the nation and around the world, she turned to Dr. Brazelton's books, read his magazine articles, and followed his advice on how to raise her two children in Omaha in the 1980s. It's fair to say that were it not for Berry Brazelton there wouldn't be a Buffett Early Childhood Fund. And were it not for the Fund, the Center on the Developing Child at Harvard University would be missing one of its most consistent philanthropic supporters of the notion it champions – that science has far more to share with policy makers than policy makers have heard to date.

In this chapter, after seven years of strategizing together as a philanthropic executive and an academic leader committed to connecting the dots, we discuss how we see early childhood knowledge, policy, and practice beginning to come together into a more virtuous circle, even though much remains to be accomplished. There was a time – until John Adams became President and set in motion change that flowered fully in the mid-nineteenth century – when public elementary education did not exist in the United States. Now it's time for another paradigm shift, focusing intently on vulnerable children from the moments of greatest opportunity, prenatally and from birth, and building from there.

New knowledge – the fruit of explosive advances in neuroscience, child development research, and economic analysis – is ready to point the way to new lawmaking at the state and federal levels. Yet public policy in the United States still sadly lags behind what we know best practice in the first five years of life should look like – the provision of basic health and early education services that build the foundations of equal opportunity and fuel the development of the nation's human capital, combined with intensive interventions for those in deep trouble. Ideology should not drive policy change in this tragically wanting American landscape, where less than 3 percent of income-eligible infants and toddlers in 2008 were enrolled in Early Head Start – the primary public funding stream for disadvantaged infants and toddlers in the richest nation on earth. Knowledge, not personal beliefs or partisan politics, should lead the way.

Translating the Science of Early Childhood Development into Policy and Practice

Knowledge, like the brain itself, is built over time. Over the past century, the continually evolving science of early childhood development has transformed our thinking from simplistic notions of a genetically driven process on automatic pilot, through the concept of a congenital tabula rasa shaped by accumulated responses to successive stimuli, to our modern understanding of a highly interactive process in which children develop within an environment of relationships that includes their family, community, and culture. Now, in the early years of the twenty-first century, rapidly expanding knowledge in neuroscience, molecular biology, and genomics is beginning to unlock a whole new level of previously hidden mysteries. To this end, we are moving from the sophisticated observation of child behavior to a deeper understanding of its underlying neurobiology. For half a century, Brazelton has been contributing to that growing knowledge base and empowering generations of thankful parents, energizing policy makers, and inspiring practitioners with clear guidance and practical advice. Today, we have a richer understanding of the biological underpinnings of that sage counsel.

Scientists are beginning to describe the mechanisms through which human individuality is shaped by early experience and embedded in the architecture of the brain. Armed with that growing knowledge, policy makers and practitioners are integrating the principles of both neuroscience and child development into a new framework to guide early childhood policy and practice. That framework, which is giving us the language and insights needed to transcend differences in political ideology and partisan politics, is deeply grounded in the following core concepts:

A sturdy brain foundation is essential. The architecture of the brain develops through a process that begins before birth and continues into adulthood. A sturdy or a fragile foundation emerges that will affect all subsequent capabilities and behavior.

Interactions matter in brain development. The interaction of genes and experience shapes the circuitry of the developing brain. As in tennis or volleyball, the child serves up an invitation to engage and his or her caretaker is either responsive or unresponsive to the child's needs. This "serve and return" process is fundamental to how the brain becomes wired in those earliest years.

Skill begets skill. Brains are built in a hierarchical fashion, from the bottom up. Increasingly complex circuits build on simpler circuits and increasingly adaptive skills emerge over time.

Cognitive, emotional, and social capacities are a package deal. Learning, behavior, as well as physical and mental health are highly interrelated throughout life. Development of each capacity affects the others.

Toxic stress damages developing brains. Although manageable levels of stress are normative and growth-promoting, toxic stress in the early years – such as from repeated maltreatment or recurrent exposure to violence in the absence of adult protection – damages the architecture of the developing brain and leads to problems in learning and behavior, as well as increased susceptibility to physical and mental illness. Just as with other environmental hazards, we must control toxic stress by addressing the conditions that cause it.

Pay now or pay more later. Brain plasticity and the ability to change behavior decrease over time. Getting it right early is less costly – to society and to individuals – than trying to fix it later. We can pay now or pay more later for society's inability to address this challenge.

We know how to improve outcomes but we must do better. We know how to measure effectiveness factors that make the difference between programs that work and those that don't. Identifying what works best for whom and learning how to bring successful services to scale should be a major priority for ongoing evaluation research.

Building on these core principles, the science of early childhood development provides a useful framework for policy makers to inform their priorities in these belt-tightening times. Policymakers should heed research as they face tough decisions about how to spend limited resources to promote the healthy development of vulnerable, young children.

Understanding letters and numbers isn't enough. A balanced approach to emotional, social, cognitive, and language development will best prepare children for success in school, at the workplace, and in life. Young children with emerging reading skills will not do well in school if they're preoccupied with anxiety or unable to control their aggressive impulses. This is not a battle between the importance of building a foundation for early literacy versus promoting emotional wellbeing and social competence. Smart policies promote a comprehensive approach toward building all these skills simultaneously in the early years.

Evidence-based programs don't mean much if the implementers don't understand the evidence. No policies designed to improve life outcomes for disadvantaged, young children will produce positive impacts if we don't invest in the education, training, recruitment, and retention of early childhood educators whose expertise matches the needs of the children and families they serve.

Children experiencing toxic stress need specialized intervention as early as possible. Successful intervention for complex problems requires substantive knowledge and technical skills. A modestly trained, warm-hearted home visitor can be a lifeline for a socially isolated, first-time parent. But a well-meaning person with limited professional expertise cannot address the complex needs of a parent with serious depression or a substance abuse problem.

Build a bigger tent. The power and sustainability of broad-based, political support and public–private partnerships are gaining traction in the early childhood world. Building a strong foundation for a healthy and competent citizenry need not be a partisan issue. The magnitude of the challenge also requires more resources than public budgets alone can provide. New champions from new places offer new possibilities.

No silver bullets. No single program will answer all unmet needs or solve all persistent problems. Supportive relationships and positive learning experiences begin at home but also can be provided through a range of informal community-based initiatives as well as a variety of formal services.

The Promising Emergence of Educare

There will be no silver bullet but a promising alternative can be seen growing today across the country, from Maine to Arizona, and Miami to Seattle. Educare attempts to embody many of the core concepts outlined above and is supported by a network of like-minded philanthropists who care profoundly about connecting knowledge to policy and practice. Neuroscience is answering the relatively easy question of "why" we should invest in our youngest children. Educare – as both a model of best practice in deeply challenged neighborhoods and a showroom for policy change – is attempting to answer the tougher questions about *what* we should do now and *how* we can do it in a variety of communities across the country.

A first class nonprofit called the Ounce of Prevention Fund created Educare on the South Side of Chicago, in what was until recently the poorest census tract in the nation. Actually, Educare was distilled there. At the turn of the millennium, this new model sought to apply state-of the-art program knowledge to one piece of mean-streets real estate. Much of that knowledge came from the Ounce's two decades of experience working in extraordinarily high-risk conditions in federal high-rise housing monoliths known as the Robert Taylor Homes. The idea that this could be such a powerful living laboratory was the brainchild of Irving Harris, a businessman-philanthropist extraordinaire. Harris died in 2004, leaving a vibrant legacy of shrewd public–private partnership on behalf of better policy for poor children.

The spirit of public–private partnership embodied in the heart of Educare rests on some simple but revolutionary ideas. The totality of the enterprise is a school, not a center, serving children from birth to age five. Wherever possible, it sits adjacent to a public elementary school to break down the mental silos that let some lawmakers think of children as not ready for "real" learning until they enter kindergarten. Because teacher–child ratios and credentials are important, every classroom is designed to have three teachers – one with a four-year degree in early childhood, one with at least a two-year early childhood degree, and an aide from the community with special training. Infant/toddler classrooms serve eight children and preschool classrooms serve seventeen. Each child remains with the same teachers from birth to three, and then moves to a preschool classroom from ages three to five. One master teacher for every four classrooms provides hands-on supervision for the teaching staff.

Every Educare family is "held" by many hands. In addition to the teaching teams, each is paired with a family support worker and supervisor to ensure that comprehensive needs are addressed. Each birth-to-five school shares the mantra that cognitive development must be undergirded by social and emotional development, with parents as fully engaged as possible. Educare aims to actualize on the streets an approach that neuroscience, developmental psychology, and economics all argue for together in theory – that the strongest possible start from the earliest possible age produces the greatest possible impact on school readiness, high school graduation, and long-term success in life.

Although it is too soon to measure its long-term impact, there are three ways so far to assess how well Educare is working as a social investment. The first is through its robust geographic growth. Communities are voting with their feet, driven by the strong appetites of philanthropies, school systems and Head Start/Early Head Start providers, for a program model that promises improved outcomes. Each Educare represents common cause between the private sector, which pays for an architecturally appropriate new building, and the public sector (school district, state government, and federal grantees) which agrees to pool resources to pay for ongoing services that meet high standards.

Within this context, it's important to note that Educare would not be possible without Head Start and Early Head Start funding, which typically makes up more than half the operating budget ($2.6 to $3 million per year) for each school (which serves 150 to 200 children). Costs per child run from $15,000 to $20,000 per year – roughly what high-quality private centers charge high-income parents. In 2005, only two schools – Chicago and Omaha – were operating and two others were under construction. At the end of 2009, eight Educare schools were up and running, four more were on track to open in 2010 and at least eight more were in varying stages of discussion and development. This is what most would call an accelerating growth curve.

The second way to measure Educare's effectiveness is through program evaluation. Thus, the Buffett Early Childhood Fund and allied funders have contracted with the Frank Porter Graham Institute at the University of North Carolina-Chapel Hill to conduct a continuous implementation study of the expanding network and add experimental research over time. Unpublished data from an initial assessment of interactions and environments in classrooms across five operating sites – Chicago, Omaha, Milwaukee, Tulsa, and Denver – show promising findings (Yazejian & Bryant, 2009). Partly because there is only one year of five-site data, these findings are very preliminary. But overall, they suggest that the earlier and more sustained the high-quality intervention, the better the results. Though primitive, this snapshot is reinforced by national Early Head Start evaluation findings, which showed that the children with the best outcomes were those who participated in both Early Head Start and Head Start.

The final way to judge Educare's effectiveness is to assess its impact as a platform for policy change. Each school reflects the determination of its private sector sponsors, in consort with their public partners, to leverage their philanthropic resources to produce greater efficiencies and enhance public policy at the state and federal levels. As such, each Educare is turning out to be an important showroom for state lawmakers. If you talk about best practice in early childhood, you draw blank stares in many a statehouse. If you show best practice in their home communities, lawmakers vote for more of it.

Illinois, where Educare began, has become a national leader in state-level early childhood policy. That success comes largely from an 11 percent infant/toddler set-aside within the state's $348 million block grant, as well as comprehensive investments in risk-focused, universal preschool. Oklahoma, spurred on by banker and oilman George Kaiser, established a pilot public–private partnership with state government that spent $15 million in year one and $25 million the following year on new infant/toddler services, with the enthusiastic support of the Governor. In Kansas – moved partly by a visit to Educare of Omaha in 2007 – the Governor broadened plans for an expansion of preschool in Kansas into a statewide birth-to-five initiative with a 30 percent birth-to-three set-aside and an expanded pilot for blending public dollars just like the Educare model.

Nowhere has the policy impact of Educare been more dramatic than in Nebraska. In 2004, the year after Educare of Omaha opened, lawmakers voted to expand high-quality preschool for four-year-olds at risk for school failure. Educare's showroom helped bolster the argument. Over the ensuing four years, the number of children served has more than doubled each year and there is a commitment to increase it eightfold, once all public schools find the physical space to devote to the program. In 2006, Nebraskans voted to amend the state constitution to acknowledge that public education begins from birth, paving the way for a new $60 million permanent endowment – $40 million in public money and $20 million from private sources – for risk-targeted infant-toddler grant-making. These dollars will flow, in an "Educare-like" manner, to public schools that are willing to partner with a community-based agency and compete for grants to deliver high-impact services averaging $9,500 per child per year. Those grants must be matched one-for-one at the local level, and must meet Educare credentialing standards.

Many of the key, early funders who anchored Educare, including the Bill & Melinda Gates Foundation, the George Kaiser Family Foundation, and the Buffett Early Childhood Fund, have become convinced that it's not enough to invest in best practice exclusively through Educare. Without better policy, they conclude, best practice can't expand. Hence, seven philanthropies are now supporting two new policy initiatives together – the First Five Years Fund at the federal level and the Birth to Five Policy Alliance for states. And all seven are making discrete but aligned investments in new knowledge generation and application, which is viewed by many as the most promising engine available to inform new policy and practice. Perhaps most important, beyond its clout in the present, all recognize that a growing knowledge base must serve the future by driving the research and development arm of an effort to reduce the intergenerational transmission of poverty. After multiple generations of modest progress in policies and programs, success must not be measured simply by increased dollars spent or by the number of children "served" by earnest yet relatively ineffective efforts. Success must be measured by the number of disadvantaged children whose lives are profoundly changed for the better.

Creating the Future of Early Childhood Policy and Practice

Over the past half century, Brazelton has translated the science of parent–child interaction and individual differences in child development in a more eloquent and more engaging fashion, and arguably for more people, than any single individual in our lifetime. The job is now left to all of us to build on that sturdy foundation and craft the next era in early childhood policy and practice.

Two key challenges currently confront the early childhood field. The first is the challenge of maintaining quality as initially successful programs are taken to scale. The second – in the face of clear evidence of the ability of effective interventions to produce positive impacts – is the obligation to do better. Addressing the first challenge requires commitment and resources. Confronting the latter requires new ideas and innovative strategies that are driven by science and are replicable in communities that do not have access to significant philanthropic resources. To this end, it is essential that we view today's best practices as a starting point, not a destination.

Four decades ago, President Lyndon Johnson inspired researchers and policy makers to design a War on Poverty which led to the creation of neighborhood health centers and Head Start, among other initiatives. Since that time, Brazelton has continued to teach us about the critical importance of early relationships while dramatic advances in neurobiology have underscored the role of positive, early experience in strengthening brain architecture and produced growing evidence that toxic stress damages brain circuits and undermines learning, behavior, and lifelong health. Over the past few years, Educare has been alerting us to the potential impact of larger community influences on child wellbeing through private–public partnerships designed to shift the odds toward more favorable life outcomes for young children living in poverty. Together these forces define a rich and compelling agenda for early childhood policy and practice.

The underlying knowledge base that helps us understand the world of early childhood emphasizes the central importance of relationships, the dramatic influences of child–adult interactions, and the extent to which young children play an active role in their own development. This framework has Brazelton's fingerprints all over it. The ultimate challenge now facing the field is clear. It's time to create a new era in early childhood policy that is inspired by science, built on best practices, and committed to a culture of innovative thinking and continuous improvement. It's time to build on the foundation that Brazelton has played such an important role in shaping and to move to the next level – to increase the return on our collective investments through greater and sustainable differences in the lives of vulnerable, young children and their parents.

References and further reading

Center on the Developing Child (2007). *A science-based framework for early childhood policy: Using evidence to improve outcomes in learning, behavior, and health for vulnerable children.* Retrieved from www.developingchild.net, accessed February 2010.

National Scientific Council on the Developing Child (2007). *The science of early childhood development: Closing the gap between what we know and what we do.* Retrieved February 2010 from www.developingchild.net

Shonkoff, J., & Phillips, D. (Eds.) (2000). *From neurons to neighborhoods: The science of early childhood development.* Washington, DC: National Academy Press.

Yazejian, N., & Bryant, D. M. (2009). Promising early returns: Educare implementation study data, March 2009. Chapel Hill: FPG Child Development Institute, UNC-CH.

30

Placing Relationships at the Core of Early Care and Education Programs

Francine Jacobs, Mallary I. Swartz, Jessica Dym Bartlett, and M. Ann Easterbrooks

Esteemed among physicians devoted to humanizing medical care, Brazelton's insistent focus has been on two figural relationships: pediatricians' relationships with children and parents, and the parent–child relationship. In his view, nurturing the former promotes the latter, and both promote the healthy development and functioning of children and families. Less heralded is the long reach that Brazelton has had in fields outside pediatrics; this chapter highlights the instantiation of his orientation within early care and education.

The Development of Brazelton's Approach to Early Relationships

For several decades, Brazelton has promoted a model of infant and family development that posits satisfying relationships as both a hallmark of thriving in infancy and early childhood and a vehicle for attaining developmental goals. Well situated with like-minded theoreticians and practitioners (e.g., Minuchin's Family Systems Theory [1974], Bronfenbrenner's Developmental Ecological Model [1979], and Sander's Organismic Perspective [1977] on infant development), Brazelton's approach is a model for relationships-based practice within pediatrics and beyond (Hulbert, 2003).

Brazelton (2000) credits Louis Sander's "model of systems regulation" (1977) as a provocation for his reflection on the contributions of internal biological systems and "external" systems (family, cultural context) to infant development. The Touchpoints framework was developed partially to overcome the limitations of "stimulus-response" paradigms of development (Brazelton, 2000).

Brazelton proposed radical changes to the organization and delivery of pediatric care (Brazelton, 1998) so that positive parent–provider alliances could enhance parental competence and promote family–child relationships. These modifications are both *structural* (e.g., altering the schedule of pediatric well-childcare to coincide with developmental "touchpoints," periods of predictable disorganization in the child's functioning that may be stress-inducing for the family system); and *process-oriented* (e.g., encouraging providers to value parental expertise, and to focus on the parent–child relationship rather than exclusively on the individual child's physical health). Brazelton noted that attending to his 13 developmental touchpoints would restructure pediatric well-child visits around issues that "truly matter to parents (e.g., feeding, discipline), rather than traditional milestones" (1998, p. 482). Professional collaboration with parents and acknowledgment of parental expertise enable parents and pediatric professionals to become allies to promote children's development and wellbeing (Brazelton, 1998). Brazelton noted that parent groups, constructed around "touchpoints," could also serve a supportive, peer community function (Brazelton, 2002).

The Touchpoints Training Model

Rather than promote an individualistic and static model of development in infancy, Brazelton and his colleagues, echoing tenets of family systems theory, embraced a positive – as opposed to the reigning deficit-based – view. The Touchpoints (TP) training model presents both strengths-based *guiding principles* and *parent assumptions* about practitioner and parental competence and roles. Presenting "developmental regressions and disorganizations" as part of positive developmental trajectories, the TP approach reframes parental distress about such disorganization to reflect dynamic rather than linear development.

Brazelton (1998) also presaged the current attention to fragmentation of services and the need for "systems of care." Since the aim of systems of care is to work as communities of practitioners on behalf of children and families, Brazelton's Touchpoints framework, emphasizing relationship building among system components, has the potential to foster change in these systems – both in the way individual practitioners engage with families and in the operations of these larger systems themselves. Effective transdisciplinary collaboration – for example, to facilitate transitions from early intervention to preschool – is one likely result.

Relationship-based Training Models for Early Childhood Providers

Brazelton's influence within the early childhood field is seen most directly in the Touchpoints – Early Childhood Care and Education (TP-ECCE) program. The increasing popularity of training focused on early relationships – e.g., under the "Infant Mental Health" rubric – can be viewed as having resulted, at least in part, from a shift in understanding about effective caregiving to which Brazelton has contributed mightily.

Touchpoints – Early Childhood Care and Education (TP-ECCE)[1] combines a range of training and supervision modalities (e.g., intensive training workshops, onsite reflective practice within child care agencies, etc.), and is offered to individuals, organizations, and communities. Providers are introduced to practical methods for supporting families through periods of developmental disorganization and growth; the context for this support is a shared partnership – parents and providers work as allies to nurture parent–child and parent–provider relationships.

The emergence of relationship-based practice with infants and toddlers is representative of a larger shift from targeted interventions for "at-risk" children to the promotion of wellness in caregiving systems (Benard, 1997; Cicchetti, Toth, & Rogosch, 2000). Research over the past three decades supports this move away from traditional deficit perspectives and affirms the basic tenet of relationship-based practice –that consistent and nurturing early relationships are the foundation of healthy growth and development (Stinson, Tableman, & Weatherston, 2000; Weatherston, 2000; Zeanah & Zeanah, 2001). Until recently, these important new findings have not been translated into effective training for early childhood professionals unequipped to support infant–caregiver relationships and the contexts in which they are embedded (Meyers, 2007; Weatherston, Moss, & Harris, 2006; Weston, 2005).

Early interventionists and childhood education providers, doulas, social workers, psychologists, and others cope with complex constellations of family strengths and vulnerabilities requiring a breadth of knowledge and skills. Much relational expertise outside the realm of traditional, discipline-specific training and education (e.g., teaching certification, social work licensure) is needed for practitioners to perform optimally.

Targeted, high-quality, professional development must bridge the gap. In their influential report, *From Neurons to Neighborhoods*, Shonkoff and

Phillips (2000) assert that, "substantial new investments should be made to address the nation's seriously inadequate capacity for addressing young children's mental health needs" (p. 6). Enhancing provider skills and knowledge is vital, although integration of early relationship development and parental mental health into standard offerings has been limited (Weatherston & Tableman, 2002). No consensus has yet emerged on what competencies an early childhood workforce ought to possess (Meyers, 2007).

A small number of statewide and local programs have led the way in developing relationship-based training derived from current research and best practice standards (see Bartlett, Waddoups, & Zimmerman, 2007; Meyers, for review, 2007). In addition, several states have developed and implemented competencies for Infant and Early Childhood Mental Health, and others are in the process of competency development (Bartlett, Waddoups, & Zimmerman, 2007). Such initiatives recognize that amelioration of risk and promotion of positive development requires coordination across "companionable" disciplines (Foley & Hochman, 2006).

During this time, questions about the effectiveness of these interventions, and about practitioners' satisfaction with them, reasonably have surfaced. TP-ECCE is among the first to undertake serious process and outcome evaluation (Easterbrooks & Jacobs, 2007; see also, for example, Mann, Boss, & Randolph, 2007). A major component of this recent evaluation[2] was documentation of the perceived effects of the training, as reported in independently conducted interviews with participant childcare providers and program directors. Below is a brief taste of their experiences with TP-ECCE.

Providers and directors at eight childcare centers shared their views about relationships with parents, and reflected on both the Touchpoints training itself, and onsite implementation of TP's Guiding Principles (GP) and Parent Assumptions (PA).

Two GPs, in particular, are central to parent–provider and parent–child relationships. GP #1 (*Value and understand the relationship between you and the parent*) encourages a range of perhaps new postures, including that providers view parents as the experts on their children (PA #1). GP #4 (*Focus on the parent–child relationship*) encourages providers to observe how parents and children interact, especially during times of reunion and separation. Many providers and directors spoke to their understanding of these principles.

GP #1: Value and understand the relationship between you and the parent

Participants emphasized the importance of valuing their relationships with parents in many ways. For example, the informant below spoke to the importance of building trust into these relationships:

> You have to let the parents trust you and let them know that you're not going to be talking to them only when there's something negative going on. Ask them how was your day? . . . Your night? How did he sleep? . . . Eat? . . . That makes them open up. . . .

Communication is often problem-focused in this field (Shpancer, 1999). Yet this provider recognized the value of communication beyond problems. Several providers described how the training changed their views and practices on this challenge. One informant noted,

> After the training, we've built communication much stronger . . . it's not just talking to them if there's a problem . . . If there was something they told us before, we bring it up, and ask how it's going. We have conversations more often now rather than just bringing up any issues in the classroom.

Another provider credited the Touchpoints training in this way:

> [I liked that we got] a lot of information about how it's important to have open communication with parents. That's the number one goal . . . it helps the child developmentally grow.

Although several providers acknowledged that challenges in this arena remained, some explicitly identified new strategies to address them. For example:

> I think I have more time, more patience . . . better communication. I take more time to talk with . . . and explain things to parents.

Another noted how she went out of her way to talk with parents she did not see on a regular basis.

> I talk to [parents all the time] and they are so happy and they talk to me. [They say], "You know, I haven't seen you in a couple of days and you really

talk to me a lot and I miss that." So I try to stay a little later or come in a little earlier because some of my kids come in before me and they leave after me.

Finally, one provider detailed changes she had seen – specifically that parents appeared more comfortable in the classrooms.

They don't come in and just drop off the kids. They stay for a little while ... The trainings helped a lot – how we have to have that verbal communication with the parents, in order to build trust, respect, and honesty.

PA #1: Parents are the experts on their children

Several interviewees' comments on parents represent a clear shift in their views of parents, from needing expert help to being experts on their children and valued caregiving partners. Endorsed by others in the field (Powell, 2001), this shift is central to the Touchpoints approach of collaboration and supporting parental mastery (Brazelton Touchpoints Center, 2005; Swartz & Hornstein, 2007). One provider credited the training as follows:

At first I was like, [the children] are with me more so I know them more, but then I realized no ... I sat back as a parent and said, "Yeah, I know my child better than the teachers ..." The parents are the experts on their child, so I sit back and I listen to them and ask them, "What exactly do you want me to help with your child? What can we do?"

A director noted:

Sometimes we as professionals ... who work with ... children have the tendency to think ... we know ... what's best for the child, but ... the films and all the discussions helped us realize that the parent knows and sometimes knows more than they think they know and more than we think they know about their children.

GP #4: Focus on the parent–child relationship

Several providers felt enhanced by this focus. One noted:

I ... never ... realized how important it is to respect the relationship between ... parents and ... child. It helped me have an open mind about

> how . . . important . . . the relationship is between the child and the parent.

Another concluded:

> Parents are the ones who are responsible for their children. They are the master-minds behind it. We need to just help support them.

Overall, providers expressed a sense of empowerment arising from the ways they had learned to be of greater service to the families in their care. These interviews offer support for TP-ECCE, and for relationship-focused training in general.

These qualitative findings are reinforced by statistically significant ones reported in the TP-ECCE evaluation (see Easterbrooks & Jacobs, 2007). Parents of children in TP-trained centers saw positive changes in their relationships with providers, whereas those in the comparison group reported decreases in the quality of this relationship. In addition, the latter experienced increasing levels of stress, whereas the former had stable levels of stress before and after TP training – a potential benefit of providers' changed attitudes and parents' positive perceptions of their relationships with providers.

Policies Crediting Early Relationships
A Long Time Coming

If relationship-focused early care and education makes sense, why hasn't it taken root in public policy – in licensing and program standards, caregiver certification requirements, childcare reimbursement criteria, training programs that would prepare the workforce to satisfy these requirements, and widely available, publicly-supported programs for young children and their families?

Brazelton might respond that the fundamental shift – the Zeitgeist overhaul – in how we conceive of young children and the effects that caregiving has on their futures – simply has still not occurred. Yet over the past four decades, with Brazelton's advocacy, incremental triumphs have been achieved that might soon move us past the "tipping point" (Gladwell, 2000) to that paradigm shift. These include federal legislation supporting early intervention services targeting infants and toddlers with disabilities (initially enacted in 1975 and more recently Part C of the Individuals with Disabilities

Education Act), parental leave (the Family and Medical Leave Act [FMLA], initially enacted in 1993), and the introduction, in 1995, of Early Head Start (EHS) – center-based and home-visiting services for low-income children, birth to three years, and their parents.

State governments have become more attentive to this population. Many have childcare licensing provisions for infants and toddlers (there are no such federal standards), fund newborn home-visiting programs, and extend undercapitalized federal programs such as EHS and FMLA. Local governments have also innovated in these areas.

In truth, however, programming and training innovations in this field usually begin in private, nonprofit agencies before attracting public attention. Public agencies then adopt the few most promising ones. Public agencies may initially act only as conveners of interested private and public parties, and then fund pilot projects for particular geographical areas or populations; it is unusual for programs focused on infants and toddlers to become statewide offerings, supported by state dollars.

This developmental course is understandable, as many policy makers argue that public dollars be reserved for programs that are proven, or hold real promise, based on empirical evidence. Evaluations to determine program effectiveness are expensive, however, and take time to produce the necessary results. This tension between encouraging innovation and funding proven approaches is not easily resolved, especially in tough economic periods.

Investments in supporting early relationships fit within this developmental framework. There are many promising training program initiatives across the country, operated by private nonprofit agencies, membership-based professional organizations (such as state Infant Mental Health associations), and colleges and universities. Many seem well acquainted with current developmental and family systems theory and research. Few have been thoroughly evaluated, though some more relationship-savvy *service programs* have demonstrated their effectiveness (e.g., McCormick et al., 2006; Olds et al., 2007), increasing the support for a workforce with these skills.

State licensing agencies have not consistently moved provider competence in early relationships into childcare licensing standards. Family childcare and relative care remain the most widely used options for infants and toddlers (U.S. Census Bureau, 2005), and are the least stringently regulated (Cochran, 2007; McGaha, Snow, & Teleki, 2001; Raikes, Raikes, & Wilcox, 2005). Some states have launched initiatives to raise the standards for those working in this field,[3] although these standards generally are not mandatory. This absence of state regulatory and certification policies represents a lost opportunity to improve the quality of early experiences for millions of young children.

Early childhood practitioners with relational skills are becoming increasingly valued – by childcare providers themselves, and other interested parties (e.g., elementary school teachers and administrators who must manage the emotional and behavior problems of children whose challenging early family experiences were not addressed in previous settings). However, until a better trained, more professionalized early care and education workforce is both required by public policy *and properly compensated* for this advancement, little broad-based, significant progress can be attained. We need that paradigm shift called for by Brazelton and others to encourage us to appropriately value and compensate the caregivers of young children.

Dare we hope that Dr. Brazelton may yet witness, in his lifetime, the realization of his life's work? With President Obama's stated commitment to early education, we can finally answer, "perhaps so."

Notes

1 See www.touchpoints.org/early_care.html for a fuller description.
2 See Easterbrooks and Jacobs (2007) for a detailed description of the evaluation's methods and findings.
3 For example, New York uses federal Child Care Block Grant funds to support Regional Infant and Toddler Resource Centers to improve childcare quality (New York State Child Care Coordinating Council, 2008). The state also has developed strategies to enhance professional preparation of infant/toddler caregivers, including a mentoring program and outreach from a four-year college (Lekies & Cochran, 2007).

References and further reading

Bartlett, J. D., Waddoups, A. B., & Zimmerman, L. (2007). *Training professionals to support the mental health of young children and their families: Lessons for Massachusetts from the national landscape.* Natick, MA: Connected Beginnings.

Benard, B. (1997). Fostering resiliency in children and youth: Promoting protective factors in the school. In D. Saleebey (Ed.), *The strengths perspective in social work practice* (pp. 167–182). New York: Longman.

Brazelton, T. B. (1998). How to help parents of young children: The Touchpoints model. *Clinical Child Psychology & Psychiatry, 3,* 481–483.

Brazelton, T. B. (2000). In response to Lou Sander's challenging paper. *Infant Mental Health Journal, 21,* 52–62.

Brazelton, T. B. (2002). Strengths and stresses in today's families: Looking toward the future. In J. Gomes-Pedro, J. K. Nugent, J. G. Young, & T. B. Brazelton (Eds.), *The infant and family in the twenty-first century* (pp. 23–30). New York, NY: Routledge.

Brazelton Touchpoints Center (2005). *Touchpoints in early care and education reference guide and participant training materials* (Version 1.0.). Boston, MA: Brazelton Touchpoints Center.

Bronfenbrenner, U. (1979). *The ecology of human development.* Cambridge, MA: Harvard University Press.

Cicchetti, D., Toth, S. L., & Rogosch, F. A. (2000). *The development of psychological wellness in maltreated children.* In D. Cicchetti, J. Rappaport, I. Sandler, & R. P. Weissberg (Eds.), *The promotion of wellness in children and adolescents* (pp. 395–426). Washington, DC: CWLA Press.

Cochran, M. (2007). *Finding our way: The future of American early care and education.* Washington, DC: Zero to Three.

Easterbrooks, M. A., & Jacobs, F. (2007). *Touchpoints early child care and education initiative final evaluation report.* Medford, MA: Tufts University.

Foley, G. M., & Hochman, J. D. (2006). Moving toward an integrated model of infant mental health and early intervention. In G. M. Foley & J. D. Hochman (Eds.), *Mental health in early intervention: Achieving unity in principles and practice.* Baltimore, MD: Paul H. Brookes.

Gladwell, M. (2000). *The tipping point: How little things can make a big difference.* Boston, MA: Little Brown.

Hulbert, A. (2003). *Raising America: Experts, parents, and a century of advice about children.* New York: Knopf.

Lekies, K., & Cochran, M. (2007). *Preparing qualified teachers for infants and toddlers: The role and function of higher education teacher programs.* The Cornell Early Childhood Program Policy Brief.

Mann, T. L., Boss, J., & Randolph, S. (2007). Infant mental health initiative pathways to prevention: A training and technical assistance initiative to increase program capacity to address infant mental health issues in Early Head Start, *Infant Mental Health Journal, 28*(2), 106–129.

McCormick, M. C., Brooks-Gunn, J., Buka, S. L., Goldman, J., Yu, U., Salganik, M., … Casey, P. H. (2006). Early intervention in low birthweight premature infants: Results at 18 years of age for the Infant Health and Development Program (IHDP). *Pediatrics, 117,* 771–780.

McGaha, C. G., Snow, C. W., & Teleki, J. K. (2001). Family child care in the United States: A comparative analysis of 1981 and 1998 state regulations. *Early Childhood Education Journal, 28*(4), 251–255.

Meyers, J. C. (2007). Developing the work force for an infant and early childhood mental health system of care. In D. F. Perry, R. K. Kaufmann, & J. Knitzer (Eds.), *Social and emotional health in early childhood: Building bridges between services and systems* (pp. 97–120). Baltimore, MD: Paul H. Brookes.

Minuchin, S. (1974). *Families and family therapy.* Cambridge, MA: Harvard University Press.

New York State Child Care Coordinating Council (2008). *High quality care for New York's infants and toddlers.* Paper presented at the Zero to Three National Training Institute, Los Angeles, CA.

Olds, D. L., Kitzman, H., Hanks, C., Cole, R., Anson, E., Sidora-Arcoleo, K., … Bondy, J. (2007). Effects of nurse home visiting on maternal and child functioning: Age 9 follow-up of a randomized trial. *Pediatrics, 120*(4), 832–845.

Powell, D. R. (2001). Visions and realities of achieving partnership. In A. Goncu, & E. L. Klein (Eds.), *Children in play, story, and school* (pp. 333–357). New York: The Guilford Press.

Raikes, H. A., Raikes, H. H., & Wilcox, B. (2005). Regulation, subsidy receipt and provider characteristics: What predicts quality in child care homes? *Early Childhood Research Quarterly, 20,* 164–184.

Sander, L. (1977). The regulation of exchange in the infant-caregiver system and some aspects of the context-contest relationships. In M. Lewis, & L. A. Rosenblum (Eds.), *Interaction, conversation, and the development of language* (pp. 133–157). New York: Wiley.

Shonkoff, J. P., & Phillips, D. (Eds.) (2000). *From neurons to neighborhoods: The science of early childhood development.* Washington, DC: National Academies Press.

Shpancer, N. (1999). Caregiver–parent relations in daycare: Testing the buffer hypothesis. *Early Child Development and Care, 156,* 1–14.

Stinson, S., Tableman, B., & Weatherston, D. (2000). *Guidelines for infant mental health practice.* East Lansing, MI: Michigan Association for Infant Mental Health.

Swartz, M. I., & Hornstein, J. (2007). Touchpoints. In R. S. New, & M. Cochran (Eds.), *Early childhood education: An international encyclopedia.* Westwood, CT: Greenwood Publishing Group.

U.S. Census Bureau (2005). *Who's minding the kids? Child care arrangements: Spring 2005, Survey of income and program participation.* Retrieved December 15, 2008 from www.census.gov/population/www/socdemo/child/ppl-2005.html

Weatherston, D. (2000). The infant mental health specialist. *Zero to Three*, 21(2), 3–10.

Weatherston, D., Moss, B. D., & Harris, D. (2006). Building capacity in the infant and family field through competency-based endorsement: Three states' experiences. *Zero to Three, 26*(3), 4–13.

Weatherston, D., & Tableman, B. (2002). *Infant mental health services: Supporting competencies/reducing risks.* Southgate, MI: Michigan Association of Infant Mental Health.

Weston, D. R. (2005). Training in infant mental health: Educating the reflective practitioner. *Infants & Young Children, 18*(4), 337–348.

Zeanah, C. H., & Zeanah, P. D. (2001). Toward a definition of infant mental health. *Zero to Three, 22*(1), 13–20.

Section III

Changing Ways of Being

31

Respect and Healing*

Sara Lawrence-Lightfoot

We lift our voices in praise of Berry Brazelton, of a life lived creatively, courageously, insightfully, intuitively, of work that has been global and local, passionate and pragmatic, of his powerful imprint on the worlds of medicine, child development, parenting, and family life, of his continuous quest to make a difference, to keep on keepin' on. What follows is a discourse with Brazelton's work, a look through the lens of my own scholarship, teaching, and writings at his influence, at the ways in which our passions, preoccupations, and perspectives speak to and echo one another.

At the center of Brazelton's work – with infants, children, parents, colleagues, caregivers, diverse communities and cultural groups – are relationships of *respect*. He helps parents understand their babies, and feel validated, strengthened, and empowered to discover their own sources of wisdom, expertise, and rhythms for raising their children. He honors cultural contexts of family life, focusing on diversity and strengths, rather than pathology and an adherence to a monolithic developmental path. These important messages, he believes, must be conveyed through words and silences, gestures and attentiveness, symbols and metaphors of respect – given and received.

* This chapter is an adaptation of Professor Lawrence-Lightfoot's lecture at the Pioneering Change Symposium at Harvard Medical School sponsored by the Division of Developmental Medicine at Children's Hospital Boston on the occasion of T. B. Brazelton's ninetieth birthday and in honor of his life's work. This event occurred on November 15, 2008, eleven days after the historic election of Barack Obama to the presidency of the United States.

In the soaring spirit of Aretha Franklin, I am honored to talk to you about "R-E-S-P-E-C-T: find out what it means to me . . . show me just a little respect." Respect is crucial to creating authentic relationships and building healthy communities, to supporting children and their capacity to live joyfully and productively, to breaking down power's asymmetries, the inequalities of knowledge, expertise, and resources, and to navigating misunderstandings and conflicts across the boundaries of race, class, culture, gender, and sexual orientation. It extends from local neighborhoods to global communities, the core of a thriving democracy and a civilized world.

The goals of educational achievement and social justice, central preoccupations in my life and work, are difficult to accomplish (both institutionally and interpersonally) given the great distance between our expressed values and our daily habits. Over the years, rhetoric about justice and respect has begun to sound over-rehearsed. We need new ways of addressing our chronic laments. The opportunities and casualties of our dual quests for excellence and diversity have been resounding notes in my research about respect as I have tried to shape a reconstructed view of this beautiful term.

Never has a dialogue about respect been timelier, demanding our attention and commitment. In recent times it has been impossible to converse about education, healthcare, human rights, or social justice without being flooded by horrific images: September 11, violence in Afghanistan, Israel and Palestine, the Sudan, Iraq, child abuse in the Catholic Church, neglect and ineptitude before and after Katrina, nooses at a Louisiana high school symbolizing slavery and oppression, the Wall Street crash uncovering the abyss between the privileged few and the marginalized many.

Even the miraculous ascendancy of our President-Elect Barack Obama – bringing so much hope, intelligence, and compassion to our world – does not make the terror disappear. During these last years of acute anxiety about our fragile world, we caregivers, pediatricians, nurses, social workers, counselors, and educators have felt a particular challenge to care for the children in our charge, to help them come to terms with these cruel events' aftermath, to find a precarious balance between grieving and getting busy.

To help children grow in this troubled world, educators must recommit to building schools that are truly inclusive, to developing rigorous standards and goals for all students, to providing the supports that they will need for us to be successful in reaching them. We must develop relationships with our students that inspire their trust, challenge their intellects, and have mutual respect at their center. The recently cast shadows of darkness and violence compel us to recognize how precious and fragile are our democratic principles, how hard it is to sustain respect, and how complex authentic inclusivity turns out to be.

I remember feeling the power and majesty of respect – and the deep connections between respect and justice – at an unforgettable moment of grace. It was April of 1986, at the burial and requiem for my father Charles Radford Lawrence II. My brother Chuck was giving the eulogy, his intimate and loving view of a very public man. Chuck's voice cracked as he recalled one of our father Charles's loveliest qualities:

> Our father Charles had a natural air of authority about him. He commanded respect without ever asking for it. In high school, my rowdiest friends – the guys who stole hub caps and crashed parties – were perfect gentlemen in my father's presence. They'd stand and say "Yes, sir, Dr. Lawrence," and answer his many questions about school and home and where their parents and grandparents were from. It was much later that I realized Dad's secret. He gained respect by giving it. He talked and listened to the fourth grade kid in Spring Valley who shined shoes the same way he talked and listened to a Bishop or college president. He was seriously interested in who you were and what you had to say. And although he had the intellectual and physical tools to outmuscle a smaller person or mind, he never bullied. He gained your allegiance by offering you his strength, not by threatening to overpower you.

In my brother's words I heard the recovery of rich meanings of respect. Through my tears, I heard the lovely symmetry and reciprocity, not the static hierarchy, the tender transfer of authority, not the power plays. I heard the deep curiosity – the urge to understand – not the arrogance of knowing enough or knowing it all. And I heard the beauty in the ordinary, daily gestures, not the drama and glory of great, public moments. My brother's words of gratitude and loving farewell have burned their way into my heart, fueled my interest in respect, and shape the way I understand its meanings.

My preoccupation with respect is fueled by these early memories of my father's natural authority. It is also haunted by the ghosts of disrespect, ancestral legacies that cast a long shadow, as well as the daily assaults of disrespect – both oblique and obvious – that all of us experience every day (small gestures of diminishment that psychiatrist Chester Pierce calls "micro-aggressions," [Griffith & Pierce, 1998]) that accumulate unnoticed and finally send us to bed feeling strangely despondent or bone weary.

My interest in exploring the underlying nature of respect is motivated by more than personal memories or our collective anguish about our treacherous world. Respect is the single most powerful ingredient in creating and sustaining trusting relationships within the human services, the cornerstone of a compassionate and productive educational culture. In the last thirty years, I have visited hundreds of schools – from poor inner-city schools to affluent suburban schools; from remote rural schools to elite, preparatory academies. I have asked students to identify their good teachers, and to tell me why they are good. The students' answers – across all settings – are the same. "Mrs. Brown is a good teacher because she respects us!" Without hesitation they explain that they feel respected by teachers who make them feel visible and worthy, who are demanding, hold high standards for them, and insist that they learn. They feel disrespected by teachers who never bother to get to know them, let them off easy, don't take them seriously or believe that they can succeed. Respect grows in relationships of expectation, challenge, and rigor. It is diminished by inattention, indifference, and empty rituals.

Respect is also a crucial aspect of schools' leadership. It shapes the ways in which principals and administrators motivate their teachers, build loyalty, commitment and a sense of community in schools, offer support, counsel, and criticism to their staffs, and assert authority and engage in decision making. Children are always watching the ways that adults negotiate respectful encounters with one another; they test adult rhetoric's authenticity to see if our words will be reflected in our actions.

This view of respect challenges traditional conceptions of respect as deference to status and hierarchy; driven by duty, honor, and a desire to avoid punishment, shame, or embarrassment. Usually respect is seen as involving debt due people because of their attained or inherent position, age, gender, class, race, professional status, accomplishments. Whether defined by rules of law or habits of culture, respect often implies required expressions of esteem, approbation or submission. By contrast, I focus on the way respect creates symmetry, empathy, and connection in all kinds of relationships, even those, such as parent and child, teacher and student, doctor and patient, commonly seen as unequal. Rather than looking for respect as a given in certain relationships, I am interested in watching it develop over time.

Respect generates respect; a modest loaf becomes many. I am interested in how people work to challenge and dismantle hierarchies rather than how they reinforce and reify them, and how the context – the situation of healer and patient, parent and child, teacher and student – shapes the ways in which people engage in respectful relationships. I consider how family roots, temperament, and life stories shape the ways in which they are able to become respectful and respected. Rather than the language of inhibition and constraint typical of a more old-fashioned view of respect, I listen for the voices of challenge and exuberance. Rather than the language of dutiful compliance, I hear the words of desire and commitment. Rather than the broad and esoteric abstractions of philosophers – so distant from the complexities of people's lives – I watch for the details of action, and try to decipher the nuances of thought and feeling.

In my book on respect (Lawrence-Lightfoot, 1999) I identify six dimensions – not to be heard as discrete ingredients of a prescribed recipe, but rather as a framework for considering the rich, experiential complexity of the term. Each dimension reveals a different angle of vision.

Empowerment: When we are respectful of others, we want to offer knowledge, skills, and resources that will allow them to make their own decisions and take control of their lives.

Healing: In showing respect for others, we hope – through our work and actions – to nourish a feeling of worthiness, wholeness, and wellbeing in them.

Dialogue: In showing respect for another, we encourage authentic communication. We listen carefully and respond supportively. We are willing to move through misunderstandings, distortions, conflict, and anger towards reasoning and reconciliation.

Curiosity: When we are respectful of others, we are genuinely interested in them. We want to know who they are, what they are thinking, feeling, and fearing. We want to know their stories and dreams.

Self-respect: In order to show respect to another, we must feel good about ourselves. Self-respect must not be confused with narcissism or entitlement. It results from a growing self-confidence that does not seek external validation or public affirmation. It is learning to live by our own internal compass – one defined by a daily, private vigilance.

Attention: When we are respectful of another, we offer our full, undiluted attention. We are fully present, completely in the room, sometimes engaged in vigorous conversation, sometimes bearing silent witness.

Healing is a dimension of respect that must be a central preoccupation and passion of professionals in every field impacted by Dr. Brazelton's work. One of its messengers is Dr. Johnye Ballenger, an African-American woman, born and raised in Louisville, Kentucky, educated at Brown, Howard, and Harvard Universities. A practicing pediatrician for over three decades, she still refers to

Dr. Brazelton as her muse and mentor. He has inspired generations of doctors like her, she says, to think differently about babies' developmental trajectories; to look at and listen to babies with a discerning eye and an open heart; to ask questions of parents that are both gentle and penetrating, challenging and forgiving; and to never shy away from truth-telling, the difficult moments of insight or disclosure in the service of health and healing. In Ballenger's distinctive voice can be heard the echoes of Brazelton's teachings.

At Children's Hospital, Dr. Ballenger works with pediatric residents; modeling and mentoring them in medicine's routines and civility's rituals. They tend to focus on symptoms and forget the child; to see pathology and be blind to health and resilience. Their preoccupation with technique, technology, and scientific rigor are all vital but insufficient for skillful practice. Their tour through medical school has probably exaggerated their paternalism, elitism, and dogma; impulses contrary to developing respectful relationships with patients. Before they become full-fledged attending physicians, Dr. Ballenger has a chance to offer alternative perspectives, introduce a little humanism, and sing Aretha's anthem on behalf of the children and families in their care. She tries to do this respectfully and strategically; recognizing how stretched and overworked the residents are; how often they feel disrespected by doctors higher on the hospital hierarchy; and how ambitious they are to hone and exhibit their doctor skills. One afternoon a week, Ballenger attends their seminar, listening attentively, deftly questioning, and occasionally offering her "two cents."

In the windowless, cramped conference room, as they chomp on their lunches, review patient records and gossip about their lives, the residents seem too consumed by the pace and strenuousness of their work to take in their environment. A voice cuts through the din of the conversation, bringing the meeting to order. Dr. Ballenger stands on the edge of the room. A black woman resident finds a chair for her. One resident begins his presentation on seizures by examining historical origins of medical perceptions of seizures in children. "The war between religion and science has been at the root of views of seizure." This historical exploration is tantalizingly brief. A presentation of the "science" ensues, and feels monochromatic, lifeless, devoid of clinical examples. The atmosphere feels dreary; the people weary. As their attention drifts, some nod off.

Johnye Ballenger intervenes only twice, bringing in clinical work's realities and patients' perspectives. Her points are brief but probing. When the speaker, making a larger point about the history of science, begins, "The delightful thing about seizures is . . ."

"Delightful for whom?" she inquires.

"For the historian," he says.

Ballenger seems to be the only one startled at "delightful" in this context. The others don't hear it or have already become locked into a perspective that sees the patient as a specimen, or as a tiny remnant of data on the historical record.

When the speaker has finished, Ballenger squeezes a question in before the group disbands. Her voice is gentle but urgent. "What language do you use to talk to parents and their children about seizures?" The question cuts through the heavy air like a refreshing breeze, but the speaker seems slightly defensive and dismissive of this central issue for practicing pediatricians. How do you communicate what you know, especially when the news is difficult to hear, the illness is difficult to diagnose, and the disease shrouded with mythology? She softens her question with praise. "Your talk was wonderful, but primary care people need to think about their relationships to patients." Her comment sparks both interest and concern.

As people rise from the table, a young white woman says, "The cultural issues are so important. This past summer I worked on a Navajo Reservation. The people there believed that seizures were a sign of incest in the family."

Later on, Ballenger expresses her frustration with the "scientific" focus's neglect of clinical practice and human relationships, that time was not protected for questions or dialogue, with the "lack of respect" that the residents show one another – the eating and nodding off, the inattention shown the speaker – that is reflected in the ways that these young doctors treat their patients. "We do to each other what we do to our patients," she says firmly.

In her second year of medical school at Howard University, Ballenger suddenly understood "the essence of respect" on rounds with her senior resident. Paradoxically for Ballenger – the activist, the doer – in that moment, she discovered that respect was expressed through doing very little when there is little to do. For the first time she saw clearly that respect can also be carried through "a certain stillness," simply by being present, attentive, and loving.

She and the resident approached an elderly black woman's bedside. She looked fairly comfortable to Dr. Ballenger. The resident told her – out of earshot – that she had "agonal breathing and would probably die by evening time." Ballenger saw nothing in the woman's demeanor indicating that she was about to die. In contrast to the resident's blunt and clinical diagnosis was the lovely way he treated the dying woman. "He asked her gently how she felt; if she needed to have her pillows adjusted. He held the glass of water so that she could slowly sip it through the straw. He just tried to make her feel comfortable. This will always be seared in my mind. This young doctor's care was so respectful, so very human. He couldn't have done more for her if he had been her son," she recalls.

Good practice requires that doctors enter into "relationships" with patients, actually "see" them, that they be respectful, tender, and gracious. The resident at Howard could not give the woman any medicine or perform any procedure that would prolong her life or reduce her pain. He could, however, offer her tenderness, the sweet attention of a son.

Johnye Ballenger's story echoes Aretha's audacious anthem, and helps us hear the deeper meanings of a respect that is generous, attentive, empathic, and generative, that is soulful, prayerful, and spiritual. Her story points to poignant lessons that have powerful implications for embodying and enacting respect in our work as doctors, nurses, medical practitioners, caregivers, and educators.

I will close with six challenging lessons that honor the work and wisdom of Berry Brazelton; lessons that join the personal and the professional, the spiritual and the clinical; lessons that search for goodness and wholeness in those we serve, and do not confuse difference with deviance; lessons for those of us who want to build relationships, families, neighborhoods, organizations, and communities animated by empathy and respect; for those of us who welcome the exciting and difficult challenges of designing rituals, practices, and protocols that are holistic, generative, and inclusive; for those of us who want to wipe away our tears – of anger and fear – and make way for wise work and lives of service.

Symmetry: We need to reconstruct our images of respect. Old ones emphasizing hierarchy, approbation, and obedience, based on habit, ritual, or law, tend to lead to relationships that are static, asymmetric, and constraining. People become stuck in their roles – of power or impotence, responsibility or irresponsibility – and are neither challenged nor inspired to try on other personas or develop new ways of being. Respect that is symmetric and dynamic supports growth and change, encourages communication and authenticity, and allows generosity and empathy to flow. The image is one of a circle, not a pyramid. Differences in power, strength, and expertise may remain, but this vision of respect creates a relational, generative symmetry.

Relationship: Respect grows in relationship, shaped by context, grounded in reciprocity and engagement, in the immediacy of the moment and the constraints of the setting. It is visceral, palpable, conveyed through gesture, nuance, tone of voice, figure of speech. One of the reasons "to diss" has become a verb spoken by all of us – not just by cool-talking adolescents – is because it seems to capture, in one sharp syllable, the potency of respect not given, the moment when we are suddenly made to feel diminished, dismissed, and demeaned. Those of us seeking to nourish respect, then, must see its embeddedness in growing relationships, and appreciate the immediate and visceral way it is transmitted.

Civility: It is important not to confuse respect with civility. Although these are related, they are not the same. Civility refers to the rituals, routines, and habits of decorum that characterize a gracious encounter, the etiquette of politeness and manners – an important but relatively surface engagement. Respect includes attention to these rituals of civility but goes deeper. It penetrates below the polite surface and reflects a growing sense of connection, empathy, and trust. It requires seeing the "other" as genuinely worthy.

Storytelling: Storytelling is at the center of respectful encounters, lubricated by genuine curiosity, authentic questions, and attentive listening. Stories allow for rapport and identification across boundaries of class, race, gender, prejudice, and fear. Through the unique and specific aspects of each other's stories, we discover the universals among us. Stories are not exclusive property. One story invites another as people's words weave the tapestry of human connection.

Family Origins: The imprint of family is powerful in shaping the ways we each negotiate respectful relationships. As we try to create relationships that are nourishing and challenging – that have respect at their center – we often confront our parents' ghosts, childhood experiences' haunts. These echoes can be inspiring; we create relationships that have the imprint of our parents' empathy and generosity. Such was the case for Johnye Ballenger, surrounded by a loving extended family – her anchor and inspiration – who believed in her capacity to achieve and serve. Others of us must work to challenge troubling generational echoes. We have to try hard not to unleash on others our parents' assaults – wittingly or unwittingly – inflicted upon us. Our determination to become healers may, in fact, be inspired by the deep residues of pain inflicted by abusive caregivers. As clinicians and educators engaged in respectful encounters, we hope to do the opposite – act out of compassion and empathy, restraint and connection – and in so doing heal ourselves.

Silence: Respect is carried not just through talk, but silence. Not an empty distracted silence, but a fully engaged silence that permits us to think, feel, breathe, and take notice, that gives the other person permission to let us know what he or she needs. At the bedside of a dying woman, Dr. Ballenger discovered the sound and radiance of silence. In nourishing respectful relationships, we must develop receptive antennae, take on the role of witness, and learn to live in the stillness. "At the still point," says T. S. Eliot in his poem *Four Quartets*, "there the dance is" (Eliot, 1943). Birth and death join at such moments, inviting our deep curiosity, our full attention. For the dying and the living, the immediate moment is the most significant. As we honor and learn from the luminous life and work of Berry Brazelton, we take his lessons and make them our own, hearing the echoes of his teachings and giving them our singular voice and commitment. Now is the time. Now is always.

References and further reading

Didion, J. (1968). *Slouching towards Bethlehem.* New York: Farrar, Straus & Giroux.

Eliot, T. S. (1943). *Four quartets.* New York: Harcourt, Brace and Company.

Griffith, E. E. H., & Pierce, C. M. (1998). *Race and excellence: My dialogue with Chester Pierce.* Iowa City: University of Iowa Press.

Lawrence-Lightfoot, S. (1988). *Balm in Gilead: Journey of a healer.* Reading, MA: Addison-Wesley.

Lawrence-Lightfoot, S. (1999). *Respect: An exploration.* Reading, MA: Perseus Books.

Index

Note: abbreviations used in the index: ECCE = early childhood care and education; FENS = Fetal Neurobehavioral Assessment System; MRM = Mutual Regulation Model; NBAS = Neonatal Behavioral Assessment Scale; NIDCAP = Newborn Individualized Developmental Care and Assessment Program; RP = regression period